This book is a study of the marrying of Anne of Cleves to King Henry VIII. It contains fascinating material – including 'demonic' interference and sexual politics at court – which differs from the usual stereotyped accounts of Anne. It also provides a rich new context of royal courtship rituals, and a startling account of the king's failure to consummate his marriage.

Henry's decision to ally himself with this German noblewoman in 1540 was in part a reaction to the Franco-Imperial treaty mediated by Pope Paul III, who renewed a suspended bull of excommunication against Henry in the hope of isolating England diplomatically. The subsequent marriage procedures, from the advent of negotiations and the portrait of Anne by Hans Holbein the Younger to Henry's Rochester greeting of Anne – in disguise – and the Greenwich nuptials, followed usual royal protocol. However, the king's sexual incapacity, which prevented the consummation of the marriage, culminated in the fall and subsequent execution of Thomas Cromwell and his client Lord Hungerford, who were both tarred with the brush of sexual heresy.

RETHA M. WARNICKE is Professor of History, Arizona State University, Tempe. Her previous publications include *The Rise and Fall of Anne Boleyn: Family Politics at the Court of Henry VIII* (1989), which was a History Book Club selection, *Women of the English Renaissance and Reformation* (1983), a *Choice Magazine* selection, and *William Lambarde: Elizabethan Antiquary* (1973).

THE MARRYING OF
ANNE OF CLEVES

Anne of Cleves

THE MARRYING OF
ANNE OF CLEVES

Royal protocol in early modern England

RETHA M. WARNICKE

PUBLISHED BY THE PRESS SYNDICATE OF THE UNIVERSITY OF CAMBRIDGE
The Pitt Building, Trumpington Street, Cambridge, United Kingdom

CAMBRIDGE UNIVERSITY PRESS
The Edinburgh Building, Cambridge CB2 2RU, UK   www.cup.cam.ac.uk
40 West 20th Street, New York, NY 10011-4211, USA   www.cup.org
10 Stamford Road, Oakleigh, Melbourne 3166, Australia
Ruiz de Alarcón 13, 28014 Madrid, Spain

First published 2000

Printed in the United Kingdom at the University Press, Cambridge

Typeface 11.5/13.5 Monotype Baskerville   *System* QuarkXPress™

A catalogue record for this book is available from the British Library

Library of Congress cataloguing in publication data

Warnicke, Retha M.
The marrying of Anne of Cleves: royal protocol in early modern
England / Retha M. Warnicke.
    p.   cm.
Includes bibliographical references and index.
ISBN 0 521 77037 8 (hardbound)
1. Anne, of Cleves, Queen, consort of Henry VIII, King of England,
1515–1557 – Marriage.   2. Marriages of royalty and nobility – Great
Britain – History – 16th century.   3. Marriage customs and rites –
England – History – 16th century.   4. Henry VIII, King of England,
1491–1547 – Marriage.   5. Great Britain – History – Henry VIII,
1509–1547.   6. Queens – Great Britain – Biography.   I. Title.
DA333.C54W37   2000
392.5′086′210942–dc21   99-30163   CIP

ISBN 0 521 77037 8 hardback

CONTENTS

PLATES

Miniature portrait of Anne of Cleves, 1539. Hans   *frontispiece*
Holbein the Younger. Reproduced by permission of the
Trustees of the Victoria & Albert Museum, London
(© V&A Picture Library)

(between pages 80 and 81)

1 Jane Seymour, queen of England. Hans Holbein. Mauritshuis,
  The Hague
2 Henry VIII, king of England. After Hans Holbein. Walker Art
  Gallery, Liverpool
3 Thomas Cromwell, 1st earl of Essex. Hans Holbein. National
  Portrait Gallery, London
4 Francis I, king of France, Jean Clouet. Musée du Louvre, Paris
5 James V and Mary of Guise, king and queen of Scotland.
  Unknown artist. The Devonshire Collection, Hardwick Hall
  (National Trust). Photo: the Courtauld Institute, London
6 Charles V, Holy Roman Emperor. Titian. Museo del Prado,
  Madrid
7 Christina of Denmark, countess of Milan and Lorraine. Hans
  Holbein. National Gallery, London
8 John of Cleves with his brother Adolph at the wedding of Philip
  the Good. Miniature from the *Remissorium Phillippi*. Algemeen
  Rijksarchief, The Hague
9 The six princes of the house of Cleves (from left to right) Adolph
  I, John I, John II, John III, William V, John William. Henrik
  Feltman. Museum of Kurhaus Kleve (Cleves)
10 William of Cleves, 1540. Engraving by Heinrich Aldegrever.
   Stadtmuseum, Düsseldorf

FIGURES

ACKNOWLEDGMENTS

I am grateful for the community of scholars, archivists, librarians, and editors who facilitated the completion of this book. At Arizona State University, I am most especially indebted to Philip Soergel, the early modern German specialist, who located important sources and contacts for me in the United States and in Germany. Other members of the departmental faculty, such as Sally McKee, Andrew Barnes, and Sybil Thornton were supportive as well. I appreciate the splendid work of my graduate student, Mary Egel, on the index. Catherine Marshall in the Languages and Literature Department put me in touch with Kathrin Ross DiPaola, an MA student from Germany now in the Ph.D. program at the University of Maryland at College Park, who completed several translations for me. Her colleague, Claudia Schlee, was also of assistance. Dhira Mahoney in the English Department forwarded evidence from medieval literature about individuals falling in love at first sight with an art form, which is essential to the analyses in Chapters 3 and 6. Finally, at Arizona State University, I am thankful for the friendly and efficient circulation and interlibrary loan staff at Hayden Library, for the assistance of the Art Slide Collection Department, and for a welcome research grant from the Vice-President for Research.

Many others in the United States have encouraged me in this research project. The participants in the Early Modern Graduate Seminar at the Huntington Library, chaired by Lamar Hill, University of California, Irvine, responded positively to a paper I gave on Henry's greeting of Anne of Cleves at Rochester. Muriel McClendon of University of California, Los Angeles, one of the seminar's participants, obtained an article for me at her university library. The Early Modern Society and the History Department at the University of Minnesota invited me to lecture on early modern protocol. Stanford Lehmberg's Ph.D. students there, Donald Biggs and especially John Currin when he was in England, subsequently forwarded sources on greeting ritual and courtship to me. Joel Harrington of Vanderbilt University advised me about the nature of German marriage contracts. My daughter Margaretha, previously at Carleton College but now at the University of Delaware, and her friend, Stephen Gardiner, at Carleton, were also of assistance.

My husband Ronald and my son Robert and his wife Cynthia, as well as Margaretha, have been consistently supportive. They were as delighted as I when I was able finally to announce that I had completed the manuscript on Anne of Cleves. They are my greatest rooters, but it is somewhat tedious to be queried regularly about how much writing I have accomplished on any given day.

I am thankful for the assistance of individuals outside the United States. Sybil Jack of the University of Sydney offered information about the estates of queens' consort. Niethard Bulst of the University of Bielefeld ordered important public documents copied for me, and an understanding librarian at Tübingen forwarded an original version of a crucial dissertation that had been accepted at the university in 1907. In the United Kingdom, I am immensely indebted to John Guy who, while on research leave from St. Andrews, agreed to read two drafts of this manuscript during his summer break. I welcomed and value highly his criticisms, recommendations, and guidance on this manuscript as I did on my previous work on Anne Boleyn. Without the skillful assistance of the archivists and librarians at the Public Record Office, the British Library, and the Institute of Historical Research, of course, no book on the Tudor court could ever be completed. Finally, I am grateful for the advice of William Davies, editor of Cambridge University Press, who is also the editor of my book on Anne Boleyn.

That I embarked upon research on the early Tudor court is largely due to the guidance of Sir Geoffrey Elton, Regius Professor of Modern History at Cambridge University, whom I met for the first time in 1984. After reading my book, *Women of the English Renaissance and Reformation* (Greenwood Press, 1983), and a manuscript on Anne Boleyn's age (later published in *Historical Journal*), which emerged from the book on Englishwomen, he suggested that I continue to research the life of Anne Boleyn. I was at once concerned and pleased. I had not heretofore considered doing further research on her, for I was then pursuing a collaborative effort on Jacobean women's funeral sermons with Bettie Anne Doebler of the English Department at Arizona State. I was pleased, however, that he considered my scholarly abilities equal to such a task and finally accepted his advice. *The Rise and Fall of Anne Boleyn: Family Politics at the Court of Henry VIII* was the result.

This present study grew out of that book. While involved in its research, I became aware of how inaccurately religious and secular rituals had been interpreted. The most obvious example was the ubiquitous speculation on why Henry VIII had failed to attend his daughter Elizabeth's christening. His absence was dictated by religious protocol, of course, and not by his disappointment that she was a daughter rather than the son he had been expecting. This awareness led me to examine Henry's greeting of Anne of Cleves at Rochester and then to embark upon a larger study of royal protocol in the courtship and marrying process.

My first findings on this research were offered at a workshop funded by the Arizona State Graduate College and by the Arizona Humanities Council in 1989. Also participating in the workshop were Elton with his former student Norman Jones of Utah State, A. J. Slavin of the University of Louisville and also visiting professor at Arizona State with his former student Joseph Block of California Polytechnic at Pomona, and two of my Ph.D. students, William Penberthy and John Wagner. I recall how attentive Elton was to the papers of the graduate students and how appreciative they were for his interest and helpful comments.

He later read and critiqued a revised version of my paper on Henry's greeting of Anne of Cleves, which thanks to Michael Moore, appeared in *Albion* in the winter of 1996. Unfortunately, my term as department chair (1992–98) and some smaller research ventures, including a few additional essays on Anne Boleyn, delayed the completion of *The Marrying of Anne of Cleves: Royal Protocol in Early Modern England*. Because it was only after his death in December 1994 that I began to examine Anne's divorce and Cromwell's fall, I shall never know whether Elton would have been able to validate my version of those tragic events, but I do hope he would have repeated what he said about my "Sexual Heresy" thesis in the book on Anne

Boleyn, that it is a "fresh and original approach." In the last decade of his distinguished career, he had decided that analyses of court politics must take into consideration themes from women's history, the history of sexuality, and family history. It is to his memory and his deep commitment to the advancement of historical studies that I dedicate this book.

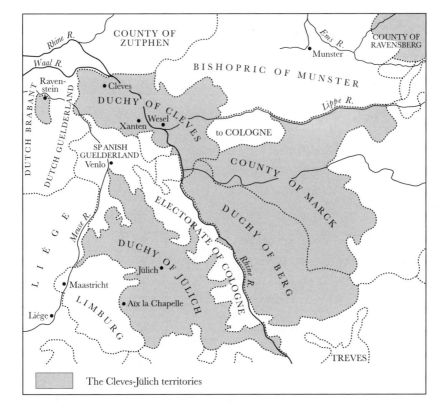

Cleves territories, early seventeenth century
Charles H. Carter, *The secret diplomacy of the Habsburgs* (Columbia Press, New York, 1964)

1 INTRODUCTION

On 6 January 1540 Henry VIII married Anne of Cleves, his fourth wife but only his second foreign-born one, with the goal of siring more male children to secure the succession. It was so expected a practice for a monarch to select a foreign bride, as Henry did in 1509 and 1540, that Erasmus felt it necessary to warn against these unions in *The Education of a Christian Prince*, which was published in 1516. In his work which was composed to provide instruction in political theory to Charles, the future Holy Roman Emperor, and later to Ferdinand, his brother and successor to the empire, this great humanist condemned these marriages because, as he observed, far from ensuring peace between the two lands, they often fostered warfare. Singling out the union of James IV of Scotland and Margaret Tudor in 1503 as an example of their realms' unfulfilled hopes for peace, he inquired: "What was gained a few years ago by the alliance of King James of Scotland since he invaded England with his hostile forces?" Erasmus's advice was the exact opposite of Thomas Hoccleve's, a fifteenth-century writer who also promoted peace. In *The Regement of Princes*, "virtually the first full fledged English manual of instruction for a prince," that was written for the future Henry V in about 1412, Hoccleve recommended wedlock between members of estranged dynasties, giving as an example, a union between Henry and, as it turned out, his future consort, Katherine of France.[1]

It is interesting that Erasmus, who had resided and worked in England, pointed to that kingdom's alliance with Scotland as an example of how dynastic unions, even relatively soon after the exchange of wedding vows, could fail in their peacemaking goals, but it is equally interesting that he omitted reference to the wars the descendants of such marriages waged in their quests for disputed

inheritances. One example of these conflicts was the on-going struggle for control of the duchy of Milan. Both Louis XII and his successor Francis I laid claim to the duchy through the marriage in 1387 of
their ancestor, Louis I of Orléans, brother of Charles VI, to
Valentina, daughter of Giangaleazzo Visconti, duke of Milan. This
genealogical claim to the duchy was at the heart of the recurrent
Franco-Imperial wars in the sixteenth century.

Unlike some other humanists, as, for example, John Colet, the
unmarried Erasmus was willing to praise the sacrament of marriage,
for, as he remarked in this advice book: "He does not die, who leaves
a living likeness of himself." Erasmus also wrote a Latin treatise
lauding wedlock, which its English translator, Richard Tavener, in
1536 ironically dedicated to Thomas Cromwell, Henry VIII's principal secretary and lord privy seal, who had been a widower for several
years. In it the humanist denounced bachelorhood as "both barren
and unnatural" and called those who remained single "traiterous
murderers" of their lineage. In other tracts, Erasmus lauded individuals who eschewed marriage; for example, he complimented Berta
Heyen for remaining faithful to her deceased husband. Even so, some
of his work offered a favorable intellectual approach to matrimony.[2]

In England until the passage of Lord Hardwicke's Act of 1753,
families were expected to proceed through five stages to conclude
marriage: (1) a contract negotiated between parents or guardians of
the bride and groom that set out dowry, dower or jointure, and other
financial matters and that was delivered at the church door; (2) the
spousals or vows to wed sworn in the future tense; (3) the proclamation of the banns three times; (4) the nuptials with vows sworn in the
present tense; and (5) sexual consummation.[3] This sequence created
the legal family, the basic social, religious, and economic unit of
early modern England. The ideal family included a conjugal couple
together with any children, wards, and servants they might possess.
The wealthiest tended to produce the most children as well as to
retain the most servants and wards in their households. At the apex
of society, among the aristocracy generally but more especially
among ruling dynasties, matrimonial selections were limited, for the
overriding issues at stake went far beyond personal decisions based
on partner preferences.[4]

Erasmus was essentially correct in that realms did often attempt to end their estrangements or hostilities through marriage alliances, as, for example, the union between Margaret and James. It was a prevailing ideal that was factored into the arrangement of truces and peace treaties. As David Potter has noted, "The game of marriage negotiations and alliances seemed to make the international system a vast family concern."[5]

The ending of hostilities was an important motive but not the only one for dynastic intermarriage. Unions between already friendly realms might deepen their amicable ties, as, for example, the union in 1537 of James V of Scotland and Madeleine of France, which confirmed the continuation of the "auld alliance."[6] Sometimes the purpose was to establish better relations between countries at peace in order to forge a network against a common enemy. When Henry began to seek a bride in 1537, he informed Sir Thomas Wyatt, his ambassador with Charles V, that he was eager to negotiate alliances with the emperor's relatives for himself, his son Edward, and his two daughters, Mary and Elizabeth. As Charles and Francis were then estranged, these marriages, if they had taken place, would have served to isolate France diplomatically.[7]

In this "patriarchal sociopolitical system," it was usually the daughters who had to leave their homes to wed husbands in strange, sometimes hostile lands.[8] The relatives of these ladies, even when they were friends of the groom's family, expected the brides to send back to their homes information about secret matters of their adopted kingdoms. If the new wives managed to give birth to surviving offspring, attempts would also be made to surround the children with advisors who were favorable to their mothers' native lands. Erasmus expressed concern for the well-being of these brides, who, like Catherine of Aragon when she wed Arthur, prince of Wales, in 1501, were expected to and often did represent their fathers' interests in their adopted homes. They were, he lamented, "sent away unto remote places" and, he suspected, "would be happier if they could live among their own people, even though with less pompous display."[9] Two years before this lamentation appeared in Erasmus's advice book, the emperor's sister, Isabella, complained to their eldest sister Eleanor about her recent marriage to Christian II of Denmark: "It is hard enough to marry a man . . . whom you do not know or love, and worse still to be required to leave home and kindred, and follow a stranger to the ends of the earth, without even being able to speak his language."[10]

Occasionally, a monarch, like the Habsburg emperor, Maximilian of Austria, grandfather to Charles, married the heiress of another principality, in his case, Mary of Burgundy. In his advice book, Erasmus expressed no concern for husbands like him who might have to reside in alien lands, for the widespread bias was that queens regnant ought to marry foreigners. In 1553 Simon Renard, the Imperial ambassador in England, informed a correspondent that if Queen Mary, who had recently succeeded her half-brother Edward VI, were to wed an Englishman, "her posterity would not have as much renown as if her husband were a foreign prince capable of assisting and protecting her." If she married one of her subjects, the danger existed that by favoring his family, she would plunge the country into civil war.[11]

In an article in the *American Historical Review* concerning Habsburg marriages, Paula Fichtner argued that marital alliances between foreign realms constituted useful diplomatic gestures because they provided a way of expressing the rule of reciprocity in international relations. The marriage established "a foundation in joint obligation" without which treaties could not be promulgated or maintained. A significant factor in these arrangements was the gift exchange by which the parties incurred obligations to each other. In the discussions leading to the agreements, much time and attention were consumed with questions of jointures, dowries, inheritances of estates, and the future possession of territories by any children produced by the unions. Often, as in the case of the Habsburg marriages, both parties contributed about equally in terms of wealth, in lands, money, or jewels, with the bridegroom's family offering more in the way of lands than cash; however, political advantage could take the place of wealth. In 1559 Charles of Austria, son of Emperor Ferdinand I, for example, was willing to forgo a dowry from Elizabeth I in exchange for permission to inherit England in the event he should survive her. Ultimately, as Fichtner argued, these unions were incapable of establishing perpetual friendly relations. Treaties failed because they were inadequate to meet the needs of the parties involved or because those needs changed over time. In the final analysis, a marriage was not strong enough to overcome the weaknesses inherent in the treaties themselves.[12]

The mutual obligation established through gift exchanges was significant, but dynasties were also alert to the possibility of extending their control over other territories through these arrangements. Claims to ancestors' principalities, as, for example, the duchy of Milan, could be the immediate excuse for aggression. The Habsburg success in utilizing these genealogical claims to obtain lands encouraged others to seek unions for their children with foreign dynasties. Ironically, the phrase, *Bella gerant alii, tu, felix Austria, nube. Nam quae Mars aliis, dat tibi regna Venus* [Let the strong fight wars. Thou happy Austria marry. What Mars bestows on others, Venus gives to thee], which refers to the method the Habsburgs used to expand their presence in Europe, was coined in 1477 by King Matthias Corvinus of Hungary, who actually intended to mock their military incompetence, not to celebrate their marital strategies. It stands, however, as an accurate description of how they achieved their dynastic advantages in the bedchamber.[13]

Charles, the prince whom Erasmus futilely advised to wed one of his subjects, was the most obvious benefactor of Habsburg alliances. By wedding Mary of Burgundy, Charles's paternal grandfather Maximilian had brought his family and Austria one step closer toward European domination through control of that wealthy duchy. Next, Charles's father Philip the Fair, the heir of Burgundy, had married Juana, heiress of Spain; Charles ultimately gained personal charge of his mother's kingdom and its overseas possessions when he became regent for her in 1516 after the death of her father Ferdinand. On the British Isles, a smaller version of the Habsburg strategy was played out in the early seventeenth century when James VI, the great-grandson of Margaret Tudor and James IV, the union that Erasmus had so deplored because it had not preserved peace between their realms, ascended the throne of England as James I.

In contrast, Henry VIII's principal purpose in marrying for a fourth time in 1540 was neither aggrandizement of the realm nor peacemaking. In 1527 he had compared his dynasty's territorial needs with those of the Habsburgs:

Formerly, the House of Burgundy only possessed Flanders, and now the Emperor has many lands and kingdoms spread all over the surface of the earth. He [Henry VIII] had not increased his father's inheritance; he had only one kingdom, small in size, it was true, but so surrounded by sea that he needed no help from anyone.[14]

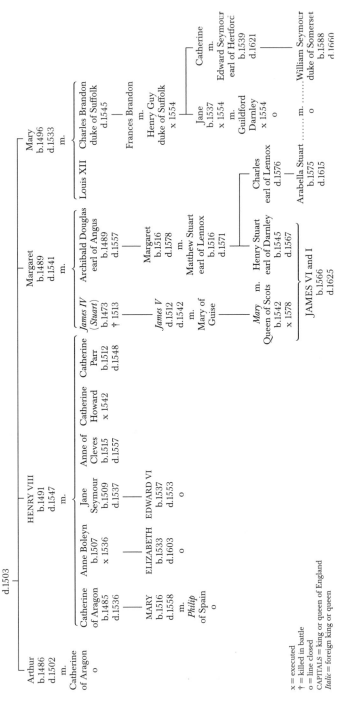

Figure 1 The House of Tudor. G. R. Elton, *England under the Tudors* (New York, 1991)

His desire for another wife was rooted in his determination to secure the Tudor succession. He and other monarchs viewed their kingdoms as family trusts to be handed down to the next generation, preferably to their legitimate sons. In 1603 James I, for example, remarked of his heir Henry: "He was not ours only, as a child of a natural father; but as an heir apparent to our body politic, in whom our estate and kingdoms are especially interested." Earlier, in 1568, Zachariah, Cardinal Delphino, had tried to persuade Charles of Austria to marry Elizabeth I with the warning that if he failed to do so, there would be "no want of persons to believe" that he had "forfeited" for himself and his "blood, both born and unborn, that great fortune, great glory and great profit and name which by all rights would have fallen on your highness and yours."[15]

Ultimately, this concern for the dynasty's continuation was the single most important reason for royal marriages. In 1553 Queen Mary confided to the Spanish ambassador that as a "private individual" who was thirty-seven-years old, she would have preferred to "end her days in chastity," but as she had ascended the throne and had assumed the responsibility of a "public position," it was her responsibility to marry.[16] By contrast, in 1539 her first cousin Emperor Charles had declined to remarry after the death of his consort, Isabella of Portugal. He rejected the suggestions of Alessandro, Cardinal Farnese, and Juan Fernandez Manrique, marquis de Aguilar, that he wed the youthful Margaret of France to cement his newly ratified French treaty with the explanation that he had a son and daughters and ought to think of them rather than of himself. Furthermore, he continued, in a sense accepting Hoccleve's earlier recommendation, he hoped for many unions between his progeny and members of the French ruling family to ensure the permanence of their peace. Throughout his life, by deeds and words, he consistently rejected Erasmus's advice against the intermarriage of foreign dynasties.[17]

Henry was not blessed with many legitimate offspring, for his two daughters, Mary and Elizabeth, had been declared illegitimate after he was divorced from their mothers in 1533 and 1536, respectively. His only legitimate child was Edward, born in 1537 to his third consort Jane, who died in childbed of puerperal fever. As Henry's elder brother Arthur had died prematurely in 1502, the king was personally aware of the slender hold his family had on the throne. In fact, Mark Hansen has determined that the expected life of a Tudor male was 10.3 years at birth and 28 years at adolescence. The expected life of a Tudor female was not much better: 18 years at birth and 28 years at adolescence. Only one-third of the Tudor offspring in the sixteenth century survived through infancy while one-half of those of the Habsburg family actually lived to reproduce themselves.[18] "More store of lawful posterity," as Henry, himself hoped for in 1539, would provide some greater assurance for his line's continuation and could be a useful pawn in marriage negotiations either in England or abroad. The first priority was the birth of another son to more firmly secure the succession, after which the birth of daughters and other sons would be welcome to cement marriage treaties.[19]

In 1540 the king selected as his wife Anne, the sister of William, duke of Cleves, from among Christendom's noble families, for diplomatic reasons at a time of religious turmoil. By early 1539 a rapprochement between Charles and Francis, as well as the renewal by Pope Paul III of the suspended bull of excommunication against Henry, had left England isolated. In retaliation and needing to marry to secure the succession, he decided to form an anti-papal network with William of Cleves, a schismatic ruler who was, like himself, neither Lutheran nor sacramentarian. Anticipating by this action a future when leaders would have to acknowledge that Christendom was permanently divided, Henry would have readily accepted the intent of a comment made by an onlooker in 1655 about the union of Philip IV and Mariana of Austria: "God give them blessed sons for the sake of Spain, the defence of the faith and above all, for peace."[20]

It is principally the sheer number of Henry's wives, six in all, that has caused the events of his reign, especially the domestic dramas, to be viewed as idiosyncratic, as though they were not in step with contemporary political and social customs. This is an unfortunate development, for it is necessary, in order to gain a fuller understanding of his reign, that his marriages be interpreted by the standards of prevailing cultural norms to determine whether they actually fell within the range of what might be termed as acceptable protocol. The most unusual attribute of his marriages might well turn out to be simply that there were so many of them, for the characteristics of each have contemporary and historical precedents and justifications. Although it was unusual for a king to divorce one wife, let alone four, or to have one executed, let alone two, the events surrounding those actions and other marital events should not automatically be dismissed as idiosyncratic.[21]

For the most part, in assessing the marrying of Anne of Cleves and Henry, only the protocol of royal unions will be examined since they have important attributes that set them apart from the practices of the English nobility.[22] The events leading to dynastic unions, including their public and private trappings, offer insights into the relationships of ruling families to each other as well as domestically to their powerful subjects. These marital alliances, which drew upon royal ceremonial rights and privileges, functioned as a "visible assertion" of their "preeminence" over their nobility and offered a sign of their growing social and political domination within their kingdoms.[23] Malcolm Vale has commented on this trend in military matters: "The fraternity of knights, regarding each other as brothers-in-arms, seems to have increasingly given way during the fifteenth century to an association acting under a sovereign."[24] The symbols of power that helped to sustain and mark this dominance were those of increasingly elaborate ceremony and pageantry: both extravagant public festivals and tournaments and less publicized ritual and protocol.[25]

Johan Huizinga's long accepted view that by the fifteenth century chivalry had degenerated into mere lavish displays while its essence, its knightly spirit, and its integrity had disappeared is no longer central to studies on this topic.[26] Scholars, such as Maurice Keen and Larry Benson, have interpreted these changes more positively as dynamic cultural developments rather than as decadence.[27] In the sixteenth century, the chivalric code of honor that extolled politeness toward women, devotion to the church, hospitality, generosity, and the individual quest for glory still resided at the core of aristocratic ideals. In hindsight, Henry,[28] Charles, and Francis, the three rulers who dominated early-sixteenth-century diplomacy, might appear to have been self-centered, greedy, grasping, and cruel, but their contemporaries believed, as Steven Gunn has observed, that they were chivalric kings aspiring to be the perfect knight. David Potter has further elaborated: They seemed "to have viewed the world around them in terms of a princely sporting event in which they engaged in personal combat with their royal competition to vindicate their honour and glory."[29]

This study of the marrying of Henry and Anne contains ten chapters. Following this introduction, Chapter 2 looks at the royal ministers, diplomatic corps, and other officials who were called upon to negotiate marriage treaties. Like diplomacy, courtship required "tact and subtlety" because its success depended "upon the appearance of sincerity" that was often "carefully calculated." As most monarchs, like Henry in 1537–40, were unable to woo their foreign brides personally, a survey of their agents at home and abroad is essential to an understanding of the marrying process. A discussion of the validity of their dispatches as evidence for court politics and events also forms a important part of this study.[30] Chapter 3 follows Henry's futile search for a bride in France and the empire in 1537–39; the candidates who were considered worthy of the queenship are identified and the reasons for the failure of his courtship of them is highlighted. In addition, attention is paid to the monarchs' strategies to make more palatable the requirement that they sometimes were required to wed brides with whom they were unacquainted. Chapters 4 through 7, which focus more narrowly on the Cleves alliance, examine the preliminary deliberations with Duke William, including an overview of religious turmoil, and provide a discussion of Hans Holbein the Younger's controversial portrait of Anne. They next detail her journey to England, her private meeting with the king at Rochester, and the wedding at Greenwich. Chapter 8 considers the reasons for the short duration of their marriage and for the fall of Cromwell. Instead of perpetuating the view that Thomas, third duke of Norfolk, and Stephen Gardiner, bishop of Winchester, led a conservative religious faction that effected the political ruin of Cromwell and his faction of religious reformers, this chapter argues that he suffered as the scapegoat for the king's inability to consummate the union with his bride. Church scholars had long believed that witches caused relative impotency, which they defined as an incapacity toward one woman, the affliction that Henry presumably suffered with Anne. Anyone who was associated, however innocently, with individuals such as Walter, Lord Hungerford of Heytesbury, who was accused of employing these allegedly demonic creatures, also came under suspicion. Hungerford and his patron, Cromwell, were executed on the same day at the Tower of London and their heads were placed together on London bridge as a warning to observers to refrain from meddling in treasonable activities. This

INTRODUCTION 🌉 11

version of Cromwell's fall examines and offers an explanation of all the extant relevant facts while it distances itself from reliance on the diplomatic rumor mill.[31] Chapters 9 and 10 address the dissolution of the king's marriage, assess their foreign and domestic ramifications, and provide a brief conclusion.

This is neither a biography of Anne nor of Henry; it is an account of his quest for a fourth wife that culminated in his failed marriage to her. It examines his marrying behavior and strategies for the purpose of relating them to the expected royal protocol and practices of early modern England. Material from the courtship and marriages of other monarchs, often from foreign dynasties, will provide a contextual framework for the study. Attempts will be made to indicate when wooing and wedding practices emerged and whether and how by the end of the seventeenth century they had been altered. This does not pretend to be a comprehensive study of early modern courtship;[32] only enough evidence, some of it substantial, will be offered to provide a window into marrying customs and thereby to provide a fuller understanding of the reasons for the making and breaking of Henry's fourth marriage.

On 12 October 1537 at Hampton Court Palace, Queen Jane gave birth to a son, who was christened Edward three days later primarily because he was born on the Feast of St. Edward. Her death on 24 October pierced Henry's great pleasure at these tidings: "Divine Providence," he lamented "has mingled my joy with the bitterness of the death of her who brought me this happiness."[1] Some time before 12 November when she was buried at Windsor Castle, royal officials had already begun private deliberations concerning a successor. In late October, as dated by the editors of the *Letters and Papers*, Cromwell instructed Bishop Winchester and Lord William Howard, the English ambassadors in France, to determine whether Margaret, a daughter of Francis, or Mary of Guise, the widowed duchess of Longueville, would be worthy replacements for Jane. Cromwell cautioned them to keep the inquiry a secret.[2]

As an introduction to the process that was to culminate in Henry's remarriage, this dispatch and Cromwell's communications with English diplomats in the Netherlands require examination for the purpose of delineating some of the themes in the marrying process, such as the search's timing, the king's likely state of mind, his dynastic concerns, other domestic issues, and foreign-policy considerations. Then a brief overview of the history and duties of the corps of officials who conducted the negotiations will provide insights into how the union of a monarch with a foreign-born lady was arranged in the early modern period.

As it was usual for a widowed ruler whose dynasty's future, like Henry's, rested on such insecure underpinnings as a sole infant boy, to seek a bride very soon after his bereavement, it is inappropriate to ridicule this Tudor king for the speed with which the search for his next wife was initiated. Certainly in 1537 his ministers and agents saw nothing amiss in seeking a replacement for Jane "that noble reine," as John Hutton, the English agent at the court of Mary, dowager queen of Hungary and regent of the Netherlands for her brother, Emperor Charles, labeled her. On 4 November 1537, the duke of Norfolk informed Cromwell that he had already advised Henry to remarry "by reason of which more children might be brought forth." Later, Cromwell revealed to Wyatt at the emperor's court, that upon the queen's decease, Imperial diplomats had suggested that Henry make an "overture" for Mary, the half-sister of John III of Portugal. Henry, himself, referred in a conversation with Eustace Chapuys, the Imperial resident ambassador, to a personal reason for pressing for an early conclusion to the negotiations. At the age of forty-six, he was "getting already too advanced in years to wait much longer" for marriage.[3]

To consider a spouse's replacement immediately upon her death was a prevailing practice. In 1480, for example, Ercole, duke of Ferrara, expressed the following condolences to Cesare Valenini, his ambassador at Milan, whose wife had died:

there is always the public good to be placed against the private and one must have patience and not break up . . . Comfort yourself as a strong man, lacking neither arms nor horses. You will find yourself another one, and you will have a new dowry and younger flesh. Don't on account of this put aside our affairs even for the shortest interval . . . and give no thought to your own particular trials.[4]

In 1537, just three months before the demise of Jane, James V of Scotland initiated a process similar to the later one of his Uncle Henry. On 7 July, the day on which James lost his wife, Madeleine, he reported her death to her father Francis I in a letter in which he also revealed that his envoy, David Beaton, would soon be bringing him another message. In the dispatch that Beaton subsequently delivered to Francis, James informed his father-in-law that he was seeking another French wife. It was far from unusual for discussions to be held about the remarriage of an individual whose spouse had not yet died. In 1539 Francis Bonvalot, abbot of St. Vincent and the Imperial ambassador in France, wrote to Charles that a union might be arranged between Henry, dauphin of France, and Mary of Portugal, since his present wife, Catherine de Medici, was in ill health.[5]

One reason for initiating the search so soon after her death was that the process could be a long-drawn-out affair, particularly if it required negotiations with a foreign power, for it was not just an alliance between two private individuals that was at stake but the union of a couple from two different countries or principalities. In addition to the usual debates over dowries and other arrangements that were the foundations of elite marriages, details that involved the diplomatic postures of the two principalities *vis-à-vis* other powers had to be weighed carefully. Who became an ally of England by the union would bring with him the baggage of his previous allies as well as that of his enemies. The monarch was not simply marrying a spouse but was cementing a public relationship that could have far-reaching political, religious, and economic consequences.

In Henry's hunt for a foreign-born wife in 1537–40, the process turned out to be by some standards relatively short – Jane died in October and her successor Anne arrived in England about two years and three months later. Compare this to the negotiations that brought Catherine of Aragon to England: The initial feelers were put out in 1487 when she was two years old, and she landed on the English coast in 1501 when she was sixteen to marry Henry's older brother Arthur. The Tudor family had hoped that she might be sent to England as a child to be reared with the prince so, having known each other for some time, their entry into married life would be a more comfortable transition for them both. As it happened, Henry was only ten years old when he met Catherine, and his youth at their first acquaintance made it easier for him, after he had grown to manhood and had succeeded to the throne in 1509, to wed his bereaved sister-in-law, a widow of some seven years standing.

It seems reasonable to accept Cromwell's statement in the 1537 letter to the ambassadors that Henry personally was ill disposed to remarry. He was forty-six years old and probably because of Jane's sudden demise after childbirth had no English candidate waiting in the wings to become his consort, as was Anne Boleyn in 1527 at the beginning of the divorce proceedings from Catherine of Aragon, and as was Jane in 1536 at the onset of divorce proceedings from his second wife. Unfortunately, Cromwell, unlike Maximilien de Bethune, duke of Sully, left no memoirs of his tenure in power. Sully recalled that when he advised Henry IV of France, a divorced man with no legitimate children, to remarry, he had responded that he feared that his second marriage would succeed no better than the first: "His mind was so violently agitated, that for a long time he could not utter a word . . . at length, recovering himself . . . rubbing his hands together . . . [he said] be it so, there is no remedy: if for the good of my kingdom I must marry, I must."[6] This was the reaction of a man who was and is still widely known for his sexual prowess, indeed, for his lechery.

Like this king, however, Henry VIII surely did not need to be unduly pressured to agree to another marriage or to be at least "indifferent to the thing," as Cromwell asserted to the ambassadors. Although he had already entered into at least two love marriages, albeit to women who although his own subjects were otherwise appropriate choices since they were descendants of Edward I, Henry, like most of his contemporaries, approached matrimony first and foremost as a sacred bond for the purpose of begetting children. Rulers eagerly anticipated the birth of an heir since their dynasties' wealth and power and, it was thought, their subjects' security depended upon it. As Cromwell exclaimed to Wyatt in 1537: "it hath pleased Almighty God, of his goodness to send unto the queen's grace deliverance of a goodly prince, to the great comfort, rejoice, and consolation of the king's majesty, and of all us his most humble, loving, and obedient subjects."[7] Royal children also increased the economic resources of their family and fostered domestic stability, for rulers sought the wealthiest heiresses for their younger sons and united their daughters to powerful subjects.[8] As about one-half of the younger royal children between Edward I and Edward IV married noble offspring, the king's kinsmen, according to Ralph Griffiths, "were well placed to provide a dependable corps of leaders within the nobility at large." Thus in 1537 domestic politics also motivated Henry to increase the number of his children, both male and female.[9]

Another of Cromwell's statements to the ambassadors about the candidate pool is especially interesting. He confirmed that "out of his tender zeal to his subjects," Henry had agreed to "the election of any person from any part that with deliberation shall be thought meet for him." A monarch could normally anticipate that his council would advise him to unite with a foreign-born lady since Henry was only the third reigning English monarch to marry one of his subjects. That his grandfather, Edward IV, had wed the widowed Elizabeth Gray was at the time and is still deemed controversial, not

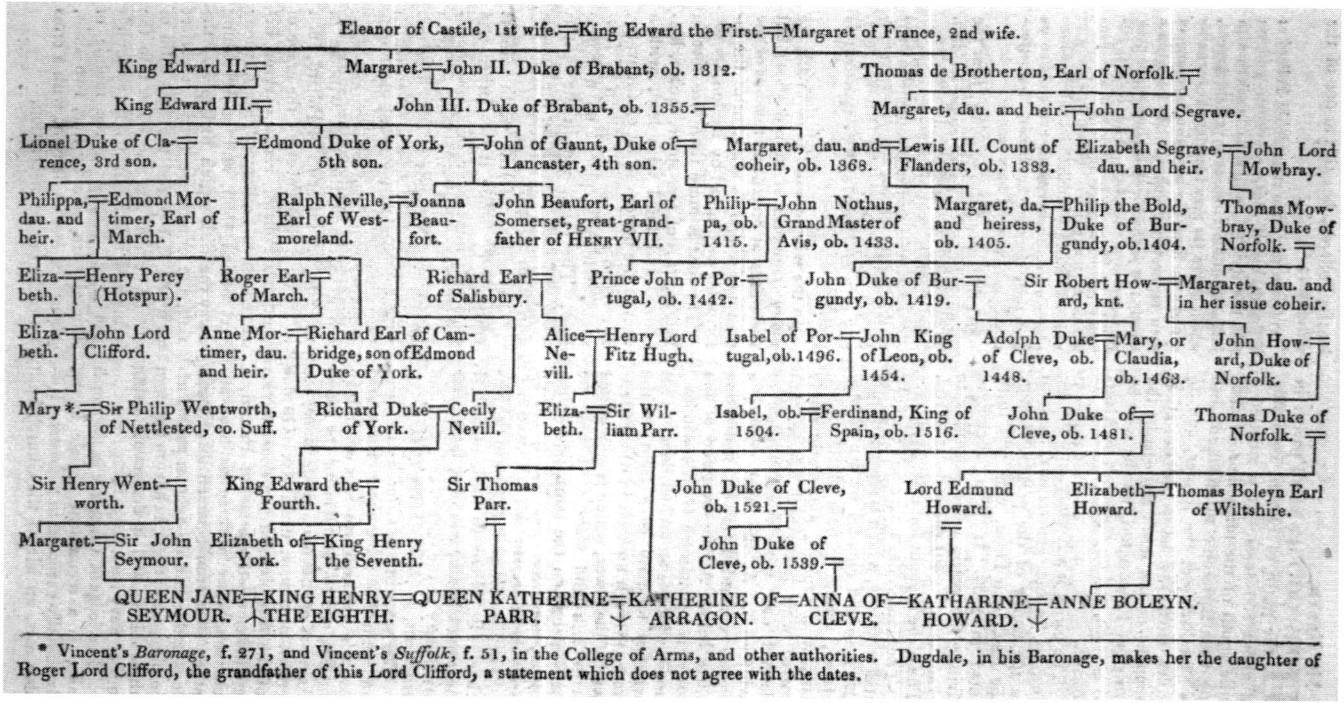

Figure 2 Royal genealogy. *The Gentleman's Magazine*, 1829

the least because it was accomplished in secret. William Camden, the Elizabethan antiquary, was to highlight that marriage's irregularity in his reminder that Edward had been the first monarch to wed an Englishwoman since the Norman Conquest. The subsequent alliance of Henry VII and Elizabeth of York, Henry VIII's parents, gained widespread praise because it was perceived as healing civil-war wounds. Henry VIII himself married four of his subjects, and of them, the first, Anne Boleyn, has forever been associated with the controversies of Reformation politics. While Jane, her successor, won favor for bearing an heir who survived infancy, another result of her marriage was her family's elevation to noble status and claim to political power. At her death it was not likely that the council, whose members included her brother, Thomas, the newly ennobled earl of Hertford, would choose to elevate another English family so high, if for no other reason than that he and his relatives might object to the empowerment of their domestic competitors. In this respect, it is noteworthy that Cromwell's son Gregory became Hertford's brother-in-law in 1537 when he married Elizabeth, the widow of Sir Anthony Oughtred and a sister of Jane and her brothers.[10]

Sometimes the ruler's marriage to his subject served to define his romantic interests. It was not to be expected that the council, the crown's major advisory institution on which Cromwell sat as principal secretary and as lord privy seal would debate the king's love life. In 1537, furthermore, with no compelling crisis, such as a civil war, threatening England, councillors were not likely to recommend a domestic union. Later, his daughter Elizabeth was to discover how controversial the possibility of wedlock with a subject, Sir Robert Dudley, future earl of Leicester, could be. Unlike her possible marriage to a foreign subject, a union with Dudley, which many feared would lead to civil war, was not a topic the privy council ever deliberated.[11]

The council, the body that deliberated another royal marriage, was, as John Guy points out, an emerging institution. The old medieval council, which was undergoing a "progressive and pragmatic" restructuring into the privy council in 1536–40 was becoming a smaller, more coherent body. During Cromwell's tenure in power, it was reduced to about nineteen members but did not gain "bureaucratic routine" until after his demise. It was to become the realm's dominant governing institution, reaching its heights in Elizabeth's reign, only to decline in importance after the Stuart succession in 1603.[12]

According to G. R. Elton, Cromwell was the first minister to enforce "the secretary's universal hold on the affairs of the realm," both domestic and foreign. As the principal secretary, Cromwell was responsible for foreign affairs and handled most of the routine correspondence. Sir John Hackett, the English resident at the court of Margaret of Austria, regent of the Netherlands, for example, noted in a letter to the king in 1534 that he wrote to him only when it was important; otherwise he addressed his correspondence to Cromwell. One of the crown's leading officers, the principal secretary, whose duties were to be split between two ministers in 1540, was the clearing house for diplomatic business and was, therefore, especially interested in how the king's marriage might bolster the realm's stance in the wider European community.[13]

After Henry's separation from Catherine of Aragon, he chose to wed two of his subjects. He may have been reluctant to seek a foreign bride when he began to court Anne Boleyn in 1527 or when he married Jane Seymour in 1536, but it is also true that he was at those times entangled in divorce crises. These domestic dramas distracted, surely even discouraged, him from looking abroad. In 1537 he was for the first time since 1509 a single man without controversy surrounding the reasons for his singleness. Free from domestic entanglements, or as he said, "at liberty from marriage," he could, if he wished, seek a bride anywhere in Christendom. Events were shortly to indicate that he would not be a silent partner in that process, for he agreed to marry a foreign-born lady fully determined to have the major voice in her final selection. By May 1538, for example, he felt it necessary to send word to Hutton in the Netherlands about his surprise that this diplomat had not written in more detail about Christina, dowager duchess of Milan, one of the ladies under consideration as his next queen.[14]

Monarchs sometimes hesitated to select a bride sight unseen. Much evidence exists to indicate that they were far from resigned to this custom and had developed a number of strategies to make the process less problematic for themselves. They asked their diplomats, for example, to view the candidates at close range, to forward detailed reports about them, and to procure their portraits. Some rulers, such as Henry's squeamish daughter, Elizabeth, even stated categorically that they would never marry anyone they had not seen. Recognizing this problem, Cromwell informed Winchester and Howard in 1537 that the king expected them to "discover what the conditions and qualities" of Mary and Margaret were and "to exhibit circumspection and diligence" in their inquiries.[15]

Cromwell also revealed that Henry wished to know "in what point and terms" James "stands toward either of them." Henry clearly sought assurances that they had not made personal commitments to the Scottish monarch and were still free to wed elsewhere. It also seems clear that one of the reasons he chose to single out these two candidates was that he hoped to prevent his nephew from negotiating another French alliance. Inquiries had already been made about whether James might wed Mary Tudor, and even if that union were to prove impossible to arrange, Henry still wanted to discourage the continuation of the Franco-Scottish alliance.[16]

It was in the midst of the controversy surrounding the king's separation from Catherine of Aragon that Cromwell had achieved power. Marital politics could not only make but could also break the careers of ministers, as his patron, Thomas, Cardinal Wolsey, learned when he failed to obtain the king's divorce from this first consort. Wolsey's failure opened the door to advancement for Cromwell who helped to accomplish the divorce through the enactment of the Reformation statutes that effected England's schism from the Roman Church.[17]

A highly skilled parliamentarian who had been ennobled as Lord Cromwell, he was fifty-two years old in 1537. Like Wolsey before him, marital politics ushered in his defeat, for on 28 July 1540, following the king's divorce from Anne of Cleves, he was executed for heresy and treason. This failed marriage was the thread that served to unravel his career and made it possible for his enemies, once he had lost royal favor, to stage-manage his execution. Although it was Henry who selected his brides, he expected his ministers to work expeditiously toward relieving him of those entanglements when they proved unfruitful or when they seemed to threaten the integrity of his lineage. Political complications involving an alliance of the papacy and the emperor helped to derail Wolsey's attempts to obtain an annulment of Henry's union with Catherine. Chapters 4 to 8 will explain how the king's marriage with Anne of Cleves was made and then broken in 1539–40 in reaction to the similar but even more threatening diplomatic complications following France's decision to sign a treaty with the emperor that had been mediated by the papacy. Unlike in 1533 when his parliamentary expertise had helped to smooth the way for Henry's divorce from Catherine, Cromwell did not or could not rise to the challenge and provide concrete remedies for relieving the king of his fourth bride (see Chapter 8).

By theology essentially still Catholic as a result of the first divorce crisis, Henry had assumed the headship of his schismatic church and had participated in heresy trials. In 1533 the Appeals Statute had made it possible for Thomas Cranmer, archbishop of Canterbury, to preside over the king's first and subsequent divorce trials without regard to the papacy. In 1537 the events of the Reformation and the reactions of Paul III and his enemies, the German Protestants, were thus to complicate Henry's quest for a foreign alliance and a wife with whom he hoped to beget another male child.

The ambassadors to whom Cromwell broke the news of the queen's death and with whom he communicated in the attempt to find her successor had already played or were to play major diplomatic roles. Brief biographical sketches of some of those involved in the negotiations in 1537–38 will help to identify the range of individuals who assisted in the wooing process. Lord William Howard was the eldest son of Thomas, second duke of Norfolk, by his second wife Agnes, and was thus an uncle to the king's second consort, Anne Boleyn. Not yet thirty years old in 1537, he was a member of the privy chamber and already had some diplomatic experience. In 1532 he had gone on a mission to Scotland to inquire about whether Mary might become the bride of James, and in 1535 he had delivered the Order of the Garter to him. While on a special mission to France in late 1537, he was ordered by Cromwell to remain there until information about the French candidates had been gathered. William was not involved in the negotiations for Anne of Cleves, although he was a member of the Calais reception party. The downfall in 1541 of another of his nieces, Queen Katherine Howard, led to his temporary imprisonment. His major contributions to political and military events occurred after Henry's death; in 1554, Queen Mary raised him to the peerage as Baron Howard of Effingham.[18]

In contrast, Gardiner, who was about forty years old in 1537, had once been an important member of the king's inner circle of councillors. Following the disgrace in 1529 of Wolsey, who was also

Gardiner's patron, Henry selected him as his principal secretary and granted him the bishopric of Winchester, the wealthiest see in England. He began to lose political influence, however, after he challenged the strategy of Cromwell, who replaced him as principal secretary in 1534, for wresting control of the canon law from the church. The next year, after Winchester defended the royal supremacy in his work, *De Vera Obedientia Oratio*, he was appointed resident ambassador to France. In Henry's reign only a few bishops were called upon for diplomatic service, although 41 percent of the missions still included ecclesiastical personnel, a figure that was to drop to 6 percent in the Elizabethan period. Until his recall in 1538, Winchester participated in most of the discussions concerning a French bride for Henry. Two years later he returned to power amidst the crisis caused by Cromwell's fall and the Cleves divorce.[19]

Cromwell's initial letter to Hutton in the Netherlands concerning a replacement for Jane is no longer extant, but from his response in December 1537, it is evident that Cromwell had asked him to identify some ladies who might be suitable brides for Henry. When Hutton, who had been the governor of the English Merchant Adventurers' Company at Antwerp and the king's agent in the Netherlands since 1536, died in September 1538, he was replaced in these positions by Stephen Vaughan, who had also been living in the Low Countries for some time and had been entrusted with various errands by Henry and by Cromwell, his patron. Ironically, Hutton had once unsuccessfully accused his future replacement of heresy. In September 1538, Vaughan joined Dr. Edward Carne and Sir Thomas Wriothesley to negotiate a marriage between Henry and the queen regent's niece, Christina of Milan. He spent most of the remainder of his life as the royal agent in the Low Countries.[20]

The other two ambassadors with Vaughan in the Netherlands had been in royal service for some time. In the 1530s, Carne, who was educated at Oxford where he became principal of Greek Hall, had gone on several missions to Rome to attempt to extricate Henry from his union with Catherine. He became one of the king's experts on the Low Countries and in the 1540s gained appointment as ambassador to the queen regent's court.[21]

Wriothesley's royal service also commenced in the 1530s when he was in his late twenties. Characterized by Walter Richardson as a "meticulous" official "who could be depended upon to execute efficiently a predetermined policy," he spent most of that decade performing secretarial tasks for Henry.[22] As clerk of the signet, for example, he controlled the ciphers used in diplomatic correspondence. After Hutton's death, he served as ambassador to the queen regent's court and returned home in March 1539 when a war with the Franco-Imperial coalition seemed imminent. In 1540 he and Sir Ralph Sadler won appointment as the king's two principal secretaries. Ultimately, he became Henry's lord chancellor and gained the title of earl of Southampton after Edward VI's succession.[23]

Charles V was another ruler whose opinion was crucial to the success of Henry's marriage negotiations since one of the candidates, Christina of Milan, was also his niece. The English ambassador with the emperor was Wyatt, the great English poet whose patron was Cromwell. Arrested at the time of Anne Boleyn's fall in 1536, Wyatt, who was then about thirty-three years old, remained in prison for one month before his release. In the next few years he served two different terms as resident to the emperor. Some months after Cromwell's death, he was arrested but pardoned by the king and died in 1542.[24]

At the beginning of the search, as noted above, Cromwell instructed the ambassadors at Brussels and Paris to obtain information about possible brides. That correspondence stands as evidence of one important means by which unions between individuals of different countries could be initiated. A review of English institutions and offices will help in following the marrying process from Cromwell's letters in 1537 through Anne and Henry's marriage in 1540 and its subsequent dissolution. The officers who went abroad were resident and *ad hoc* ambassadors, some of whom were gentlemen of the privy chamber, and heralds.

The diplomatic corps had an interesting development. Rulers in early Christendom had sent messengers, sometimes called *nuncii*, to other princes for the purpose of negotiating matters of mutual interest, especially the marriage treaties that formed a considerable part of their workload. These diplomats had a variety of names besides *nuncii*: sometimes they were addressed as ambassador, a name that first spread in Italy in the high middle ages, occasionally orator, a term that ultimately supplanted ambassador in Venetian documents, and even legatus, a title that could be but was not always associated with the papacy. At the end of the fifteenth century, these terms were still used interchangeably, but the word ambassador was ultimately to triumph. Partly to provide their arrival with a ceremonial touch, the diplomats carried with them letters of credence as well as oral messages to the host courts.[25] On these missions they represented their rulers' views, or as Sir Francis Walsingham, ambassador to France, said in 1571: "I left my private passions behind me, and do submit my self to the passions of my prince."[26]

Starting in the twelfth century with the revival of Roman law, rulers also appointed agents, called procurators, with the power to "negotiate *and* conclude" treaties. This office, which first appears in English documents in 1193, is the antecedent of the modern ambassador plenipotentiary. Like the less powerful envoys, whom they supplemented but did not replace, procurators had several names, such as ambassador or orator. From the early thirteenth century they began to act as proxies in marriages on behalf of their rulers. This practice spread fairly rapidly and ultimately initial proxy unions preceded most of the nuptials of couples who hailed from different native lands.[27]

At first both types of ambassadors were *ad hoc* appointees. They were dispatched on specific missions and returned home when their tasks were accomplished or when it was determined that it was impossible for them to be completed. By the mid-fifteenth century, some Italian governments began to require the less powerful ambassadors to remain at the political units to which they sent frequent messages. These ambassadors resided at their appointed posts for indefinite lengths of time and proved to be of assistance to other diplomats, especially those with full powers, who arrived on special missions.[28]

Henry VII began the English practice of employing resident ambassadors. The first identifiable ones are John Stile, who resided in Spain from 1505 to 1510 and from 1512 to 1517, and John Spinelly, whose origins are somewhat obscure but who was certainly employed in the Netherlands early in the reign of Henry VIII. The development of a permanent corps for the management of foreign relations was, according to Charles Carter, "the most significant mark of modern diplomacy." One major disadvantage of the system was, however, that, in an age when communications were slow, the resident's information about his homeland became somewhat dated.[29]

A ruler might decide to appoint two residents to important courts, one of higher status to handle discussions with the monarch and one of lesser status to collect news and to witness his official acts. An occasional *ad hoc* ambassador might also be sent on a special assignment to these same courts. This was how England often conducted French diplomacy. When, for example, Winchester first arrived at Paris in September 1535, he worked with Sir John Wallop, already there as the English resident. It was the duty of Wallop, also a member of Henry's privy chamber, to acquaint Winchester with recent events in the kingdom and to instruct him concerning matters of protocol that were relevant to his mission. In the spring of 1537 when Wallop returned home, Winchester carried on alone as resident but was later joined by Sir Francis Bryan of the privy chamber and Thomas Thirlby, future bishop of Westminster. In 1538 Edmund Bonner, future bishop of London, and a series of *ad hoc* diplomats replaced Winchester and his two colleagues. Bonner had actually expected to be joined in his residency by a member of the privy chamber but that appointment was never made.[30]

As noted, some of the above named ambassadors were also gentlemen of the privy chamber. Their appointments are interesting because they served Henry in England in a personal rather than in a public capacity. David Starkey has pointed out that the privy chamber, which emerged as the third household department in the reign of Henry VII, gained a new hierarchical staff in 1518–19 that included gentlemen at the highest levels. The purpose of this restructuring seems to have been to provide Henry's personal servants "parity of status" with those of the French king. David Potter has claimed that it was the use of these "second-rate" men as ambassadors that made it possible for France to outwit England in foreign relations, especially in Germany. Ministers at courts abroad clearly understood what their domestic capacity was; in 1537 Gian Matheo Giberti, bishop of Verona, referred to Bryan as one of Henry's "principal mignons." From the later Tudor period, the duties of these men were limited to domestic matters.[31]

"Trafficking in news," according to David Queller, was the resident's prime duty, although he could also possess full powers to negotiate and conclude treaties. Governments demanded frequent letters from their ambassadors, who were, as Lope de Soria wrote to the emperor from Venice in 1539, "duty bound to report all they hear and learn." Sometimes they obtained information so sensitive that it had to be communicated to their governments in cipher. In England a favorite place to gather news was at St. Paul's Cathedral, where gentry, lords, courtiers, and professional men walked up and down the center aisle conversing with each other between 11:00 a.m. and noon and again between 3:00 p.m. and 6:00 p.m. The expectation that they should collect information was so great that ambassadors sometimes felt it necessary to apologize for their lack of it, as did Richard Pate, ambassador to the Netherlands in 1540, who lamented to Henry: "This court is the closest in the world, I think, for news."[32]

Their news was, as Joycelyne Russell reported, "an endlessly stirred whirlpool of information, misinformation, and . . . disinformation." They sometimes bribed courtiers for information, although this practice did not, of course, ensure the transmission of accurate facts. These bribes, as Charles V noted in 1537, might be rich jewels, money, or even pensions. The diplomats were occasionally somewhat disingenuous. In 1538 Cromwell, who had received a pension from Francis, informed the English ambassadors in Paris that Louis de Perreau, sieur de Castillon, had offered to forward Henry's letters to them by the French courier. Since the king could not refuse this offer without displaying distrust, Cromwell had decided to send this message to them by the French courier as though it were actually Henry's packet of materials.[33]

At the end of the seventeenth century, Abraham van Wicquefort, who wrote a "text-book of diplomatic practice," confirmed that it was "lawful" for diplomats "to corrupt" the ministers of the courts where they resided. By this time some countries, such as France and Spain, had succeeded in developing well-structured intelligence networks to supplement the work of their ambassadors. It was actually because residents functioned as intelligence gatherers that a few monarchs had at first been reluctant to admit them into their realms, and when they did, made attempts to isolate them in their embassies and to have them spied on in turn. A vague line existed between the job as fact gatherer and as spy.[34]

But as they were thus "suspected" of being spies, van Wicquefort warned them "to suspect every body," for as he noted, princes had "their agents, who make it their business to acquire the confidence of the ambassador" in the hope of passing off "false news" to him. In the 1530s Cromwell had certainly functioned as one of Henry's most successful councillors by ingratiating himself with diplomats, especially with Chapuys, to pass on "false news." Cromwell had also sent Vaughan, the future diplomat to the Netherlands, to spy on Chapuys when he visited with Catherine of Aragon shortly before her death in 1536. In addition, in his treatise that was translated into English in 1603, John Hotman warned diplomats against hiring servants from the country to which they were assigned for fear these hirelings would act as spies. He even recommended that ambassadors take their wives with them to supervise their households in order to prevent its members from revealing sensitive information to outsiders. It was far from unusual for the most high-ranking servants of the diplomat's staff to sell documents, even ciphered dispatches, as occurred in 1541 when Chapuys obtained a copy of a letter from Francis to his embassy in England. Governments were also concerned that the ambassador, himself, might accept bribes. According to Garrett Mattingly, this fear caused some monarchs to hesitate to appoint a resident, whose long tenure might make it possible for him to develop intimate relationships with the host prince and his ministers that might tempt him to accept bribes from them.[35]

The diplomats' service as spies meant that they also had to be careful not to reveal sensitive material inadvertently. In the spirit of the need for secrecy, they often had to pass on inaccurate facts and to prevaricate, duties that some found offensive. In 1539 Bonner complained to Cromwell that it was difficult for him to "dissemble" and speak graciously to the French king and his servants. Henry Wotton, the English ambassador to France in 1604, made the famous comment about this duty: *Legatus est vir bonus peregre missus ad mentien dum reipublica causa* [an ambassador is an honest man sent abroad to lie for the good of his country].[36] Despite the ubiquitous awareness that ambassadors acted as spies, many authors of treatises maintained that their persons were "sacred" and that they were, like friars and pilgrims, under special papal protection. Even the houses of ambassadors were considered "inviolable." This theory was seldom followed to the letter; rulers routinely sought to uncover evidence about the intelligence that ambassadors were gathering at their courts; sometimes they confiscated diplomatic pouches. Occasionally, they even imprisoned the ambassadors themselves, as occurred in England and Spain in 1528. After the English minister who was sent to escort the Imperial ambassador to an audience with Henry retained him in custody, Wolsey announced that the diplomatic prisoner would be released as soon as the English resident in Spain was freed.[37]

That these ambassadors operated as spies, and were widely known to be spies, was not a bizarre practice within the political culture. Many individuals, from military leaders to courtiers, were on the alert to uncover secret information about their countrymen for their rulers, who rewarded them for this intelligence with office, prestige, authority, and financial windfalls. Ambassadors also had to worry about the activities of fellow diplomats. In 1538, for example, Cromwell asked Bonner to spy on Winchester, whom he was replacing as resident in France. Thus, early modern sovereignty, defined by John Archer as "a system of political power organized around the court" of a ruler, was bound up with intelligence gathering and spying as well as with the better-known culture of display, that is the visible processions, ceremonies, and entertainments.[38]

Other diplomatic controversies arose from the demands princes made in the name of status and protocol. The *ad hoc* ambassadors of the late middle ages and early modern periods with full powers to negotiate and to conclude treaties were sometimes of the nobility. Governments expected ambassadors who were charged to carry out important negotiations to be of appropriate quality to handle those matters. Edward II, for example, had halted marriage negotiations between England and Portugal in 1325 because the Portuguese *nuncii* were of insufficient status. About 200 years later in 1541, Chapuys reported the French ambassador's dismay when he learned that Henry planned to appoint Sir William Paget, clerk of the privy council, whom he characterized as "a man of very little stuff and still smaller quality," to negotiate a marriage between Mary Tudor and Charles of Orléans. In his book on diplomacy, Hotman also complained about rulers who sent "grooms of the chamber, cloakbearers, and others of baser sort unto the greatest princes of Christendom," and lamented: "And God knoweth how they handle many times the affairs of their masters." Later, van Wicquefort confirmed this opinion: "It is impossible for a man of vile condition, duly to represent a great prince unless it be upon the theatre, and to divert the people."[39]

More specifically, in the wooing process the looks and character of the negotiators held great significance. Hotman warned that it was inadvisable to choose "an old and melancholy man to treat of a marriage with a young princess, and make love unto her in the behalf of his master," for "she would not so willingly see or hear him as one that were more youthful and gallant." He also advised against selecting a person who was "bleary-eyed, crooktbackt, lame, or otherwise misshapen."[40]

As their governments' representatives, their treatment in terms of material goods and of protocol not only identified the relationship of their country to the host realm but also signaled whether they were making an appearance worthy of the rank of their princes. As Francis Thynne pointed out: "Our ancestors were in times past so careful of their honor, and that every man should be furnished according to his degree, that they left not undetermined, with what troops of horses everyone should be furnished when he went ambassador." The diplomat's retinue, like that of the archbishop of Rheims who arrived in England in 1440, could include hundreds of individuals besides the usual secretaries who handled correspondence and the steward who oversaw the household budget. Most ambassadors lived less lavishly than this archbishop, but Winchester seems to have employed numerous servants, and according to Bonner in 1538 kept a expensive household. He countered with the charge that Bonner was besmirching Henry's honor by living "wretchedly" on 10 shillings a day. It was important for the ambassador to live well to mark his master's liberality.[41]

"Diplomacy without ritual," as David Kertzer has pointed out, "is inconceivable. Protocol is ever important, and the right symbols must be manipulated in just the right way."[42] A standardized ritual developed around an ambassador's arrival and departure; it was usually more lavish for the special envoy than for the resident. These ceremonies not only helped to make countries appear powerful but also offered signals of their respect for each other. It was the duty of the host country to dispatch individuals of suitable rank to greet the ambassador. In England on important occasions the welcoming party went all the way to Dover; at other times it stopped at Canterbury. After the diplomat's arrival, if he were of sufficient status, he might be escorted in a public procession to his initial meeting with the ruler. According to English custom, agents assigned to the kingdom had to delay their visits to diplomats of powers friendly to their own realms until after they had been summoned to this first royal audience. For the procession to meet the king, civic leaders might decorate the streets with fountains of wine and stage pageants with musical accompaniments. This ceremonial increased in splendor into the early seventeenth century.[43]

At court, during his audience with the ruler, the ambassador might also be met with great ceremony. In 1538, for example, Castillon noted that the English court was extremely ceremonious even on feast days. The newly arrived ambassador handed over his credentials and gave a set speech in which he explained the reasons for his mission. "Speaking," as Peter Burke has observed, "was an art, a kind of performance, which mattered even more" in the early modern period than it does today. In addition, the non-verbal language, the posture, gestures, and tone of voice were also ritualized to lessen miscommunications and to enhance the ability for understanding at a time when Latin reigned as the diplomats' language, although French and Spanish, but not English, were sometimes utilized.[44]

During the ambassador's stay, the courtesy with which the ruler and his ministers treated him indicated the relationship of their countries to each other. In 1540, for example, Wallop, who had returned to France as resident, noted the condescension of Francis, who had escorted him through his private chambers at Fontainebleu. For this reason, princes of friendly countries tried to appoint ambassadors with whom the host rulers felt comfortable. In 1540 Anne de Montmorency, grand constable of France, told his resident in England that he should make himself agreeable to the king and his councillors. The emergence of new, antagonistic relations between realms could be signaled by the exchange of openly hostile envoys for friendly ones. In the event, however, that the two principalities concluded a treaty, a grand fête or other entertainment might be held to honor the resident. Finally, at his recall home the host ruler granted him a farewell audience and offered him gifts, the nature of which depended on his social rank and the warmth of feelings that existed between their two countries. The decision to withhold these courtesies signaled strained relationships. In 1522 occurred, noted Sydney Anglo, a most "unpleasant negative use of public ceremony in Tudor diplomacy," for because of deteriorating Anglo-French relations, the Venetian ambassador was the sole mourner at the funeral of the French ambassador who had died at his London post. When such circumstances arose, a diplomat, as did Castillon in 1539, might plead to be recalled out of fear that the host ruler might do him an injury.[45]

An even more controversial question was the ceremonial status ambassadors demanded on behalf of their principals. This was a significant issue, for their ranking indicated the relative importance of their homelands to each other. Although, in the early seventeenth century, Hotman could confidently write that "almost everyone . . . knoweth the degree and place that is due unto them," sufficient doubt existed about the status princes deserved or thought they deserved that their diplomats were sometimes called upon to defend their place or rank.[46]

A keen rivalry had emerged between France and Castile in the fifteenth century. Although generally the superior standing of France had gained recognition, conflict erupted between the two realms on this issue: In 1459 at the Congress of Mantua, for example, the Castilian representative had an armed force eject the French ambassador from his seat of precedence. This issue was not laid to rest, as it was hoped it would be, by Pope Julius II's list in 1504 that named the realms in the following order: the Holy Roman Empire, France, Castile, Aragon, Portugal, England, Sicily, Scotland, Hungary, Navarre, and Cyprus. Competition between Spain and France became particularly acrimonious in the Stuart period. In the reign of James I, to lessen their disputes, the two country's ambassadors were usually never invited to the same court masques. Their on-going rivalry finally led to a bloody encounter in London in 1661 in which the Spanish gained a momentary victory. The carriages of the French and Spanish ambassadors fought a battle for first place in a procession assembled to greet the Swedish ambassador. It left a French postilion dead, "hamstrung" two of the French coach horses, and almost precipitated a war between Louis XIV and Philip IV. Consequently, Charles II banned the participation of diplomatic coaches in processions, and Philip decreed that henceforth his ambassadors would decline to attend occasions where their first-place rank might be disputed.[47]

Besides Franco-Spanish conflicts, disagreements among other realms about their ranking occasionally occurred. Henry VIII, for example, did not recognize that John of Portugal held a position superior to him at either the French or the emperor's court. In 1538, after a protest from him about rankings at the Imperial court, Charles's privy seal, Nicholas Perrenot, sieur de Granvelle, wrote an explanation to Henry that placed his ruler firmly on the fence on this issue. Granvelle admitted that while the emperor "could not possibly affirm that the king of Portugal ought to precede [Henry] . . . at the same time honesty and close relationship" prevented Charles, who was married to John's sister, from denying Portuguese precedence. Henry later disingenuously informed Castillon that Granvelle's message indicated that the emperor did not wish to accord Portugal a superior status to that of England. That summer, as Winchester was preparing to return from France, his instructions to Bonner stated that the English ambassador was to be placed after the Imperial but before the Portuguese agents on ceremonial occasions. If the diplomat failed to gain the placement he thought appropriate, his recourse was either to decline to attend the event or to go incognito as a private citizen.[48]

By the end of the seventeenth century, the number and lavishness of diplomatic ceremonies had declined. Van Wicquefort noted that all "superfluous civilities" had been done away with because the English had been made aware that their ambassadors were not given lavish receptions abroad. Henceforth diplomats were met at Gravesend, conducted from there to the Tower in royal barges, where they were transferred to coaches belonging to the court and transported to their own houses or to the lodgings provided for ambassadors. This was the scaled down practice that prevailed throughout the continent, but exceptions could be made for extraordinary occasions, such as royal marriages, which demanded a greater ceremonial presence.[49]

This description of the diplomatic corps did not apply to all territories. In some units, such as the Netherlands, which was an appendage of the Empire, one or more resident English agents, such as Hutton and Vaughan who also served as governors of the Company of Merchant Adventurers, were retained and were styled ambassadors, although the embassies were not credited with a permanent status like those at France and Spain. A few states, like the German ones including the duchy of Cleves, did not have resident diplomacy. Even the most routine matters had to be negotiated by special envoys, whose status was generally similar to that of a minor resident. A second group of entities was too insignificant to be involved in international concerns or, like the duchy of Milan, had come under the control of a foreign power.[50]

Although one or more resident or *ad hoc* ambassadors might already be present at a court and could, therefore, make inquiries about brides for their prince, other means of discovering information were available. A second extraordinary embassy might arrive with instructions to perform one task publicly but to do another concerned with wooing matters *sub rosa*. A royal relative or even a lower level "functionary," such as a merchant, a scholar, a tourist, or a cleric with contacts abroad might be asked unofficially to discover information that would be useful in deciding whether a monarch should initiate negotiations to marry a particular lady.[51]

Another agent who could be sent abroad was a herald. The office of herald had developed out of the medieval office of minstrel, when some of the household staff had begun to specialize in devising pageants. The first reference to them in the English records occurred in 1290 when a knowledge of armorial bearings was already essential to their duties. By the end of that century, a well-developed system of the officers of arms had emerged under the authority of the lord high constable. In 1420 the first official chapter of the heralds was held at which were present three kings of arms and four heralds. While lords and knights often retained heralds and pursuivants (junior heralds), kings of arms served only sovereigns by whom they were crowned with much ceremony. In 1484 Richard III incorporated the heralds and granted them Coldharbour House, but his successor, Henry VII, confiscated the building and voided the incorporation, although he did confirm a rotation of kings of arms, heralds, and pursuivants for attendance at court. In 1555 Queen Mary granted them Derby House, which burned down in the Great Fire of 1666, but the site with a new structure remains the headquarters of the College of Arms.[52]

The growing elaboration of the tournaments that heralds orchestrated increased their prominence, for from Edward III's reign they had both military and diplomatic functions. Their duties included carrying declarations of war and even challenges for personal duels between rulers, such as the one Francis sent to the emperor in 1528. They framed ordinances for the royal household, made up lists of precedences for functions such as weddings and banquets, assisted the marshal at coronations, acted as masters of ceremonies, supervised funerals, and at least from 1530 visited communities to identify armorial families.[53]

They were sometimes accredited as *ad hoc* ambassadors in the late fifteenth century, but it is not clear which herald was the first to possess diplomatic status, for most were only messengers. There is general agreement, however, that Henry VII employed Roger Machado, Richmond, Norroy, and Clarenceux, king of arms, as ambassador, primarily on missions to France. In Henry VIII's reign, Thomas Benolt, Windsor, Norroy, and Clarenceux, king of arms, fulfilled ambassadorial duties on missions, such as the one to Scotland in 1516 when he was required to obtain ratification of the Anglo-Scottish truce. Officers of arms may have gained acceptance as ambassadors because their membership in an international order gave them passages of safe-conduct; rulers through whose countries they traveled could not, for example, imprison them.[54] These safe-conducts could not protect them from the anger of a monarch to whom they delivered a hostile message. In 1528, for example, the emperor arrested the two heralds who brought him declarations of war from England and France. Even while some heralds acted as ambassadors, therefore, most continued to function as messengers.[55]

In the seventeenth century their duties and powers began to wane. Their local visitations to identify armorial families came to an end in 1686. By then their control of funerals had been compromised, and because of the professionalization of the diplomatic corps, they no longer served as ambassadors. Sir John Borough, Norroy, Garter, king of arms, who died in the service of Charles I in 1643, for example, went on missions in which his duties for the most part seem to have been those of an escort and a clerk. In the course of the sixteenth century, furthermore, with changes in the character of armor, heraldry had ceased to be a means of recognition in the field, and in the seventeenth century, war games, such as jousts, which the heralds had supervised, went out of fashion. Even less dangerous sports traditionally associated with heraldry came to be entirely eclipsed. Thus, officers of arms essentially became genealogists, topographers, and antiquaries with the duty of maintaining coats of arms and of preserving their manuscripts at the College of Arms, although they continued to play an important role in royal and noble ceremonies and processions.[56]

As might be expected, these councillors and diplomats generated a plethora of documents. First, signaling their appointment, letters of credence identified the quality of the minister. Without these credentials, which were shown to the host rulers, the new appointees lacked authority to represent their governments. Next, when appropriate, letters of procuration empowered them to negotiate and to conclude treaties. Then, the councillors issued instructions for the diplomat's discussions with the foreign rulers, any relevant evidentiary documents, and letters of safe conduct or passage. Some princes asked to read the instructions, which the envoys were warned not to produce. Since presenting a foreign government with the instructions came to be seen as an act of friendship, some princes began to send two sets of instructions, one to be revealed to the host ruler and one to be kept secret. In 1539, although the instructions of Charles de Marillac warned him to keep official documents a secret, he confessed to Montmorency that, since there was no sensitive information in them, he had shown them to Henry to alleviate his suspicions. So that Marillac could continue to share some of his messages with Henry, the diplomat also requested that nothing confidential be included in Francis's letters to him. During the ambassadors' residency, further instructions were sent to them, and they were expected to send back dispatches regularly, to make reports as appropriate, and to compose relations or final reports when their tours ended.[57]

It is interesting that in some sense most of the diplomatic, personal, and governmental corps of offices utilized to effect Henry's marriage in 1540 were in the early rather than the later stages of their development. All of them, even the heralds, were either at the heights of their powers or reaching toward them early in the sixteenth century, but they were to decline in significant ways in the late Tudor or the Stuart period. The relatively new office of resident ambassador won wide acceptance in the early sixteenth century when much emphasis was placed on ceremonial affairs. It was to observe this elaborate protocol well into the Stuart period but no further. As the diplomatic corps was increasing in the number and the kinds of its agents, the privy council was undergoing the opposite kind of development.[58] Restructured out of the old royal council, it was to reach its heights in the reign of Elizabeth and then to decline significantly. Like the ambassadors, the heralds had developed a hierarchical structure and, for a short time, played significant diplomatic roles. As ceremonial festivities for ambassadors were decreasing in the seventeenth century so, also, were the duties of heralds diminishing. In the meantime, the privy chamber whose members had been utilized for public business enjoyed a shorter period of diplomatic service than did the officers of arms. Already on the wane in Elizabeth's reign, the privy chamber went into permanent decline after the Stuart succession.

Chapter 3 briefly examines the failure of these royal ministers and diplomats to arrange a treaty of marriage for Henry with either an Imperial or a French bride. Ultimately, his foreign policy floundered on the success of Paul III in mediating a truce and then an alliance between Charles and Francis that Henry viewed as both threatening his realm with isolation and opening up the possibility of a combined Franco-Imperial crusade against him. In reaction to these events, Cromwell and he were to look to Germany for a bride.

3 CANDIDATE POOL

In the winter of 1536 before Jane's death, Henry and Charles V had been attempting to arrange a marriage for Mary Tudor, Henry's daughter by his late wife Catherine of Aragon, who was also the emperor's aunt. The proposed husband was Don Luis, brother of John of Portugal and Empress Isabella, the wife of Charles. One of the concessions Henry hoped to negotiate was the emperor's grant of Milan to Don Luis.[1] Both Mary's targeted bridegrooms and her father's potential brides and the eagerness with which they were courted provide insights into how this duchy for which Louis XII and Francis I had spilled much blood intruded into England's foreign-policy schemes.[2]

In this chapter the competition for Milan emerges as an interesting twist in Henry's search for a wife. A brief account of his attempts to gain access to it through diplomacy serves as a backdrop to a discussion of the candidates he wooed or considered wooing and to an examination of contemporary romantic marriage etiquette, including portrait exchanges and inspection strategies. Finally, the progress of his courtships will be traced to their unsuccessful conclusions in 1538–39 with some attention directed to Paul III's crucial intervention in the negotiations.

France had a genealogical claim to Milan, as Francis I and Louis XII could trace their lineage back to Valentina, daughter of Giangaleazzo Visconti of Milan who had wed their ancestor, Louis of Orléans. In the marriage contract, Giangaleazzo had promised that if the Visconti family failed in the male line, Milan would go to Orléans's descendants, but in 1447 when Filippo Maria Visconti died without male heirs, Francesco Sforza defied this pledge. The husband of Bianca, an illegitimate daughter of this last Visconti duke, Francesco established control over the duchy in 1450.[3]

Some sixty-five years later, Francis, the great-grandson of Valentina Visconti through two different lines of descent, ascended the French throne bent upon eliminating Sforza rule in Milan. Control of this duchy, which was the doorway to Italy, would permit France to escape the threat of Habsburg encirclement. Francis conquered Milan only to lose it to Imperial forces in 1521. Four years later, after he had again taken the duchy, he was captured by Charles following a rout at Pavia and spent slightly more than a year as his prisoner. He was released after he agreed to wed the emperor's sister Eleanor, dowager queen of Portugal. In 1527 still hoping to gain control of Milan, Francis sent another army into Italy, only to have it suffer another disastrous defeat.[4]

Then in November 1535 the death of Francesco II, the last Sforza duke of Milan whose widow was Christina, a niece of the emperor, appeared to open up new opportunities. The next January, Francis, who was negotiating an alliance with the emperor's enemy, Suleiman the Magnificent, sultan of the Ottoman Turks, intruded into Savoy, an outpost of northern Italy that he claimed as his inheritance through his mother Louise, half-sister of its ruler, Charles III who was also the emperor's brother-in-law. As Francis well knew, to attack Savoy was to attack the emperor. In a counter thrust, Charles V, as the suzerain of Milan, penetrated briefly into Provence while his armies seized the county of St. Pol in Picardy on the Flemish frontier. In control of Savoy and hoping to draw the northern war to a close, Francis agreed to a truce in 1537 and began to seek possession of Milan through a marriage between one of his sons and a relative of the emperor, whose dowry would include the duchy.[5]

England had long been interested in Milan. In 1368 Edward III's son Lionel, duke of Clarence, had traveled to Lombardy to wed Violante Visconti, sister of Giangaleazzo who had been attempting to expand his influence through a series of dynastic alliances. Many in England unrealistically expected that with Milan as a base, Clarence might become king of all Italy, but these hopes ended with his death in October, a few months after his June wedding. Relations between England and Milan continued to be close, and the possibility of Richard II's marriage to Catherine Visconti, daughter of Duke Bernabo, was raised. When papal politics helped to derail this alliance, Richard wed Anne of Bohemia. At first his Lancastrian successors, especially Henry V, invested their resources in northern

Europe where they hoped to protect their French conquests, which, however, except for the port town of Calais were lost forever in 1453.[6]

While the French were expelling the English from their borders, a variety of important Anglo-Italian contacts were being developed: In 1445 Henry VI married Margaret of Anjou, a daughter of René I who was a pretender to the crown of Sicily; in England, Milanese and Venetian ambassadors joined legates of a renewed papacy to conduct diplomatic and religious matters; enthused by the spirit of humanism, English scholars studied classical languages and literature in Italy; after the death of Elizabeth of York in 1503, Henry VII, the patron of Italian scholars and artists such as Polydore Vergil and Pietro Torrigiano, contemplated wedding Giovanna, widow of Ferrandino the Younger, king of Naples. Upon the elder Henry's death in 1509, his namesake successor maintained contacts with Italian rulers principally through the activities of his agents at Rome. After Jane became his wife in 1536, in response to French territorial ambitions but also to counter papal maneuvers to effect peace between Francis and Charles, Henry chose to pursue options for extending English influence into Italy through the marriage of his daughter to the Portuguese infante.[7]

Jane's death seemed to increase the likelihood of Henry's influencing the settlement of Milan by making it possible for his next marriage to be a factor in the negotiations. Shortly after her demise, as noted in Chapter 2, Cromwell questioned diplomats abroad about possible successors. In France he inquired about Margaret, who was born in 1523, and Mary of Guise, who was born in 1515. It is interesting that Henry was willing to consider a French bride, for in 1536 shortly after the execution of Anne Boleyn who had spent her youth in France, he had rejected a French candidate with the retort that he had already "had too much experience of French bringing up and manners." In 1537, however, when it was learned that James, his twenty-five-year old nephew, intended to wed Mary of Guise, the Tudor monarch decided to pursue the possibility of marrying her while rejecting Margaret, allegedly on the grounds that she was too young for him. It is likely, as noted earlier, that his motive for competing with James for Mary was to interfere with the continuance of the Franco-Scottish pact, for Scotland was widely regarded as England's "natural" enemy.[8]

Cromwell's other message required Hutton in the Netherlands to seek out names of potential brides.[9] The first of his four candidates was Margaretha, the fourteen-year-old daughter of Lord Reinoud III van Brederode, who was a captain-general in the emperor's army in Picardy, and his deceased wife Philippote, niece to Eberhard de la Marck, cardinal of Liége, who had assumed responsibility for the girl's dowry. An attendant of the queen regent, Margaretha was, according to Hutton, "of a goodly stature," "vertuous," "sad," and "womanly," but her beauty was only "competent." Since Henry had rejected Margaret of France because of her youth, he may also have considered Brederode's daughter, who was about the same age as the princess, too young. In addition, he surely was disinclined to marry a dependant of Cardinal Liége, who was a friend of Reginald Pole, a Yorkist descendant with a claim to the English throne and who had completed a volume in 1536 that promoted the restoration of papal supremacy in England. Characterizing Henry's methods as Turkish, Pole lamented the death of Thomas More, the king's divorce from Catherine, and the treatment of the rebels in the Pilgrimage of Grace. In December 1536, Pope Paul III raised Pole to the College of Cardinals and the following April empowered him as his legate to travel across France to meet with Catholic sympathizers in England. Using his diplomatic clout, Henry forced Pole's expulsion from France and thwarted his aim to reside at the queen regent's court, but he could not prevent Pole's taking refuge in Liége's dominions where he was entertained, as he boasted, "with liberality." In August, less than two months before Jane's death, Pole returned to Rome, and under these circumstances, it is unlikely that Henry ever gave Liége's relative serious consideration as his bride. She was to wed Pierre Ernst, count of Mansfeld in 1542.[10]

The second candidate, Frances van Luxembourg, widow of Jan van Egmond, second count of Egmond, was, Hutton noted, of "goodly personage." Like Margaretha she belonged to a prominent Netherlands family: only the Nassau princes of Orange exceeded the Egmonds and van Brederodes in wealth and landed estates. The Brussels home of the van Brederodes was even comfortable enough for the queen regent to select as her residence for a time in 1533. The countess must have been a youthful looking forty-year-old lady, for, according to Hutton, her age did not show in her face. Although she had proved to be fertile, having been delivered of one daughter and two sons who lived to adulthood, she was indisputably too old to wed for the principal goal of childbearing. Unlike Margaretha she remained unmarried.[11]

The third and fourth ladies Hutton knew only by reputation and rumor. He had learned that Christina of Milan was beautiful, but had heard "no great praise" of the personage or the "beauty" of Anne, a daughter of John III of Juliers–Cleves. In 1537 no compelling reason existed for Henry seriously to consider wedding a daughter of John, whose heir William was intent upon gaining control of Gelderland against the emperor's wishes. Christina soon emerged at the top of Hutton's list amidst rumors that her uncle, the emperor, would marry her to the heir of Juliers–Cleves to settle the Guelders dispute.[12]

By early 1538 the negotiations with the Habsburgs were enlarged to include Henry's wooing of Christina, or as he said in his January letter to Wyatt at the emperor's court, he "might honour the said duchess by marriage, her virtue, qualities and behavior being reported to be such as is worthy to be much advanced." He also required Wyatt to claim responsibility for her selection from the bridal pool. This was a frequently used convention, for if the diplomat's ruler appeared too eager for an alliance, his bargaining position might be greatly diminished. In 1538, for example, when Henry remarked to Castillon that Francis had first suggested a marriage between one of his sons and Mary Tudor, the diplomat quickly took credit for initiating that proposal.[13]

Born in February 1522, the duchess of Milan was only slightly older than Margaret of France, but Henry seems to have believed that her experience as a wife of a considerably older man would offset her youthfulness. Imperial documents comparing Christina to her cousin, Mary of Portugal, another niece of Charles who was briefly considered for the English alliance, support this speculation. The daughter of the deceased Manuel I and his wife Eleanor of Austria, who had since married the French king, Mary was a half-sister of Don Luis, a potential husband for Mary Tudor. In early 1538 the Imperial ambassadors reported to Charles that because of "her age and position," Henry believed that the duchess was "a more convenient" bride for him than the infanta. Since Mary, who had been born in 1521, was a bit older than Christina, this statement seems odd, but as the infanta had never been wed, the comment surely reflected Henry's preference for the lady with marital experience. The emperor agreed that the duchess was a better choice for him because of "her age and corpulence, as well as the near resemblance of their complexions resulting from their births in corresponding climates with similar modes of living." While he was ready to promote a winter-spring marriage between his niece and Henry, he declined to enter such a union. In 1539 after the death of his empress, one of the reasons he refused to woo Margaret of France was, as he remarked, because he was too old for her. The age gap between them was twenty-three years but that between Henry and the Imperial nieces was thirty years or more. Most brides probably also preferred husbands nearer their own ages. In 1468, for example, when Elisabetta, sister of Galeazzo of Milan, married Marquess Guglielmo VIII, Paleologo of Montferrat, who was five times her age, she lamented: "I always feared I'd have an old husband, and now I have one." In fact, although various factors sometimes led to these lopsided unions, the general wisdom was that the bride and groom should be about the same age.[14]

In 1537 Henry hoped to use his marriage both to prevent a rapprochement between the emperor and Francis and to cement a closer relationship with one of their governments. Either he would marry the duchess of Milan, obtain a Portuguese husband for his daughter Mary, and resume the cordial relations with the emperor that the divorce from Catherine of Aragon had shattered, or he would wed Mary of Guise and thereby block a renewal of the Franco-Scottish alliance. The Guise marriage, which Henry favored most, would also commit England and France to a deeper friendship. In a 1539 letter to Cromwell, Wriothesley, who had been in the Netherlands for some five months attempting to arrange the king's alliance with the duchess of Milan, recalled how amazed he had been to learn that Henry had at first preferred Mary of Guise to her. A union with Christina remained attractive, however, and might well lead to Imperial marriages for the younger Tudors. In early 1538 rumors even spread in England that she was to become the queen.[15]

The timing of his consort's death was far from helpful to Henry's achieving the diplomatic coup he envisioned, for two political shifts had recently occurred. First, internal politics had made France less friendly to England. The recent return to favor of Montmorency strengthened the influence of ministers, such as Jean de Guise, cardinal of Lorraine, who worked to end the expensive Italian wars with the emperor. French diplomacy between 1537 and 1540 was guided by the constable and other policy-makers whose desire for rapprochement with Charles led to a chill in Anglo-French relations.[16]

The second shift was the intervention of the bishop of Rome, as Henry styled Paul III, in the Franco-Imperial hostilities. This move was not unprecedented, for by the fifteenth century papal mediation was an accepted factor in international diplomacy. Rulers often ratified treaties at religious ceremonies where they swore solemn oaths to enforce the agreements. From his accession in 1534 when he was sixty-seven-years old, Paul, whose birth name was Alessandro Farnese, had pursued goals that were both self-serving and laudatory. He secured wealthy spouses and high church offices for the children of his natural offspring, whom Julius II had legitimized, but partly to combat the Turkish threat, Paul also genuinely worked to end religious divisions. Henry was surely trying to counter this papal leadership when he offered to mediate the dispute between Francis and Charles, for he was concerned that Paul's involvement might leave England entirely out of the negotiations. Indeed, English isolation was a papal goal. As soon as Paul succeeded in persuading the empire and France to adopt peaceful relations, he planned to call a general church council at Mantua, a site that had aroused some resistance since it was an Imperial city. In 1545, of course, the council did meet at Trent thanks mainly to the perseverance of Paul. In the meantime, Henry required his ambassadors to advise Francis to refrain from relying on papal mediation to end his dispute with Charles and considered adding a clause to the treaty between Mary and Don Luis that would commit the emperor to denounce the summoning of a council, although he did later concede the need for such an assembly but demanded that it be held in a neutral place like Cambray. Paul had begun to meet with limited success as the hunt for a Tudor bride was launched, since Francis and Charles were then moving toward a rapprochement that would end in their signing an agreement at Toledo in 1539.[17]

A closer look at Henry's top candidates in 1537–38 and the strategies he adopted to overcome his inability to become acquainted with them will set the stage for the discussion (in Chapter 4) of his courtship of Anne of Cleves. Despite Hutton's remarks, the king decided to select her as his bride and to ally with her homeland in order to counter these intensified diplomatic shifts and Paul's assertiveness.

The top Imperial candidate was Christina, the second daughter of Christian II who was deposed as king of Denmark in 1523, and his wife Ysabeau, a sister of the emperor. In 1533 when she was not quite twelve years old, she had married the thirty-eight-year-old duke of Milan, a semi-invalid who died two years later. In their marriage contract the duke had agreed to relinquish to her elder sister Dorothea, who was born in November 1520, his new duchess's claim to her paternal inheritance. This concession to Dorothea, who at the age of fifteen became the wife of fifty-year-old Frederick, count palatine (elector in 1544), was an issue Henry raised in the negotiations, for he clearly expected the agreement to be voided in the event that Christina actually became his bride. The queen regent and her advisors expressed concern about Henry's demands, however, for they believed that a union of England and Denmark would pose a greater threat to Imperial power than the union of Juliers–Cleves and Guelders.[18]

The dowager duchess was widely reputed to be a beauty, and Hutton, who first saw her in late 1537 when she returned to Brussels from Italy, claimed that she resembled Mary Shelton, a cousin of Anne Boleyn who had been popular with the gentlemen of the privy chamber. Hutton explained to Wriothesley then still in England: "She is not so pure white as the late Queen [Jane Seymour] whose soul God pardon." Later, he reported that although she knew Italian and German, she mostly spoke French and lisped "which does nothing misbecome her." When Wriothesley and Vaughan encountered her at Brussels in late 1538, they added that she was "a goodly personage of stature higher than either of us, and competently fair, but very well favored, a very good woman's face, a little brown." Wriothesley found her charming: After an audience with her in early 1539, he observed to Cromwell how beautiful she was and regretted that she might be "bestowed where she could not like."[19]

The diplomats' information about the Imperial candidates was made in writing, but as Cromwell had instructed William Howard to return with an oral report, his opinion of the French ladies was not recorded. Wallop, who arrived in England before William, seems to have informed Henry that Mary was large in stature, for the king told Castillon that, as he was "big in person," he required a "big wife" (*qu'il est gros et grand personnage et qu'il a besoing de grande femme*). Wallop also lauded the looks of Mary who was fair skinned with blue eyes and bright red hair.[20]

She was the eldest daughter of Claude, duke of Guise, and Antoinette of Bourbon, sister of Charles, duke of Vendôme. Guise's father René II, titular king of Naples, Sicily, and Jerusalem, duke of Bar and Lorraine, could trace his ancestry back to John II of France through his son Louis of Anjou. At René's death in 1508, his estates had been divided: His heir, Antony, had retained the Bar and Lorraine inheritance and title while his younger son, Claude, had assumed ownership of the Guise estates and had become a French citizen. He and his wife's brother, the duke of Vendôme, were particular friends of Francis.[21]

In 1534, Guise's eldest daughter Mary had wed Louis, duke of Longueville, prince of Neufchatel and grand chamberlain of France. One of the wealthiest noblemen in France, he was the descendant of Jean, count of Dunois, the "Bastard of Orléans," who had gained renown as Joan of Arc's artillery officer. Mary gave birth to Longueville's heir Francis in October 1535 and to a second son Louis in August 1537, about two months after her husband's death at Rouen. Her fertility proved to be deceptive, however, for both these sons and those of her future Scottish husband James died before they reached adulthood, leaving only a namesake infant daughter to inherit the Scottish throne in 1542. As the duchess of Longueville, Mary had been present at the wedding of James and Madeleine in 1537 and seems to have become acquainted with her future husband at that time.[22]

Responding to English inquiries, Francis remarked that he would be greatly honored if Henry were to marry one of his subjects but insisted that Mary had been promised to James. Francis offered Marie of Vendôme to Henry instead, but Castillon reported that he remained "amorous" of Mary of Guise and refused to believe that she was unavailable. Clearly, Henry, who was unacquainted with Mary, was pressing for this alliance, but not because, as was alleged, he was in love with her. He was worried both about a Franco-Imperial truce and about the renewal of the Franco-Scottish alliance. According to David Potter, the goal "for a small country of medium power like England," was "to survive in the changeable and unpredictable waters of European diplomacy." Henry seems to have believed that his survival depended on making friends with other rulers while preventing them from forming alliances that would isolate him diplomatically. France's willingness to agree to a marriage treaty with England, especially if it involved a lady who had been promised to James, would provide Henry with a measuring stick by which to judge French friendliness toward him and toward other powers: namely, Scotland, the empire, and Rome. This was a diplomatic approach that continued throughout the early modern period. In 1579, for example, when Elizabeth decided to explore marrying Francis, duke of Anjou, brother to Henry III, she did so to obtain an alliance that would "provide her with security" against the Spanish, especially Philip II.[23]

Suspecting that Mary was unenthusiastic about the Scottish union, Cromwell sent Sir Peter Mewtes, a gentleman of the privy chamber, to visit with her at Chateaudun Castle, the Longueville headquarters, on two different occasions in 1537–38. Mary, who had been displeased to learn about these wedding plans for her in August, barely two months after her husband's death and about one month after her latest confinement, informed Mewtes that she would do as Francis requested but that she was not promised to James, leaving open the possibility that she preferred Henry to his nephew.[24]

The attempt to block the Franco-Scottish agreement was not unusual, for, in fact, many proposed matches were never concluded. In 1537, for example, the duchess of Milan traveled to Brussels specifically to marry William of Cleves, but attempts to implement their contract that had been signed in October stalled over the question of Guelders, although his agents continued to press for the union. Furthermore, it was likely that Henry assumed that his courtship of Mary should be favored over that of his nephew because of England's greater wealth and more prestigious rank relative to Scotland. When it became clear that Mary would wed James, Norfolk remarked that it was Francis's loss, for in creating a bond of international friendship, none would consider Scotland an equal to England.[25]

Henry declined to accept Marie, the eldest daughter of Charles de Bourbon, duke of Vendôme, who was born in 1516, as a substitute for Mary of Guise because he would not take, he said, the leftovers of the king of Scots, who had previously rejected her. Francis had a special concern for Marie's welfare and had tried to settle her future in 1532 by betrothing her to James, who had then protested that he preferred Madeleine, one of the king's daughters, as had been promised in the Treaty of Rouen. Momentarily, because of her ill health, her father had persuaded him to accept Marie instead. Then, when James traveled to France in 1536 to inspect both ladies, he chose the fragile Madeleine over Marie, perhaps because the latter seems to have had a "misshapen back." Francis remained unsuccessful in finding a husband for Marie, who died in 1538 still unwed.[26]

By heritage she was eminently qualified to become a royal bride, for she could trace her ancestry back to Louis IX of France, through his son Robert, count of Clermont. Her late father, who had been an important royal minister, served as the Grand Huntsman of France and also as president of the council when Francis was Charles's prisoner. The king had recognized him as "first prince of the Blood and head of the House of Bourbon." His wife, Frances of Alençon, was sister-in-law to Margaret of Alençon, the king's sister who had married as her second husband Henry d'Albret of Navarre.[27]

Crucial to James's success in wedding Madeleine was that the princess, realizing that it was probably her destiny to wed a foreigner, seems to have had an ambition to achieve queenly rank and to have intervened to overcome her father's reluctance. They were married in France in January 1537, and it was her death in Scotland the following July that caused her widowed husband to seek another French wife to continue the "auld alliance" and to compete with his English uncle for the Guise marriage.[28]

The targeted candidates clearly also had concerns about the personal qualities of their potential grooms. Before she wed Ferdinand of Aragon in 1469, Isabella of Castile had, for example, sent her chaplains to Aragon and France to collect information about her suitors. Similarly, in 1538 when Gran Battista Ferrari, an attendant of the duchess of Milan, returned from a visit to England, his mistress inquired about its monarch. Confirming that Henry was in good health, Ferrari spoke of his "benignity, comeliness, abundance, and bountifulness." Although a summons to supper ended the discussion, she later resumed her questioning of Ferrari. This incident indicated her interest in the marriage and belied later gossip about her negative attitude toward Henry. In 1539, moreover, George

Constantine, who had lived as a religious refugee in the Netherlands for some years, reported that he was unsure whether the bride who demanded pledges before she would consent to the English union was the duchess of Milan or Anne of Cleves, but he suspected it was the German lady.[29]

Absolutely no evidence substantiates the claim, which first surfaced in the seventeenth century when it was known that two of Henry's wives had been executed, that the duchess of Milan had refused to wed him because, as she remarked, she possessed only one head, but that if she owned two, "one of them should be at his Majesty's service." When Wriothesley, who believed that she would rather be a queen than a duchess, heard "malicious" rumors about Henry at the queen regent's court, he asked Christina her opinion of the king; she responded that she considered Henry "a noble prince." Carne also thought she favored the English marriage. In January 1539 the queen regent even informed her brother that:

If the king of England would seriously mend his ways and proceed to conclude the marriage in earnest, not merely to sow dissention between His majesty and the king of France this would no doubt be the most honorable alliance for the duchess and the most advantageous for the Low Countries.[30]

The next step in the search was for envoys to interview the ladies and for artists to paint portraits of them, a practice that could develop only after the emergence of the genre of portraiture in the modern sense. State portraits with reasonably accurate representations can be traced only to the early fourteenth century, as for example, the one commissioned by Robert, king of Naples, in 1317.[31] Unlike these formal renditions, the likenesses exchanged in courtship were, according to Andrew Martindale, initially "small, portable and private." This type of portrait had its first appearance in Simone Martini's creation of an image of Laura for Petrarch in 1336. Some years later, Pandulph Malatesta utilized this method for his two likenesses of Petrarch. These representations provided evidence of admiration and love, for they were "a reminder of life and in the first instance an evidence of friendship."[32]

Their first recorded appearance in marrying protocol occurred in the reigns of Charles VI of France and of Richard II of England. In 1384 the French king's advisors sent an artist to Scotland to create an image of Egidia, daughter of Robert II, but before the painter arrived, she had already married a countryman. Artists next traveled to Bavaria, Austria, and Lorraine and, after viewing the miniatures they painted, seventeen-year-old Charles was said to have fallen in love with fourteen-year-old Isabella of Bavaria, whom he wed in 1385. Eleven years later when Richard II was wooing Isabella, this same queen's young child and namesake, a miniature of her was sent to him.[33]

Martin Warnke has argued that the portrait exchanges emerged within a literary context: "Classical literature, courtly romance, and oriental fairy tales that had long been acquainted with the motif of the portrait that 'set the heart on fire.'" It was part of a grander development in which courtship began to utilize the affective language and conventions of romantic love that acted as a veneer for the actual political and economic motivations for the marriage. Romance and chivalric tales, which drew inspiration from classical authors, such as Ovid, and medieval writers, especially Celtic ones, were extremely popular. It is important to an understanding of the literary impact on marrying practices that evidence of it can first be discovered near the end of the fourteenth century when, according to Richard Green, "some degree of literary facility came generally to be regarded as an appropriate accomplishment for members of the ruling class."[34]

While romances ritualized many existing practices, within a few decades of their composition in the late twelfth century, evidence of their fictional events and names began to appear in society: the earliest tournament designated as a round table was held at Cyprus in 1223, and Edward I and Eleanor reportedly had the grave of Guenevere and Arthur at Glastonbury opened up in 1278. At the end of the fourteenth century, furthermore, when portrait exchanges emerged, the Barrois, French, and Aragonese courts were widely reputed to be courts of love. It was even erroneously claimed in 1400 that a judicial court of love rendered judgments in amorous matters in France. In England Richard II also utilized festivities from the romance tradition to celebrate his marriage to his first wife, Anne of Bohemia.[35]

Literary romance, which usually proceeds through the five stages of sight, conversation, touching, kissing, and coitus, had a far-reaching impact on courtship ritual. Obviously, the portrait or image offered the first opportunity to suitors who had never met for "eyeliking" or love at first sight. One of the most popular pieces for 300 years after its composition was *The Romance of the Rose*, written in French between about 1230 and 1275 by Guillaume de Lorris and Jean de Meun. It contains the tale of the sculptor Pygmalion who created a female image of ivory "so exquisite that it seemed as alive as the most beautiful living creature." Ultimately, he wed her and prayed successfully to the gods, especially to Venus, for her transformation into a real woman. His story is doubly significant, since Pygmalion fell in love not only with an art form but also with it at first sight. It is interesting that in two of Petrarch's sonnets honoring the Laura portrait created by Martini, the poet referred to Pygmalion.[36]

That references to portrait exchanges in courtship protocol can first be found in French records is not surprising, for Charles VI's father and his uncles had adopted cultural forms that were renowned throughout Europe. Charles's son-in-law, Richard II, also presided over a court that had began to rival French achievements; art historians, according to Joan Evans, even think of his deposition in 1399 "with a certain regret."[37]

The emergence of the notion that portraiture should be realistic meant that a practical reason existed for the adoption of portrait exchanges, for wooers could expect to obtain relatively accurate representations of their potential spouses.[38] Renowned artists such as Jan van Eyck, the Flemish miniaturist, sometimes accepted commissions to convey the likenesses of the ladies to their suitors. In 1428, for example, van Eyck traveled to Portugal to paint Isabella, the future wife of Philip the Good of Burgundy. As the fear grew that artists might flatter their subjects, monarchs attached detailed instructions to their commissions. In 1442 when Henry VI of England contemplated marrying one of the daughters of John IV of Armagnac, his advisors instructed Hans the painter to portray them "in their kertells simple, and their visages, like as you see their stature, and their beauty and color of skin, and their countenances, with all manner of features." Later Henry received a miniature of his future consort, Margaret of Anjou.[39]

The candidates also obtained portraits of their prospective grooms. In 1396 Richard II sent miniatures of himself to Isabella's parents, and in 1399 Louis II of Anjou is thought to have had a likeness of himself conveyed to his bride, Yolande of Aragon. In the Lancastrian period this practice spread and it, too, had become the norm by the Tudor century. In 1505 when Maximilian tried to persuade the recently widowed Henry VII to wed his daughter, Margaret, regent of the Netherlands, he not only sent two likenesses of her to England but also commissioned Flemish-trained Michael Sittow to paint a portrait of the king, which was presented to the regent but without the intended result, for both rulers remained single.[40]

As the sixteenth century wore on, the crown brought portrait painting under increasing scrutiny. Elizabeth's decision to license artists in 1563 was, according to Roy Strong, the "first of a succession of attempts to control royal portraiture." Some monarchs may even have been reluctant to permit artists to paint them because the likenesses in some mysterious way were thought to partake of the nature of the subject; attempts were made, for example, to dispose of Elizabeth by destroying images of her. Despite these fears, portrait exchanges remained a vital part of courtship protocol, and in 1613 it was even reported that Frederick V, count palatine, had fallen in love with Elizabeth Stuart when "his eye lighted" on her picture at Heidelberg. By the eighteenth century, however, the importance of the portrait had shifted, for by then the gift of one to a lady carried with it the promise that the suitor would soon arrive to meet his beloved in person.[41]

In 1537–38, when Henry began to seek a new wife, he asked that portraits of the candidates be procured for him. The instructions of Mewtas, the first royal agent dispatched abroad to converse with a candidate, required him to obtain a likeness of Mary of Guise. Although Francis denied that she was available, Mewtas was directed when he visited her, if she were free and if her father permitted, to have her picture "truly made, and like unto her, and bring the same hither with him." These orders were not carried out because it had already been decided that she would marry James.[42]

It was at the queen regent's court that an artist executed the first likeness of a bride for Henry. In March 1538 Philip Hoby, a groom of the privy chamber, and Hans Holbein the Younger, a German painter resident in England whose masterpieces are renowned for the detail and accuracy of their compositions, traveled to Brussels to obtain a portrait of the duchess of Milan. To Hutton's consternation they arrived on 10 March, after an agent had already left for England with an inferior image of her by Bernard van Orley, who had painted her in a brilliant gown even though she normally wore mourning clothes. Having heard of Holbein's skill, Hutton attempted unsuccessfully to recover van Orley's portrait.[43]

When Hutton reported Holbein's commission to the duchess, she responded that she must have her aunt's consent to sit for the painter. The queen regent's permission having been given, Christina posed in her mourning clothes for Holbein the next day in a three-hour session in which, according to Hutton, he completed a "very perfect" sketch of her. After they had returned home with the likeness, Chapuys learned that Henry was pleased with it. Considered by many critics to be one of his best efforts, Holbein's frontal portrait executed from the sketch was the only full-length, life-size painting of a lady that he produced. Her simple dress served to highlight her natural beauty, which was confirmed by the later opinion of Pierre de Bourdeille, seigneur de Brantôme, that she was "one of the loveliest and also as accomplished a woman as" he had ever seen.[44]

Hoby, who was fluent in French and Italian, also secured an audience with the duchess and returned home armed with information concerning her demeanor, conversation, and looks. He had been instructed to "well note her answers, her gesture and countenance with her inclination, that he may at his return declare the same to the king's majesty."[45]

Henry's instructions to Hoby and Holbein were actually far less intrusive than those of his father to the three ambassadors who were sent in 1504 to inquire about the attributes of Giovanna of Aragon, the younger dowager queen of Naples. He required them to gather detailed answers to twenty-four questions that ranged in subject matter from her attendants, her property, her countenance, her language skills, her stature and bodily features, including the size of her breasts, her demeanor, the color of her hair and skin, her facial features, including whether hair grew over her lips, the sweetness of her breath and how she smelled, to her eating and drinking habits. He also instructed the ambassadors to "enquire for some cunning painter" to make a "very semblance" of her, but the queen would not permit her portrait to be painted.[46]

Henry VII's detailed questions about his candidate provide an interesting perspective to his son's efforts to obtain information about his potential brides. Even so, scholars have sometimes ridiculed Henry VIII's inquiries. In fact, there was some delay in his obtaining feedback about a viable French bride because he refused to seek a replacement for Mary of Guise until notice of her wedding to James in May 1538 had clearly removed her from the candidate pool. After learning of this ceremony, the government called upon Bryan, who had been in France since April, to assist in selecting another lady for the king. That summer Bryan began to collect portraits of Louise of Guise, a younger sister of Mary, who was born in 1521, her cousin, Anne of Lorraine, who was born in 1522, and even Marie of Vendôme, who had earlier been rejected. Bryan had actually traveled to France with Thomas Thirlby to replace Winchester, but their mission had been changed. They received instructions to join the bishop, who was to remain at his post, to negotiate a marriage between Mary Tudor and Charles of Orléans and to persuade the emperor to grant Milan to Orléans. In the meantime discussions with Charles V about her union to the Portuguese infante and about Henry's to the duchess of Milan continued.[47]

While Bryan was pursuing these duties, Hoby and a painter, probably Holbein, recrossed the channel. In June they were at Le Havre to execute a portrait of Louise of Guise, who along with her father had accompanied Mary to this port on her progress to Scotland. At least one anonymous Scotsman admired Louise, who was in 1541 to marry Charles of Croy, prince of Chimay and future duke of Arschot, more than her elder sister. According to Castillon, this Scotsman wondered why James had chosen a widow when he could have had a young sister, the most beautiful woman he had ever seen. Castillon also assured Henry that Louise was the "very counterpart" of Mary, "beautiful," "graceful," and "clever". At Le Havre Holbein may also have succeeded in painting a portrait of her cousin Marie of Vendôme.[48]

Henry was subsequently to learn of Renée, another Guise daughter who was born in 1522 and who was to become the abbess of St. Peter's, in Rheims. In August 1538, when Hoby and Holbein arrived at Joinville to obtain her portrait, she had already departed for Rheims, but Louise was at home and although she was unwell, they were able to speak with her. That Henry was willing to consider Renée as his bride evoked some French sarcasm. The constable quipped to the Imperial ambassador at Paris: "I have no doubt that as the king of England considers himself a pope in his own kingdom, he would have preferred the nun to any other daughters of the royal blood in France."[49]

Hoby and Holbein had also visited Nancy, the headquarters of the duke of Lorraine, the older brother of Guise, to obtain a portrait of his daughter Anne. Nominally, as Lorraine's duke, he was a feudatory of the empire, but in reality he acted as an independent prince. Technically, Lorraine owed allegiance to France as well as to the empire, since he did homage for the duchy of Bar to both, one-half to France and the other half to the emperor. In 1540 the duke sided with the empire when he arranged for his daughter to marry René, prince of Orange, an ally of Charles. In 1541 his heir Francis also married another Imperial ally, the duchess of Milan, whom Henry had unsuccessfully wooed in 1537–39.[50]

Even before the portraits of the ladies could be collected, Henry suggested another strategy to Wyatt at the Imperial court. The proposal was that he should meet with the candidates and their families at Calais, because, as he explained:

His Grace prudently considering how that marriage is a bargain of such nature as may endure for the whole life of a man, and a thing whereof the pleasure and quiet, or the displeasure and torment of the man's mind doth much depend, thinketh it to be much necessary both for himself and the party with whom it shall please God to join him in marriage, that the one might see the other before the time they should be so affianced, as they might not without dishonor or further inconvenience break off.[51]

He clearly viewed their portraits and the testimonies of their beauty as insufficient evidence. Like James in 1536, Henry felt anxious enough about the ladies' attributes to propose meetings with them, which, as it turned out, proved impossible to arrange.

Throughout the summer of 1538, Henry and his agents attempted to schedule a rendezvous with them at some convenient place. In July, Bryan asked Francis if he would permit his sister Margaret of Navarre to escort them to Calais where Henry could become acquainted with them. After rejecting this request, Francis sent word to Henry to send some trustworthy individual to see them. Later, Montmorency, who was pressing for an Imperial truce, complained to Castillon about Bryan's demands; he thought it was absurd that Henry wanted young ladies to trot on display like horses for sale (*ne sont point dames pour envoyer trotter sus la monstre*). He went on to request that either a daughter of Vendôme or of Guise should be chosen and that Bryan should send new portraits and reports about her to England.[52]

It was not uncommon for princes and their families to seek to view potential spouses. As Geoffroy de la Tour-Landry IV, the fifteenth-century knight of the Tower explained: "And they should be seen if they were well shaped and like to bear children and that they had such things as women ought to have." A long history of individuals inspecting future mates existed. As early as 1253, for example, Alfonso X had informed the future Edward I that he would have to journey to Castile so that it could be ascertained whether he was "worthy in mind and body" to marry the infanta. In 1538 the Spanish court still favored this procedure, for just before Francis refused Henry's request for a meeting with his cousins, Anthony de Castelnau, bishop of Tarbes, his resident at Toledo, wrote to him concerning a proposed marriage between his son, Orléans, and the infanta of Castile, a daughter of the emperor. Tarbes noted that it would be necessary for Orléans to visit Toledo because the empress wished to see him before approving the match.[53]

References in Imperial communications about Henry's proposed Calais rendezvous were, therefore, understandably far less mean-spirited than those in French dispatches, although the Habsburgs did believe, as Charles, himself remarked to his wife in 1536, that a fine distinction existed between a princess being "offered" and being "demanded." In 1623 Sir Charles Cornwallis, ambassador to Spain, was to echo this sentiment in his relation concerning Prince Charles's courtship of a Spanish infanta. The diplomat wrote that the daughter's "sex giveth [her] ever the privilege to be sought." This gender difference, the male seeking and the female being sought, also affected queens regnant, some of whom proved to be squeamish about discussing their marriage plans with negotiators. In 1554, for example, Queen Mary announced to a Spanish embassy that "It was not known for a maiden queen thus publicly to enter on so delicate a subject as her own marriage." In fact, treatises on the behavior of maidens advised them to concentrate on remaining chaste and to leave matrimonial matters to their parents. Given these expectations, if a queen regnant of mature years felt awkward discussing her marriage publicly, then almost certainly a young lady's parents would have considered it inappropriate for her to travel to a convenient place to be inspected by a potential husband.[54]

In August 1538 Castillon wondered whether Henry might imitate the Scots king and journey incognito to see the ladies, himself. In

September 1536, as noted above, although James possessed a portrait of Marie of Vendôme, he had actually traveled to her home on the Loire River with John Tennant, keeper of his wardrobe, whose servant he pretended to be. Marie, to whom he had earlier sent a likeness of himself, however, recognized him almost immediately. That he adopted a disguise was not an unusual act for him, for he enjoyed roaming about his own realm dressed as a poor traveler. His subjects called him "*gaberlungie* (beggar-man) king."[55]

Like the portrait exchange, the incognito visit borrowed from romance conventions, for the fiction was kept up that the disguised suitor and the lady would fall in love with each other at first sight. The widespread practice of masking was, of course, much older than this tradition, for it can be traced from pagan days to the Christian period through the mummers' attempt to assist the changing of the seasons with their imitative magic that is essentially the vestige of fertility rites.[56]

Victor Turner has also revealed the importance of disguise in the liminal phase of tribal rites of passage. Normally, a point arrives in these rites when a disguised neophyte enters an ambiguous state, loses status, and assumes a passive or humble demeanor. In the liturgical ceremonies of the Christian mass, Turner has identified "truncated" forms of these liminal phases. The bride, for example, enters liminality when she wears a veil for the formal wedding celebration.[57]

In the twelfth century authors began to compose romance stories in which individuals, particularly knights errant, entered truncated liminal states. The heroes participated in initiation rites to become knights or to join secret societies, often incognito.[58] Sometimes they wore disguises in courting their ladies with whom they usually fell deeply in love either in anticipation of their first meeting or suddenly upon first sight.[59] In addition, they appeared in unidentifiable armor at tournaments to prove that they were able to gain their ladies' love and to win the mock combat by their virtue and prowess rather than by their reputation or lineage. In Baldesar Castiglione's *The Courtier*, Federico Fergoso expressed this sentiment: "It would not be right for the prince to choose to play the part of the prince himself. . . ."[60] Disguise thus provided the prince an opportunity to prove himself superior to others by his qualities, for as Lloyd Davis has pointed out, disguise was "a cultural touchstone for ideas about character."[61]

Influenced by romance literature, fourteenth-century monarchs began to don disguises as part of their entertainments. In England, Edward III appeared in tournaments, as, for example, in 1334 when he dressed up as Lionel, a relative of Guenevere's Sir Lancelot.[62]

Medieval suitors occasionally had visited prospective brides incognito to determine whether or not to wed them. In the tenth century, for example, Henry the Fowler entered a nunnery in disguise where he observed Matilda whom he subsequently carried off and married.[63] By the late fourteenth century, this inspection process had begun to reflect romance culture. In 1380 when Juan I of Aragon visited the court of Duke Robert of Bar, then reputed to be a court of love and a chief resort of troubadours, with the intention of viewing the duke's daughter Yolande, he went in disguise as a troubadour of Lanquedoc. At first sight in imitation of the knights errant of romance, he allegedly fell deeply in love with her but instead of ignoring protocol, he gave her his signet ring and returned home where he successfully pursued his courtship through appropriate channels.[64]

It was this tradition that James recalled when he visited Marie's home in 1536, although he did not wear the disguise of a troubadour or a minstrel. He appears to have established a precedent that his great-grandson, Charles of England, followed although in modified form. Charles traveled to Spain disguised as John Smith in 1623 with the intention of persuading his intended to marry him, rather than of viewing her to see if he wished to conclude the alliance. Peter Thomas has claimed that the prince "never outgrew the habit of a sentimental gallantry," and, indeed, it confirms the cultural heritage of this adventure that Edward, Lord Herbert, the resident ambassador in France in 1623, quoted in his autobiography the remark of the duke of Savoy that the journey was a "Trick of those ancient knight errands." Another diplomat, Sir Henry Wotton, referred to Charles's "joy in chivalry."[65]

In May 1538 Henry became extremely ill and was no longer healthy enough to jaunt about the countryside visiting the homes of potential brides. He had the added concern that if he ventured too far into alien territory he might be captured and held for ransom, as was Francis after Pavia. As the ladies could not accept his Calais invitation, he proposed in August that they be asked to visit their families' estates which lay near this port town where he could send an envoy of rank equal to them for an interview; he seems to have been aware that Marie of Vendôme's grandmother resided near Calais and that some Guise property was situated near Amiens. In a dispatch home, Castillon speculated that since Henry was the only Englishman of rank sufficient to be called the equal of the ladies, he might well journey to France in disguise, as James had earlier done.[66]

Henry's request for a meeting with the ladies, although somewhat unusual, was not quite as ridiculous as Francis and his advisors claimed. In July 1538 after a conference between the emperor and the French king at Aigues-Mortes, Castillon reported that Henry was "marvelously cooled" toward France and advised Francis to agree to a Calais meeting. He recommended this concession because he believed that if Henry were to wed a French lady, he would never enter an Imperial alliance.[67]

Henry expressed both personal and public motives for seeking this interview. "By God!" Castillon quoted him in August 1538: "I trust no one but myself. The thing touches me too close. I wish to see them and know them some time before deciding" [*Pardieu . . . je ne m'en fye de personne que de moy. C'est une chose qui touche de trop près. Je les veux veoir et hanter quelque temps avant que de m'y arrester*]. Castillon tried vulgar ridicule to distract him from that viewpoint since Francis opposed his proposal: He laughingly suggested that Henry could sleep with each lady in turn, retaining the most accomplished one for himself, and then inquired as to whether that was how the knights of the round table used to treat their ladies. It is interesting that the ambassador referred to these knights in his discussion, for fictional practices did have great influence, as has been noted, on early modern courtship. In response, the king was said to have blushed but kept up the attack, for more was at stake than just a bride's selection on the basis of her personal qualities, since, as he also informed the ambassador, he was determined not to wed unless either Charles or Francis preferred his friendship to that which they enjoyed together. Clearly, he was attempting to use the marriage to carve out a better diplomatic understanding with one of these two rulers.[68]

The exchanges about a Calais conference occurred during the summer of 1538 as the emperor and Francis were moving toward a reconciliation. The ten-year truce they agreed to was partly the fruit of Paul's determined labors. While stationed at Nice, he had met separately with Francis at Villanuova and with Charles at Villafranca to effect this agreement. Although it was not the definitive peace he had sought, the pope was able to persuade them to send plenipotentiaries to Rome for further discussions. A July storm drove the emperor's ship to Aigues-Mortes where Francis, as noted above, met with Charles on board the vessel and then accompanied him to the castle on the lagoons west of the Rhone where they exchanged promises of loyal friendship.[69]

After learning of this diplomacy, Bryan ceased collecting portraits of the ladies and left for home in August so unexpectedly that the French did not have time to present him with the usual parting gift, a signal of the growing rift between their kingdoms; he returned with the news that the French ministers had been very cold to him. At first Henry may have hoped to avoid a confrontation with France, for he complained that Bryan, as well as Thirlby and Winchester, who had recently been replaced by Bonner, had been deceitful, and in September he characterized Bryan as a drunkard. With Bryan's departure, however, the Anglo-French marriage schemes fell into abeyance, Winchester mentioning them only once more in his August instructions for Bonner in which he noted Francis's refusal to permit the Calais visit.[70]

By October, when the queen regent and the French king were meeting together, Henry had changed his tune and had begun to expound upon French incivility. It must have galled him that Mary of Hungary and Francis, accompanied by the ladies of their courts, were meeting together at Compiegne when both had turned down his Calais invitation. In fact, none of Henry's potential brides was with them. The queen regent had left her niece behind at Brussels, and, of the relevant French ladies, Anne of Lorraine was at home nursing her ill father; Louise of Guise was still indisposed; and Marie of Vendôme had recently died. In an audience with Castillon, Henry complained about Bryan's discourteous reception. The subsequent unfavorable treatment of the French embassy in London, both in terms of lodging and entertainment, signaled English hostility toward their king, for as Marillac was to note, they viewed the caressing of ambassadors as a sign of friendship. This hostility was short lived, however, for Henry began to seek the friendship of Francis again when the marriage negotiations with the emperor ground to a halt over two issues: the queen regent's delays and papal politics.[71]

As early as July 1538, even as he was working on a French rapprochement, the emperor had sent a commission to his sister to negotiate both the marriages of Don Luis to Mary Tudor and Christina to Henry. In the document the emperor gave the queen regent full powers to conclude the alliances, relieving her thereby of the necessity of waiting for his final approval or ratification. Without sufficient authority written into the text, the other party, who customarily demanded to inspect it, might refuse to negotiate. Earlier that year, when French councillors had raised with Winchester the possibility of a marriage between Mary Tudor and Orléans, the bishop had protested that they did not possess sufficient authority to negotiate such an agreement.[72]

Although Charles had invested her with the powers necessary to conclude the treaties, the queen regent delayed the deliberations. In September she complained that she had heard Henry had been seeking a wife in France and elsewhere and in mid-November she refused to enter into negotiations because, as she reported, Charles had not provided her with sufficient details about Christina's dower and patrimonial rights or about Dorothea's cessation of her claims to the crowns of Denmark and Norway. In addition, the emperor had failed to identify which property and what rank he intended to bestow upon Mary Tudor or which lands the descendants of her union with the Portuguese infante would inherit. Questions were also raised about Mary's legal status in England. On another occasion, the queen regent stalled the deliberations because of the absence of a principal minister, Philip de Croy, duke of Arschot. On 20 November, when her advisers finally displayed their authorizations for inspection, the English ambassadors expressed concern that the documents did not specifically appoint them to act for her. In response, she promised them a "testimonial" to approve in advance any pledges her ministers made on her behalf. In the meantime, the emperor was assuring English diplomats that he had invested his sister with the appropriate authority.[73]

By late November when the peace negotiations with France were succeeding, Charles belatedly sent word to Henry that he could not grant Milan to the Portuguese infante for fear of offending Francis. The emperor also expressed doubts that the pope would dispense with the impediment of consanguinity (blood relationship) between Don Luis and Mary. As both were grandchildren of Ferdinand and

Isabella of Spain, they were first cousins and thus related within the prohibited fourth degree of kinship; the Fourth Lateran Council of 1215 had not only forbidden unions such as these but had also defined the impediments to marriage within the fourth degree of affinity (carnal intercourse with a relative of the intended spouse) and of public honesty (betrothal to a relative of the intended spouse). The Council extended the impediment of spiritual relationships only to the individuals who had actually participated in the sacraments of baptism or confirmation. One reason Paul was hostile to the marriage of Mary and Don Luis was that he had been seeking to influence Milan's disposition. He was opposed to an Italian duchy falling into the hands of Portugal, France, or England and hoped to obtain Milan for his grandson, Ottavio Farnese, future duke of Parma, and his wife, Margaret, the emperor's natural daughter.[74]

A disappointed Henry responded to Charles's message about the marriage of Mary to Don Luis and about the duchy of Milan in a letter of 28 November to Wyatt in which he asked his ambassador to inquire who it was that the emperor thought the princess should wed. Among those whom Henry proposed was William of Cleves, a candidate whose name had surfaced as a possibility as early as 1530.[75]

The Habsburg rulers were obviously waiting for the outcome of the deliberations about a Franco-Imperial pact. Onlookers began to observe signs of their growing amity for each other and of their diminishing friendship toward England: in December at the Louvre Francis was seen wearing the insignia of the emperor's chivalric Order of the Golden Fleece, and at Brussels Vaughan reported the queen regent's cold behavior toward him. These were signals that Francis and Charles had tentatively agreed to a treaty, which was to be signed at Toledo on 12 January 1539, that pledged they would conclude no separate alliances with England.[76]

The event that sent Henry moving back toward a French rapprochement was Paul's assertiveness. On 17 December 1538 a few days after Charles and Francis had secretly agreed to their alliance, the pope announced that he was planning to renew the suspended bull of excommunication against Henry, first promulgated in 1535 in response to his divorce from Catherine of Aragon who had died in January 1536. The bull removing Henry from access to the sacraments was a public sign that the pope objected to his marriage to the duchess of Milan. Whether or not he had been the legal husband of Catherine, who was Christina's great-aunt, he had certainly been betrothed to her and had sired children with her. Without a papal dispensation, the duchess could not become his wife, for the blessings of Cranmer were no longer, if they ever had been, a viable option. The decision of Charles that papal approval would be needed to validate his niece's match with Henry should have come as no great surprise, for Hutton had earlier warned that the duchess had said she would never disobey God's laws. It is likely that Henry had continued courting Christina in the hope that if Charles could be persuaded to approve the marriage, it would create a rift between him and the pope.[77]

The renewal of the bull of excommunication, which was published in January 1539, signaled Paul's determination to isolate England diplomatically. In a dispatch to the emperor, he referred to the "nefarious deeds of that most cruel and abominable tyrant" and demanded a termination of trade relations and diplomatic ties between his realm and the Imperial kingdoms and their dominions. If asked, the pope would certainly refuse to permit Christina to marry a man whose soul he had just damned to hell. Usually, even the faithful who dared to interact in routine matters with excommunicated people, as, for example, praying with them or traveling with them, were required to do penance for their behavior. Henry, of course, did not seek papal approval; in May 1538 he had said he would refuse to ratify a treaty in which the pope was a "meddler," but without it an Imperial candidate would decline to marry him.[78]

The papal authority to dispense with marriage impediments had been well established by the death of Innocent III, the convener of the Fourth Lateran Council. His successors followed the example he had set in either issuing or withholding bulls of dispensation for political reasons. Before the reign of Henry, papal refusal to dispense with these impediments had prevented English expansion on the continent. In the years 1366–68 Charles V of France succeeded in dissuading Urban V from granting to Edward III a dispensation of the impediment of consanguinity for his son, Edmund, earl of Cambridge, and Margaret of Flanders, the richest heiress in Christendom. In 1369 she wed Charles's brother, Philip of Burgundy, and her wealth and estates helped to lay the groundwork for the Valois Burgundian duchy. The decision to grant the papal dispensation hinged in part on the question that was asked during inquiries about whether an impediment should be removed: Would "the bonds of peace and friendship between parents, kinsmen and friends . . . be better preserved and increased by their marriage?" Paul's response to this query concerning a union between Henry and Christina would have been, of course, a resounding no.[79]

Despite these setbacks, English diplomats at Brussels continued to discuss the possibility of Henry's alliance with Christina. In the meantime, Cromwell speculated that Charles actually preferred either the heir of Cleves or of Lorraine for his niece. Deliberations about her English union were brought to a close by the emperor's remark on 15 February 1539 that the marriage could not take place without a papal dispensation. Thus, as Castillon had earlier predicted, Henry would discover that the pope and the emperor were "one"; at least they were "one" on this issue. Even before Charles's final word was given concerning his niece's marriage, English commissioners had departed for Germany to discuss the marrying of Henry and Anne.[80]

Edward Hall's account of the king's courtship of Anne was inaccurate in some important details. In his chronicle Hall claimed Charles had first proposed that Henry wed the duchess of Milan and that the Imperial council "so dallied with the king, that shortly he left off that suit." Hall surmised that Charles's intention was "to have brought the king to sue to the bishop of Rome for a license, which thing the king's majesty soon smelled and perceived. . . ." The chronicler further asserted that when Duke William of Cleves heard that Henry was no longer wooing Christina, he made suit to the king on behalf of his sister. But as Chapter 4 reveals, when the English ambassadors arrived in Germany they sought to raise the possibility of this union with the duke elector of Saxony and with William's and Anne's ailing father, Duke John. It was only in February, after his father's death, that William entered into his inheritance, and in March two English ambassadors arrived at his court to initiate the negotiations that would lead to the marriage of Henry with his sister.[81]

4 ❧ CLEVES SELECTION

The lady Henry selected to be his bride in 1539 was Anne, daughter of John III of Cleves, nicknamed the Simple, and Maria, heiress to Juliers. After presenting information about her family's duchies and dominions, which were mostly located in the strategically important Lower Rhine River Valley,[1] this chapter examines the role of her relatives in the diplomatic and religious culture of the 1530s for the purpose of establishing a framework for her marriage to Henry. It will next turn to the attempts of the English government in 1538 to destroy the perceived threat of Yorkist intrigue and in 1539 to counter the claim that in seeking a Cleves alliance the king had committed his realm to further, perhaps Lutheran, reform. Both the arrest of members of the Pole family loyal to papal authority and the enactment of the Six Articles to root out heresy are related to Henry's decision to select a bride in Cleves. After an analysis of English negotiations in Germany to arrange the marriage, including a review of the letter of Nicholas Wotton, the ambassador to Cleves, in which he described Anne's character and upbringing, the chapter concludes with the dispatch of German commissioners to England.

Like the Italian city-states Juliers–Cleves was situated in one of the most hotly contested areas in western Christendom. Both the fifteenth-century rise and expansion of Burgundy and the sixteenth-century competition of the Valois and Habsburg dynasties impacted upon it politically and diplomatically. The Juliers–Cleves duchies had once been separated into four dominions. Juliers, with 1,628 square miles, reached out from the left bank of the Rhine westward to the Meuse River; to the north and east of Juliers but unattached to it lay Cleves, with 868 square miles, located on both sides of the Rhine just south of the county of Zutphen. Berg with 2,040 square miles lay immediately south of Cleves on the right bank of the

Rhine, and Mark with 911 square miles bordered Berg on its eastern edge.[2]

Utilizing marital strategies similar to those that created the Habsburg empire, one German house had succeeded in uniting these territories, which had grown to a population of about 400,000 in 1550. In 1368 the counts of Mark had acquired Cleves through a marriage with the heiress of its last count, and in 1417 the Cleves–Mark dynasty had won ducal status. This was a significant elevation, for while there were approximately a hundred counts in German-speaking lands, the number of secular dukes and princes, a status that only the emperor could award, varied from about fifteen to twenty-five. Customarily these noblemen, who enjoyed the trappings of royal status, led a warlike existence. In 1423 Adolph II, duke of Juliers–Berg, for example, had unsuccessfully attempted to regain Guelders, which his family had controlled since 1371 but had recently lost. The marriage in 1510 of his descendant Maria, daughter of William IV of Juliers–Berg, to the namesake heir of John II of Cleves–Mark brought Juliers–Berg to Cleves as the bride's dowry. When John III inherited his patrimony in 1521, he had been serving as duke of Juliers since 1511, the year of his father-in-law's death.[3]

Although nominally an Imperial fief, the Duchy of Juliers–Cleves, like other principalities in the Holy Roman Empire, was virtually independent. It possessed ruling estates, courts without appeal, a territorial army, and an independent foreign policy. Under John III's leadership the dominions prospered principally because he eschewed warfare. With good government, shrewd economies, and a relatively peaceful foreign policy, the core of which was neutrality, he secured a sound financial base. He levied taxes only for the marriages of his daughters and for the diplomatic and religious concerns of the empire, most especially the Turkish offensives and the attack on the Münster anabaptists in 1535. As he died on 6 February 1539, it was his son William who was called upon to arrange Anne's marriage to Henry.[4]

Anne also had two sisters, for her mother had given birth to four surviving children, Sybilla in 1512, Anne on 22 September 1515, William in July 1516, and Amelia in 1517. The lineage of the children was distinguished. Of Henry's six wives only Catherine of Aragon's was more impressive, for Anne could not only trace her ancestry back through the Cleves line to Edward I of England by way of the marriage of his daughter Margaret to Duke John II of Brabant, but she could also claim descent from King John II of France. Her ancestor, Adolph IV of Cleves, who died in 1448, had elevated his progeny to the status of princes of the blood by marrying Mary, daughter of John the Fearless, duke of Burgundy and a grandson of King John.[5]

The Cleves family had subsequently played an important role in Burgundy. Adolph IV's son, John I, who died in 1481, had been reared at the court of Philip the Good, his mother Mary's brother. John's expensive tastes reportedly led his father to mock him with the words: *Da kompt Jonneken mit den bellen*; literally the phrase means "here comes Johnny with a loud noise," such as a cough or bark, but *bellen* was probably used to ridicule his courtly, perhaps self-important, way of speaking French, the language of the Burgundian court. Referred to by a chronicler in 1468 as "the mighty prince the duke of Cleves," John went on a pilgrimage to the Holy Land in 1450, the jubilee year, and served as an adviser to the Valois dukes of Burgundy until the decease in 1477 of the last one, Charles the Bold, son of Philip the Good. John's brother, Adolph, lord of Ravenstein, was also a ducal counsellor, and their sister Mary met her future husband, Charles, duke of Orléans, in the apartments of Duke Philip's wife, Isabella. In 1462 Mary gave birth to Orléans' heir Louis who was to succeed as the twelfth of his name to the throne of France.[6]

Both John I's namesake heir, who also was educated at the Burgundian court, and his brother's son, Philip of Ravenstein, were childhood companions of their cousin Mary of Burgundy, heiress to Charles the Bold. They were situated high enough in political circles for their names to be proposed as her husband when she succeeded her father as ruler in 1477. After her marriage to Maximilian, future Holy Roman emperor, Philip of Ravenstein led a resistance against her Habsburg husband and was forced to remain in hiding at Sluys from 1488 until 1492 when his father Adolph died and he was allowed to assume his position as lord of Ravenstein. At his death in 1528, his cousin John III of Juliers–Cleves inherited his property, which juts southward from the Meuse River into Brabant.[7]

Despite this estrangement, the Cleves family enjoyed close relations with the Imperial rulers. In 1508 John II attended Maximilian's court at Worms, and in 1516 Adolph, his younger son, accompanied Charles, the grandson of Maximilian and future emperor, on his travels to Spain. John III, himself, was a member of Charles's train when he journeyed to England in 1522, thus providing an opportunity for him to become acquainted with the Tudors some eighteen years before their families were allied by Henry's marriage to Anne.[8]

John was known for his enthusiasm for splendid clothing, and his estates were pivotal in the adoption of new ideas and social patterns, since the Lower Rhine was the principal route by which French culture penetrated into Germany.[9] He was also, as noted above, the descendant or relative of nobility who had enjoyed close ties with the Burgundian court, the elaborate protocol of which was widely admired and copied. Both his grandfather, John I of Cleves, and his great-uncle, Adolph of Ravenstein, had been members of the Order of the Golden Fleece and had participated in lavish entertainments.[10]

In 1454, for example, after the Turks had captured Constantinople, Philip the Good held a series of banquets to inspire his knights to join a crusade against the invaders. He selected his nephew John I of Cleves to host the first feast at the palace of Lord Valeran des Aubeaux at Lille. John, whose motto was *Candida nostra fides* [our faith is spotless], cleverly utilized a family legend about an ancestor who had met with the heiress of Cleves and had departed from her mysteriously in a boat guided down the Rhine by two white swans. On the principal table at the Lille banquet was a splendid arrangement: A knight bearing the Cleves colors commanded a sailing ship that a silver swan drew by a golden chain affixed to its golden collar. At the end of the table stood a model of the castle of Cleves with a ship floating on the Rhine. John's brother Adolph announced that the knight of the Swan would appear at the third banquet, the Feast of the Pheasant, which Duke Philip planned to host, and challenge all comers to a tilt. Adolph attended the banquet disguised as the Knight of the Swan and fought with an opponent at close quarters, but the joust was discontinued after both had fallen beneath their horses and been badly bruised. His son Philip of Ravenstein, also gained recognition as a typical "example of Burgundian courtly chivalry."[11]

Most of the great households, including that of Juliers–Cleves, imitated the Burgundian court, retaining ceremonial officers, such as stewards, marshals, cup-bearers, and heralds. Indeed, many extant records have specific references to heralds and marshals at Juliers–Cleves. In addition, documents dated between 1511 and 1539 provide evidence of over fifty payments to musicians, including canters, at the court as it moved from Wesel to Düsseldorf, to Duisberg, and to Recklinghausen. The orchestra was normally composed of eight to ten instruments, including trumpets, a harp, and a lute.[12]

In January 1539 as his courtship of Christina of Milan was ending, Henry began seriously to consider a match with Anne, a daughter of this German house. Diplomats had raised the possibility of a marriage with her twice previously. The first time was, of course, in 1537 when in response to Cromwell's request for names of eligible ladies, Hutton had listed her with three other candidates. The second time occurred in the summer of 1538 when the king, who had heard reports of Anne's union with Francis of Lorraine the previous January, was still seriously seeking an Imperial or French wife. Despite these rumors of her Lorraine marriage, Francis Burchart, vice-chancellor of Saxony, proposed her as a possible bride for Henry in discreet conversations with Cromwell. Along with other envoys of the Schmalkaldic League, Burchart was in England attempting, without success as it turned out, to negotiate a treaty with the king. From 1531 to its defeat in 1546–47, this Lutheran League, which was headed by John Frederick, duke elector of Saxony, and Philip, landgrave of Hesse, served as the emperor's chief opponent. Inevitably, when a member of the royal family was free to wed, envoys at treaty-making opportunities like this one proposed suitable matches for that individual. Wary about the German presence in England, both the Imperial and French resident ambassadors passed on rumors to this effect to their governments. In June, Chapuys reported that the king had sent an artist to Cleves to paint a portrait of William for Mary and one of his kinswomen for Henry. English records do not corroborate this claim, although in July at Brussels, Hutton had heard rumors that some Scottish and English ambassadors were at Cleves. A few weeks later, Castillon revealed to the constable that Henry had spoken approvingly of Anne's reported alliance with Francis and Mary's proposed one with William. Then when Cromwell also lauded William's temper, disposition, and qualities to Chapuys, the diplomat began to suspect that he was slated to be her husband. The statements of Henry and Cromwell about William, whose possession of Guelders was viewed as a threat to Habsburg hegemony in the Netherlands, may have been thinly disguised attempts to pressure the emperor into approving the more coveted alliance for Mary with Don Luis of Portugal.[13]

Only six months after Henry had volunteered that he approved of Anne's marriage with Francis of Lorraine, he decided to woo her for himself. Her brother's dispute with the emperor over Guelders and the Habsburg–Valois rapprochement seemed to be a propitious moment for him to begin the Cleves courtship. William's claim to Guelders derived from his Juliers ancestors who had lost the duchy to the Egmonds in the early fifteenth century. On the paternal side, he was also related to Charles, the present duke of Guelders who was a grandson of Katherine, daughter of Adolph IV of Cleves, and her husband Arnold of Egmond. Despite his October 1537 commitment to wed Christina of Milan, William signed a contract at Nymwegen in January 1538 to marry a daughter of Lorraine in the hopes of persuading her father, Antony, who had a claim to Guelders, to support his takeover of Guelders at the request of its troubled estates, which had recognized William, the heir of Juliers, as their "liege lord," in defiance of their ruler Duke Charles. Shortly before his death in June 1538, the childless Charles validated William's actions by bequeathing his duchy to him, thereby ignoring his promise in 1528 to cede it to the emperor, who had briefly gained the upper hand over him militarily.[14]

William's subsequent diplomacy hinged on persuading the emperor to accept his control of the duchy, but Imperial advisers repeatedly warned Charles V that the unification of Guelders and Juliers–Cleves seriously jeopardized the Netherlands' security. Even without the addition of the Guelders' coastline, Juliers–Cleves already held a formidable position. Not only did it lie across the Rhine River, the vital route connecting the Habsburgs to their Italian holdings, but it also penetrated north and east toward the heart of the Netherlands. It was spread across one of the most significant military and economic sites of western Europe. The important junction of the Rhine and Lippe Rivers and the stronghold of Wesel lay within its borders.[15]

As Guelders's ruler, William was potentially even more dangerous than his predecessor Charles, a "robber-baron-princeling," who, according to James Tracy, is remembered primarily for his many raids into Holland. The duchy provided William with access to the Zuider Zee and control of three branches of the Rhine River – the Waal, the Lek, and the Nedeerijn. With the resources and the strategic position of this territory, he had the capacity to destroy Dutch commerce and to force the Habsburg Netherlands to fight a second front during any future war with France, the traditional ally of Guelders. Although Francis was moving toward a peaceful co-existence with the emperor in 1538, Charles V had no reason to expect that a truce between them would be everlasting.[16]

From time to time before he made the decision to match himself with a daughter of Cleves, Henry and his realm had enjoyed a variety of contacts with its inhabitants. Evidence of Cleves denizens can be found in the public records and among those documents is one dated 1512 concerning some feudal possessions that the duke of Cleves held of Lewis, count palatine. In 1519 the diplomat Richard Pace attended the duke's court at Düsseldorf, and in 1522 John III had, of course, traveled to England in the train of the emperor.[17]

In 1530, eight years after John's visit, Sir Herman Ryngk proposed to Henry that Mary Tudor wed William of Cleves to strengthen the realm in case of a war with France, Spain, or Burgundy. His dispatch requires attention because it provides testimony about the strength of Cleves. A wealthy Hanseatic merchant of the London Steelyard, Ryngk mostly resided at his home in Cologne, near Düsseldorf. For a fee he, his father, and son executed various commissions for the Tudor family. They purchased goods, supplied war materials, delivered letters, raised loans, and unearthed information, such as that which was contained in this letter about a possible husband for Mary. In his dispatch Herman revealed that John possessed three powerful duchies, two countships, and many populous towns and that he would be able to raise an army sufficient to defend England at perilous times. The duke's heir was fifteen years old, well learned, able to speak Latin and French, of medium height, with brown complexion and sound in body and limbs. In 1538 William Lok, Henry's merchant/buyer in Brussels, was to add that William was "very wise and hardy and much beloved." Twenty-seven years later, Adam von Zwetkovich, baron von Mitterburg, recommended to Maximilian II that William be selected to accompany Charles of Austria to England to woo Elizabeth, because of all the German princes he was the most skilled in French and Italian manners. As William was also polite and virtuous, Mitterburg believed the queen would welcome his presence.[18]

Since he was hoping to promote a match between Mary and William in 1530, Ryngk discussed only his sisters' important connections and made no reference to their looks and education. Four years earlier in September 1526, he explained, the eldest child Sybilla had become the wife of John Frederick, then the future duke elector of Saxony, who was a mighty prince with many allies. Since 1527 the second daughter Anne had been affianced to Francis, heir of Antony, duke of Lorraine, Calabria, and Bar, who had been born on 23 August 1517. Their marriage covenants stipulated, according to Ryngk, that Guelders would descend to Francis, the grandson of Philippa of Egmond, who was the sister of Duke Charles. Ryngk's assertions concerning Anne's status in 1530 clearly contradicted a rumor he himself had reported to England in February 1528, which has been repeated almost verbatim in many modern histories, that her union with Francis had been broken off, that she would marry a Danish prince, and that Guelders would be ceded to the emperor. Clearly, Ryngk's dispatch of 1530 which indicated that the covenant agreed upon between Cleves and Lorraine was still viable left his readers to infer that the rumors he had reported of its revocation in 1528 had been false. The youngest child Amelia, he added, was in her minority and had not yet been affianced, and, indeed, was to remain unmarried.[19]

Ryngk's description of the power of Cleves must have persuaded the king to consider an alliance with the duchy, for in late 1531 an embassy arrived to negotiate a match between William and Mary. The next spring after having learned the reason for the mission, Chapuys discussed it with Norfolk, who conceded that John was rumored to be mad and that it was not known whether William would be similarly afflicted. Even so, as a husband for Mary, the council preferred William to James of Scotland. Two years later in October 1533, Vaughan informed Cromwell from Brussels that John bore some grudge against Henry; perhaps he was miffed that the negotiations had stalled because of events surrounding the king's divorce from Catherine of Aragon and the birth of Elizabeth. Special note must be taken here of the above dates concerning this Cleves initiative. Both before Cromwell gained appointment as the principal secretary and before the enactment of the Reformation statutes, the English government had seriously considered an alliance with this duchy, and it may well have been the schism from Rome that derailed further discussions about it.[20]

In 1539 ducal religious policies may also have motivated Henry to consider a Cleves marriage. Like him, its rulers were doctrinally Catholic, but John's strategy for peace had led him to enter into alliances that were anti-papal and in the case of his eldest daughter even Lutheran.[21] The official religion of Cleves may be described as Erasmian, although at least since 1491 the duchy had been strongly influenced by the quiet inwardness and moralistic ideals of *Devotio Moderna*. Hoping to avoid disputes that might lead to disorder, John had banned Lutheran writings in 1525 and 1530, had condemned the sale of indulgences and had ordered preaching to be "without self-interest" and "free of charge." In 1532 he issued a set of regulations that encompassed a practical ethical religion, looked to the writings of the Church Fathers for guidance, and emphasized the need of the clergy to be resident and to educate their parishioners. Specifically, the regulations set out instructions for preaching, for celebrating holy days, and for the saying of prayers, and defined the nature of the sacraments. The humanist, Conrad von Heresbach, took a copy of these orders to Freiburg for a review by Erasmus, who seems to have approved of them, and in 1533 the duke granted him an annual pension. That same year Henry's agents at Nurenburg confirmed that John had rejected papal authority and had reserved to himself the collation to benefices; two years later, however, a papal agent, Pietro Paulo Vergerio, bishop of Capo d'Istria, claimed that the duke had expressed a willingness to attend the general council that Paul was planning to convene at Mantua. Besides Heresbach, who served as William's tutor, John employed other Erasmians: John Ghogreve, the chancellor, Dr. Henry Olisleger, the vice-chancellor, and Dr. Carl Harst, a diplomat sent to England in 1540. John's patronage of humanists led Philip Melancthon to charge that their presence in Cleves retarded the advance of the Reformation.[22]

It was John's conservative reforms that bolstered Henry's decision to foster a closer relationship with him. The English overture can be interpreted partly as a response to Paul's aggressive stance against England and his public support of the Yorkist claimant, Cardinal Pole. After Paul appointed Pole to the College of Cardinals, rumors began to circulate that he would be willing to switch his cardinal's hat for England's crown. Henry correctly believed that Paul not only intended to effect his realm's isolation but also to oust the Tudor dynasty, for an England controlled by the Pole family would assuredly return to the papal fold.[23]

During 1538, as Paul was successfully promoting peaceful relations between Francis and Charles, Henry's ministers were investigating Cardinal Pole's communications with his English connections. In August, Geoffrey Pole was arrested for corresponding with his older brother and managed to save his life by revealing information about the activities of other Yorkist claimants. His confessions about their communications with the cardinal, of their plans to flee England, and of their dynastic ambitions lay behind their subsequent trials and executions. In November, Henry Pole, Lord Montague, as well as two other Yorkist descendants, Henry, marquess of Exeter, and Sir Edward Neville, were arrested and later executed. Altogether some sixteen persons died. The elderly matriarch of the Pole family, Margaret, countess of Salisbury, was attainted by parliament in 1539 and languished in the Tower until her execution in 1541.[24]

In the meantime, Henry had reacted to the Franco-Imperial truce and to papal diplomacy in several ways. (1) He held some ships of Spain and the Netherlands in English ports in response to the seizure of English ships in the Netherlands. (2) He increased defensive fortifications in southeastern England. (3) He ordered musters to be held. (4) He began to charge aliens the same import duties as his subjects with the hope that since Netherlanders would benefit the most from this reduction, they would pressure the queen regent for peace. (5) He sought both a Protestant alliance and the marriage to Anne of Cleves. Like Henry, the leaders of the Schmalkaldic League, which reached the zenith of its power in 1539–40, were opposed to the "bishop of Rome's tyranny" and to his goal of convening a general council to heal the split in Christendom.[25]

As early as February 1538 some months before the arrest of Cardinal Pole's brother, the emperor had begun to worry, unnecessarily as it turned out, that the German heretics would succeed in converting Henry to their beliefs. For diplomatic reasons, the English king was willing to exchange embassies with the League leaders, but he persisted in rejecting their entreaties for Lutheran reform and categorically denied their petition to attack "three heads of papal idolatry:" (1) prohibition of communion in both kinds; (2) private masses; and (3) enforced clerical celibacy.[26]

Despite these divisions, negotiations between England and the League continued, for as Christian III of Denmark promised in May 1539, the confederacy would be able to assist Henry in his struggle against "the yoke of the Roman Pontiff." The Danish king clearly understood Henry's attitude toward the papacy. Recently, as he was preparing for the defense of his frontiers, Henry had referred to Paul as that "most pestilent idol, enemy of all truth and usurpation of princes." By this statement, he confirmed his belief that popes had seized the religious privileges and rights of secular rulers.[27]

Besides the papal threat, other considerations encouraged the English to seek a German alliance. In an April 1538 dispatch to Charles, written some months before the promulgation of the Franco-Imperial treaty, Chapuys repeated the recent denial of the royal councillors that they were worried about a rapprochement of France and the empire. His private rejoinder to this claim, "taunt" he called it, was that unless they had succeeded in forming a German alliance they were either quite worried or had "entirely lost their senses." Later, he predicted that Henry would marry his daughter to William of Cleves and form a defensive alliance with other Germans in response to the Franco-Imperial treaty. In fact, as Castillon believed, the general wisdom in Christendom was that Henry felt secure only when the emperor and France were estranged from each other.[28]

Despite the king's assertion to the German princes and to Christian III in 1538–39 that the English goal was to support any prince who worked against Popish tyranny, rumors still circulated that he was a Lutheran and that he planned to use the proceeds from the dissolution to promote heresy and revolution abroad. If believed, these claims could place the realm in jeopardy, for if an excommunicated ruler like Henry were a doctrinal heretic and not just an enemy to papal power, the case for a united Catholic front against him would be greatly strengthened. His councillors soon began to refute this speculation about his faith. In January 1539 Chapuys informed the emperor that Cromwell had been assuring the French ambassador that the only English innovation was the denial of papal authority. In addition, much ado about Henry's animosity toward Paul enlivened public entertainment. That summer, for example, two galleys fought on the Thames River in the presence of the king; the victor bore the royal arms and the loser the papal arms.[29]

A controversial response to the allegations about his heresy and perhaps also to the discovery of an anabaptist sect at Calais was the king's decision in the spring of 1539 to assent to the Six Articles, a conservative doctrinal statement, the final text of which he personally edited. The statute confirmed, among other usages, transubstantiation, private masses, and clerical celibacy. It was thought that its enactment would stifle rumors that the reason he was attempting to marry the daughter of a German duke was because he had converted to Lutheranism.[30]

While privately Alexander, Cardinal Farnese, vice-chancellor to Paul, was predicting that the emperor would settle German affairs before breaking with England, Henry and his ministers were pressing for a Cleves alliance in anticipation of, or at least in fear of, a more immediate rupture.[31] In mid-to-late January 1539, amidst speculation in London and Brussels that Henry had decided to marry his daughter to William of Cleves, Cromwell delivered two sets of instructions to Christopher Mont that detailed his duties at a diet of the Schmalkaldic League at Frankfort, where he was to meet with the duke elector of Saxony.[32] A native of Cologne, Mont had become a denizen of England in 1531 when he entered Cromwell's service, making himself useful as a translator. Two years later he undertook the first of many prolonged missions to obtain news on German religious and political affairs.[33]

In the first set of instructions to Mont, who was acquainted with Melancthon and other reformers, the king required him to discover from the duke elector the inclination of the duke of Cleves and his family toward the "bishop of Rome" and to inquire whether, if they were papists, they would be willing to change their opinions. Henry's other concerns focused on anabaptist activities and League policies.[34] Following the convention that agents should initiate the first marriage proposals or, at least, should appear to have initiated them, Cromwell dictated Mont's second set of instructions in which he outlined two possible alliances. If the duke elector seemed to favor a union between Mary and William, Cromwell reported, Mont should confer about it with his vice-chancellor. Were Burchart to request a portrait of her, Mont should respond that pictures of high-ranking ladies were never sent abroad and that since the vice-chancellor had recently seen her in England, he could personally testify to her appearance and accomplishments. As potential husbands had been obtaining images of royal daughters for over one hundred years, and as the king's painter, Holbein, had executed portraits of candidates for Henry in France and the Netherlands, this statement was patently untrue. It probably reflected doubts about William's interest in an English marriage, since rumors continued to circulate, despite the Nymwegen Contract, that he would wed the duchess of Milan to settle the Guelders controversy. If he wished to receive Mary's portrait, he would first have to indicate a strong desire to wed her. Ultimately, as it turned out, the duke elector refused to support this marriage proposal because of her illegitimate status.[35]

Cromwell also instructed Mont to obtain information about the elder of the two unmarried Cleves daughters. He should send back descriptions of her shape, stature, and complexion, discover if she had qualities the king might find attractive, and obtain her portrait. If possible, it would be useful if Mont should somehow persuade her family to offer her in marriage to Henry, thus overriding, probably because of the discrepancy in the social and political status of their dynasties, the prevailing tradition attested to by the emperor that ladies ought to be demanded, not offered in marriage.[36]

It is not entirely clear why the English had decided to approach John's son-in-law first about these alliances, but it was true that Henry hoped that the proposed treaty with Cleves would result in a political, rather than a religious, agreement with other powerful German princes. Although John and William had refused to convert to Lutheranism or to join the league, they still relied heavily on Saxony's support, particularly in the perilous times following their seizure of Guelders. As it turned out, Saxony initially approved of Henry's marriage to his sister-in-law, partly because he and his associates were hoping to use it to persuade William to join the League as a Lutheran convert. It is also possible that the earlier rumor about John's madness was partially true. In mid-to-late January 1539, he could easily have been either senile or simply unapproachable because of a serious illness, for he died on 6 February. Consequently, since Mont was due to be at Frankfort for deliberations with members of the Schmalkaldic League in any case, it must have seemed appropriate to ask him to raise the marriage issue with the duke elector at that time. Ultimately, Saxony, who was some thirteen years older than William, proved to be as knowledgeable about and as interested in the arrangements for Anne's marriage as was her brother, who was surely at his father's deathbed and incommunicado on 27 January when Mont, who had departed England a week earlier, arrived at Antwerp.[37]

On 10 March Cromwell responded to letters sent by Mont and his colleague, Thomas Paynell. Although Paynell was not included in the draft of the original instructions, he was later added to the mission. He arrived with Mont at Antwerp and was present with him on 17 February at the Frankfort Diet. An Austin friar and canon at Merton who had been educated at Oxford, Paynell was a translator and author of many religious works. He had accepted an annual pension of £10 at his abbey's dissolution in 1538 and for a short time was tapped for diplomatic service to Germany.[38] He later served as Henry's chaplain.

The messages of Mont and Paynell to which Cromwell responded on 10 March were dated 18 and 19 February and are no longer extant. In them, the two ambassadors admitted that they had made no progress in their attempts to further the Cleves alliance. The long delay in Cromwell's response to them may have been due to problems in obtaining their letters, for the weather frequently hindered channel crossings, but in this case their reports had probably led to discussions about how to proceed in the negotiations. Cromwell informed them in his 10 March letter that the king had decided to send Nicholas Wotton, Edward Carne, and Richard Beard to Cleves. He asked that they inform Saxony of this decision, obtain assurances from Burchart that the duke elector favored the marriage, and confer with the new English diplomats at Cleves.[39]

Their instructions authorized the Cleves negotiators, whom bad weather had stranded at Dover until 15 March, to offer William any match that seemed reasonable, to inform him that Henry was willing to marry in his dominions, and to request him to send ambassadors to England with a portrait of an appropriate lady. If the proposals pleased the duke, they should reveal that Henry would be glad "to honour his house and family" by marrying his elder unmarried sister with whom they were expected then to arrange an interview. Finally, they should discover the duke's views on the gospel, the bishop of Rome, the Schmalkaldic League, and the emperor.[40]

In the meantime, on 5 March, five days before Cromwell wrote to inform them about the Cleves embassy, Mont and Paynell had finally been able to report some successful results in a letter that the lord privy seal did not receive until 18 March. In it, they revealed that the duke elector had promised both to promote the king's marriage with Anne and to forward a portrait of her to England, but that unfortunately Saxony's long-time court painter, Lucas Cranach the Elder, was, for the moment, too ill to undertake this commission. The English ambassadors had also learned that everyone "praised the beauty" of Anne "as well for the face, as for the whole body, above all other ladies excellent." One observer had even told them that she excelled the duchess of Milan "as the golden sun excelled the silver moon."[41]

On 22 March, Cromwell, who had earlier sent them some further instructions from the king, requested that Mont and Paynell return home from Frankfort by way of Cleves and confer with Wotton and Beard about the attributes of the selected bride and other matters. Two weeks later Mont and Paynell were still at Frankfort where they had succeeded in discussing the proposed marriage on 3 April with the Cleves ambassadors and in a separate meeting with Ghogreve, the duke's chancellor. On 23 April the two Englishmen were back in London, confirming to Cromwell that Saxony was willing to support the match but also warning that the issue was far from resolved, since the Cleves councillors, with whom they had discussed it, had not yet returned home.[42]

Only two of the three commissioners originally appointed to negotiate the marriage reached Cleves. Before they departed, it had been decided to station Carne at Brussels where he spent most of the late winter cooperating with the other English ambassadors there. In late February he traveled to Guelders with Vaughan probably to discuss a defensive treaty with William.[43] From the outset Wotton and Beard assumed responsibility for the deliberations with the duke and his vice-chancellor, Olisleger. Recently appointed as groom of the privy chamber, Beard was attached to the embassy with Wotton, an experienced royal minister, as an aide rather than as a serious negotiator, for it was his duty to supervise the forwarding of dispatches home. In one of his later letters to the two envoys, Cromwell instructed Beard to bring Anne's portrait to England when it was obtained, leaving Wotton, who had been composing the dispatches, to continue the deliberations. The future dean of Canterbury and York, Wotton had earned the degrees of doctor of civil and canon law and of divinity probably at an Italian university. This mission was not the first the doctor had undertaken abroad for the king, for in 1530 he had accepted assignments to solicit support from foreign universities for Henry's divorce from Catherine of Aragon. He was also to serve the king's three children after their accessions but from personal choice he clung to relatively humble positions, for he refused a bishopric from Henry and later the archbishopric of Canterbury from Elizabeth.[44]

On 23 April 1539 the same day that Mont and Paynell briefed Cromwell in London, he informed Henry that he had once again requested Wotton and Beard, who had been gone from England for over a month, to obtain Anne's portrait. To this date, they had made little progress in their mission, perhaps partly because of family matters concerning first the death of John in February and then the illness in March of William, whom Wriothesley had heard lay near death's door with a swollen face and body and a "deadly flux," symptoms that led to speculation that he had been poisoned.[45]

Henry and his ministers were increasingly anxious to conclude a German alliance, primarily because they feared a Franco-Imperial invasion. A Flemish fleet cruising in the channel had them on edge and recent diplomatic maneuvers created more tension. In February when Chapuys left his post before his replacement's arrival, Cromwell charged him with violating protocol and with prejudicing Anglo-Imperial relations. His recall and Wriothesley's almost simultaneous transference home caused both Cromwell and Mary of Hungary to suspect each other's motives. She also expressed deep concern about the mission of Carne and Vaughan to Guelders. Two months later Castillon's departure for France and the seizure of English ships in the Netherlands had Henry and Cromwell concerned that war with Frances and the emperor was imminent.[46]

At Cleves that spring the English diplomats continued to encounter delays in accomplishing their mission. On 3 May Wotton detailed some of their difficulties in a long letter which both he and Beard signed. Because of the Frankfort Diet and the deepening Guelders dispute, they revealed, they had been unable to obtain a response from William about the marriage proposals. The duke had recently departed for Düsseldorf, leaving Olisleger behind at the town of

Cleves to discuss the matter with them, but the vice-chancellor had requested instead that they meet him at Xanten where he was scheduled to attend an emergency council meeting. When that business was finished, he promised to accompany them to Düsseldorf for deliberations on the marriage alliance. The reason for this awkwardness in conducting business derived from decisions John III had made when he inherited Cleves in 1521. Although his court remained highly itinerant, he resided principally at Düsseldorf in Berg and at Düren in Juliers. He convened the formal sessions of his council at Xanten in Cleves, however.[47]

In May 1539 after the adjournment of the council meeting, Olisleger was forced to confess to the waiting English diplomats that they had needlessly journeyed to Xanten, for the duke had amended his instructions. Instead of escorting them to the court at Düsseldorf, he must leave for a conference on the Guelders dispute that the queen regent had requested at Brussels. Before departing he was still willing to discuss the marriage with them, but, for those deliberations, they must return to the town of Cleves.[48]

After reaching Cleves, the Englishmen had to wait a full day before hearing from Olisleger that he would confer with them on the morrow, which was May Day, at which time they learned that the delay had been caused by the late arrival of some of the duke's councillors who brought his instructions with them. William had raised two impediments to proceeding with the negotiations: (1) When the Frankfort Diet ended, he had planned to confer with the duke elector concerning the English initiative but because of family and international emergencies, his brother-in-law had been forced to return to his duchy without meeting with William. (2) Since he was unclear about what dower his sister Anne should have, about the arrangements that ought to be made if she should be widowed, and about the conditions the king would require before entering into an alliance, William wished first to learn Henry's opinions about these issues. After presenting this unsatisfactory news to them, Olisleger revealed that he would have portraits of both the duke's unmarried sisters, which had been painted some six months earlier and were stored at Cologne, delivered to them within two weeks.[49]

The astonished Englishmen replied that if William waited until he could speak with his brother-in-law personally, the business might be delayed indefinitely because princes did not often have opportunities to meet with each other. Moreover, they did not understand the need for the two leaders to converse about the marriage: the duke elector had already assured Burchart, Mont, and the Cleves ambassadors at Frankfort that he favored the alliance. As to the request that Henry first explain what financial conditions would be required, Wotton and Beard, who must have been surprised that the duke did not seem more eager to marry his sister into the higher ranking Tudor family, objected that it was not customary for their king "to desire of other men" that which "other men rather ought for a great benefit to desire of his majesty." Their response dovetails with the expected behavior of an inferior to a superior ruler. Conference protocol, for example, dictated that the greatest leaders should arrive first. Less exalted princes would then come to find them. Wotton and Beard further charged that the duke was looking for delays and using "colored excuses."[50]

They had been pleased to learn about the availability of the two ladies' portraits, especially the one of Anne, since their instructions had required them to obtain it. As they had not requested one of Amelia, they may have found this concession somewhat surprising. Sir Charles Cornwallis's relation about the English attempt in 1611 to negotiate a marriage between Anna, the elder Spanish infanta, and Prince Charles, has a revealing comment about a similar incident. The Spanish ministers had responded to the proposal for Anna, who was reportedly already betrothed, by offering her younger sister instead. Normally, negotiators, like Cornwallis, balked at the substitution of a younger sibling principally because of her less favorable inheritance rights. He soundly condemned the Spanish ministers' unsuccessful maneuver, for, as he wrote, they had "no advantage in point of honour, that a daughter whose sex gives ever the privilege to be sought, being offered, hath not been accepted."[51]

In 1539 when offered likenesses of both the unmarried daughters of Cleves, Wotton and Beard seemed willing, for the moment at least, to accept the younger lady's candidacy. Instead of protesting at Amelia's inclusion in the negotiations, they took the opportunity to assert that they were unable to swear that the portraits were faithful representations since the faces of the ladies, when they had seen them, had been well hidden under a "monstrous habit and apparel." Having assured the envoys that the images were true copies,

1 Jane Seymour, queen of England

2 Henry VIII, king of England

3 Thomas Cromwell, 1st earl of Essex

4 Francis I, king of France

5 James V and Mary of Guise, king and queen of Scotland

6 Charles V, Holy Roman Emperor

7 Christina of Denmark, countess of Milan and Lorraine

8 John of Cleves with his brother Adolph at the wedding of Philip the Good

9 The six princes of the house of Cleves. From left to right: Adolph I, John I, John II, John III, William V, John William

10 William of Cleves, 1540

11 Sybilla of Cleves, duchess of Saxony

Olisleger chided them: "Would you see them naked?" Had Amelia and Anne been infants, the immediate rejoinder would have been yes.[52]

In response to their troubled reaction, the vice-chancellor inquired directly what it was that Wotton and Beard thought should be done. They replied that since the journey to England did not take very long, some five or six days, and could be accomplished at no great charge, the duke should immediately send commissioners to offer Anne in marriage to Henry. Once in the realm, they could learn what conditions were necessary to effect the alliance.[53]

Olisleger then elaborated about his difficulties. The duke governed a small principality that had a limited number of councillors, some of whom had to stay with him at Düsseldorf; others had to attend the regent at Brussels; still others had to remain at Guelders. For the moment, none could be spared for an English mission, but if Henry were willing to wait until about Whitsuntide (25 May), when the agents dispatched to Brussels should have returned, William would send an embassy to him at that time.[54]

Next, Olisleger revealed why William had wished to delay the negotiations until after he had spoken with John Frederick. The deceased duke of Juliers–Cleves and the present duke of Lorraine had, Olisleger confessed, reached an agreement concerning their children's marriage in 1527. After the two fathers had sealed documents detailing the arrangements, John had subsequently paid certain sums to Charles of Guelders, the mediator of the match who had appointed Francis of Lorraine, Anne's future husband, as his heir. Cleves had, therefore, fulfilled the promises he had made on behalf of his daughter. In fact, the dukes of Lorraine, Juliers–Cleves and Guelders had actually signed off on two documents in 1527. One, the wedding contract, which was dated 5 June, detailed the inheritance rights of Sybilla and her husband as well as those of Anne and Francis. Eight days later, on 13 June, the three dukes also signed a friendship agreement, which incorporated the text of the marriage contract. The vice-chancellor denied that because of these documents, Anne was "ensured" in wedlock, since only the dukes had confirmed and ratified the contents of the contract, leaving the possibility of another marriage for the intended bride and groom, who had not, or whose proxies had not, sworn binding oaths to each other.[55]

This information led the English diplomats to ask why, since she had not entered into a *per verba de presenti* union with Francis, her brother was delaying the present negotiations, an inquiry that prompted the vice-chancellor to explain the nature of William's business with his brother-in-law. Cleves had been concerned enough both about the honor of his father, who had approved the Lorraine match, and about the arrangements dictated by the contract, that he had requested Saxony and one other individual (whose name Wotton and Beard could not remember), to speak with Lorraine about these issues. The duke elector might also be able to resolve the dispute of the present dukes of Lorraine and Cleves over the possession of Guelders, since Antony maintained that he was its rightful owner as the nephew and heir of Duke Charles. As noted above, John had paid sums of money to Charles to confirm his approval of the marriage covenants that had set out the rights of Antony's son Francis to the duchy. None of the several arranged appointments of Lorraine and Saxony to discuss these matters, Olisleger claimed, had been kept. Actually, unbeknownst to the English diplomats, the duke of Lorraine, who had been refusing to concede Guelders to William, had sent ambassadors to Cleves as late as 6 February 1539 with instructions to implement the contract of 1527 that would result in Anne's nuptials with Francis and the transference to him of Guelders.[56]

The question of who had the best claim to Guelders was even more complicated than the explanation put forth in the ambassadors' letter. At one time or another, Duke Charles had looked upon King Francis as his heir. At other times, he had seemed to favor, as he did in the pacts of 1527, his grandnephew of Lorraine. In 1538 he had willed his duchy to William of Cleves. The younger brother of the duke of Lorraine, the powerful duke of Guise, was also an interested party to the succession crisis and expressed a desire to recover his family's rights to the duchy. Furthermore, before King Francis and Charles had signed their peace treaty in 1539, they had each made promises to others concerning Guelders's future. King Francis, to whom Charles of Egmond had agreed to grant the reversion of his duchy as late as 1535, actually supported Lorraine's succession, while the emperor, who had renewed his family's rights to the duchy in a treaty with the deceased duke of Guelders in 1528, had, in an attempt to heal the rift in Christendom, even offered it to Saxony if he would agree to attend a general council meeting.[57]

Olisleger's revelations concerning these covenants of 1527 greatly disturbed Wotton and Beard, for, as they protested, Saxony might never succeed in persuading Lorraine to agree to any terms. They reminded the vice-chancellor that the deceased John long since had honorably carried out his part of the bargain, while Antony reportedly had failed to follow through on the arrangements outlined in the pact and might well delay acting on his promises indefinitely. Wotton and Beard complained to Olisleger: "The further we go, the more delays . . . appear in this matter."[58]

Concerned about their reactions, the vice-chancellor excused himself to converse with some of the duke's councillors who had recently arrived. Half an hour later, he returned to inform them that two options were possible. (1) Wotton and Beard might tarry at Cleves until he and his colleagues returned from Brussels at which time some of them could be appointed to depart for England. In the meantime, the portraits of the ladies would be made available. (2) The two Englishmen might leave for home with the likenesses, and when the duke's councillors returned from Brussels, William would send a response to their king.[59]

After Wotton and Beard explained that they must remain in Germany at Henry's pleasure, Olisleger advised them to reside at Cologne where they would be near William's court at Düsseldorf. At the completion of the Brussels conference, he promised, the duke would either send ambassadors to England or send a direct answer to the king's inquiries. The interview having been concluded, Olisleger and other ducal advisers departed by wagon for Brussels where they had safely arrived before 11 May.[60]

Next, Wotton and Beard detailed in their letter to Henry the worst possible interpretations that they could imagine might be placed on Olisleger's explanations. When the emperor had learned about their mission, they speculated, he must have hoped to disrupt the negotiations by instructing his sister to summon the Cleves commissioners to Brussels to discuss Guelders's future. At this meeting, Wotton and Beard worried, Mary of Hungary might well reveal that the emperor would permit William to retain Guelders if he would be willing to pay a high enough price. He could marry the duchess of Milan, whose financial resources would be transferred to the emperor rather than to her husband. By these comments the two Englishmen indicated how unaware they were of the Habsburg resolve to wrest

Guelders from William. Wotton and Beard also speculated about Lorraine's actions. Instead of relinquishing his son's marriage to Anne, which would force him to repay to her brother William the money their father John III had earlier remitted to Guelders, Antony might well insist that the wedding take place and, in return for some reasonable sum of money from Cleves, renounce his claim to Guelders. Finally, they conjectured that William was deliberately delaying his response to Henry until one or both of these actions occurred, for, as they commented about his sister's place on the marriage market, her brother "knows well enough that her beauty will get her a good husband, though she have not the duke of Lorraine's son at all."[61]

At the end of this dispatch, they reported that they planned momentarily to depart for Düsseldorf, and unless the duke had business to transact with them, they would leave his court for Cologne. There they hoped to obtain the portraits of Anne and Amelia that would be forwarded to England as soon as possible. Cologne was a convenient place for them to reside, for they would be able to collect information and gossip at its famous cathedral, where, as was customary at St. Paul's, two daily perambulations took place.[62]

While the Cleves embassy at Brussels was encountering difficulties in resolving the Guelders dispute, the English government was considering how to respond to Beard's and Wotton's letter about the written promises between Lorraine and Cleves. One of the issues that must have concerned Henry and Cromwell, but that had not been raised in their letter, was Olisleger's admission that John had remitted money to Guelders without requiring that permanent vows be sworn between Anne and Francis to protect his investment. Another troublesome matter was the unexpected inclusion of Amelia in the negotiations. They may well have wondered why Olisleger had willingly offered them a portrait of her when they had requested one of Anne only.[63]

By the end of June the English government had decided to send a third ambassador to Cleves: William Petre, who had earned the degree of doctor of civil law at All Souls, Oxford, in 1533. At first a client of the Boleyns, he had secured Cromwell's favor and had been appointed deputy for him in his capacity as vicegerent in 1536. His zealous service as a visitor of the greater monasteries won him advancement from chancery clerk to master in chancery. After having prepared a bill for the enactment of the Six Articles in 1539, he was next ordered "to proceed with all speed to Cleves."[64]

Although his mission seems to have been aborted, his instructions provide interesting insights into the strategies the English next considered. They required that Wotton and Petre meet separately with William and his mother, or, if expedient, with them together. After expressing thanks for their good will, the diplomats should solicit as much information as possible from them, but especially from the duchess about the pacts signed by her late husband and the duke of Lorraine. It was important to obtain the views of Anne's mother both because William had been too young in 1527 to be privy to the arrangements and because traditionally rulers' wives were consulted about marriages for their female relatives, particularly their own daughters. While Henry was seeking a fourth wife in 1538–39, for example, Queen Eleanor of France was exerting herself to find a husband for Mary, her daughter by her late husband Manuel I, but to no avail partly because her stepson, John III, who had custody of his half-sister, proved to be unwilling to support her efforts. Although it is not relevant to the marriage of Anne, who was twenty-three in early 1539, it is also noteworthy that royal women sometimes attempted to delay the nuptial ceremonies of their young female relatives beyond the canonically accepted twelfth year.[65]

In his instructions to Wotton and Petre, Cromwell further informed them, in a sense anticipating Cornwallis's later reaction to the Spanish offer of a younger infanta, that Henry regarded the elder unmarried daughter, whose virtue and wisdom he had heard praised, as the more suitable bride, but before a final commitment was made, they should inspect all relevant documents to ascertain that Anne was at liberty to marry. If the duke should maintain that she had been promised beyond retraction, an obvious reason for him to have promised portraits of both sisters, but that Amelia was still available, Petre and Wotton should respond that they believed that either lady would suit the king but that they must raise the matter with him again. Henry hesitated to accept the substitution of Amelia for Anne because her hereditary rights were less favorable than those of her older sister. Thus keeping Henry's options open, Petre and Wotton should also meet with both ladies, and if Beard had not already forwarded their portraits to England, some images should be sent immediately with a statement declaring how realistic they were.

To questions about a dowry, they should explain that in general the king preferred virtue and friendship to money.[66]

In July Beard returned to London perhaps in response to new instructions. If he brought back with him the two portraits Olisleger had promised, the king considered them inadequate, for Beard escorted Holbein to Germany and by early August they were at Düren. Having quickly finished sketches of both Anne and Amelia, Holbein departed for England before the end of the month. These were probably sketches in crayon, which he used as models for his finished portraits, as he had the earlier ones of Christina and the French ladies. He painted the image of Anne, which is now at the Louvre, on a parchment fastened down on a wooden panel, and chose a dark-green background to set off her figure. The portrait, which is almost three-quarters length long, less than life-size, depicts her in a frontal view with her hands folded. Dressed in a bejeweled cap and an elaborate gown of red velvet that had bands of white linen with embroidery, she wore two gold chains and a cross around her neck and had several rings on her fingers.[67]

To many modern viewers her face in Holbein's portrait, which seems to be overwhelmed by all the jewelry and finery, is at least "pleasant" although not extraordinarily beautiful. It is noteworthy, however, that Wotton, who had earlier referred to her as a beauty who would do well on the marriage market, was of the opinion that the artist had made an accurate portrayal of her. Stories surfacing in the seventeenth century, perhaps because Holbein had been born at Augsburg, that he painted a portrait of Anne which greatly flattered her, are clearly false. One of the leading characteristics of his work is its clarity and truthfulness of representation, for it exhibits "a beautiful form sustained by an uncommon objectiveness, a minute observation of reality and of the individual features, a balance of shape and a geometric structure of the composition." When Henry was later divorced from Anne, he complained bitterly about his ministers' activities but not about the artist's honesty or the ambassadors' efforts.[68]

English reactions to the negotiations varied. In June, Castillon's replacement, Charles de Marillac, who had arrived in late March, noted that the formerly pensive king was appearing on the Thames in the evening where harpists and chanters were entertaining him. He was said to be taking great pleasure in painting and embroidery and had sent abroad for masters of these arts and for more musicians. Observers interpreted this display as a sign of his desire to remarry. In 1538 when the king had been similarly entertained after receiving a portrait of the duchess of Milan, Chapuys had also speculated that this kind of public demonstration signaled his eagerness to wed again.[69]

By July 1539 rumors were circulating in England that Anne would be Henry's bride. Marillac reported the news to his court, and both the earl of Hertford and Charles Brandon, duke of Suffolk, indicated to Cromwell that the match would greatly please them. In August, Constantine also referred favorably to Anne in a conversation with John Barlow, dean of Westbury, in which he claimed she was a better bride for Henry than Christina, whose marriage would have required a papal dispensation.[70]

While these rumors were circulating in England, Wotton sent Henry a dispatch from Düren on 11 August that contained less than satisfactory news. Responding to the king's inquiry dated a month earlier, Wotton explained that William had been refusing to proceed with the negotiations until after the duke elector contacted him. On 7 August Saxony had finally informed William that he was sending some councillors to Düren, who were authorized to accompany Olisleger and Werner von Hochsteden, the grand master, to England to negotiate the treaty. Unbeknownst to Wotton, Saxony had ceased to favor the marriage because the passage of the Six Articles seemed to end German hopes that the union with Anne might not only lead Henry to rethink his doctrinal position but also encourage Cleves to join the League. As late as 31 August Saxony was still complaining to William that he was opposed to the match but that since the negotiations had proceeded so far, he would accept it.[71]

In his 11 August dispatch Wotton also forwarded to the king the unwelcome news that he had not been able to obtain a copy of the written covenants agreed to by the duke of Lorraine and the deceased duke of Juliers–Cleves in 1527. William's ministers had informed him that the documents would either be sent to him or be delivered to Henry with an explanation of why Anne was still free to wed. Despite this failure, Wotton could at least inform the king that the council of Cleves was willing to declare that as she had not personally promised to marry Francis, her father's pledges did not bind her.[72]

The English ambassador further revealed without explaining the reason for his actions that he had been attempting secretly to obtain a copy of the marriage agreements between Anne's sister Sybilla and the duke elector.[73] It is possible that Wotton thought these documents would provide insights into the covenants signed in 1527 by John with Antony of Lorraine, whose heir had been appointed to receive Guelders when he married Anne. Questions about the Guelders succession and about the financial details of Anne's dowry seem to explain why her elder sister's husband had remained an interested party to the marriage negotiations.[74]

In the 11 August letter, Wotton also described in detail some of Anne's qualities and traits. The duchess has raised her, he said, as she had Sybilla in her own household "and in manner never from her elbow, the Lady Duchess being a wise lady and one that very straitly looks to her children." Although he believed that Anne's gentle nature made her mother loath to permit her departure, an earlier report to Cromwell had indicated that the duchess approved of the English marriage for her daughter. In her leisure hours Anne occupied herself mainly with needlework, for she cannot, Wotton explained, "sing nor play any instrument, for they take it here in Germany for a rebuke and an occasion of lightness that great ladies should be learned or have any knowledge of music." Moreover, she could speak and write only German (low German), but as she was bright, Wotton thought she would be able to learn English quickly. He reassured Henry that he did not think she was "inclined to the good cheer of this country," meaning the drinking of spirits, for, as he noted, her brother was abstemious. Finally, he reported that Holbein had painted "very lively" or faithful likenesses of both Anne and Amelia.[75]

Wotton's comments need examination because writers have usually relied upon them to prove that Anne was an inappropriate wife for the king. It is important in evaluating her candidacy to study the statements made about her prior to her marriage and to leave the negative reactions of Henry in January 1540 for a later discussion. Four references to her appearance, including two by Wotton, had now been conveyed to England along with an image of her.

Hutton, who made the first of these statements at Brussels in 1537, reported that he had heard no "great praise neither of her personage nor beauty." When his comment, which has received much press in modern histories, is read in association with Wotton's above letter, it becomes clear why Hutton had heard no "great praise" of her. Unlike the duchess of Milan or Hutton's other candidates, Anne never attended the queen regent's court where he was headquartered. Since she could speak only her native tongue, furthermore, and had remained in her mother's household, probably very few, if any, of the courtiers at Brussels whom Hutton could have approached about her, even if they had visited Juliers–Cleves, would ever have had an opportunity to see her at close range, let alone speak with her. John III did not entertain resident ambassadors who might have had more opportunities to interact with his family than had the extraordinary envoys assigned to his dominions. Even some individuals, like Burchart, whom it might be expected to have visited Cleves, had not done so at this time. As noted earlier, Wotton and Beard, who were wooing her on behalf of their monarch, actually resided at Cologne, rather than at her brother's court, while awaiting the return of Olisleger from Brussels. Had Hutton heard any specifically negative comments about her at Brussels, as he had about Margaretha van Brederode, he would surely have repeated them in his dispatch.[76]

The next dated statement about her appearance came from Mont and Paynell at Frankfort where they were able to speak about her with some individuals, one of whom had claimed she excelled the duchess of Milan in beauty. This informant might actually have had the opportunity to see Christina in Anne's homeland, for on her journey from Pavia to Brussels in 1537, she had crossed the Brenner Pass to Innsbruck. Then, she had traveled along Lake Constance and down the Rhine to Heidelberg and Cologne. Afterwards, she went by land to Aix-la-Chapelle in Juliers, to Maestricht, and thence to Louvain and Brussels. While in Juliers, Christina visited Anne's mother and may have spent some time with Anne and Amelia as well.[77]

The third reference to Anne's appearance is in Beard's and Wotton's letter of 3 May in which they predicted, even after complaining that they had been unable to see her so well as they would have liked, that her beauty was such that her brother would have no difficulty in finding a husband for her. Subsequently, Wotton must have had an opportunity to visit with her again, for, as was noted above, he ended his 11 August letter with the explanation that

Holbein's painting of Anne, whose looks he thought made her highly marriageable, was a faithful image.[78]

Modern historians have also deplored her simple education. Far from criticizing her upbringing, however, Wotton indicated that her mother had been "wise" to keep her under her charge. Since she had been destined to become the bride of Francis of Lorraine from an early age, it was not necessary for her family, even if that had been their custom, to send her to another household to obtain an education or to attract an appropriate suitor. Many royal and noble women kept their daughters at home until they were old enough for married life. No one was better suited, it was thought, to prepare them for their future as rulers' wives. Her mother seems also to have accepted the contemporary view that female nature was so weak and vulnerable that daughters needed more careful guidance than sons. To protect their virtue, parents and guardians watched girls closely and kept them busy with religious devotions and needlework. The qualities that were encouraged in them were modesty, chastity, humility, reticence, and maturity of gestures. Female instruction stressed controlled eye and eyebrow expression and warned against permitting eyes to rove or to flit about from place to place. Wotton made no mention of the specific religious training of Anne whose mother was almost certainly a conservative and strict Catholic, for in 1528 she had been the patron of Jacob von Hochstraten, dean of the Dominicans of Cologne who had accused the humanist John Reuchlin, the first German Hebraist, of betraying the church. Although the duchess had also appointed as her confessor Dom Joannes Justus Larspergius, prior of the Charterhouse of Our Lady of Compassion at Cantave, Melancthon actually identified her religious advisors as members of a humanist circle who were enemies of the Reformation.[79]

Like most gentlewomen, Anne spent her leisure moments doing needlework. Indeed, her education seems somewhat less severe in this respect than that of Anne of Denmark who married James VI of Scotland in 1589. Anne's mother, Queen Sophie of Denmark, ruled her ladies with an "iron hand." They rose at daybreak, spent the day at their spinning wheels, were forbidden to wear jewelry, and ate plain foods. In 1540 Wotton's comments about Anne's domestic skills surely reassured her future husband, for, as noted above, Marillac reported rumors that the king had developed an interest in embroidery. It must be remembered that Henry was principally seeking a wife to bear him children not a lady courtier to amuse him. The questions he posed about her looks and temperament arose not merely from his own personal need to have an attractive wife but also out of concern that she possess appropriate traits to pass on to his children. For their sake and the sake of his dynasty, he was interested in entering into a legal arrangement with a lady who displayed social propriety and moral responsibility.[80]

Impressed by Anne's intelligence, Wotton also predicted that she would readily learn English; since in the Tudor century only the English spoke their native tongue, the king and his ministers anticipated that like most other foreign brides, she would at first have to communicate with her husband through interpreters. It was perhaps for this reason that rumors claimed that Cranmer had protested seeking a consort in another country because it would be "strange," if Henry married someone with whom he could not communicate. Cromwell reportedly retorted that no suitable Englishwoman was available. Actually, Catherine of Aragon, who knew neither English nor French, had only a slight linguistic advantage over Anne when she arrived in England since she could at first converse somewhat with Arthur only in Latin. Some English ladies who were ambitious to go to court did learn French but only a handful were classicists. As almost no English person studied German, the Hanseatic merchants were often utilized as interpreters. For Anne's lack of foreign language skills, her mother should not be greatly condemned. The Cleves family, perhaps because of its earlier association with the Valois Burgundian court, did have a tradition of providing French instruction to its children. It is not possible to ascertain, whether after the Habsburg ascendancy in Burgundy Cleves's daughters as well as its sons, like Anne's brother William, had continued to share in this learning. On the whole, its culture was more cosmopolitan than that of Juliers, where Anne's mother was raised, or, for that matter, than that of many of its neighbors. Unlike William, neither Christian II of Denmark nor the duke elector could speak French. Indeed, it was not a favored language at any other German court. In 1570, for example, when Elizabeth of Austria married Charles IX of France, she could speak only German, Spanish, and some Latin. Those parents who wished their children to learn French sent them abroad for language study.[81]

Some writers have also cited Wotton's comments about music and alcohol to create negative characterizations of Anne. By English courtly standards it was unfortunate that she had not learned how to sing or to play an instrument, but this lack of training did not mean that she and her mother were incapable of appreciating good music. The Juliers–Cleves court possessed an orchestra of eight to ten musicians and some canters, and records indicate that Duchess Maria personally favored harp music. It is more likely than not that Anne also enjoyed listening to the musicians and was quite capable of admiring her new husband's musical skills.[82] Except for her lack of this training, Anne's education seems similar to that usually provided for aristocratic Englishwomen, including her predecessor Jane Seymour, a sample of whose needlework was still in existence in 1652. There is no evidence that Queen Jane knew any language except English.[83]

Wotton also assured Henry that he had no reason to believe that Anne was a great imbiber of spirits, probably he meant wine since beer was only beginning to gain popularity in Germany. According to the duke of Sully, when Henry IV was considering remarriage in 1599, he claimed that if he married a German princess, he would feel as though he were in bed with a "wine-barrel." The decision of Wotton to send his king reassurance on this score said more about the general European attitude toward German culture than it did about Anne's personal habits. It was part of the prevailing stereotyping to characterize Germans as sots: In 1546 Bernardo Navagiero, Venetian ambassador to the Imperial court, described Germans as "insubordinate, proud, and drunken"; Wotton may have believed his king held a similar opinion. In 1533 when Frederick, count palatine and future brother-in-law of Christina of Denmark, visited England, his secretary, Hubertus Thomas Leodius, reluctantly endured a drinking bout with Henry. Feeling thirsty, the king had sent for two goblets, the first containing beer and the second wine, and then asked Leodius to choose a goblet and drink its contents down in one draught. Henry had then allegedly boasted "that Englishmen, yea the king, himself, could drink in true German fashion." While Henry drained his goblet of beer in one swallow, it had taken Leodius four swigs to down his wine! Apparently, he had tried to refuse the challenge by revealing to the king the count palatine's decision to join with other German noblemen in forbidding the custom of "equal-drinking." This was the practice that Henry forced upon Leodius with the retort that Frederick had no authority in England.[84] By his behavior the king actually confirmed the opinion of some who thought the English were "sottish and unrestrained in their appetites."[85]

On balance, Wotton's comments about Anne had a favorable impact. None of his news except his inability to obtain copies of the covenants of 1527 between the dukes of Lorraine and Juliers–Cleves seems to have caused any concern. By 1 September Marillac had learned that Holbein had returned with the portraits of the sisters and that the Cleves diplomats were on their way to England to negotiate an alliance with Henry.[86] They had not as yet left Düsseldorf, however, for William's credence to his ambassadors, Olisleger and Wilhelm of Harf zu Altorf, the prefect of his court, who replaced Hochsteden, as was earlier rumored, and two Saxony envoys, Burchart and Sir John a Dolzig, was not dated until 4 September. Two days later they departed for England and within a month the agreement for the marriage of Henry and Anne was concluded.[87]

5 TRAVELING BRIDE

In September 1539 the Cleves–Saxony embassy reached England prepared to negotiate a marriage treaty with the king's commissioners. Nothing Henry had learned about his selected bride had dampened his interest in welcoming her brother's ambassadors to his kingdom. Although the dispersal in early summer of the Flemish fleet that had been cruising off Holland and Zeeland had eased tensions somewhat, he still viewed the German alliance as his best response to the Franco-Imperial treaty signed at Toledo in January. Henry was later to inform Marillac of four reasons for wedlock with her: (1) He had long desired an alliance with the Germans whom he esteemed. (2) In the event of an attack on his realm, Cleves would be able to provide a diversionary military action. (3) He could use this relationship to soften some of the German religious innovations. (4) As he was anxious to have more children, he believed that no better wife than Anne could be chosen: she was of a suitable age for childbearing, had a healthy disposition, was elegant in appearance, and had other admirable traits (*qui est en aage requis, disposition de santé, stature élègante, et avec d'aultres grâces de nature*).[1]

This explanation, which is corroborated by his other statements and actions, indicates that Henry did not expect the Cleves alliance to lead to further religious reform in his realm. It is true that before the passage of the Six Articles, Burchart and his colleagues had viewed the marriage as an opportunity both to lure Cleves into the League and to press their reformed cause in England. It is equally true that some of their Lutheran allies, such as Christian III of Denmark, who identified Henry's enemies narrowly as papists, knew this hope was futile.[2]

The two principal reasons for him to remarry were the desire to have in his own words, "more store of lawful posterity," and the need for an ally to assist his kingdom against invasion. He seems not to have given as much credence as Cromwell to the rumors at Antwerp that the Franco-Imperial peace would not last. Henry had, nevertheless, continued to probe for a softening of their friendship. In August he informed Marillac that Gian Giacomo, marquis of Marignano, an Imperial commander, had proposed to surrender Parma and Placentia to him in exchange for protection against Habsburg retaliation. Henry admitted he had declined the offer because he feared that Charles and Francis would misinterpret his actions as an attempt to gain control of Milan, but he had since been wondering whether Francis would find the proposal attractive. In response to the request of the wary Marillac for a written statement concerning Marignano's proposition, Henry agreed to send a report about it to Francis, whose subsequent lack of interest in the enterprise was probably disappointing but surely not surprising.[3]

This chapter examines the marriage negotiations between Cleves and England to set the stage for a discussion of the organization of the queen's household and of the arrangements for her removal to England. It also details her progress from Cleves to Calais and the almost simultaneous journey of the emperor through France to the Low Countries to settle a Ghent rebellion and to respond to the Anglo-Cleves alliance. The chapter ends with her arrival on English soil.

The first news that the German commissioners were shortly to begin their mission was probably contained in letters that Burchart's servant brought to the realm on 19 August. About two weeks later, on 1 September, Marillac informed Francis that the Cleves embassy, which included Saxony ambassadors, had departed for England, but he also assured his king that he was certain Henry was desirous of as many friends as possible and would gladly also welcome a French alliance. On that same day Marillac wrote in more detail to Montmorency about these matters. He speculated that Henry, who had recently vowed that he was content with his lot in life and preferred to remain on his island, defending it from invasion rather than attacking his neighbors, was still trying to set Francis and Charles against each other. He also revealed that Philip Maioris, dean of Cambray, the Imperial ambassador who had replaced Chapuys, was none too pleased to hear about the expected German embassy.[4]

Marillac's information was basically correct except that the

Germans had not yet begun their journey. Their instructions and commission having been dated at Düsseldorf, 3 and 4 September, respectively, they left for England on 6 September and reached their destination some eleven or twelve days later. Complicating arrangements for their welcome was the slightly earlier arrival of another German traveler, Frederick, count palatine, the husband of Christina of Milan's sister Dorothea. Although Henry had been suffering from a cold, he had recovered enough by 13 September, the day the count palatine landed at Dover with Arthur, Lord Lisle, deputy lieutenant of Calais and an illegitimate son of Edward IV, to agree to meet with him in a week or so. The king not only arranged for a horse litter and two mules to transport them to their lodgings at Dover where civic officials welcomed them with sixty great shots of artillery but he also asked the London magistrates to prepare an honorable reception for Frederick when he arrived on 16 September.[5]

Momentarily, the count palatine's visit distracted attention from the anticipated Cleves–Saxony embassy. Rumors circulated, which turned out to be correct, that Frederick was seeking financial assistance to recover Denmark for his deposed and imprisoned father-in-law, Christian II. Others wondered, especially members of the French government, whether he also planned to promote a marriage between Christina and Henry to thwart the Cleves negotiations. The speculation that Frederick might try to interfere with Henry's marrying plans was reasonable, given the opinions of his Habsburg in-laws and prevailing diplomatic conventions. Both the emperor and the queen regent were opposed to the union because they feared it might result in Henry's providing aid to the Lutheran princes in an all-out assault on Imperial power in Germany.[6]

In addition, it had become customary for monarchs to work against alliances that were considered detrimental to their kingdom's security. Louis XI of France, for example, had futilely lobbied against the issuance of the papal dispensation that had permitted Charles the Bold of Burgundy to marry Margaret of York in 1468. If anything, these tactics were to grow in intensity during the early modern period. In 1553 both the Venetian and French ambassadors attempted to prevent the wedding of Queen Mary and Philip of Spain, and in 1661 the Spanish ambassador actually hoped to dissuade Charles II from marrying Catherine of Braganza, who had hitherto led a sheltered life, by slandering her maidenly conduct.[7]

Shortly after the count palatine's entry at London on 16 September, the Cleves embassy, along with Dolzig and Burchart from Saxony, reached England with full powers to conclude a marriage treaty, the terms of which had received preliminary approval at Düsseldorf. On 20 September and again on 27 September, in order to facilitate the deliberations, which the English hoped would also include a defensive alliance with Cleves that the duke elector and other German princes would join, Cromwell attempted to persuade the concerned Saxony ambassadors that Henry was "not inclined toward" the Six Articles and held out the hope to them that the next parliament might even soften the religious settlement. As was their usual custom, the king's councillors were providing diplomats with the information that their principals wished to hear, undoubtedly hoping that the Germans would not discuss this version of Henry's religious stance with their French and Imperial counterparts in England. Cromwell had reason to believe that the German diplomats would find his comments credible, for in July he had received a friendly letter from Alexander Alesius, a Scottish refugee who had resided in England for four years from 1535 until earlier in 1539 when he had removed to Wittenberg. Indicating how secretive Henry and his advisers were about their true beliefs, Alesius explained that he had told his Lutheran friends that the bishops, not Cranmer, Cromwell, or the king, were the authors of the Six Articles.[8]

On 21 September, the day after the first of Cromwell's meetings with the Cleves–Saxony embassy, William, earl of Southampton, lord high admiral of England, who was at court, forwarded Henry's thanks to him for entertaining the Germans. Southampton further required him specifically on the king's orders to send for the Cleves ambassadors and to

bid them as heartily welcome, as [he] could devise; declaring unto them, that their coming is marvelously agreeable unto his majesty; offering them all the gratuity [he] can devise; and further to declare unto them, that [the king] hath appointed the Count a time to be at Windsor on Tuesday . . . and he shall have audience on Wednesday; which thing was appointed, [before] his Majesty knew of their coming.

After assuring them that it was not Henry's intent to extend preferential treatment to the count palatine, Cromwell was to learn whether they wished to attend court while Frederick was there or to

tarry until after his departure. To emphasize the gravity of the negotiations, Southampton also forwarded to Cromwell the king's
command to refrain from questioning the Tower prisoners whom
only three days earlier he had been instructed to examine closely.
Until this business was over, Cromwell was "to put all other matters
out of [his] head saving this [the king's] great weighty causes, and
sharp [his] wit to attend only unto the same."[9]

Although rumors claimed that the count palatine's visit caused
William enough concern to dispatch three more envoys to England,
his commissioners were prepared to attend court while Frederick
was still there. On 23 September Henry greeted both German dele-
gations at Windsor and the next day hosted a banquet for them.
Hubertus Thomas Leodius, the count palatine's secretary and councillor who kept a record of the festivities, reported that Frederick
(because of his noble rank) sat opposite the king and above the
Cleves ambassadors at the banquet: the rights and obligations of
individuals in the sharing of food at these events thus reflected their
rights and privileges in society at large.[10]

The many courses of food served in golden dishes, the exquisite
tapestries of worked gold on the walls and floors, and the pleasant
music played on several different instruments greatly impressed
Leodius. Henry provided splendid entertainment such as this only
for important guests on special occasions like church holidays, weddings, and treaty signings. This banquet stands as a prime example
of the conspicuous consumption that was calculated to impress
foreigners with the king's wealth and power and thus to increase his
realm's prestige in Christendom. Since, except on regular feast days,
Henry normally ate in his privy chamber to avoid "ceremonial intrusion" on his dining habits, his presence at this banquet indicated his
interest in the upcoming negotiations and his wish to honor the
German ambassadors. According to Felicity Heal, even lower down
the social ladder, such "generosity and good behavior as a host were
no mere matter of personal preference . . . but a matter of public
concern."[11]

The minute attention paid to ceremonial display at mealtime and
other important events can be traced to the ordinances first drawn
up by Dauphine Humbert II of Vienne in 1336. By the end of the fifteenth century only the Prussians in western Christendom lacked
written guidelines detailing the procedures to be followed at meals

and specifying the clothing to be worn by each guest according to his rank and the season of the year. The elaborate instructions for the English court, which had first been recorded in 1493, described a practice that had long been in place, for the courts of Henry VI and Edward IV had gained reputations for their strict, almost excessive protocol. Diplomats also regularly characterized Henry VIII's court as ceremonious.[12]

Both Lord Lisle and his agent, John Husee, informed Honor, Lady Lisle, that the king had graciously welcomed and entertained at his own expense the count palatine, who had been greeted outside Windsor and escorted to his lodgings at the Dean's House by Suffolk and one hundred horsemen clad in velvet. According to Edward Hall, both sets of Germans had been "continually . . . feasted for eight days and hunted, with all pleasure that might be showed unto them. . . ." Having made a point of observing Frederick's London entry, Marillac expressed a different view. On 3 October he claimed that the English treated the Cleves diplomats more favorably than the count palatine, who had come to the kingdom, the ambassador had been able to confirm, to obtain aid for the recovery of Denmark for his father-in-law. The Frenchman had also heard that the marriage of Anne and Henry had been concluded and guessed that the ten ships that were being outfitted would be used to convey her to the realm. In fact, the actual treaty was not signed until 4 October, one day after his comment and three days before Frederick and Lisle left for Calais. Meanwhile the pope, who had been futilely proposing that the Franco-Imperial pact be strengthened by the marriage of Francis's daughter Margaret to the recently widowed emperor, worried that the count palatine had been mediating an Anglo-Imperial treaty.[13]

The king's authorization to negotiate his marriage, which was dated 24 September, the day of the banquet, named six men: Cranmer, Thomas, Lord Audley of Walden, the lord chancellor, Suffolk, Cromwell, Southampton, and Cuthbert Tunstall, bishop of Durham. As they began their deliberations, Henry continued to entertain the German visitors. On 27 September he hunted and dined with them and on 30 September he dined with them once more. In his discussions with Burchart, the king, as Cromwell had done on 21 and 27 September, adopted a somewhat conciliatory religious stance in hopes of persuading the Lutherans to enter into a defensive alliance with England, even making the vague, but friendly, pledge that he was seeking nothing less than the "evangelical truth." He further explained that he could not alter a statute like the Six Articles, for only parliament had that authority. Although no evidence dated in the autumn of 1539 confirms that he also discussed Anne's marital status with the Cleves diplomats, his later sworn testimony and that of his councillors indicate that he had warned that when they returned with her to England, they should bring with them the documents that proved she was free to wed him. It is reasonable to assume that he did make this request since Wotton had been futilely attempting to obtain those records for months. Moreover, Olisleger had actually brought with him a few extracts from the treaty and contact of 1527 that contained information about the Cleves inheritance rights that were to be addressed in the English agreement. For unexplained reasons it was decided at Cleves not to provide him with complete copies of those documents that would have made it possible for Henry's churchmen to determine the kind of vows that had been sworn on Anne's behalf. It took less than two weeks for the diplomats to come to an agreement on the Anglo-Cleves marriage. Considering the length of time these deliberations could take, the commissioners had moved with great speed. Because these documents detailed financial matters, conditions, deadlines, and sometimes even contingency plans to substitute one spouse for another, they were completed with great care, often after lengthy debate. The haste with which they acted can be attributed partly to the king's anxiety about the Franco-Imperial treaty and to his willingness to leave the friendship pact for separate discussions with Cleves. He personally felt inclined to move with dispatch because, as he himself pointed out, old age was fast creeping up on him.[14]

The treaty covered eleven customary topics. The first four clauses stated that the proxy union would be concluded in England with Olisleger and Altorf representing Anne and that William would, if he could get a safe conduct for her through Habsburg dominions, have her conveyed at his expense to Calais within two months. Henry promised to arrange for her voyage across the channel, where the nuptial ceremony would take place. If the safe conduct could not be obtained, William would send her to an appropriate seaport from whence he would have her transported to England in a convoy of ships at his own expense.[15]

Items five and six detailed the financial settlement. In accordance with a custom that had reemerged in the eleventh century, Anne's brother had promised her a dowry: 100,000 gold florins (25,000 English marks sterling), 40,000 of it to be paid on the wedding day and the remainder within a year. By this means, families had agreed to provide for the transmission of some of their property to female children. In their turn, Henry's ministers guaranteed Anne a dower of 20,000 gold florins, thereby establishing a ratio of five to one between the dowry and dower that was typical in early Tudor marriage settlements. The dower, which normally guaranteed a wife, if she were widowed, rights to one-third of her husband's estates, had gained general acceptance by the twelfth century. It could only be collected, however, if it were granted at the church door before the nuptial ceremony.[16]

In the event that Anne was widowed without children and decided to return home, the treaty permitted her to keep her dresses and jewelry and guaranteed her 15,000 gold florins in two yearly payments for life, which, if Henry's heirs so chose, could be redeemed for the lump sum of 150,000 gold florins. Although the sealed grant of the dower would not be sent to her brother until the day of the nuptials, a true copy would be forwarded to him ten days before her departure for England.[17]

The next five clauses dealt with the inheritance of her brother's dominions, the carrying out of the terms of the treaty, and its confirmation. The inheritance details were based in part on the marriage contract of Saxony and Sybilla as well as on extracts from Anne's marriage documents of 1527. The Saxony ambassadors were especially interested in these clauses for it was their duty to protect the rights of Sybilla, who would become William's heir if he should die without lawful issue. If she, in turn, should die without legitimate children, Anne would inherit the family estates. In the event of Sybilla's succession, a sum of 160,000 gold florins should be paid within four years to her two sisters or their heirs. Sybilla must also grant Anne for life the castles of Burdericum in Cleves with 2,000 gold florins a year, Casterium in Juliers with 2,000 a year, and Benradum in Berg with 1,000 a year. If Anne should inherit her family's property, Henry pledged to pay her younger sister Amelia and her heirs 160,000 gold florins. However, if Sybilla should acquire the dominions, and if either of the other two sisters should die without heirs, the duchess was obliged to pay the surviving sister the deceased's share of the aforesaid florins. These arrangements clearly highlighted the reason the king had preferred Anne to Amelia as his wife, since her portion or dowry and her place in the line of succession were superior to those of her younger sister. It also should be noted that although the English inquired about the claims of Anne to Guelders, the treaty did not address this issue, reportedly because the rights of her and her sisters to that duchy had not figured in the previous marriage covenants.[18]

In the final two clauses, William promised to keep Henry informed about the arrangements for her journey to England so that she could be appropriately welcomed. Henry, John Frederick, and William were obligated to confirm the treaty by letters patent under their hands and seals. The German rulers would send their confirmations to the king and he would forward his to them.[19]

One interesting aspect of this treaty is that it lacked clauses dealing with the Anglo-Cleves diplomatic relationship. That issue was left for a separate agreement to which the king's Great Seal was attached in February 1540. With Saxony's reluctant approval, William could proceed with his sister's match but not with a defensive agreement that included the duke elector, who was refusing to enter into an alliance with England while the Six Articles remained in force. Henry continued to hope, however, that Saxony might change his mind and join in a Anglo-Cleves pact against the emperor, France, and Rome that treated "honest causes besides the cause of religion." For John Frederick, who was to make it clear in March 1540 that he rejected this restriction, the only just cause for an alliance was religious. As later evidence indicates, William also was not eager to sign off on a defensive pact with England. While his inability to resolve the Guelders dispute with the emperor had led him to agree to the English marriage, he still hoped to settle the controversy through diplomatic channels, and, out of concern that a defensive pact with England might completely alienate Charles, the duke had decided to stall on that agreement. In other words, he was being less than forthright with Henry: he wanted the king's aid against the emperor if it were needed, but he was reluctant to assent to an official pact against him while he was still attempting to win Imperial consent to his control of Guelders. A brief comparison of the text of the treaty between England and Cleves in 1539 to that of the Treaty of Medina del Campo between England and Spain in 1489 will serve to highlight how separating these two issues deviated from the English norm. The treaty of Medina del Campo had twenty-six clauses, the first sixteen of which treated economic, military, and political relations between the two kingdoms. It was not until its seventeenth clause that references were made to the union of Catherine and Arthur. The final ten items outlined the financial settlement, succession rights, and arrangements for her journey to England. Even a marriage agreement drawn up in late 1539 for Mary Tudor and Philip, duke of Bavaria, yet another German visitor to the realm that autumn, pledged that England and Bavaria would aid each other if another power attacked them. Philip, the younger son of Rupert, who was a brother of the count palatine and Ludwig, elector palatine, had arrived in England just a few weeks after the departure of his Uncle Frederick.[20]

The marriage contract of Henry and Anne was signed before noon on 5 October, the day after the treaty was concluded. Olisleger and Altorf, her procurators, agreed to a notarized statement on her behalf that completed an indissoluble union with the king *per verba de presenti*. That this solemn event took place in England seems to have been a change in the original plans, for Cromwell indicated in his September "Remembrances" that a noble person had to be selected to go to Cleves "to make the spousals." He probably assumed this appointment would be made because the initial vows were usually sworn in the bride's homeland. Unfortunately, no description has survived of the betrothal ceremony, but it undoubtedly followed the protocol that had been utilized in the union of Joan, dowager duchess of Brittany, and Henry IV, the only other English king to marry his bride's procurator. At Eltham Palace in 1402, when Henry wed Antoine Riczi, the agent of the dowager duchess, the king placed a ring on his finger and swore the appropriate vows.[21]

It was in the early thirteenth century that ambassadors with full powers to negotiate treaties had first begun to wed their princes' brides. These unions had become fashionable because parents had been reluctant to send their daughters to foreign lands without establishing elaborate safeguards for their virtue and marital security. While proxies could act for their principals in the nuptials as well as in the betrothal ritual, they most commonly did so in the preliminary ceremony. In 1225, for example, the archbishop elect of Capua, as

Emperor Frederick II's procurator, betrothed him to Yolanda de Brienne of Jerusalem in the Church of the Holy Cross at Acre, astonishing her countrymen that a valid union could be made between a bride and groom who were separated by the Mediterranean Sea.[22]

By the fourteenth century, monarchs routinely appointed proctors to wed their foreign-born brides before they set out for their new homes where the marriages would be concluded in nuptial rituals.[23] Female rulers also wed the proxies of foreign-born princes. In 1554, for example, Philip of Spain insisted on a ceremony between his procurator and Queen Mary before his departure for her kingdom. Prior to the ritual which took place in England in a room where the Holy Sacrament stood, the queen swore that she had not agreed to marry out of carnal affection but for the "honor and prosperity" of her kingdom and the "repose and tranquility" of her subjects.[24]

After the Reformation, as Henry had experienced in his courtship of Christina, schismatic monarchs sometimes had difficulty obtaining papal dispensations that permitted them to wed Catholic ladies. Because of this complication, in one instance, at least, a proxy union had to be waived and the bride's family once again forced to trust the groom. In 1662 Charles II signed a document declaring that Catherine of Braganza was his wife. She could neither be betrothed nor married by proxy in Lisbon except by Catholic service, which, because Charles was officially a heretic, required a papal dispensation. Since Alexander VII, like many of his faith, did not recognize that Portugal existed separately from Spain, he refused to issue that dispensation. Other variations could occur, however. In 1625 Urban VIII approved the union of Henrietta Maria and Charles because he believed that she would be able to assist persecuted Catholics in England.[25]

Two other wedding customs briefly require examination: the type of vow taken and the nature of the ritual. The decretal letters of Alexander III, pope from 1159 to 1181, set down the basic guidelines for matrimony, which were modified by more than thirty sets of canons and statutes between 1200 and 1342. These regulations, which were generally applied in England until the middle of the eighteenth century, authorized a two-step procedure that principally required the consent of the bride and groom. Vows sworn in the future tense (*per verba de futuro*), which were often referred to as the espousal or fiancells, were recognized as an announcement of the intention to marry. In this case, the appropriate English words were "I will take." This marriage remained incomplete unless it was followed by coitus in which case canon law recognized it as an indissoluble union. The final *sponsalia*, which were sworn in the present tense (*per verba de presenti*), were interpreted as completing the union that had begun with the earlier ceremony. The appropriate English words were "I take," and, even without sexual union or a church wedding, they created an indissoluble marriage.[26]

Over time the rituals varied somewhat from this pattern. First, the nuptial ceremony came to incorporate both the future tense of the espousal and the present tense of the concluded marriage. Secondly, a subtle switch occurred in fiancells between members of foreign dynasties, whether proxies were used or not. To make the marriage treaty more binding, the *per verba de presenti* wording replaced the *per verba de futuro* in the preliminary ritual. The present tense established an indissoluble union that more easily satisfied the bride's parents who feared that an intended husband would abandon their daughter and leave her helpless in a foreign land.[27]

When Patrick, earl of Bothwell, as the proxy of James IV of Scotland, wed Margaret Tudor in 1502 he took the following vow:

I Patrick, earl of Bothwell, procurator of the . . . right high and mighty prince, James . . . King of Scotland . . . having sufficient authority, power, and commandment to contract matrimony *Per Verba De Presenti*, in the name of and for my sovereign lord, with you Margaret . . . daughter of the . . . high and mighty prince . . . Henry . . . king of England, and Elizabeth queen of the same . . . contract matrimony with you Margaret, and take you . . . for the wife and spouse of my said sovereign . . . James, king of Scotland, and all other, for you, as procurator foresaid, forsake . . . during his and your lives natural, and thereto as procurator forsaid, I plight, and give you his faith and truth, by power and authority foresaid committed and given to me.[28]

In royal betrothals, the *per verba de futuro* vow might still be sworn if an impediment prevented completion of the marriage. An impediment could arise from the youthful ages of the spouses, who by canon law were supposed to be fourteen if they were male and twelve if they were female, although, as a practice, consummation of the union was often delayed until the bride was fifteen. That the appropriate papal dispensation had not arrived would be viewed as yet another impediment. In 1524, for example, when the emperor's sister, Catherine, and John III of Portugal were wed, they swore the *per verba de futuro* vow because the bull that would legalize their union, since their family relationship fell within the prohibited degrees, had not yet arrived. Upon its receipt, they concluded their marriage with the *per verba de presenti* vow.[29]

In the course of time, as other rituals had increased in complexity, so had the initial proxy service. From the first, it seems to have included, whenever appropriate, the joining of hands and the exchange of rings and kisses, which were ancient wedding usages. Other more elaborate chivalrous behavior sometimes accompanied this vow, a good example of which occurred in the alliance in 1514 of Henry's sister Mary with Louis, duke of Longueville, the proctor of her groom, Louis XII. The union took place publicly in the Great Hall at Greenwich in the presence of the king, queen, and the whole court. After Louis' authorization for Longueville to represent him was read, the duke and Mary exchanged *per verba de presenti* vows in French. He placed a ring on her right hand, gave her a kiss, and signed the marriage schedule. Immediately afterwards, Mary changed into a nightdress and lay down; with one of his legs bared to the thigh, Longueville reclined beside her and touched her body in a symbolic consummation of the marriage.[30]

This seems to have been an ancient procedure on the continent, for Sir John Froissart noted in his chronicle that it was performed in a proxy union in 1385 between Margaret of Hungary and Louis, future duke of Orléans, "according to the custom in such matters required." Variations existed, however. In 1501 when Margaret of Austria and René, the Grand Bastard of Savoy, acting for his brother, Duke Philibert, participated in this ceremony at Dole in front of a throng of people, no single women were permitted to witness it, for maidens were considered highly susceptible to sexual license and in need of special protection even from symbolic con-summations. While stretched out with each other on a bed with only his thigh bared, Margaret and René exchanged a few words, after which he arose and successfully asked her for a kiss. The more cau-tious Germans, according to Nicander Nucius, a member of the Imperial embassy to England in 1545, kept their thighs covered. By contrast, the bride and groom had both their legs unclothed in Italy: Bona of Savoy and Tristano, who represented his brother, Galeazzo Maria, duke of Milan, adopted this procedure in 1468.[31]

Increasingly in the early modern period the symbolic consummation seems to have become less popular. By 1589 Danish custom, for example, required only that the procurator sit on the bed beside the bride, and in seventeeth-century France and Spain the practice went out of fashion entirely. It is likely that the 1514 performance of Longueville and Mary Tudor was the first and the last of its kind in England.[32]

A procedure definitely missing from Henry's marriage to Anne was the obligatory banns, which had been mandated at the Fourth Lateran Council in 1215. The banns, an announcement of an approaching nuptial wedding, were required to be proclaimed three Sundays in a row at the parish church where the ceremony was scheduled to occur. In 1540 Cranmer probably issued an episcopal license waiving this procedure, as he had in 1536 for the king's union with Jane Seymour and would do so again in 1543 for his marriage to Katherine Parr.[33]

After the ambassadors had departed for Düsseldorf, which they reached on 20 October, Henry and Cromwell sent special instructions and a new credence to Wotton to handle discreetly a device intended to increase friendship with the duke, probably an authorization to proceed with the defensive pact that was finally approved in February 1540. Cromwell pointed out to Wotton that it would ease the king's "contentation." He also outlined some activities that Anne and her mother should attend to as they were preparing for her journey and revealed that messages of congratulation were being forwarded to her, along with "rich and princely" gifts. Next to the vows, the exchange of gifts, principally from the groom to the bride, was the most significant feature of betrothals. They provided circumstantial evidence of a contract and part of a "system of reciprocity," according to Marcel Mauss, "in which the honour of giver and recipient [was] engaged." By tradition, the groom was expected to present elaborate gifts, especially jewelry, to his new spouse. As it was also customary for him to write a personal letter to her, it is possible that one of the messages placed in Wotton's packet was a note to Anne from Henry.[34]

Even before the treaty and contract of marriage had been signed, the king's ministers had begun to make plans for her journey. As she was due to arrive in two months, this anticipation was essential, for marriage to a foreign lady required a vast amount of coordination and communication, not only with her family but also with the rulers of dominions through which she might have to travel to reach her new home. The union of Anne and Henry was not only a private matter but also a public affair that had already attracted widespread attention. The first signal to Marillac that the treaty had been signed was, as noted above, on 3 October when he reported the outfitting of ten English ships. Actually, a week earlier, Henry had already sent a message to William, alerting him to the need for speed in making the final arrangements because of winter's approach. The bearer of the letter to Cleves was a sea captain whose mission was to learn the name of a friendly port where English ships could pick up Anne and convey her to the kingdom. Peter Barber has suggested that an extant chart that highlights Harderwijk in Gelderland, a port that Anne's brother controlled, was the one selected for her embarkation. Since the duke of Bavaria landed there in February 1540 on his way home, the chart was probably drawn up for him. Surely this port was not selected as the place to begin Anne's voyage, for Marillac characterized it as "little frequented and rather dreaded by mariners, rather a roadstead than a port."[35]

How she should be transported to her new country had greatly concerned the Cleves negotiators, who agreed that if it must be a sea voyage, which would take approximately three times as long to accomplish as the usual channel crossing, William, not Henry, would have to bear the expense. They had protested rather vigorously against this mode of transportation, however, because, as they said, she was "young and beautiful" and the sea air might ruin her complexion. They warned:

the time of the year being now cold and tempestuous she might there, though she were never so well ordered take such cold or other disease, considering she was never before upon the seas, as should be to her great peril and the king's majesty's great displeasure.

They also expressed concern about a possible Hollander attack if the emperor failed to grant her safe conduct on the seas around his dominions. No doubt they feared more for her safety than for her complexion because crossing the sea to England could be treacherous. In 1589, for example, Anne of Denmark, who was sailing to Scotland to marry James VI, was stranded in Norway.[36]

The Germans were probably concerned about other factors as well. Without denying that they sincerely feared for Anne's safety, they surely also had the expense of this transportation in mind. Until the duke had obtained Guelders, his family's dominions had been without seaports; supplying ships to convey his sister to England was thus probably stretching both his finances and ability to accomplish. Anne's countryfolk were, moreover, not noted for their love of the sea. An old German proverb cautioned: "Whosoever would learn to pray, let him go on a ship." Consequently, Henry, whose fleet was being outfitted, would surely have assumed responsibility for conveying Anne to his kingdom. It would not be the first time that an English fleet had delivered a bride to her groom. In 1468 sixteen ships had escorted Margaret of York to Sluys where she was greeted by Dowager Duchess Isabella, the mother of her husband, Charles the Bold. The voyage had taken one and one-half days.[37]

These difficulties about Anne's transportation as well as its cost were undoubtedly two of the reasons that Henry had not pressed to see his bride before their marriage, as he had done in 1538 when he proposed meeting with the French and Imperial candidates. At that time, Francis, Mary of Hungary, or the relatives of the women would have had to bear the expenses of their journeys to Calais or its vicinity, which was much more accessible to them than England was to Cleves. There was yet a third reason. In 1538 Henry had been striving to play Francis off against Charles in a competition for his friendship. He had attempted to discover which ruler most desired an alliance with him, but as both had snubbed him, he had felt compelled to turn to Cleves for a bride. It was still important to him that he meet a lady before committing himself to matrimony, but for England diplomatically, he believed, it was crucial that the union be entered into speedily without allowing for this personal concession.

To the relief of the parties involved, on 27 October the queen regent and the emperor granted permission for Anne to travel through their dominions. This decision may have come as something of a surprise to William and his ministers, for rumors at Antwerp had indicated hostility in the Low Countries to the Anglo-Cleves treaty. Indeed, rulers sometimes chose not to guarantee safe passage through their realms to the brides of unfriendly monarchs. That November the instructions of Cardinal Farnese, Paul's legate to

Charles, required him to relate to the emperor the circumstances under which he should refrain from granting Anne a safe conduct through his territories.[38]

The financial settlement in the marriage treaty proved to be somewhat ephemeral. Anne's brother could spare meager funds for her wedding since he was preparing for the possibility of an expensive war with the emperor over Guelders, which ultimately was lost to him after a ruinous military defeat. Even so, William had not utterly refused to finance his sister's marriage, as had John III of Portugal, who had made it clear earlier in 1539 that he would not provide a dowry for his half-sister Mary, since he had to pay for his daughter's wedding.[39]

In contrast, William agreed to arrange his sister's marriage, but, as he could not afford a suitable dowry for her, Henry had authorized his commissioners to sign a separate document forfeiting the 100,000 gold florins. The sum, which had first been agreed to and then waived on 6 September at Cleves and waived again on 6 October at London, had constituted a rather substantial amount for a second sister. Their father had granted Sybilla a dowry of 25,000 gold florins at her marriage to the duke elector and had promised Anne 30,000 gold florins for her nuptials with the son of Lorraine. The difference between Anne's two dowries arose, of course, from the relatively greater status and wealth of England *vis-à-vis* Lorraine's. Henry's willingness to relinquish her dowry meant that had she been forced to travel to England by sea, he would probably have also borne that cost which the bride's family was usually expected to bear.[40]

The reason for including a dowry in the treaty, even though it was forfeited, and for indicating that her brother would pay for her travel expenses, if she journeyed by sea, was to save face for all parties involved. The failure of William to provide his sister with an appropriate dowry, if the fact were made public, would signal his family's weakness, even poverty, and would constitute a humiliating blow to his honor.[41] On the other hand, a monarch like Henry could be greatly criticized if his commissioners were unable to negotiate lucrative financial arrangements. In his chronicle, published in 1548, for example, Edward Hall referred to the "unprofitable marriage" of Henry VI and Margaret of Anjou.[42] In another chronicle written before 1471, the anonymous author took the government of

Richard II to task for purchasing Anne of Bohemia from her brother, Emperor Wenceslas, who received 10,000 marks and bore no share in the expenses of her journey. In addition, if the suitor displayed too much eagerness, the size of the dowry might also be negatively affected. As Henry and his ministers had been pressing for the Cleves alliance for several months, their clout in financial matters had surely been somewhat diminished.[43]

Even before they had learned that the emperor would be willing to permit Anne safe passage through his dominions, Henry's ministers had begun preparing for her arrival. Appointments to her household, the purchase of goods, and preparations for the nuptials were complicated enough, but her receptions and lodgings at Antwerp, Calais, Deal, Dover, Canterbury, Sittingbourne, Dartford, and finally Greenwich also had to be arranged and ships had to be made available for bringing her across the channel from Calais, or in the worse scenario, across the sea from another port.

One of the first decisions about her household was made in October, a few days after the departure of the Cleves commissioners. The king approved the sending of Mrs. Gilman, alias Parker, with four servants to Cleves, perhaps for the purpose of acquainting Anne with her new kingdom. As Mrs. Gilman, who was to join the queen's privy chamber, was impoverished, Henry had ordered Anthony Denny to send word to Cromwell that he must see that she was appropriately attired and furnished. Richard Beard, a member of the earlier Cleves embassy, was appointed as her escort. The king's actions were extraordinary, for normally bridegrooms did not send ladies to attend their foreign-born brides. The closest parallels to this can be found in the appointment of male servants to perform errands for them. In 1468 the duke of Milan had dispatched five tradesmen to Bona of Savoy to secure goods for her, and in 1508 Charles, the future emperor, had sent John Cerf to wait on his betrothed, the future Henry VIII's sister Mary, whom he, of course, never wed.[44]

Except for Mrs. Gilman, the other English people who won posts in Anne's household awaited her arrival. Rulers did not always select ladies of the privy chamber for their brides in advance, as Henry and his ministers were doing, but some did for political or financial reasons. In 1679 Don John of Austria, an illegitimate half-brother of Charles II of Spain, who was opposed to the king's marriage to

Louisa of Orléans, filled up her household with his friends and allies. In 1539 competition for places in Anne's privy chamber was keen. Two of Lord Lisle's stepdaughters, Anne and Catherine Basset, sought the assistance of their mother in becoming maids of honor. Only Anne succeeded in gaining this appointment, and in December she thanked her mother for the recent information she had sent about her new royal mistress, who had been stranded at Calais because of bad weather. Lady Lisle had revealed to her that the queen was "good and gentle to serve and please," news that her daughter believed would greatly comfort the king who was looking forward to his betrothed's arrival.[45]

After the marriage, the greatest cost the crown would have to bear for the queen would be the expenses of her household, including the privy chamber. Clearly, Henry's ministers sought to channel as much of these funds as possible into salaries for their clients. By November, Cromwell was responding to requests for these positions. Lisle, who had hoped to become her lord chamberlain, had to give way to Edward Manners, first earl of Rutland. Jane Roper also lobbied unsuccessfully for her son-in-law to become the queen's attorney, and John Gostwick failed to place a young client in the queen's wardrobe. The luckier John Grenville did win appointment as the queen's sergeant-at-arms. In addition, other domestic servants, such as cooks and scribes, had to be hired and livery for them had to be provided. The stable had a high priority on the agenda, since Anne required horses for exercise and for royal progresses. John Husee wrote to Lady Lisle in November that he could not obtain the head and plate she had required for her new saddle, even though he had already paid for them, because the gilders were so busy catering to the king's and queen's needs. He did not specify whether Henry was obtaining plate for Anne's saddles or for other enterprises.[46]

Henry's household was also preparing for his bride. The marriage provided him with an excuse to reconstitute the Band of Spears or Pensioners. Sir Anthony Browne became captain of fifty new spears whose duties included standing guard in the presence chamber where the king's official audiences with important dignitaries took place. In their velvet or damask doublets and with their gold chains and pole-axes, the gentlemen pensioners, who accompanied Henry to Anne's public reception, were bound to impress her and her attendants. The king's stable needed £200 worth of new provisions, and

Whitehall Palace, especially the queen's lodgings, required repairs. Tents had to be erected for her Blackheath greeting and new privy kitchens and jakes had to be prepared for her at Greenwich. Furthermore, London Bridge had to be reinforced with 100 halberts from Greenwich and with 100 sheaves of new arrows and thirty-one new bows from the Tower of London, which was also scheduled for repairs.[47]

Instructions with information about where they should assemble to greet her were delivered to many of the king's subjects. On 23 November, for example, letters, like the one sent to Christopher More of Losely, Co. Surrey, summoned numerous gentlemen and their servants to London on 10 December to prepare for her reception at Blackheath Common, the place where the king was planning to greet her publicly for the first time, despite rumors that he would journey to Canterbury for this meeting. The gentlemen were required to "ride in coats of black velvet with chains of gold about their necks" and to "have gowns of velvet or some other good silk for their change accordingly."[48]

Before these arrangements were finalized, royal advisers had already decided who was to sail to Calais to meet her there and had set aside sums of money to defray the expenses for her journey across the channel. These greeters also needed to have elaborate attire and an appropriate number of servants, or as Cromwell indicated in a memorandum, "A device to be made with how many persons every personage shall have in his company at the said meeting, according to degrees." He had also to arrange that the lodgings at the places where she and her train were to spend the night were suitably furnished with beds, plate, and other necessities for their comfort.[49]

By December Henry Middleton had earned a reward of some £11 for bringing the post from Cleves to England. Since haste was needed, the ministers could not wait for merchants returning from Antwerp to deliver them as usual. Indeed, on 8 November Cromwell complained to Wotton in a message carried to him by Philip Hoby about the failure of English diplomats to send word to the king and his council as to how rulers were reacting to the news of his marriage. Because of the brief time remaining before Anne's departure, Cromwell had directed Hoby to return immediately with her brother's letters and the ambassadors' dispatches. About two weeks later, Vaughan responded to a letter from Cromwell that had been delivered by Francis Picher, one of the king's reliable couriers, with an apology for the delayed communications. Vaughan had earlier been admonished, he reminded Cromwell, not to cause the king great expense by relying on the post rather than the merchants who traveled between Antwerp and London. He promised henceforth to dispatch the letters from Cleves more speedily and if given permission to accompany the queen to brief Cromwell on recent events in the Netherlands. In the meantime, his council having approved the contract, the duke of Cleves had sent the humanist, Conrad von Heresbach, to Henry with his confirmation of it. On 21 November, Heresbach arrived at Hampton Court and on 2 December having completed his mission, he sailed to Calais with Southampton, who was planning to escort Anne across the channel. Eight days later Herebach reached the ducal court, carrying with him the copy of the marriage contract that Henry had signed on 10 November.[50]

In the meantime, on 7 November, the duke of Cleves ordered all the gentlemen who were appointed to accompany Anne on her bridal journey to assemble in the town of Cleves on 25 November dressed in their appropriate clothing and armor. On 26 November, beginning their slow journey to England that was to cost her brother the sum of 18,608 gold florins, Anne and her attendants left Düsseldorf for Cleves where these gentlemen joined her train. Completing only about 5 miles on some days, she traveled in a horse-drawn chariot, which structurally was a small wagon "with carved and gilded standards from which a canopied nacelle was slung on ornamental chains." When he saw it in England, Hall described it as "well carved and gilt with arms of her country curiously wrought and covered with cloth of gold, all the horses were trapped with black velvet, and on them rode pages of honor in coats of velvet . . ." Usually, noble and royal women rode in chariots like this one when they traveled great distances. It was similar in design to the vehicles that transported Mary Tudor to her nuptials in France in 1514 and Henrietta Maria to the coast for the channel crossing to England in 1625. For her journey, Anne's brother-in-law, the duke elector of Saxony, had loaned her thirteen trumpeters who played loud music to proclaim her arrival at the towns on her itinerary. The addition of the trumpeters lent a festive air to her travels. One of the reasons monarchs had begun to increase the number and use of musicians at their courts was their more frequent scheduling of ceremonial occasions such as these. The towns through which Anne planned to journey having been notified, their leaders made preparations for her arrival. From Cleves, she traveled to Ravenstein, Bertingburg, Tilburg, Hoogstraaten, and thence to Antwerp on 4 December.[51]

For her security and protection, the emperor had instructed his commander, Floris d'Egmond, earl of Buren, and his master of the ordinance, Ferry de Melen, to escort her to Gravelines from Antwerp, the principal city and greatest commercial mart in his dominions, which had up-to-date harbor facilities, bonded warehouses, and a sound credit system. Her entry into Antwerp, recently characterized by John Hale as the "Venice of the North," was the first on her journey for which a description has survived. Evidence of citizens welcoming distinguished personages on their initial visits or entries such as this, which were modeled after ancient Roman triumphs, can be found in English documents from the thirteenth century. One of the earliest on record was Queen Eleanor's entry into London in 1236. Escorted by Henry III, she was greeted on horseback by the mayor, aldermen and principal citizens, who were dressed in robes of embroidered silk. The ceremony included no pageantry, for poetry and music were first added to English entries in 1298 when the citizens honored Edward I's victory at Falkirk.[52]

In 1539 the welcome Antwerp offered Anne attracted much attention. Four miles outside the town with "four score torches burning in the daylight," fifty of the merchants, dressed in velvet coats and decorated with chains of gold, met Anne and escorted her to the English house on Old Bourse Street that had been prepared for her. Subsequently, Lord Buren feasted her attendants while Vaughan and the merchants entertained her. According to Wotton, who brought Cromwell up-to-date about the queen's procession to Antwerp, Lord Buren confessed that he had never seen so many people gathered at any entry, even the emperor's. This reference to her entry's popularity was surely somewhat exaggerated, for no pageants were produced for her welcome. Charles's first Antwerp reception had occurred in 1520 after his election as emperor to celebrate the *jocundus adventus*, the entry of a new lord into his city or territory where he had certain rights and privileges. The special entries, such as his, employed pageants and triumphant arches to honor the heritage and power of the monarch. Indeed, as Richard Pate was later to inform

Henry on 15 May 1540, bad weather had caused the rehearsed and prepared pageants to be omitted at the emperor's most recent Antwerp reception. Only guns, which were shot all night, and lights greeted him, a scaled down welcome that seems comparable to Anne's in 1539. The pageants that bad weather had prevented for this Imperial entry, as R. Malcolm Smuts has cautioned, however, while so important to modern scholarly analysis, "bear little relationship to what most spectators actually saw." Even when a series of pageants were produced at a reception, most witnesses would have been able to see only one of them and probably could not have heard the actors' voices above the crowd's roar. In 1625, for example, at Henrietta Maria's entry into Amiens, a spectator complained that he could not hear the speeches of the girls dressed as marine goddesses who presented the queen with the keys of the city. It was the "sheer spectacle of the court" or in this case the train of Anne of Cleves as it moved into town behind the blaring of trumpets that seems to have impressed the citizenry.[53]

Wotton characterized the merchants' reception of the queen, which Cromwell had helped to orchestrate by mail, as a "goodly sight." These wealthy Englishmen belonged to the Company of Merchant Adventurers, which Vaughan headed as governor, that possessed a royal license to export to the continent cloth woven from English wool, then considered to be the finest produced in Europe. The demand for this cloth was so great that exports of it to Antwerp doubled between 1500 and 1550. The members of the company, whose headquarters had been moved here in the first half of the fourteenth century, were either residents of or frequent visitors to the town in which they held their markets twice a year.[54]

In his letter from Antwerp, Wotton provided Cromwell with details about Anne's attendants. In all, eighty-eight of her country folk, mostly the younger ladies and gentlemen, were planning to remain with her in England. Besides Mrs. Gilman and her four servants, Wotton named Lord Wissem's widow, who was the governor of Anne's five gentlewomen. Lady Wissem had five servants and the ladies under her charge had three. In addition, Wotton counted eight pages, one of whom was her cousin, Francis, heir of the count of Waldeck, and an aged steward named Tennagel with six servants. Eight gentlemen with twelve servants, a secretary, a chaplain, and an unspecified forty others made up the remaining number.

Accompanying them were the dignitaries who planned to return to their homes. From Saxony came Burchart and Dulzig with ten servants and from Cleves Lord Wirich of Dhun, Count of Falkenstein and Limburg and lord of Overstein with seven servants, Hochsteden with five persons, and Olisleger with six attendants.[55]

Numerous others in her train were not expected to attend the wedding, although the king's ministers could still extend invitations to them. Usually, like Cosimo I, duke of Florence, who was also married in 1539, the groom tried to limit the number of his bride's attendants. The most obvious reason for this action was to decrease expenses, but it is also true that anyone of her escorts could function as her family's partisan. Among those who were not scheduled to cross over to England, Wotton counted another thirty-two individuals, including the trumpeters, who, after they reached Calais, sought permission to visit the kingdom. When Southampton learned that Anne, evidencing either a love for the blaring of trumpets or a fondness for arriving in towns amidst festive music, favored their request, he approved it. Some other officers with their servants and two ladies made up the final count. In all, the train numbered 263 persons and 228 horses.[56]

Wotton provided Cromwell with useful information about both the social standing of Anne's attendants and German gift-giving customs. He listed the ladies and gentlemen in the order of their rank so that the lord privy seal would be able to make the necessary seating and procession appointments. This information was crucial to the arrangement of wedding events. Not only did Cromwell wish to refrain from insulting anyone with unsuitable placement but he also desired to avoid confrontations about this issue. In 1626, for example, when Gaston, duke of Orléans, brother of Louis XIII, wed Mary, duchess of Montepensier, two ladies fought with pushing and scratching over the question of their ranking in the wedding procession.[57]

Wotton had also inquired about German gift-giving customs. According to Sir Michael Mercator of Grave, who had frequently been of service to the English government, on the morning after the wedding a nobleman gave his wife a *morgengabe* as a reward for the surrendering of her virginity, the value of which he was free to determine. The husband should give *bruidstuckes* (probably *Brautstuckes*), which could be either rings or brooches for the ladies and either velvet or silk doublets, jackets, or gowns for the gentlemen. Normally the bridegroom gave only the individuals who had actually performed services at the marriage feast these rewards, but he could offer them to anyone he thought appropriate. Vaughan had also raised this issue with Richard Harman, a merchant adventurer in Antwerp who refined somewhat upon Mercator's information. Harman reported that the queen should provide only the ladies with gifts, which could be garlands, little rings, or brooches and that the king should give caps or doublets, jackets or gowns, and chains to his gentlemen. He assured Vaughan that both the duke elector and the landgrave of Hesse had followed these procedures at their weddings. The value of the gifts that a bridegroom presented to his foreign-born wife's attendants also signaled his wealth and power, and he undoubtedly wished the amount to be publicized. In 1468 the duke of Milan even sent a list of the gifts and their value to Louis XI, brother-in-law of his new bride, Bona of Savoy, who had hitherto resided at the French court.[58]

Obtaining gifts for Anne to welcome her to England and its dominions had already taken up some of his ministers' valuable time. Apparently, the duke of Bavaria, who planned to greet her at Blackheath, did not have a token he thought appropriate for the queen. He did possess a cross that he considered too valuable to offer her, but as Wriothesley informed Cromwell, he thought the duke could be persuaded to part with it. Before Anne's departure for Calais, Lady Lisle, who sought positions in the queen's household for her relatives, had already sent her a present, and across the channel Cranmer was gathering money to be presented to her in a cup at her entry into Canterbury. For this sum Cromwell had sent 50 sovereigns to the archbishop, who was hoping to raise an additional 50 angels locally.[59]

From Antwerp the procession traveled through Bever, Stecken, Tokkyn, to Bruges, which it had expected to reach on Saturday, 6 December, but as the horses could not go over the Scheldt because of its low water, the arrival was delayed until Sunday. From Bruges, Anne journeyed through Dambrugh, Newport, and Dunkirk, where she heard a sermon by a catholic priest that some members of her train characterized as seditious. After an investigation, Southampton was able to reassure the king that it had not posed "any danger or hazzard" to him or the realm but conceded that it had been "full of unfitting words." Because of bad weather, Anne did not actually reach Gravelines, which was situated a few miles from Calais, until 10 December, although Olisleger and Vaughan, who had received permission to join the queen's train at Antwerp, had predicted she would be there some two or three days earlier. Antoine Brusset, a resident of Gravelines, where she had been welcomed with a "shot of guns," wrote to Lord Lisle that he had reserved for her the best lodgings available. While she rested there, Lord Buren and Brusset lobbied for a position in her household for the widow of Jan Adams, a trusted servant of Henry's. The purpose of Brusset's letter to Lisle was to seek his assistance in obtaining this position for her.[60]

Anne's welcome at Calais was more elaborate than her earlier entries. Captured from France in the Hundred Years War, Calais had become the English staple port for the export of wool in the fourteenth century. Initially a prosperous market, the staple, and along with it Calais, had fallen into a state of decay by the sixteenth century. Over time the Merchant Adventurers' increased export of their cloth to Antwerp had led to a decline in the demand for wool at Calais. Despite the decay of the wool trade, Calais remained important to the crown because of its mint that processed bullion into English coins. In his "Remembrances," Cromwell listed some of the tasks that needed to be accomplished to make the welcome there a success. He arranged for payments of some £400 to the English greeters: £20 to each of the lords and over £13 to each of the gentlemen. He also solicited the king's opinions about who should be members of the receiving party. On a personal note, Cromwell had to provide £40 for his son Gregory's journey there and £100 for his nephew Richard Cromwell's participation in the Blackheath reception. He listed the gifts that would be given to the Germans in Anne's train who were not scheduled to accompany her to England. Southampton, who was characterized by a Italian diplomat as "wise, active, and of good experience; one of the best captains in England," took charge of disbursing these rewards to her country folk.[61]

Since November the Calais inhabitants had been preparing for her visit. Among other items William Thynne had obtained £200 for "certain provisions" against her coming. In addition, the town officials had Lantern Gate, the principal gate of the town, painted and had the king's house, the Chequer where Anne was to be lodged, refurbished. When she arrived at the English pale on Thursday 11 December between 7:00 and 8:00 a.m., Lord Lisle, his spears, and officers in velvet coats with chains about their necks were there to welcome her. His party having combined with hers, they then rode toward Calais and when they approached St. Peter's within a mile of the port town, they were received by Southampton, who was apparelled in

a coat of purple velvet, cut on cloth of gold, and tied with great aglettes and trefoils of gold, to the number of four hundred, and baldric-wise he wore a chain, at the which did hang a whistle of gold set with rich stones of great value.

His noble attendants, including Lord William Howard, were dressed in cloth of gold and purple velvet with rich chains of gold. Among the lesser aristocracy present were Bryan, Sir Thomas Seymour, Gregory Cromwell, and some forty other gentleman attired in satin damask and velvet. Trailing behind them were 200 yeomen in red and blue cloth. Anne and her train continued on to Lantern Gate to view the king's ships, the *Lion* and the *Sweepstake*, which, decorated pleasantly with 100 banners, pencels, and flags of silk and gold, were to transport her across the channel. On them were 2 master-gunners, 200 mariners, 31 trumpets and a double-drum "that was never seen in England before." Their uniforms had also been one of the many items for which Cromwell had made arrangements.[62]

Led by the trumpeters, the queen entered the town, which lay between its walls in a parallelogram, and immediately gunners on the two ships fired 150 rounds of ordnance that "made such a smoke that one of her train could not see one another." Lady Lisle and her ladies met Anne and escorted her down the street on both sides of which stood 500 soldiers in the king's livery, the mayor and the aldermen, who presented her with 50 gold marks, the commons, and the merchants of the Staple, who gave her a purse with 60 gold sovereigns. They formed a line through which she passed to the Chequer. The customary entry required civic officials, as they did at Calais, to assemble along the route of the royal procession. After dinner the next day, the lord admiral took her to view the ships again, provided her with a banquet, a light meal of dessert and wine, and then escorted her to the jousts that were held in her honor.[63]

Originally she had been scheduled to cross over to Dover on 12

December when the tides would normally have permitted her to leave at 5:00 a.m. but on 13 December it was Southampton's and Wotton's duty to inform Henry that the weather was preventing their passage. They arranged for nine men to lie outside the walls to notify them immediately of any improvement in the weather. As soon as a change was noted, trumpets would signal the news throughout the town. Reminding Henry that men could not control the sea or the wind, they swore to bring Anne to him as soon as humanly possible. They also reported that the Cleves ambassadors had given the lord admiral a horse with a black harness and a steel saddle in gratitude for his favoring the marriage and had requested him to advise Anne about the behavior expected of her. Southampton had responded that as a faithful servant of the king, he would be glad to promote love and affection between her and her husband.[64]

During the next fourteen days of the weather delay, they entertained the queen with the "best pastimes that could be devised." It was noted that she "kept open household" and that she was attempting to become better acquainted with her English subjects, whose language she could not yet speak. In the letter in which Southampon and Wotton gave Henry their weather report, they also forwarded news to him about his consort. She had, they said, required Olisleger to ask the lord admiral to teach her a favorite card game of the king's. They had played "Sent," which she had apparently learned rather easily, for she played "with as good a grace and countenance" as Southampton had ever seen in a noble lady. Card games were one of her favorite pastimes and consumed many of her leisure hours in England as well.[65]

After the game was over and in accordance with her country's customs, she invited the lord admiral and some of his colleagues to sup with her because, as she explained, she desired to see the behavior of Englishmen "sitting at their meat." At first Southampton had refused her request because the English royal family did not usually eat with company: indeed, Tudor monarchs required more privacy in their domestic lives than did either German rulers or French kings. After she had required Olisleger to repeat the request two or three times, Southampton finally accepted her invitation on behalf of himself and nine of his countrymen, including Lord William, Bryan, and Gregory Cromwell. He characterized her manner while eating as regal.[66]

The excuse she gave Southampton for wishing to sup with her new subjects was that she wished to learn something about their table manners, but also she may have been homesick. Margaret Visser has pointed out that as children individuals learn their status and place in society through the eating patterns of their family. In a foreign land comfort can sometimes be found through the enactment of the daily routine of one's upbringing.[67] New eating customs, which Anne had begun to experience, often confounded foreign-born wives: in 1679 Louisa of Orléans, the new Spanish queen, was disappointed at being required to eat in private and by the lack of her native French dishes. Ultimately, her husband Charles II gave her leave to dine in public. A few decades earlier when Anne of Austria, the queen of Louis XIII, entered France, she immediately expressed her longing for Spanish bread and the snow with which drinks were cooled at her table.[68]

An incident that occurred a few days after Anne of Cleves had supped with her English subjects seems to confirm that she was feeling somewhat homesick. The lord admiral, who had been sending messages to England on fishing boats, wrote that at her request in the presence of Bryan, Gregory Cromwell, and Richard Morison, he had opened a packet of letters from Flanders. She had been hoping, she had confessed, that it might contain some messages for her from home.[69]

In October, as England began arranging for the queen's arrival, France began preparing for the emperor's visit. On 8 October just a few days after Henry's and Anne's proxy marriage, in response to a request of Charles who shrank from a voyage through the channel in late autumn, the constable had invited him to pass through France on his return to Brussels from Madrid where he had been mourning the empress's death. His visit would gratify Francis and might silence those who wished to sow jealousy between the two allies. When Henry learned of the visit, he was concerned enough to send a special envoy to uncover as much information as possible about the intentions and activities of the emperor and Francis. The November instructions for Wyatt, who had earlier served as Imperial ambassador, directed him to go to the French town where the king and the emperor had arranged to meet. After accompanying Bonner and Richard Tate, ambassadors to France and the empire, respectively, to audiences with their rulers and informing them that Wyatt was to become the new Imperial ambassador, he should relate to the two allies how pleased Henry was to learn of the peaceful relations that continued between them. The king directed Wyatt to observe closely the answers, reactions, and gestures of both monarchs in the hope of learning from them the reason for Charles's presence in France. "In this culture," as Peter Burke has pointed out, "Speech and – its accompanying gestures – were of crucial importance in the presentation of self, and every word was part of a performance. . . ."[70]

A few days later Vaughan informed Cromwell from Brussels that he had heard rumors about why the emperor was journeying to Flanders but that he did not want them repeated to the king because he had not been able to confirm them. The emperor supposedly had three reasons for visiting his northern dominions: (1) The mutiny of some of his towns, especially Ghent; (2) England's alliance with Cleves and thus with Guelders, which he greatly disliked; and (3) the confederacy between the English king and the German princes. It was rumored inaccurately, as it turned out, that in response to these events the newly widowed emperor would deepen his friendship with Francis by marrying his daughter Margaret. Certain in the knowledge of French amity, the emperor could then overpower his towns, secure Gelderland, "assay" the German princes, and work some "displeasure" against England. Vaughan also revealed that the count palatine and his company, who had just arrived, were spreading negative reports in Flanders about the kingdom, especially about Henry. It is curious that these negative opinions were credited to the count palatine, for his later visitors indicated that he appreciated the "great goodness" shown him in England and felt a love and zeal for the realm.[71]

From Charles's arrival near Bayonne on 27 November, the people of France entertained him lavishly, and the citizens of Bordeaux, Potiers, and Loches, where he met his sister Eleanor and Francis on 12 December, provided him with splendid entries. The two rulers continued northward toward Paris, celebrated Christmas at Fontainebleu, and reached the capital on New Year's Eve. His journey partially mirrored that of Anne who had left Cleves on 26 November just about the time he had entered France. The day after he met Francis, she arrived at Calais where she was forced to celebrate Christmas. When two days later the weather cleared, she landed at Dover and was with Henry on New Year's Day at Rochester while Francis was entertaining Charles at Paris.[72]

That Cromwell pressured Henry who "refused to believe that the friendship between Charles and France would endure" into this marriage because of his need to "consolidate the Reformation" has become an accepted interpretation of this disastrous union. An examination of the extant evidence from 1539, the year the marriage was negotiated, which was discussed both in this Chapter and Chapter 4, does not support this assertion.[73] First, diplomats sent to Cleves were not individuals normally associated with Cromwell: Wotton had long served the king and Beard was a member of the privy chamber. Secondly, they mostly addressed their dispatches to Henry, not to Cromwell, presumably in accordance with the procedure outlined in 1534 by John Hackett who sent only the most important messages directly to the king. Later, in December, when Southampton informed Cromwell about the Calais weather, the lord admiral reported that his letters to him were incomplete because he assumed that he had access to the ones addressed to the king. Southampton further explained that he had assigned two clerks to keep Henry up-to-date about his consort's activities at Calais. A comparison of this procedure to the French ambassador's in England reveals an important difference. Marillac usually wrote letters to both the constable and the king on the same day, but in contrast to the English habit the ones he sent to Montmorency were longer and with greater detail (*toutes le particularities par le menu*) than those dispatched to Francis (*la substance*). Thirdly, although the six commissioners appointed to negotiate Henry's marriage had included Cromwell and two who have been associated with him (Cranmer and Audley), the other three, Bishop Durham, Suffolk, and Southampton have usually not been considered his allies. Fourthly, as noted above, it was Henry who orchestrated the timing of the ambassadors' arrival at his court and who ordered Cromwell to concentrate his efforts on the "weighty matters" that they had come to discuss. Afterwards, the king sent instructions to Cromwell about arranging for Mrs. Gilman to join Anne's household.[74]

The documents that would have been useful for an inquiry into the degree of Henry's involvement in the courtship of Anne, but which are unavailable because they never existed, are letters that a Cleves resident ambassador could have written in 1539 concerning his conversations with the king about Anne. Unfortunately, William did not employ residents although, after his sister's marriage, he did send the equivalent of a resident to England to be of assistance to her. These non-existent letters would have served as useful counter-parts to the dispatches in which the French and Imperial ambassa-dors reported on their exchanges with Henry about the various candidates under consideration in 1537–39. Without the Cleves letters, although Henry's conversations with Marillac are invaluable in dispelling the notion that he was disinterested in wooing Anne, it becomes easier to downplay his desire for this union. Unfortunately, not only did William lack residents in 1539 but he also delayed sending a special embassy to England until mid-September. At their arrival, the die had already been cast, for Henry and Anne were to wed.

That fall and winter those who were with the king reported that he was in good spirits. In October Richard Cromwell even reported to his uncle that Henry, who was "in health and merry," had conversed agreeably about the Cleves affairs. In December while Anne was stranded at Calais, Cromwell sent word to Southampton that the king, who had suffered a similar weather delay in 1532, was con-cerned enough about her well-being to admonish the lord admiral to keep her and her train entertained so that "they may think the time as short as the tediousness of it will suffer." His hospitable attitude in the face of the mounting costs incurred by the delay was admirable. All the towns in which Anne was scheduled to spend the night had to be kept in readiness for her arrival. Stationed both at Dover and Sittingbourne, for example, were two gentleman ushers, who had to remain there a total of thirty-five days at 5 shillings each per day. Also at these places were two yeomen and five grooms who had to be paid for thirty-nine days, the yeomen at 2 shillings each per day and the grooms at 20 pence each per day.[75]

And, except for the expense, why should the king not have been in good spirits? Everyone from several walks of life who had seen his consort had praised her looks, her good disposition, and her quiet dignity. In November Michael Mercator, who had visited Cleves in April, and as noted above, had researched German gift-giving prac-tices, sent Cromwell a description of her. A resident of Grave, which lay near William's dominion of Ravenstein, Mercator wrote: she was attractive, had sense and wit, as well as good manners and grace [*gracieuse et vertueuse noble dama Ana, bien prudence et bon esprit, bonnes maniéres et grâces*]. One month later, on 13 December, confirming the positive statements of Wotton, Beard, Mont, Paynell, the Cleves procurators, and Mercator, the lord admiral, reported from Calais that he had informed the German ambassadors that because he had heard good reports of Anne's "notable virtues" and "her excellent beauty," which he perceived "to be no less than was reported in very deed," he was happy to advance the marriage. Six years later, in 1545, Nicander Nucius, who seems not to have met the then divorced queen on his visit to England, wrote that he had heard that she was a "masculine" woman (a reference to her height) of "great beauty."[76]

6   ROYAL GREETER

While Charles visited with Francis at Loches and Fontainebleu and Anne remained at Calais, Henry's ministers were completing the arrangements for her reception. Although rumors had spread in November that the king, who was then at Hampton Court, would journey to Canterbury to complete his marriage with her, his first official meeting with her was scheduled at Blackheath Common. Adjoining the town of Greenwich, the common lies about 2 miles from Placentia or Pleasure, the palace that in 1570 William Lambarde, the Kentish antiquary, lauded as "pleasant, perfect, and princely." When on 23 December the king left for Greenwich, as Cromwell remarked, "to enter his new order," he must have gone by barge, the usual method of travel to his riverside homes. As he awaited Anne's arrival, the holiday celebrations commenced. The Children of the Royal Chapel were, for example, rehearsing a play that was to be performed for him on New Year's Day after supper.[1]

On Saturday 27 December, the weather at last cleared enough for the lord admiral in command of a fleet of fifty ships to convey Anne and her train across the 30 mile stretch of sea that lies between Calais and Dover, a trip that took between twelve and fourteen hours. At 5:00 p.m. they disembarked at Deal in the downs, a fishing village situated half a mile from the shore and separated from the sea by a great artificial bank.[2] After welcoming Anne, Thomas Cheyney, lord warden of the Cinque Ports, escorted her to the newly built castle on the town's south side; one of three fortifications that had been erected for defense in reaction to the Franco-Imperial alliance, a large force of laborers was still putting on the finishing touches in December. In its handsome apartments where she rested a few hours before continuing her journey, she was attended by Suffolk and Catherine, his duchess, Richard Sampson, bishop of Chichester,

127

George, Lord Cobham, and a great number of other ladies and gentlemen. After she had supped, she removed to Dover Castle, which stands about a quarter mile outside the town proper. As a traveler approaches from Deal, the stone bulk of the castle's towers and ramparts, which had recently been repaired, "suddenly fills the whole foreground."[3] The castle, which is over 300 feet tall and occupies 35 acres, has the appearance of a small town, but since she did not arrive until about 11:00 p.m., her first view of it was somewhat limited. She was scheduled to stay in its refurbished royal apartments until the morning of 29 December when she would recommence her travels.[4]

Crossing the channel, which she had finally accomplished, was often an unpleasant business, for the horrors of the passage are a recurrent theme in contemporary accounts. Those travelers who completed the voyage without storms beating them back to Calais or without arriving in England seasick often wrote with relief to their friends about their safe passage. In 1445 one of Anne's predecessors, Margaret of Anjou, the wife of Henry VI, had suffered a particularly difficult crossing and was seriously ill when she finally reached the coast.[5]

Unlike Margaret, Anne must have escaped seasickness, for Suffolk and Cheyney did not refer to it in their message written to Cromwell at Canterbury on the evening of 29 December. They reported that they had not left Dover until about 11:00 a.m. when the baggage and freight that had accompanied Anne's train had finally been unloaded. Despite the fierce morning storm that had blown hail and rain into her face, she had decided to set out on the 16 mile trek to Canterbury although she was traveling in a chariot with only a canopy to shelter her from the elements. The route her train followed was Watling Street, the usual path of travelers going between Dover and London. After one night each at Canterbury, Sittingbourne, Rochester, where the king planned a private visit, and Dartford, she was to meet him publicly at Blackheath.[6]

Her resolve to continue the journey had pleased her escorts because had she decided to spend the night of 29 December at Dover, she would not have reached Canterbury until 30 December and Sittingbourne until New Year's Eve. Since she was due to rest on New Year's Day, the second major festival of the Christmas season, the first being Epiphany and the third being Christmas Day, she would have had to remain two nights in Sittingbourne. Suffolk and Cheyney considered this itinerary unacceptable because Sittingbourne was a rural community of one parish with housing barely adequate to meet the queen's needs. It was the only stage on the route to Greenwich where a monastery or royal palace was unavailable, and lodgings for her and her train had had to be reserved at nearby gentlemens' houses. No separate reception party had been appointed to greet her at this unincorporated town, which could offer little in the way of entertainment. If she had decided to remain at Dover on 29 December, Suffolk and Cheyne had considered extending her stay at Canterbury through New Year's Day, but this alternative was far from attractive, for it entailed another delay in her already belated arrival at Blackheath Common.[7]

On Barham Down some 3 miles from Canterbury, Cranmer, Thomas Goodrich, bishop of Ely, and numerous gentlemen met her and her train and escorted them to St. Augustine's, a dissolved Benedictine abbey, which lay outside the city walls and which had been appropriated in 1538 for the use of the royal family. In 1539 it still held the gilded shrine that housed St. Augustine's body. Suffolk and Cheyney reported to Cromwell that the citizens had greeted her with torchlights and a round of gunfire and that about fifty gentlewomen attired in velvet bonnets had welcomed her in the great chamber of the queen's lodgings, which had been remodeled for her visit. Laborers had hurriedly been burning charcoal in earthenware pans to dry out the rooms that had barely been finished before her arrival. She may have continued to share meals with her English escorts, for the two letter writers related that in her joy at meeting so many of her subjects she seemed to have forgotten about the stormy weather and was merry at supper.[8] That same day Cranmer lamented in a letter to Cromwell that no more than six score gentlemen, besides his own company, had attended him at the reception.[9]

On 30 December she continued her progress, her train having been enlarged by members of the reception parties from Deal, Dover, and Canterbury. After spending that night at Sittingbourne, which still had a free chantry dedicated to Thomas Becket, she rode on to Rochester. Norfolk, Thomas Fiennes, Lord Dacre of the South, William, Lord Mountjoy, the barons of the Exchequer, and many other gentlemen, dressed in coats of velvet with chains of gold, received her at Rainham Down, about two miles outside Rochester, and escorted her to the Bishop's Palace which stood south of the Cathedral, an unsuppressed Benedictine foundation. When it was dissolved two months later, Henry gained control of the palace in which royal lodgings had been set aside since the fourteenth century. Given a rumor circulating in December that Anne would refuse to depart for England until all the abbeys had been pulled down, it is ironic that on New Year's Eve she was to be entertained in one not yet suppressed.[10]

This chapter identifies the king's private encounter with Anne at Rochester as one of the ceremonies that early modern rulers performed to honor their foreign-born brides when they arrived at their new homes. Other important topics in this chapter include his negative reactions to her appearance that must be analyzed in association with her brother's failure to send to England a copy of her marriage contract with Francis of Lorraine, her official reception at Blackheath Common, the timing of the royal wedding, and the settling of her jointure.

Heralds were usually present to direct the movement of participants on ceremonious occasions and to record the proceedings in minute detail. A reading of the chronicle of Charles Wriothesley, Windsor herald, leads to the conclusion that he was either in the king's party at Rochester or had access to an eyewitness account of another herald, such as Gilbert Dethick, Hammes pursuivant and later Richmond herald, who received £4 for attending Anne at her arrival.[11] That the herald scribe did not meet her party until she reached Rochester can be inferred because he offered only slight information about her nights at Dover, Canterbury, and Sittingbourne and failed to note her landing at Deal. Furthermore, his reference to the mode of transportation by which Henry returned to Greenwich makes it reasonable to speculate that he was a member of the king's party that descended upon Rochester. His description is as follows:

and on New Year's day at afternoon the king's grace, with five of his privy chamber, being disguised with cloaks of marble with hoods, that they should not be known, came privately to Rochester, and so went up into the chamber where the said Lady Anne looked out at a window to see the bull baiting that was that time in the court, and suddenly he embraced her and kissed, and showed her a token that the king had sent her for her New Year's gift, and she being abashed, not knowing who it was, thanked him, and so he communed with her; but she regarded him little, but always looked out of the window on the bull baiting, and when the king perceived she regarded his coming so little, he departed in [an] other chamber and put off his cloak and came in again in a coat of purple velvet; and when the lords and knights did see his grace they did him reverence; and then, she, perceiving the lords doing their duties, humbled her grace lowly to the king's majesty, and his grace saluted her again, and so talked together lovingly, and after took her by the hand and led her into another chamber, where they solaced their graces that night and till Friday at afternoon; and then his grace took his leave and departed thence to Gravesend, and there took his barge, and so went to Greenwich that night, and she rode to Dartford that night and lodged there till the morrow. . . .[12]

At the end of June, after his arrest, Cromwell, who was not a member of the Rochester party, referred to the meeting in two letters to the king, one of which was written in response to inquiries seeking evidence for the divorce. Cromwell recalled that Henry had explained that he was going to Rochester "to nourish love" and that upon his return he complained that Anne was "Nothing as well as she was spoken of." If he had earlier been aware of information that he had since learned, he lamented, he would never have permitted her to enter the realm.[13] That his motive for the trip was "to nourish love" makes it possible to identify his welcome of her as part of the accepted protocol for the grooms' greeting of foreign-born brides. As early modern monarchs were expected to perform this ceremony, its history will be briefly addressed.[14]

In the late fourteenth century various romantic themes from fiction began to appear in courtship ceremonies, the motive of which was to stimulate affection between strangers whose marriages had been arranged before they met. The love at first sight motif, a kind of enchantment, as explained in Chapter 3, gave rise to portrait exchanges in royal courtships and to the inspection of potential wives by rulers in disguise.[15] As a corollary to these chivalric impulses, monarchs also began to don disguises to greet their foreign-born brides. The ruler who originated this practice may have been Louis II, titular king of Naples, Sicily, and Jerusalem, who was also a first-cousin of Charles VI of France. In 1399 he mingled among the spectators at Montpelier in the guise of a simple knight, seeking to view his bride Yolande, daughter of Juan I of Aragon, as she arrived at its castle on her way to their nuptial ceremony at Arles.

Louis was said to have fallen deeply in love with her at first sight and to have approached her carriage to kiss her hand. It was also noted that the bride did not guess who her admirer was, but that her mother understood him to be her son-in-law.[16]

As this ceremony developed, even if Yolande did not recognize Louis, the new wife usually guessed the identity of the would-be lover. As was probably acted out by Anne of Cleves, part of the game was for the lady to pretend not to know who the intruder was, but who else would play the would-be lover? Who else would dare to kiss the king's consort? No private citizen would presumably dare to be so familiar with the royal betrothed. In the romances the disguises were also often penetrated by the knights and on occasion by the ladies themselves. Sometimes the literary disguises were so transparent that jokes were made about them.[17]

After Louis greeted his bride, almost half a century may have elapsed before another monarch performed this ceremony in disguise. Louis and Yolande were the parents of René of Sicily, whose daughter, Margaret of Anjou, traveled to England in 1445 to wed Henry VI. She was extremely ill when she arrived at Portsmouth, as noted above, and was carried ashore by William, marquess of Suffolk. The next day she removed to a convent named God's House on the outskirts of Southampton at which Henry apparently went privately to see her although no eyewitness account of this encounter has survived. In 1458, some thirteen years later, Raffaelo de Negra, an envoy in the kingdom, informed his principal, Bianca Maria, duchess of Milan, about an informant's claim that Henry, accompanied by Suffolk, both of whom were dressed as squires, had visited Margaret to obtain a private glimpse of her. He had knelt and presented her with a letter ostensibly from the king and had remained on his knees watching her while she read it, paying no attention to him whatsoever. When the marquess later informed her of the identity of the letter bearer, she was said to have been vexed because she had kept him on his knees so long.[18]

In its early stages solid evidence for the development of a ceremony is often lacking. Still, it may be conjectured that Henry VI had heard stories about how his wife's grandfather had disguised himself to greet her grandmother. It is the kind of romantic tale, although somewhat archaic, that would have spread through royal networks. With his interest in the less martial side of chivalry and his desire to welcome his bride, Henry apparently took the opportunity afforded by her illness to visit her in disguise.[19]

The details of Henry VI's greeting of Margaret more nearly conform to Henry VIII's greeting of Anne than to those of similar ceremonies on the continent. As it emerged across the channel, monarchs followed the lead of Louis in attempting to view their ladies in the open streets; later rulers sometimes followed their brides' processions for miles. The next disguised greeter after Louis may have been Henry IV of Castile. In 1454 while traveling incognito, the Castilian king and four companions almost converged near Badajoz with the train of his second wife, Juana of Portugal. He hovered at a distance "peering between tamarisks" and followed her for several miles.[20]

Probably only one fifteenth-century ruler without the status of king or regent adopted this protocol. He was not, as might be expected, the head of the Burgundian-Valois dynasty but of the Sforza house of Milan. In 1468 when Galeazzo Maria, duke of Milan, welcomed his bride, Bona of Savoy, he pretended to be his brother, Sforza Maria, duke of Bari. The encounter between Henry IV of Castile and his wife may have been accidental, but clearly the duke of Milan had orchestrated his private meeting. It is possible that his mother Bianca, whose envoy had some years earlier sent her a description of Henry VI's chivalric greeting of Margaret of Anjou, had imparted this information to her son, who, like Charles the Bold, had great social and political ambitions. By performing this ritual, the head of a relatively new ruling dynasty chose to associate himself with the chivalric princes of Christendom.[21]

Two major factors distinguish the English ceremony of 1540 from that of 1445: an eyewitness account has survived of Henry VIII's greeting and his performance was more elaborate than Henry VI's. Renaissance monarchs recognized the value of borrowing gestures from chivalric tradition and encouraged their officials to create increasingly sophisticated protocol. While Henry VI reportedly disguised as a squire with one attendant had given Margaret a letter, Henry VIII, along with five attendants, was attired in a cloak of marble and brought a present for Anne, probably because it was New Year's Day, the traditional gift-giving day. The visit of Henry VI was much shorter than that of Henry VIII who, unlike his predecessor, ended the ceremony by confronting his bride. As Olisleger pointed out in his journal, the king could not keep up his disguise during the entire visit at Rochester since he planned to spend the evening there.[22]

The ceremony also became more elaborate on the continent. In 1543 when Maria of Portugal entered Badajoz, her bridegroom Philip, whom his father, Charles V, had recently named regent of Spain, already had arrived. No danger existed of his party converging with his bride's procession, as had occurred in 1454. In disguise Philip followed Maria all the way to Salamanca, "dashing along the streets of a town to see her face as she passed, now watching from the window of a house or an inn." When she learned that Philip was peering at her from a house in Salamanca, she held up a fan to hide her face but an attendant pushed it away so that he could see her.[23]

In contrast to the ceremony across the channel, the version performed in the northern part of the British Isles, like the one in England, took place indoors. In 1503, for example, James IV, who was scheduled to greet his bride Margaret Tudor at Edinburgh, met her privately for the first time at Dalkeith Castle. Disguised as a hunter, the king in a jacket of crimson velvet with a lute swung over his shoulders entered her chamber. The Somerset herald in attendance on Margaret kept minute details of this and other events of her trip to Edinburgh.[24]

The royal greetings of foreign-born brides may be viewed as a microcosm of power politics and chivalric ideals in early modern Europe.[25] Usually only bridegrooms who were kings or regents wore disguises in these ceremonies. In 1501 Arthur was without a disguise when he met Catherine of Aragon at Dogmersfeld, and in 1554 Queen Mary was in her formal royal dress when she welcomed Philip at Winchester.[26] Thus by these ceremonies, which functioned as "ritual signs of dominance," male rulers were set apart from their heirs, from female monarchs, and from their nobility, a gulf that has usually been interpreted as a sign of their growing social and political preeminence.[27] The "symbolics of power" that marked this dominance were those of increasingly elaborate ceremony, both public festivals and less publicized royal protocol.[28]

By interpreting Henry's incognito visit to Rochester as idiosyncratic, modern historians[29] have been unable to perceive that it gave him an opportunity to demonstrate his premiere status in his realm, to reaffirm to his peers his "royal dignity," and to prove himself a chivalric ruler with courteous manners.[30] Performing the ceremony was a mark of his nobility, and since his contemporaries held the ideals of correct social etiquette in high esteem, they would have viewed his omission of it as a deliberate insult to his wife.[31]

Any variation in court etiquette caused great concern. In 1456 when the future Louis XI of France visited Burgundy, for example, he sought to give Duchess Isabella precedence over him by walking a few steps behind her. This condescension astonished her because it was widely accepted that the king of France and his immediate family outranked all other princes. After debating the issue with her for over a quarter of an hour, he insisted that she proceed hand-in-hand with him. She obeyed his request but with mortification because the denial of his superior status put her in the humiliating position of infringing the rules of protocol.[32] Another example of this concern for etiquette can be found in an incident that occurred during the emperor's meeting with Francis in 1538. Charles was astounded when Catherine de Medici, the dauphin's wife, tried to serve him a towel with one knee on the ground. He refused her offer because it was a "dishonor" to be served in such a way by so high a lady.[33]

Monarchs abroad continued to greet their foreign-born brides in disguise well into the seventeenth century, but Henry's reception of Anne was the last in which an English king participated. In 1623, before his accession, Charles I had already seen his future bride Henrietta Maria when he traveled incognito through France on his way to Spain to woo the Spanish infanta. Plainly dressed, although wearing an "outsize periwig," he had watched her rehearsing a masque in the *Grande Salle*. In 1662 their son Charles II, who lacked his father's chivalric impulses, nonchalantly walked into the bedroom of his consort Catherine of Braganza and introduced himself to her. His French cousin Louis XIV may have been the last early modern monarch to perform the private greeting ceremony in disguise.[34]

On 3 June 1660 Louis had been wed by proxy to Maria Theresa at Fuenterrabia on the frontier of Spain in the presence of her father Philip IV. The next day Philip took Maria Theresa to meet Anne of Austria, his sister and Louis' mother, at a pavilion that had been set up in the middle of the Bidassoa River. To obtain a glimpse of his betrothed, Louis approached incognito the doorway of the chamber where they had assembled and braved the teasing remarks of the courtiers in attendance for a few minutes before withdrawing. As Maria Theresa and Philip entered their barge and crossed back to the Spanish side, Louis, still incognito, followed them on horseback along the riverside. Whatever the Sun King came to stand for in the future, it can be said with this parting episode that here he represents the sunset of medieval chivalry.[35]

Since the greeting in disguise had become an accepted ceremony, the charge that an impatient Henry VIII impulsively dashed down to Rochester to see his bride must be laid to rest. It could even be argued that he was not all that eager to greet her, for he failed to make the trip to Canterbury to receive his new wife, as some of his predecessors had done, and as it was rumored he would do. He lingered at Greenwich until she had reached Rochester, a town that was much closer in distance to him than Winchester was to his daughter Mary when she met Philip of Spain there in 1554 and than Exeter was to his predecessor Henry IV when he greeted his spouse Joan of Brittany there in 1403. In 1445 Henry VI had definitely demonstrated much more impatience than Henry VIII since he traveled all the way to Southampton to visit his sick consort.[36]

By this standard the most impatient bridegroom of all was James VI of Scotland, the future James I of England. In 1589 he decided to cross the seas to rescue Anne of Denmark whom stormy weather had stranded at Norway. Surely, the story of his grandfather James who sailed to France to fetch his bride Madeleine some forty years earlier was familiar to him. Of course, unlike his ancestor, he did not travel incognito, but he did compare himself and Anne to Hero and Leander. Not normally known for chivalrous acts, James as king of England celebrated the Arthurian myth by announcing he would create 1,000 new knights in imitation of Arthur and by giving the name of Great Britain to the unified kingdom of England and Scotland in honor of that legendary monarch.[37]

Sixteenth-century princes donned disguises more frequently than their predecessors for reasons they had not fully appreciated. Charles VI of France had been one of the few earlier kings to appear in disguise in courtly entertainments,[38] although there is also evidence that his cousin Philip the Good of Burgundy exchanged his usual black doublet for a green one on May Day and announced: "This is the livery of love." In England courtly masking had spread in the reign of Edward III, who like most of his contemporaries usually employed disguises for practical purposes, for journeys, in tournaments, or in warfare, rather than merely as a means of entertainment, although it was noted at the Christmas feast in 1348 that he and eight of his chamber knights dressed up in green garments embroidered with pheasants' feathers.[39]

Henry VIII was the first English monarch to participate regularly in maskings unassociated with tournaments or warfare. In 1509, for example, Hall noted that he had gone into his consort's chamber dressed up as Robin Hood. In the decade before he wed Anne of Cleves, other references can be found to his disguised doings. In 1536 just after his marriage to Jane, he attended a wedding and masquerade dressed up as a Turk. Two years later after Holbein returned with the portrait of Christina of Milan, Chapuys noted that Henry had been masking while visiting Lady Suffolk. The king could not be, the ambassador alleged, "one single moment without a mask." Finally, on 15 September 1539 shortly before the Cleves embassy arrived, Bryan informed Cromwell that the king had been merry at a mask the previous evening.[40] Even so, Henry's behavior was less intrusive than that of some of his contemporaries, especially James V and Francis I, who roamed the streets of their capitals in disguise.[41]

Also, adopting a disguise was not a practice in which only young monarchs like James indulged. In 1538 when the emperor was thirty-eight-years old, he went incognito to a banquet where he engaged in some flirtatious exchanges with a lady, who pretended not to recognize him when he took off his mask. Although Charles had not welcomed his wife Isabella in disguise when she arrived in Spain, their son Philip, as noted above, did perform this ceremony for his foreign-born brides. In 1570 when he was fifty-one, a few years older than Henry when he met Anne of Cleves, the Spanish king obtained his first view of his wife, Anne of Austria, while mingling incognito among the courtiers welcoming her to Segovia.[42]

Secondly, to return to June 1540, the imprisoned Cromwell recalled that the king had complained after the Rochester meeting that he had found her "Nothing so well as she was spoken of,"[43] a remark that has usually been interpreted as a disparaging comment on her face, the beauty of which, of course, lies in the eye of the beholder. In a analysis of her appearance, it is not necessary in order to find a means of complimenting her looks to compare her

favorably to Queen Jane, whom Holbein painted when she was pregnant in a somewhat stiff pose, for some of Anne's contemporaries
clearly found her appearance pleasing.[44] It does seem odd, moreover,
that the king instantly found a lady so repugnant whom men from
different social ranks had claimed was attractive. Caution should be
used in assuming that he was referring to her face specifically,
although it is true that hardly any other part of her body, except for
her hands, was then visible for his inspection.

It is essential to restate that Cromwell was a prisoner in June when
he provided this information in response to inquiries that were being
made to unearth evidence for the royal divorce.[45] All the other testimony about Henry's negative feelings toward Anne was contained in
depositions gathered especially for the July divorce case. The witnesses thus had to recall facts that had occurred between five and
nine months earlier. In at least one detail Cromwell was in error, for
in the chronology of events, he claimed that the wedding had been
held on Monday (5 January) rather than on Tuesday (6 January).
This might seem a minor point but the exact day should have been
relatively easy to pinpoint because it was the twelfth day of
Christmas, the Epiphany, the major festival of the Christmas
season.[46]

All the documentation obviously must be examined with great
care; despite this discrepancy in Cromwell's letters, they are much
more trustworthy as evidence of what actually occurred than are the
sworn depositions. He was neither answering questions for his
defense nor officially for the divorce trial, since he was required only
in response to the council's inquiries to write down the events for the
king as he remembered them. The difference in the way the two
kinds of evidence was collected is significant, for as Malcolm Gaskill
has recently revealed, statements in early modern criminal cases
often contained fictions: deponents created evidence, which reputa-
ble and respected judges accepted, to represent what they believed
had actually occurred. They thus "demonstrated their conviction
through fictionalized narratives." Gaskill characterized this as
sincere behavior that arose from a different "ordering of reality in
the early modern period . . . a lost social context of communication"
that slowly disappeared after 1700.[47]

With Gaskill's study in mind, it is essential to note whenever possible how the deponents' memories differed from Cromwell's. In July

all individuals questioned about the Rochester visit confirmed his statements about Henry's negative reaction to Anne. Sir Anthony Browne, master of the horse, who accompanied him on the visit, recalled that he had confessed on the return to Greenwich, "I see nothing in this woman as men report of her, and I marvel that wise men would make such report as they have done." The king had, Browne also claimed, been so disappointed that he had deferred giving her his New Year's present, a "partlet furred with sables and sable skins for her neck, with a muffler furred and a cap," until the next morning when he ordered Browne to deliver it with a "cold message." He further recalled that Henry had not spoken twenty words with her. Browne's testimony that the king had manipulated the gift-giving custom to insult his bride was surely a fictionalized account, for it is evident at other occasions, Anne's Greenwich reception, for example, that he disguised his personal feelings and publicly honored her. Even the critical Marillac, who participated in the entry, admitted that she had been received very graciously. About two years later in December 1541 after the divorce, her brother's ambassador, Carl Harst, reported that she had sworn to him that Henry had never acted in a disrespectful manner toward her.[48]

While characterized as private, the Rochester meeting was far from secret: It occurred in a large chamber with her German attendants and many members of the English aristocracy present as witnesses. In an setting such as this, as Raymond Firth has remarked, the acts of hosts and guests tend to be "rigid and highly prescribed," a claim that reflects Michel de Montaigne's comment that "Ceremony forbids us to express natural and lawful things, and we obey it." Wriothesley's chronicle, moreover, disputes Browne's assertion. According to the herald, the disguised Henry had actually shown her "a token that the king had sent her for her New Year's gift." It is possible that Browne was confused or merely forgetful but it is more likely that he was fictionalizing the evidence to accord with how he remembered Henry's private reaction. The alleged "cold message," for example, with which the gift was presented to Anne would have lost most if not all its effect in its translation into the German language that was required for communication with her. Browne also had a personal reason to twist the evidence; by placing this spin on the Rochester events and helping to create firm evidence of the king's innermost feelings and thus support his grounds for the divorce, Browne might hope he could make up for the earlier blunder of his half-brother, Southampton, who had offended Henry by so greatly praising her beauty in his letters from Calais. Regardless of when she received the gift, surely the king had not deliberately insulted his wife, if for no other reason than that those who witnessed the ceremony would have assumed the snub was a disrespectful gesture toward her brother and her homeland. As to Browne's other assertion that the king's conversation with her was so brief as to be rude, all his exchanges with her had to be made through interpreters and in this kind of setting could not have been lengthy. Wriothesley said only that they "talked together lovingly" and that Henry led her into another chamber where they "solaced their graces." In contrast to Browne's recollections about the king's brief, rude treatment of her, two other contemporary accounts, in addition to Hall's chronicle, all confirm that he shared a meal with her that holiday night, and Cleves records also indicate that he dined with her on Friday morning before departing for Greenwich.[49]

Most of the king's councillors and members of the privy chamber actually remained ignorant of his negative reaction to her for several weeks. Since only a few of them swore in the July depositions to having had personal knowledge of his disenchantment with her at Rochester, clearly Browne's claim that Henry took the opportunity to insult her by momentarily withholding her present was inaccurate. This was a ritual of exchange that occurred annually on New Year's Day: the amount of the gift, how it was to be offered, and to whom were clearly defined. Had it been delivered in a manner calculated to insult its receiver, all the English in attendance would have recognized the snub that was intended. Those who were aware of Henry's disenchantment in January were only two doctors, John Chamber and William Butts, and six other men: Cromwell, Suffolk, Southampton, Russell, Browne, and Heneage. Whether the other four councillors, Cranmer, Audley, Norfolk, and Tunstall, who met with Henry on 3 and 4 January at Rochester and Greenwich concerning his domestic tangle, were told of his repugnance is not known. The most revealing comment about this veil of secrecy can be found in the testimony of Anthony Denny of the privy chamber, who participated in the Greenwich entry. He swore that after the queen's arrival and for a long time after that, he had misunderstood Henry's feelings about Anne, for "he took evermore occasion to praise her to the king's highness," who "would never approve those praises, but said ever, she was no such as she was praised for." Finally, just before Lent, which began on 11 February in 1540, Henry told Denny he could not have affection for Anne because "she was not as she was reported" and then mentioned specific parts of her body, her breasts and stomach.[50]

It is noteworthy that Denny's testimony, which corroborated Cromwell's earlier reconstruction, links the phrase "she was no such as she was praised for" with parts of her trunk that were hidden to all men but the king, as her husband, and not with her face and hands that were available for all to inspect. This link seems to make the events of June and July somewhat more understandable, for ultimately most of the blame for the marriage's failure was placed on Cromwell, who had not seen her on the continent, while almost everyone else, who had seen her there, continued to enjoy royal favor. In 1540 Wotton was returned to Cleves as ambassador and later gained a unique position in the church as the holder of a deanery in both the newly structured cathedrals of Canterbury and York. In 1547 he served as one of the executors and supervisors of the king's will. After Cromwell's execution, Henry awarded his office of lord privy seal to the apologetic Southampton. Vaughan returned to his diplomatic duties, Beard served as Anne's gentleman usher, and Michael Mercator continued performing "right acceptable service" for the king at Grave.[51]

Until his death from the plague in 1543, Holbein was identified as the king's painter in royal accounts and pursued his artwork unaffected by the fall of Cromwell, who had been ennobled as the earl of Essex a few weeks before his execution. No contemporary or near contemporary account hints that Henry had been displeased with Holbein's portrait of Anne, and it was widely believed that the king greatly admired the artist's skills. Carel van Mander's *Book on Picturing*, published in 1604, contains some tales about Holbein and Henry, one of which relates Holbein's dispute with an anonymous English earl whom the painter threw down the stairs. The king's response to the earl's complaint about this treatment was: "I tell you, earl, that if it pleased me to make seven dukes of seven peasants, I could do so, but I could never make of seven earls Hans Holbein or any as eminent as he."[52]

Among the greeters in England Marillac was the only diplomat to write down his description of Anne in January 1540. Before examining his remarks, it must be pointed out that it was customary for foreign envoys who wished to prevent a royal marriage or who resented the rejection of their candidates, such as Anne of Lorraine or Louise of Guise, to disparage the actual selection. In 1661 the hostile Spanish ambassador, for example, mendaciously claimed that Catherine of Braganza was deformed. Given this convention, Marillac's comments were mild. Although he attended Anne's reception, which he dismissed as a "quantity of large chains," his position in the procession had not offered him an opportunity to obtain a clear view of her. The judgment of those who had seen her at close range, he assured Montmorency on 5 January, was that she was neither as beautiful nor as young as everyone had said. However, he went on to admit that Anne, who was rather tall, a trait that her contemporaries found especially pleasing in a woman, was reportedly the most beautiful German lady at the entry, for all her attendants were said to be inferior to her in appearance. When these details were repeated in France, the interpretation of Cardinal Farnese, who forwarded the news to Paul, was that she was "old and ugly." In his letter to Francis, also written on 5 January, Marillac explained that she was of "medium beauty" [*beaulté moyenne*].[53] It is noteworthy, however, that two years later in 1542 when Cleves was his country's ally, he informed Margaret of Navarre that Anne was "said to be half as beautiful again" since she left court [*plus belle de la moietie*]. His comments about her appearance are even more interesting when they are compared to his remarks about Katherine Howard's looks. In July 1540 he had heard that Katherine was a lady of *grand beaulté* but in September, after he had seen her, he described her as a lady of indifferent beauty [*de beaulté médiocre*]. A reasonable inference is that he considered Anne at least as pleasing in appearance as Katherine.[54]

If not her face, perhaps the cause of Henry's disenchantment was that she was German; perhaps her clothes or her manner of speaking offended him. To Montmorency in the above cited letter of 5 January, Marillac went on to claim that even if her attendants had been beautiful, and his informants did not think they were, their unfashionable clothes would have caused the ladies almost to be described as ugly.[55] This prejudice against German styles continued throughout the Tudor century. In 1596 the diplomat Henry Wotton, for example, laughed at German ladies who were "most pitifully attired." It is true that Henry VIII was known to favor French fashions but as he had seen a portrait of Anne in her native style, her clothing was surely not unexpected and it could easily be changed. On the Sunday after the nuptials, Hall noted that she was apparelled in the English fashion with a French hood "which so set forth her beauty and good visage that every creature rejoyced to behold her," except, as was later made clear, her husband. Ironically, in 1568 as Charles of Austria began to court Henry's daughter Elizabeth, Zachariah, Cardinal Delphino, approved of the match because, as he observed, the English were descendants of German forefathers and "reason and necessity demand that blood should seek kindred blood." He also spoke of the "predilection" of the English for the German people.[56]

Their language, which may have sounded guttural or "grating" to some,[57] was later characterized by Henry Wotton as "cousin-german" to English, and in 1540 was far from being a new sound for the king's ears. During the fall and winter of 1539–40, many of Anne's countrymen visited his court. Even Philip of Bavaria, whose suit of Mary was under serious consideration, could converse with her only in broken Latin and through interpreters since he lacked a knowledge of French or English.[58]

In modern studies it is usually asserted that Henry eagerly and hurriedly charged into the chamber to see Anne, unrealistically expecting to fall in love with her at first sight. The only "suddenly" the herald mentioned was the kiss he bestowed upon his bride, who had hitherto concentrated on the bull-baiting, one of the usual holiday sports in England. Since, as has been noted, protocol dictated this private meeting, his visit is not evidence of a personal impatience to see her. He undoubtedly rode over from his barge at Gravesend; for that was the route he was to take on his return trip to Greenwich. It was the obvious route, for most passengers and goods traveled by river between London and Gravesend, the "gateway" to the port of London.[59]

Before performing the ceremony, he surely took time to rest from the rigors of the river, which often had strong winds that could be a challenge to boatmen, and from riding on horseback from Gravesend to Rochester on a wintery day. Probably, he warmed himself before a fire, perhaps washed his hands and face, an action that was considered a gesture of good manners and courtesy, and surely enjoyed some refreshment. Appropriate arrangements also had to be made for the greeting. Although the herald failed to mention that Browne had preceded Henry into the chamber, the master of the horse recalled that he had delivered a message to Anne from the king concerning his New Year's gift. It is likely that his task was simply to ascertain which lady she was so that he could assist Henry in identifying her. Some time might have also had to elapse after the king's arrival to give interested parties an opportunity to gather for the ceremony. The tides, not Anne's schedule, would have had to guide the timing of his arrival at Rochester. On a similar occasion in 1625, although he was not in disguise, when Charles reached Canterbury for his greeting of Henrietta Maria and learned she was eating breakfast, he delayed his welcome until she had finished her meal.[60]

In 1540 Henry could easily have conferred about the marriage arrangements with Wotton before the greeting ceremony and certainly, according to Browne, he discussed them with her commissioners and his councillors afterwards. Altogether, he spent about twenty-four hours at Rochester, probably waiting for the adjustment of the tides to make possible his return to Greenwich.[61] During that interval he would have had opportunity to learn that Anne's brother had failed to keep his pledge to Wotton at Cleves and his embassy's promise to the king at Windsor. He had not furnished the records that could prove conclusively that Anne was free to wed Henry. The absence of this documentation greatly concerned the king whose claim, that he had informed the Cleves ambassadors when they had arrived at Windsor armed only with extracts from the Lorraine treaty and contract, that he must have proof that she was free to marry before the nuptial service could be held was corroborated by the July depositions. Suffolk, not only alone but also in a joint statement with Audley, Canterbury, Norfolk, Southampton, and Durham swore that at Windsor the previous October the ambassadors had promised to bring the appropriate records with them when they accompanied Anne to England. The king must have begun to suspect a cover-up of her marital status, and it would have been reasonable for him to recall with concern the unexpected offer to him of Anne's younger sister Amelia, whom he had not sought as a bride. From almost the moment he saw his queen, Henry must have viewed her as potentially a married woman. She was "Nothing so well as she was spoken of," he complained. Beginning with that negative attitude, from then on every time he saw her he found something else to criticize.[62]

It is impossible to argue that his reaction to her would have been positive had the relevant documentation been forthcoming. If it could actually be proved, however, that he had learned before he performed the greeting ceremony that her brother's ambassadors had failed to bring with them copies of the contract and treaty, it would be argued here that their failure to do so actually set Anne up for the king's negative opinion of her. It lingers as a suspicion. What can and must be maintained is that the question of whether or not she was free to marry was so significant that even had Henry found her appearance pleasing, he would still have ordered his councillors to investigate whether her Lorraine marriage continued in force. Under these circumstances, he could obviously claim after he had seen her that she was not the lady he had anticipated since he had been expecting a maiden entirely unencumbered by previous contracts. Clearly, he was uninterested in, even fearful of, entering another union that violated divine law. According to the July testimony of George, Lord Cobham, the Younger Pallant, one of Anne's German attendants, had also voiced that concern in his disclosure that, in order to ensure the legality of her union with Henry, some unspecified papists had requested Paul to dispense with her previous contract. Pallant had also speculated that had Henry known of this request, he would never have agreed to wed Anne out of concern that he would be violating God's laws. In August, after the divorce had been concluded, Wotton and his colleague, John Clerk, bishop of Bath and Wells, reported to the king in a joint letter from Cleves that Pallant had denied that he had made these statements to Cobham, but that he had also declared that he and another countryman considered themselves Henry's sworn servants and planned to return to England to seek royal pensions. By these comments, Pallant seemed to be holding out the possibility that he might confirm Cobham's fictionalized comment if a stipend were made available. For their part, Wotton and Clerk promised to do all they could to prevent his journey to the kingdom.[63]

On 2 January as Henry was complaining to Cromwell about

Anne at Greenwich, she was settling in for the night at Dartford in the suppressed priory of the only Dominican nuns in England. After its dissolution some eight or nine months earlier, Henry had ordered it remodeled as a royal palace. On 3 January Anne's official reception at Greenwich, which lies only a few miles from Dartford, was scheduled to take place.[64] Until after it was concluded, the king could not convene another meeting of his councillors to discuss his domestic dilemma, for three of the original treaty negotiators, Suffolk, Southampton, and Canterbury were with the queen and planning to accompany her to Greenwich.

Henry decided to hold the reception as scheduled and as Christopher Barker, garter king of arms, and Thomas Hawley, Clarenceux king of arms, had proclaimed in London and Southwark on 2 January. At the foot of Shooter's Hill on Blackheath Common, several tents and pavilions of cloth of gold had been erected to serve as a waiting station for Anne and her ladies. A wide lane had been cleared of ground cover between the tents and the gate of Greenwich Park, a "most delightful spot of ground, extending as far as Blackheath." This reception, more clearly than the previous entries for Anne, demonstrates how the placement and movement of its participants, who were required to arrive by 8:00 a.m., represented their relationship to each other within the social hierarchy. At the gate were placed twenty-four Hanseatic merchants of the Steelyard on horseback; then along both sides of the pathway were grouped Englishmen by rank: the officials and merchants of the city of London, gentlemen, knights, and the fifty gentlemen pensioners who all wore velvet coats and chains of gold.[65]

About noon Norfolk, Suffolk, Cranmer, and others who had joined her train in Kent escorted Anne to the reception area. As she and her party came down Shooter's Hill, her lord chamberlain and some of her other English officers and servants greeted her. Anne's new almoner, Dr. George Day, made an eloquent oration in Latin to which Olisleger responded. Then the king's nieces, Lady Margaret Douglas and Frances Grey, marchioness of Dorset, his widowed daughter-in-law, Mary Fitzroy, duchess of Richmond, and many other ladies, including Eleanor, countess of Rutland, and Anne, countess of Hereford, welcomed her. The queen alighted from her chariot, thanked and kissed them, and after her new officers and councillors had similarly saluted her, she entered her pavilion to partake of refreshments, some wine, fruit, and spice, to enjoy the warmth provided there, and to change her clothes. Undoubtedly, it was a chilly day but the weather was not extremely bad or the reception would have been delayed.[66]

When Henry learned that she had arrived at her pavilion, he began his progress through the park. Leading his procession were twelve trumpeters, his privy councillors, and members of his privy chamber, all on horseback and wearing richly decorated coats. Next, in their appropriate order came the barons accompanied by Sir William Holles, lord mayor of London, the bishops, the earls, the dukes, including Philip of Bavaria, the Imperial and French ambassadors, Cromwell as lord privy seal, Audley, the garter king of arms with the other officers of arms, and the sergeants at arms. Henry Grey, marquess of Dorset, carried the king's sword of state. After him at some distance, Henry rode forward on a fine horse trapped in rich cloth of gold. He wore a purple velvet coat, trimmed with many rich jewels and embroidered with flat gold of damask that hung so low, according to Hall, the "ground little appeared." Following him were William, Lord Sandes, his lord chamberlain, Browne, as master of the horse leading the royal horse of state by a long rein of gold, the pages, and Sir Anthony Wingfield, captain of the guard, all well mounted and in rich coats. When Henry stopped near where the spears stood, his attendants withdrew to each side of him, leaving him astride his horse in the middle of the lane.

As he approached, Anne emerged from her pavilion dressed in a rich gown of raised cloth of gold without a train in the German style. On her head was a cap with pearls set off by a cornet of black velvet and around her neck rested a chain of rich stones. Mounted on a fair horse also draped with rich cloth, she followed her gentlemen, her councillors both English and Cleves, her officials, among them her lord chamberlain, Norfolk, Cranmer, Cheyney, and others. Behind her rode her master of the horse, Sir John Dudley, leading her horse of honor. Then came all the ladies according to their rank, with her yeomen and servingmen bringing up the rear. Anne proceeded down the lane to the king, who moved forward toward her, paused as she came closer, than took off his hat, saluted and embraced her. Hall continued:

she likewise not forgetting her duty, with most amiable aspect and womanly behavior received his grace with sweet words and great thanks. . . . O, what a sight was this to see so goodly a prince and so noble a king to ride with so fair a lady of so goodly a stature and so womanly a countenance, and in especial of so good qualities. . . .[67]

In their appointed order the greeters rode back through the park to the wall of the suppressed Observant Friar's House, the land of which adjoined the palace, where all the men dismounted except for some of the king's attendants who continued on to the palace door. The ladies, some of whom rode in chariots including the one belonging to the queen, traveled to the court gate. As they passed the wharf, they could see Londoners sailing on the Thames in many kinds of craft that had been decorated with banners and flags. Earlier a guard rail had been erected to avoid anyone "by press of people" being pushed into the river in his/her eagerness to view the crafts on which were men, women, and children singing and playing instruments. Among the vessels was a barge, called the *Bachelor's Bark* with a foist that shot great pieces of artillery. Inside the palace's inner court where the king and queen dismounted, as he embraced and kissed her, they could hear a gun at the Tower of Greenwich shoot a loud peal. He then escorted her to her privy chamber.[68]

Thousands of people, including the queen's attendants, had participated in the ceremony: Marillac estimated the number at 5,000–6,000. Careful planning had been required to coordinate the placement and movement of so great a crowd of people. Fourteen whifflers had ridden from the park to the queen's pavillion to see that all the participants followed the directions that had been distributed to them. Although entries such as these could be quite noisy, Marillac complimented its organizers, for he thought it had been very well conducted with *silence et san aulcune confusion*. According to Hall, it was late in the evening before this great host was disbursed, most of them returning to London. Many spectators must have crowded into Greenwich to witness the reception, for as Sir John Hayward was to comment about Elizabeth's London entry in 1559: "The people are naturally both taken and held with exterior shows."[69]

Even so, it had not been so elaborate a welcome as had been prepared for Catherine of Aragon in 1501. That Anne's wedding was held at Greenwich meant that it would necessarily have to be a less extravagant affair than that of Catherine, who had made her entry into London amidst pageants, the flowing of wine, and the waving of tassels and banners. Anne's more low-key reception can be explained by several factors. First, the timing of her arrival was inconvenient, for she had been expected in early December, about two months after the treaty was signed, a relatively short period of time for the welcomers to create and to produce pageants. The weather may have also discouraged the preparations. In addition, her arrival was to take place during one of the periods in which the church forbade marriages, between Advent, 27 November and the octave of Epiphany, 13 January. Licenses could be obtained to hold weddings at this time but scaled-down celebrations usually accompanied them. Finally, and extremely important, was the expense, for she brought with her no dowry to help defray the cost of her reception. Scheduling it at Blackheath meant that the greater expense of the London entry, which the crown would have had to subsidize, could be avoided. As R. Malcolm Smuts has also pointed out, the elaborate royal entries with pageants were becoming increasingly rare in the Tudor period and tended to coincide with coronations. During the seventeenth century, civic entries for rulers went entirely out of fashion. The few remaining royal processions, usually for coronation celebrations, funerals, and weddings, were detached from civic entries. In London the lord mayor's show increasingly took over as the kingdom's regular festive occasion.[70]

Between the reception on 3 January and the wedding on 6 January, much activity occurred at the palace, most of the evidence for which, as noted above, comes from statements made some five to six months later. When he left Anne, Henry returned to his privy chamber and reportedly called to Cromwell who awaited him there: "My Lord, is it not as I told you? Say what you will, she is nothing so fair as she hath been reported; howbeit she is well and seemly." The word "fair" is so vague it could mean a specific attribute, such as the color of her skin, or it could mean a general comment on her appearance. Cromwell recalled that he had responded with sorrow at the king's reaction and had confessed he thought she had a "queenly manner," a statement with which the king agreed. Henry's admissions that Anne was "well and seemly" and had a "queenly manner" seem curiously at odds in the context of his announced dislike of her person. He ordered Cromwell to assemble his councillors, specifically Canterbury, Norfolk, Suffolk, Audley, Southampton, and

Durham, to discuss the marital tangle. That same day according to the July testimony of John, Lord Russell, who had also accompanied Henry to Rochester, the king asked him if he thought she "so fair and of such beauty as report had been made me of her."[71]

Cromwell and the other councillors were required to meet with the Cleves diplomats to learn what commissions they possessed, to examine the friendship covenants sent to Wotton that had required ratification at Cleves, and to inquire about the validity of the marriage contract between Francis of Lorraine and Anne. When these issues were raised with Olisleger and Hochsteden on Saturday evening, they requested a delay to prepare their response. In a meeting that took place the next morning (Sunday, 4 January) while the king and queen, who was "richly apparelled," attended mass, the ambassadors were said to have expressed astonishment at the inquiries. They admitted they lacked a commission to treat with the covenants that had been delivered to Wotton at Cleves and restated that the contract between Francis and Anne, which had been made in their minority, had been revoked. Olisleger and Hochsteden offered to remain in custody until a copy of the articles for the friendship treaty that the duke had ratified and a copy of the revocation of Anne's contract with Francis could be forwarded from Cleves. In both of Cromwell's letters written at the end of June, he recalled that they had promised to send a copy of the repudiation of the contract but not the original document itself.[72]

Before the nuptials it was entirely appropriate for Henry to request evidence of Anne's eligibility to wed, and the Cleves diplomats should have, indeed must have, expected that moment, perhaps even dreaded it. Their alleged astonishment had to have been rooted in pretense for at least three reasons. First, weddings throughout most of Christendom, including German-speaking lands, began by asking about impediments that would prevent a union between the bride and groom. Unlike today's practice this was not a perfunctory question: church courts punished spouses who failed to disclose impediments and even accomplices who aided them. Confirming the validity of a marriage was also essential for establishing children's legitimacy. In the registers that Cromwell ordered parishes to keep in 1538, priests more faithfully entered marriages than burials and christenings because of the need to document the legal status of offspring. It was also common in England, when one of the two partners was a stranger to the parish in which the marriage was to be held, for him/her to present testimonial letters to the priest to prove that he/she was free to wed. In Roman Catholic countries, papal dispensations permitting unions forbidden by the church were routinely inspected before the ceremony could be held. When Richard, duke of York, espoused Lady Anne Mowbray in 1477, for example, the priest refused to begin the service until a dispensation permitting them to wed was produced, since they were related within the forbidden degrees. Secondly, on 4 January for Wotton this was clearly a *déjà vu* experience, as he had repeatedly requested a copy of the Lorraine contract. Thirdly, the king, as he claimed, had himself told the Cleves diplomats at Windsor in September (when they arrived with extracts from the treaty and contract of 1527) that he would need to have written evidence that she was not bound by earlier commitments before he could proceed with the marriage.[73]

So essential was the presentation of evidence at the wedding to prove the bride and groom were free to marry that relatives who were eager for a crucial alliance, such as the one between Isabella of Castile and Ferdinand of Aragon in 1469, might even have the relevant document forged. Although Isabella desired this match to solidify her position in the Castilian succession, she had made it clear to Ferdinand that she could not wed him without a dispensation. A forged one was produced, for otherwise the marriage would not have taken place. Later, Sixtus IV issued them a general bull of dispensation.[74]

In 1540 Henry did not believe he had any realistic option but to marry Anne, for at that moment Francis was entertaining Charles at Paris. It had been the threat of their alliance that had led Henry to select a German bride in the first place. When Cromwell reported the Cleves ambassadors' replies to him, he exclaimed with displeasure that he was "not well handled." He did not wish to marry her, he protested, but she had traveled such a distance and great preparations had been made for the wedding. He also worried about driving her brother "into the hands of" the emperor and the French king "being now together." After dinner when Henry met with his councillors, he required that they ask her to swear both before them and some notaries that she was free from all other marriage contracts. When he learned she had completed the oath, Cromwell recalled that he had cried, "Is there none other Remedy, but that I must needs, against my will, put my neck in the yoke?" No other remedy was at hand and the wedding preparations continued.[75]

Suffolk and Southampton, individually, and the councillors, jointly, maintained in their depositions that the king had caused the nuptials to be delayed for two days from Sunday to Tuesday. But it appears from the rather more detailed statements of Cromwell, who unlike these deponents had been at Greenwich directing the arrangements for Anne's arrival, that it was the Cleves ambassadors who created the delay by requesting that they be given time to prepare their report, which was presented at the aforesaid Sunday meeting. As noted earlier, Cromwell also recalled incorrectly that the nuptials had taken place on Monday rather than on Tuesday. In addition, he failed to indicate that the king had interfered with the preparations for the wedding but remembered only that he had lamented his inability to call it off. Surely, the ambassadors would not have requested a delay to prepare their response had the ceremony originally been scheduled for Sunday.[76]

It is likely that Cromwell remembered Monday, 5 January, because it was the day on which the nuptials had been set to take place once it was learned that Anne would be at Greenwich on 3 January. Usually the service was held at least two and sometimes more days after the entry of the foreign-born spouse. In 1501 Catherine of Aragon and Arthur were married two days after her London reception, and in 1403 Joan of Navarre and Henry IV were wed two days after her Winchester greeting. Many other examples of a similar time-lag between the reception of the foreign-born consort and the celebration of the nuptial service can be found. Various housekeeping reasons could cause the delay, from the desire to prepare her wardrobe for the wedding to the need to familiarize her and her attendants with her new realm's customs. For most brides going from one major ceremony to another on back-to-back days would have surely been an exhausting and probably an impossible ordeal, particularly as weddings, which were accompanied by the nuptial mass, had to be scheduled before noon. As Anne had been in transit in inclement weather for some time, two nights' respite following her public reception, which was not completed before late afternoon or even early evening, would almost certainly have been prearranged.[77] It may well be, however, that when the ambassadors received permission to delay giving their report until Sunday, the work on the wedding arrangements was disrupted while his councillors prepared for the meeting with them. In requiring the matter to be investigated, Henry could not have anticipated whether the inquiry would take two days until Tuesday or even three until Wednesday. If he did interfere with the arrangements, they were halted for only one day, for on Monday, 5 January, the Cleves ambassadors made a sworn statement concerning Anne's contract with Lorraine and the king confirmed the necessary charters for her jointure.[78]

The notarial instrument that Olisleger and Hochsteden signed in Cromwell's chamber, which lay on the north side of the palace, had been drawn up by Anthony Hussey and Robert Johnson. In it the ambassadors confirmed that Charles of Guelders had mediated a contract of marriage between Anne and Francis of Lorraine when they were minors, and that afterwards in the presence of witnesses, Henry de Grioff, chancellor of Guelders, had declared the agreement null and void. Within three months from 5 January, the ambassadors promised to produce copies of this revocation and of two marital pacts agreed to by the dukes of Lorraine and Juliers–Cleves in 1527. In their conversations with the councillors on Sunday, Cromwell recalled, they had promised only a copy of the repudiation, but Henry obviously demanded that they swear under oath to send the treaty and contract of marriage as well. Even by sixteenth-century travel standards, a lead time of three months seems rather long, unless, of course, the Germans were anticipating either that a diligent archival search would have to be made to unearth the original documents or that the duke would delay acting upon their sworn promise. When they were later departing for home, Olisleger promised Cromwell that he would advance the business as quickly as possible. The witnesses to this notarial instrument were Cromwell, Cranmer, Audley, Southampton, Tunstall, Wotton, Petre, and John Oliver, dean of the Royal College at Oxford.[79]

On that same day, the king certified two different documents detailing Anne's jointure. One in the amount of about 327 marks was a slightly different version of an earlier draft, dated by the editors of the *Letters and Papers* in October 1539. The original of this and another one in the amount of about 4,377 marks are in Düsseldorf archives. Copies of them, as well as of a third document in the amount of about 312 marks, can be found in England. It is noteworthy that Anne enjoyed income from lands that traditionally had been set aside for queen consorts, including her predecessor, Queen Jane. It is a comment on the haste of the Cleves ambassadors, each of whom was granted £100 as a departing reward, that they forgot to take with them their copies of Anne's financial settlement. Olisleger wrote to Cromwell asking that they be sent either to Gravesend or Dover where he would collect them.[80]

Unlike the dower, the jointure, which first emerged in the thirteenth century, did not need to equal one-third the value of the husband's estates. Increasingly, however, because the dower could only be attached to lands in which the husband was seised, since the property held in use was exempted, the jointure came to replace it. It required a husband's settling certain estates jointly on himself and his wife during their lifetimes and on the survivor alone after the death of one spouse with provisions and safeguards for the transmission of the property to their heirs after the death of both spouses. The Statute of Uses of 1536 had stipulated that the widow could not have both a jointure and a dower. By law, the jointure, which provided a wife with an income for her household, had to be ratified and approved before the marriage was completed, in this case on 5 January, the day before the wedding. When a bride agreed to a jointure before her marriage, she could not later renounce it for the dower.[81]

With these documents confirmed, the nuptials that were probably delayed from Monday to Tuesday were back on track, and Chapter 7 begins with this ceremony. About the events that had transpired in England since New Year's Day 1540 at Rochester, the comments of William Thomas, who defended the life and actions of Henry in 1546, seem appropriate: "Universally in all things I do find one singular and perfect rule, which is this, that the outward appearance is always preferred before the inward existence, and that most commonly do all things otherwise appear to be than as they are indeed." Thomas, who may never actually have seen Anne of Cleves, also claimed that "the king loved this woman out of measure: for why? her personage, her beauty, and gesture did no less merit it."[82]

7 QUEEN CONSORT

Although the exact hour on which it occurred was not recorded, a notarial instrument was signed on Henry's wedding day in the presence chamber, his ceremonial room that was situated on the north side of the palace. As it is likely that an official meeting such as this would have been scheduled early that morning rather than in the afternoon after the marriage, he had probably instructed his councillors to gather there before 7:00 a.m. to witness the signing by Hochsteden and Olisleger on behalf of William of Cleves of a document in which they acknowledged that Henry was an orthodox Catholic whom the papacy had treated unjustly. By requiring this sworn statement, he was denying through them to their ruler and his allies that the union with Anne would lead to the spread of further religious reform in England. Audley, Norfolk, Suffolk, Cromwell, Southampton, Sussex, Russell, Tunstall, Sir William Kingston, comptroller of the household, and John Godsalve, clerk of the signet, witnessed the instrument. Cranmer was not present perhaps because he was preparing for the nuptial ceremony at which he was to officiate.[1]

At 8:00 a.m., according to Hall, the king and his gentlemen entered the gallery next to his closet where the wedding was to occur. He was attired in a rich gown of cloth of gold decorated with silver flowers and black fur and in a satin coat tied with large diamonds.[2] As he was being dressed for the service, Cromwell later remembered, the king had been called upon to settle some last minute confusion about Anne's escort. It had been determined that Henry Bourchier, earl of Essex, would fulfill this duty, but when he failed to appear in a timely manner, the king appointed Cromwell as his replacement, but why he was selected is not clear. Henry may have turned to Cromwell, a baron since 1536, because he had already decided to grant him the earldom of Essex at the demise of the present aged lord, who had no legitimate male child and whom an Italian diplomat had two years earlier described as "an old man, of little wit and less experience, without power." In addition, as lord privy seal, Cromwell held a place superior to that of an earl in ceremonial functions such as this. Shortly after he reached Anne's chamber, however, Essex arrived, permitting Cromwell to return to Henry, who exclaimed, "My lord, if it were not to satisfy the world and my realm, I would not do that I must do this day for none earthly thing."[3]

In the meantime, Anne's ladies were dressing her for the ceremony. It was only in the nineteenth century following the marriage of Victoria to Albert that white became inextricably linked to the bride's wedding dress. For her attire Anne chose a splendid gown of cloth of gold embroidered with flowers in pearl without a train in the German fashion. Around her waist was clasped a belt with rich gems and around her neck a jeweled collar. As was usual for first weddings, her long hair, which was blonde, trailed down her back. From the fourteenth to the seventeenth century brides arranged their hair in this style to signal their virginity.[4] On Anne's head, around a coronal of gold and precious stones, was entwined a garland of rosemary branches that symbolized remembrance and constancy. Although rosemary, an evergreen shrub of the mint family, was often carried or strewn on the ground at English weddings, Anne is the only identifiable royal bride in the kingdom who wore a garland of it on her head, a practice she introduced from her native land. The garland also symbolized her maidenhood.[5]

In his journal Olisleger related that Anne's attendants were Lord Wirich of Dhun, count of Falkenstein and Leimburg and lord of Overstein, who represented Cleves, and John a Dolzig, who represented Saxony. The duty of the tardy Essex was to lead the queen's procession to the appropriate room in the palace. As it was also an English tradition that two bachelors should accompany a bride to her wedding, it is possible that the king selected the widowed Essex for this task because one of her two German escorts was still married. If this suggestion is correct, then that Cromwell was also a widower may have been another reason for the king to turn to him as Essex's replacement. Hall, who mistakenly identified Hochsteden, rather than Dolzig, as her second male attendant, said that Anne entered the gallery "with most demure countenance and sad behavior" and curtsied before the king who positioned himself to her right.[6] Cranmer probably used the Sarum Rite for the service, since it was the one on which he later based the liturgy for the Edwardian Prayer Books; he also used it for Katherine Parr's wedding in 1543. Compiled between the late twelfth and early thirteenth century, the Sarum Use was, as Kenneth Stevenson has pointed out, the "richest expression of marriage in vernacular devotion."[7]

Before he began the ritual the archbishop had first to inquire whether they were at liberty to wed. Olisleger put in his journal a detailed version of Cranmer's words. He first asked the king and then the queen if either had come to this solemn occasion with deceitful intentions, to which inquiry both in turn openly and freely replied, "No." Then he warned them in the name of the Father, the Son, and the Holy Ghost that if they knew of any impediment to their union, they should immediately identify it. Both in turn answered openly and freely that they knew of none. Next, Cranmer turned to the gentlemen and ladies who had gathered to witness the ceremony and warned them in the name of the Father, the Son, and the Holy Ghost that if they knew of any legal obstacle to the wedding, they should immediately reveal their information. They answered unanimously that they knew of none. When on the infrequent occasion someone at the wedding alleged an impediment, it was usually the existence of a previous indissoluble marriage. To counter any claims that Anne was already married, Henry may have already provided Cranmer with a copy of her sworn statement that she was at liberty to wed and of Hochsteden's and Olisleger's notarial record that the contract into which she had entered in her minority had been revoked. The licenses to waive the usual banns and to hold the service on a forbidden day, in this case, a feast day, which Cranmer, as archbishop, had surely issued, were normally read before the vows were said. Next, the couple was asked to affirm their consent to the union: "Wilt thou have this woman. . . ?" and "Wilt thou have this man. . . ?" When their consent was established, the nuptials could begin.[8]

On behalf of her family, Overstein initiated this familiar sequence by delivering Anne to the king,[9] who following protocol would have held her right hand in his right hand and pledged his troth in the present tense: "I, Henry take thee, Anne, to my wedded wife. . . ." After the withdrawal of his hand, she would have taken it and repeated: "I, Anne take thee, Henry to my wedded husband. . . ." Upon the release of his hand, he would have placed on the priest's book gold and silver coins that were thought to signify the inner love that would always exist between them, and a ring, which, Hall reported, was engraved with the words, "God send me well to keep." If the ring, which Olisleger described as golden with a very precious stone, had not previously been blessed, it was then blessed. Either way, Cranmer returned it to the groom who by tradition would have taken it with the three main fingers of his right hand and, saying the appropriate words, put it initially on the first finger or thumb, then on the second, next on the third, and finally on the fourth finger of the left hand, which it was believed had a blood vein that ran directly to the heart. Following this exchange and before the recital of the appropriate psalm, Cranmer blessed the bride and groom, wished them a fertile union, and pronounced them man and wife. He also blessed those gathered in attendance with wishes of peace and prosperity.[10]

After prayers were said, the king and queen went "hand in hand" into his closet to hear the Mass of the Trinity. Since it was not Henry's first marriage, the canopy or care-cloth that four ecclesiastics usually held over the heads of the bride and groom was probably omitted. Before communion, Cranmer turned to the altar, said the *Agnus Dei* and then the *Pax Domini*. As was customary in the English ritual, he would have given the kiss of peace to the queen on the cheek. Following this sequence of events, Olisleger recalled, the king kissed and embraced her. After receiving the Eucharist, Hall reported that the married couple "offered their tapers" and then partook of wine and spices," the customary wedding refreshment. Gilbert Dethick, Hammes pursuivant, later received 53 shillings, 4 pence for proclaiming the queen's title and style.[11]

After the ceremony, as the king returned to his privy chamber, Suffolk and Norfolk, two married men as tradition required,[12] escorted Anne to her privy chamber, her ladies trailing along behind them. Sometime after 9:00 a.m. Henry entered his closet dressed in embroidered crimson velvet, and she came to hers in her wedding apparel. Together they walked in procession to the traditional wedding feast, where they sat together under a cloth of state as was customary. After the completion of the meal, which was held to celebrate the alliance of their two families, Hall, who did not stipulate how long it lasted, recorded that they returned to their privy chambers where she changed into a gown that was furred with sables and a cap with a coronet rich in pearls and stones. With her ladies, who were similarly dressed, she attended evensong, probably because the wedding was held on the Epiphany. Otherwise, the custom was to spend the time between the wedding feast and supper in dance and song. Following the service, she supped with the king after which banquets, masks, and other festive events were held.[13]

This chapter examines the events following the nuptials that were to culminate in Henry's divorce from Anne, and in Cromwell's execution. The wedding entertainment, the king's failure to consummate the marriage, issues concerning the queen's household and attendants, renewed Anglo-French initiatives, information about the new Cleves ambassador and the Lorraine contract are then investigated. The chapter concludes with Anne's removal to Richmond.

In listing the amusements provided for the married couple on the evening of their wedding, Hall mentioned masks but did not specify which kind, a vagueness that supports Sydney Anglo's claim about the "fluidity" of terms with which writers referred to entertainment. The words, masks and disguisings, were used interchangeably for quite different activities. Before 1528 abundant evidence exists, especially on Twelfth Night, of disguisings or elaborate pageants, usually mock sieges, in which disguised knights attacked a fortress that housed ladies who ended the battle by surrendering and dancing with their conquerors. This pageantry, which required transporting scenery on wagons into court, was introduced into England in 1501 for the wedding of Catherine and Arthur. It was an adaptation of long used Italian and Burgundian revelry. Although English disguising had previously signaled elaborately costumed dances performed by members of the royal household, pageantry itself was not new to the realm, for it had been included in civic entries and celebrations since the end of the thirteenth century.[14] The other kind of mask was much less elaborate, for it simply involved gentlemen, often numbering Henry, leaving a banquet and returning in disguise to dance with the ladies.[15]

After 1528 little detail has survived about disguisings. This omission may be the result of the accidental destruction of evidence, but it seems more likely to indicate a "waning interest," as Anglo has suggested, "in lavish spectacle for its own sake." The expense of producing the sieges must also have led to their decline. Like every-thing else about Anne's wedding, a smaller scale then Catherine of Aragon's was the order of the day. The masks at the festivities in 1540 probably involved only disguised gentlemen entering after supper to initiate dancing with the ladies. If Henry participated in them, Hall did not make reference to him.[16]

In the early Stuart period elaborate disguisings called masques in which members of the royal family acted and danced, became popular but also grew increasingly expensive to orchestrate. The Civil Wars put an end to them, for Charles and Henrietta Maria per-formed in their last one in 1640.[17] After the Restoration, their heir Charles II essentially chose not to revive them although one was pro-duced in 1674. Going abroad in disguise also remained popular in his reign, but he banned this practice in 1671 after two of his natural sons, who were returning from a party incognito, killed a watch-man.[18]

Considering that Anne was a foreign-born bride, the festivities accompanying her wedding were remarkably slight. Except for the amusements on Tuesday evening, no other entertainment was held before the jousts on the following Sunday, unless Hall failed to recount some of the events. Usually the celebrations, which included banquets, dancing, songs, outdoor sports, and other kinds of merri-ment, lasted for several days. Providing entertainment at weddings was an old tradition in Christendom, for when Constance, daughter of William the Conqueror, married Alan, duke of Brittany, for example, six days of marriage feasts had ensued. In 1501 the festiv-ities for Catherine had lasted for more than a week, and in 1537 the revelry for James and Madeleine had endured for a fortnight. These grand celebrations continued into the seventeenth century, for in 1613 when Elizabeth Stuart married Frederick of Palatine, non-stop masques, torchlight processions and martial games were held over the course of a week even though the court was officially in mourn-ing because of her brother Henry's recent demise.[19]

It is unlikely that in 1540 Henry curtailed events because of his disappointment with Anne. The original decision to hold the wedding at Greenwich was surely intended to keep down costs and the number of activities honoring the day. In addition to the concern about expenses, the religious factor loomed large in the decisions about the festivities. From the day on which his marriage contract was signed, Henry knew full well that Anne was due to arrive some time between Advent and Epiphany, a period in which the Church, as explained in Chapter 6, forbade marriages. To complicate matters further the delay caused by the request of the Cleves ambassadors for time to prepare their report about the Lorraine contract meant that the wedding actually fell on a feast day, the Epiphany. Cranmer undoubtedly issued them a license to dispense with the ban of wedlock on a feast day and during a forbidden period. Usually, however, prolonged celebrations did not accompany the ceremony. Thus, their festivities, except for the traditional wedding feast, were those typically held in honor of the Epiphany.[20]

Following the entertainment, if the usual custom was followed, Anne's ladies undressed her and put her to bed. The groom then arrived, was undressed by his attendants, and lay down beside her. The Sarum Use provides for the officiating priest to enter the chamber and bless the bed, an old fertility rite that the Church had long embraced. One of his blessings includes the words, "watch over your servants as they sleep in this bed, protecting them from all demonic dreams." Finally, the priest concluded his efforts to exorcise them from the dangers of impotence and infertility by sanctifying and sprinkling them with holy water.[21]

Ribald curiosity governed this night, as Brantôme explained, "when everybody was eavesdropping, as is the custom."[22] This scrutiny amounted to more than mere prurience, for it was important to the completion of diplomatic agreements for witnesses to confirm that a marriage with a foreign-born spouse had been consummated and was, therefore, indisputably concluded. In all royal marriages, of course, the couple's sexual union had important legal and financial ramifications and also signaled the possibility of a pregnancy that would result in progeny.[23] Sometimes interested parties could be quite intrusive. In 1469 after Isabella and Ferdinand were bedded down, witnesses, probably notaries who were stationed at the chamber door entered at the appropriate moment and took the bed-sheet which amidst the blaring of musical instruments was displayed to the assembled courtiers.[24]

An intense interest in confirming the completion of the marriage continued throughout this period. In 1538 when Paul learned that the alliance of his grandson, Octavio Farnese, future duke of Parma, with the heretofore reluctant Margaret, natural daughter of Charles

V, had been consummated, he gratefully rewarded her with some jewelry. In 1613 when James I quizzed his Elizabeth and Frederick in their bedchamber about their wedding night together, he learned to his satisfaction that their marriage had been consummated.[25] Sometimes the grooms boasted of their prowess: In 1468 Galeazzo Maria of Milan informed Louis XI about the consummation of his marriage to Bona of Savoy, and in 1514 on the morning after his wedding to Mary Tudor, Louis XII bragged that he had "crossed the river" thrice that night. Not bashful about his conquests, Charles II made it clear to his ministers in 1662 that he was satisfied with the results of his first evening with Catherine of Braganza.[26]

No extant record indicates just how much eavesdropping English royal couples had to expect on their wedding night. It is clear from the evidence presented in 1529 at the Legatine inquiry into whether Catherine was a virgin when she married Henry that heralds normally stood watch near the bedchamber door. Two of them, Thomas Wriothesley, garter king of arms, and Thomas Tong, Norroy king of arms, gave testimony to the legates' court about her nuptial evening with Arthur. The stationing of notaries nearby to confirm the consummation, as occurred at Isabella's and Ferdinand's wedding, seems not to have been an English practice, although it was later alleged that the bloody sheet of Catherine and Arthur was sent to her parents. It is also known that on his wedding night with Henrietta Maria, Charles demanded privacy. When he reached the chamber where she awaited him, he bolted the doors, all seven of them. After his two attendants undressed him, he locked them out, too.[27]

Anyone who attempted to eavesdrop outside Henry's bedchamber on the night of his nuptials may not have heard anything interesting to report. According to the July testimony of Dr. William Butts, the king had decided not to consummate the marriage on that feast night, although on the third and fourth nights, he attempted sexual union but unsuccessfully. The doctor's information seems to contradict the recollections of Cromwell who remembered speaking to the king about his feelings toward Anne the morning after their wedding night: "The morrow after his majesty was married as it pleased his highness to talk with him of his affairs and weighty matters he asked his grace whether he liked her any better than afore." In his response, Henry did not specifically state that he had suffered sexual dysfunction, although he did admit that "his nature hath abhorred her." It is possible that, as the doctor testified, the king had delayed attempting consummation of the marriage until the third night, but that despite this voluntary abstinence he had learned enough about her physical features to assert, as Cromwell recalled, that he found them offensive. Given his disenchantment with his bride, it might be tempting to argue that he delayed attempting sexual union for personal reasons, but as he wished to follow marriage law and tradition scrupulously in order to beget a normal male child, he had good reason for waiting until the third night after his wedding. First, he was married to Anne on the Epiphany, a feast day, when it was popularly believed if conception occurred the resulting offspring would be lepers, epileptics, or possessed by the devil. Secondly, a tradition extending back to Pope Gregory I, which was hardly ever observed, held that consummation should be postponed from one to three days after the wedding to dispel any notion that the couple had begun their sexual relations with lustful intentions.[28]

In pre-modern society, sexuality, as Mercea Eliade points out, "like all functions of life" was "fraught with sacredness." Clerics warned spouses not to approach the marriage bed enraged with "boiling lusts" but to "sanctify" it "with prayer" in order to make themselves ready for the holy duty of increasing God's children.[29] Ministers of all Christian persuasions from the medieval through the early modern period expressed a similar attitude toward human sexuality.[30] Infertile women hoping for conception went to great lengths to appease God. In the late fifteenth century Anne of Brittany, wife of Charles VIII, went on a pilgrimage to Plessis-les-Tours, the retreat of St. Francis de Paule, a holy man whose prayers were said to ensure that barren women would have children. Not only did Henry and Catherine of Aragon complete pilgrimages to the shrine of Our Lady of Walsingham, but the queen also wore the coarse habit of the third order of St. Francis under her clothing. Later, Dorothea, wife of the count palatine, imitated his mother in going on pilgrimages and wearing holy girdles in hopes of conceiving. By the end of the seventeenth century, however, some infertile wives, like Catherine of Braganza, were also seeking natural cures at health spas.[31]

The view that God would personally intervene to make childbirth possible for pious women and men permeated society: It was expressed in romance literature as well as in religious works. In *The*

Romance of Sir Tryamoure, a fifteenth-century text, can be found the following stanza:

> Therefore the king, as I understand
> Hath made a vow to go into the Holy Land,
>   To fight and not to flee,
> That God Almighty should help them so
> A child to get between them two,
>   That their heir might be.
> When the king his vow had made,
> And at the Pope the Cross taked,
>   To bed them were they brought;
> That night on his lady mild
> As God would, he gat a child,
>   But they of it wist nought.[32]

Henry had seemed to echo the sentiment of this poet in his 1519 letter to Pope Leo X in which he discussed going on a crusade: "If our longed-for heir shall have been granted before the expedition sets out to do battle with the Infidel, we will lead our force in person."[33]

It is difficult to believe that once he attempted consummation Henry, given his reluctance to put on the "yoke," would have elaborated about his experiences, even had they been successful. Clearly an old pro in handling the sexual innuendoes of his courtiers, he must have, in fact, made gestures or comments that led them to believe the marriage had been consummated, for few were aware of his impotency in January. Indeed, he may have at first admitted the problem only to Cromwell who recalled his comment that after he had "felt" her "breasts and belly," he concluded she was not a "maid," and asserted, "if she brought maidenhead with her" to England, he had not deprived her of it. In one or two conversations that took place after Candlemas (2 February) and before Shrovetide (10 February), he also confessed that he had continued to lie with her nightly or every second night but without success. During Lent, Henry probably rigorously obeyed the church's ban on intercourse on holy days for he would have welcomed a respite from his attempts to pay the marital debt. After Easter (28 March) he seems to have resumed those efforts, for, as he admitted to Cromwell, he had tried to make his heart consent to sexual union but an "obstacle" had prevented him from performing the act. It was about Whitsuntide (16

May) that his attendants generally began to learn of his marital woes.[34]

It is possible that, besides Henry and Anne, only Cromwell and the two doctors knew the truth for the first eight days or so after the wedding. Southampton recalled in June, that on 14 January Cromwell had revealed the problem to him, but Henry himself had not discussed it with him until shortly before Easter. The only other deponents in the divorce trial who admitted to having had knowledge of his impotency were two members of the privy chamber. Denny affirmed that he had known about it since a little before Lent when Henry had complained to him that her breasts were slack, and Heneage swore that he had been aware that the king mistrusted her virginity and had been incapable of completing the marriage with her but did not specify when he had learned of these matters. It is interesting that Henry did not reveal his impotency to Browne and Russell, the two members of his privy chamber whose intimacy with him was such that they could testify in July that they had known he was unhappy with Anne from the Rochester meeting. That at least from 9 January Henry lay regularly with Anne masked the reality of their married life. He would not have had to suffer through a whole night with her, for monarchs did not always literally sleep with their consorts. A visit of an hour or two every second night or so would have provided sufficient evidence for most of their attendants to assume they were having marital relations.[35]

Cromwell also revealed the couple's difficult relationship to one more individual, the earl of Rutland, Anne's lord chamberlain, but it is unclear exactly what the nature of the comments were or even when the discussion between them took place. In a letter to the king on 12 June, the recently imprisoned Cromwell remembered that after her unfulfilled evenings with Henry, Anne had often tried to speak with him about their problems but that he had "durst not." When he had finally revealed these wifely pleas for assistance to Henry, the king had responded that it might help matters if Cromwell conversed frankly with her. But because he had lacked, as he alleged, an opportunity to initiate this conversation, Cromwell had delegated to her lord chamberlain the duty of encouraging her to behave more pleasantly toward her husband. His recommendation arose from the contemporary notion that a woman must act in an attractive or receptive manner for a man to respond to her physically. Cromwell did not indicate that he mentioned the king's actual incapacity to Rutland, who may or may not have spoken to the queen about her wifely behavior. Since the union remained unconsummated, Cromwell admitted he had repeated his advice to the lord chamberlain when he and her other councillors came to Westminister in late May to request licenses for the departure of her maidens to Cleves. It was not unusual for a monarch to accept assistance such as this from his trusted councillors in dealing with a foreign-born bride. In 1625, for example, when Charles experienced difficulty in his relations with Henrietta Maria, he turned to George, duke of Buckingham, for advice.[36]

Henry's problem was, as he had articulated it to Cromwell in January, that when he had the opportunity to feel her physical features, her breasts and belly, he had confirmed the fears that had worried him since their Rochester meeting. He was persuaded that she was legally a married woman and therefore by his way of thinking no longer a maiden. Even though William Thomas could warn in his study of the king that outward appearances often cloaked the reality of the inner person, his contemporaries, as he also lamented, generally believed that outward attributes did actually reveal the inner condition.[37] The Catholic description of Anne Boleyn as a witch, Sir Thomas More's portrait of Richard III as a Satanic hunchback, John Ponet's depiction of Winchester as a demonic creature are examples of this mind-set. Henry's references to Anne's body, although not so problematic as those descriptions, belong to that cultural bias.[38]

Besides the loss of her hymen, a maiden was thought to be physically different from a married woman in other ways. Brantôme, whose opinion seems to have echoed Henry's, defined a virgin as one with a smooth belly and tiny erect breasts. Some writers claimed that the "clear and sparkling" urine of maidens was transformed into a muddy color after sperm corrupted her body. In 1905 Martin Hume criticized Henry's "incredible grossness" in complaining about the looseness of Anne's belly and the slackness of her breasts, but they were the physical evidence, which the king and his attendants quickly understood: they were proof that she had failed to bring her maidenhead with her to England. She was not his lawful wife but the spouse of the heir of Lorraine.[39]

Early modern Christians did not recognize the psychological

dimension of impotency as it is understood today. Their theories on the cause of male incapacity, which were drawn in part from witchcraft lore, will be explained in Chapter 8, for as W. H. Trethowan has pointed out, it was not until the late nineteenth century that the "medio-psychological nature" of impotency was understood. Given Henry's complaints about Anne's appearance and his doubts that she brought her maidenhead to England, it seems likely that he was unable to consummate the marriage for "psychogenic" or "inhibitory" reasons, as explained by Vern Bullough and Bonnie Bullough, that is, because of his suspicion, even fear, that she was someone else's lawful wife. After all, as Henry had anticipated, Cranmer had warned him in the wedding ceremony in the name of the Father, the Son, and the Holy Ghost, to confess if he knew of any impediments to the marriage with Anne; although the king had feared she was already married, he had permitted the service to be held for diplomatic reasons. After the exchange of vows, which must have struck him as a deceitful act, he attended mass and partook of the Holy Sacrament of the Altar without the benefit of confession. In early modern society, according to Mark Breitenberg, there also existed a "pervasive masculine anxiety toward female chastity and women's sexuality in general." One of the commonest forms of psychosexual impotence was the incest taboo, the fear that the spouse was actually a mother or a sister. The cause of Henry's incapacity was similar to that of the incest taboo, for it can be surmised that his anxiety about Anne's legal right to be his wife was particularly intense because of his deep desire about obeying the letter of God's laws concerning matrimony. Clerics and scholars had consistently argued that marriage was a special sacrament because God had personally bestowed it upon humanity; that it was a direct divine gift set it apart from the other sacraments that had been presented through the agency of lesser beings. Henry had the "dogged conviction," as Eric Carlson has observed, that if he played by God's rules he would succeed in his goals, that is, if he obeyed the strictures of marital law, as expressed in the Bible and in the ecclesiastical code, God would bless him with male children. The problem, the king had concluded, lay not in the sacred corpus of law but in his failure or the failure of his wives, with the exception of Queen Jane, of course, to comply with it faithfully.[40]

Even though Henry and Anne were struggling with their sexual relationship in private, they appeared as a contented couple in public. On the morning after the wedding, Anne's demeanor persuaded Olisleger that she was delighted with her husband and pleased with the traditional *morgengabe*. He had presented her with lavish and expensive gifts: precious belts, pearl rings, and beautiful dresses. In his last letter to Cleves before he departed on 19 January, Olisleger continued to comment on their harmonious life together. In the meantime, members of the king's household, who mostly did not know about this great disparity between the private and public lives of their monarch, were completing arrangements for the jousts that were to be held on Sunday, 11 January. Because of the restrictions of canon law, the king had probably decided to delay the games until a few days after the Epiphany wedding in order to distinguish them from the necessarily limited marriage celebrations. It was not an unusual time for scheduling the competitions, since in previous years the court had held them in early January. Even so, since the thirteenth century, when women had first appeared at them as spectators, tournaments had often been associated with wedding festivities. Women's attendance at the games soon led their producers to introduce into them pageantry, music, and disguises in imitation of romance literature. Indeed, the immense popularity of the chivalric tales, in which tournaments were depicted as romantic interludes, had played a major factor in taming their brutal eleventh-century structure when they were melees with two opposing groups of as many as 200 men fighting against each other across country over several miles of territory.[41]

In time the games had come to play a role in marking the center of royal authority, as Clifford Geertz has explained, for they expressed in festival form the status of the monarch as liege lord and as the source of political power.[42] They had also become more diversified in their organization, for the melees had begun to give way in the thirteenth century to jousts in which two mounted warriors rode at each other with rebated lances. In the early fourteenth century, a tilt or barrier was put in place to prevent the horses from crashing into each other. Coexisting with these jousts were tourneys in which groups of mounted knights, usually armed with swords, competed against each other, but in a confined area rather than in a wide-ranging territory; by the Tudor period, they consisted of knights fighting in single combat with swords or other weapons. The barriers, the third kind of martial game that Anne witnessed while queen, provided for foot combat in which warriors fought, either singly or in groups, with swords or long staves over a waist-high wooden barrier that sometimes was situated indoors. The pageantry of these martial sports, often referred to generically as tournaments, had by the Elizabethan period assumed as much, if not more importance, than the mock battles themselves.[43]

The Sunday jousts, according to Hall, pleased Anne's countrymen greatly. The noise at these events could be deafening. Besides the blaring of music, heralds rode on the field calling out messages and signaling scores and faults. The shouting of spectators and the ringing of blows also accompanied the thunder of horses' hoofs racing down the lists.[44] It was probably because jousts offered an individual knight opportunities to be praised by spectators for his heroic feats, that they emerged as the most popular of the war games. Between 1485 and 1640 in England, well over 140 of them were held, 8 of which accompanied royal and noble marriages. A substantial reason for this popularity was that they emerged as the principal event in Elizabeth's accession day festivities. After Charles I abandoned these tournaments, his descendants failed to revive them, probably because they were expensive to produce but also because they were no longer fashionable.[45]

Their inherent danger had made them lose favor earlier in France than in other parts of Christendom. In 1559, to honor his daughter Elizabeth's marriage to Philip II of Spain, Henry II participated in a joust in which a splintered lance penetrated his visor and killed him. His widow Catherine de Medici subsequently forbade these games at court. By the reign of Louis XIV, the tournament had dwindled to the horse ballet, described by George Kernodle and Portia Kernodle as "an elaborate figured military parade," and to the carousel, "a ball game somewhat like polo . . . the knights of the new age strutted and danced their horses about the field."[46]

In the meantime, matters concerning Anne's countrymen who were preparing to leave England and other arrangements for her household still required the crown's attention. According to Hall, when the Germans had been "highly feasted . . . very sumptuously," they took their leave but not before they had received "great gifts," both "plate and money." Actually, as noted above, Hochsteden and Olisleger did not leave for home until 19 January, eight days after the jousts. On 12 January, a few days before their departure, Cromwell, as well as other royal councillors, had met at his London house with some of the Cleves lords, the duke of Bavaria, the vice-chancellor of Saxony, and Ludwig von Baumbach, the ambassador of the land-grave of Hesse. Cromwell may have wanted to engage in follow-up conversations with Olisleger and Hochsteden about their promise to forward to England within three months official copies of the con-tract and treaty of 1527, a copy of the document repudiating these agreements, and a signed copy of the new Anglo-Cleves defensive treaty that prevented them from entering into a separate alliance with Francis, Charles, or Paul. Their failure to bring a ratified copy of this covenant with them may have been the reason that the indig-nant king decided to insist on another article that would bind England and Cleves even more closely in commercial and military matters. He wanted guarantees, for example, that if William decided to wage war against the emperor over Guelders that the duke would agree first to reveal his plans to his English ally who might be drawn into the conflict. Cromwell also discussed with them the possibility of William's marriage to Christina of Milan. With both the Saxony and Hesse diplomats in attendance, England's religious stance was also a topic on the agenda, for the king was still hoping to persuade the temporal electors to enter into the Anglo-Cleves alliance that would shortly be concluded. Cromwell once again hinted that the next par-liament might amend the Six Articles, which, of course, the king alone could not do. The lord privy seal also invited them to send Melancthon and other theologians to England to discuss the relig-ious issues under dispute. Henry and his advisors were walking on a diplomatic tight rope between the Germans who were pushing for further doctrinal reform and the Hapsburg and Valois monarchs who feared his conversion to Lutheranism. Inevitably, the marriage had caused questions to be raised abroad about the orthodoxy of his faith. From the Imperial court on 7 January, Wyatt had brought Henry up to date about his audience with Charles in which the dip-lomat had emphasized that the only change the king, who was con-tinuing to punish sacramentarians and anabaptists vigilantly, had made in his religious establishment was the expulsion of the bishop of Rome's authority. The emperor's response had been that papal power "touches our faith."[47]

The next month, on 24 February, John Butler, an Englishman living at Strasburg, wrote confidently to Henry Bullinger that the state of religion in his homeland had become much more secure since Henry's marriage to Anne, a "pious woman by whom it is hoped the Gospel will be diffused." One month later, on 29 March, he lamented to Bullinger that the state of the faith was the same but that he still hoped for further reformation.[48]

Before Olisleger departed for Cleves, he had tried to assist the Lisle family in obtaining an appointment for their daughter Katherine as a maiden of honor. On the same day as the wedding, Olisleger informed Lord Lisle that when he had spoken with the queen's "goodwill" to both Cromwell and Henry, he had learned that all the maids had been appointed and that no exception would be made for any lady. Major changes had recently occurred in the privy chamber. The queen's household records indicate that of the three girls who were each paid 50 shillings as maidens of honor at the Christmas quarter, only two remained to serve her, one of whom was Anne Basset. Sometime, perhaps by late December, another four were chosen, among them Katherine Howard, the daughter of Norfolk's brother Lord Edmund and Joyce Culpepper.[49]

Lady Lisle was not easily put off. She quizzed John Norris, one of the king's gentleman ushers, about Anne's household, and she wrote to her daughter Katherine, who was residing with her stepfather's cousin the countess of Rutland, an attendant of the queen, to discover who might be able to influence these appointments. She also admonished her daughter Anne to assist her sister in gaining this post. Both Katherine and Lady Rutland suggested that Lady Lisle contact Mother Lowe, the supervisor of the queen's German maids. The reason to press for these positions was clearly evident in Anne Basset's response to another inquiry from home. She assured her mother that she had spoken about Katherine to the king, who responded that Bryan and others had also been recommending their friends to him for this position. Henry indicated a reluctance to make any more appointments until some of the present maidens had been preferred elsewhere, and he also wanted to be certain that the selected lady was "fair" and "meet for the room." Anne reported that although he was grateful for her mother's gift of codiniac, it had not been a propitious time to speak to him about Lord Lisle's business. Obtaining positions for her daughters that made it possible for them to approach Henry directly was thought to be, and could be, a distinct advantage in resolving the family's various problems.[50]

Obviously, word had not leaked out beyond the king's most trusted advisors about his marital problems. Except to inform Southampton and Rutland, Cromwell seems wisely to have kept the matter a secret from everyone else. On 15 January Vaughan, who had returned to Brussels, wrote that he had received Cromwell's message about the royal marriage and that he was glad the lord privy seal had found "his judgment true of the queen." On 18 January, Henry himself kept up the subterfuge in a letter to Anne's brother in which he promised to act sincerely concerning their friendship and the marriage. This message may have been carried by Wotton who arrived at Cleves on 9 February with letters from the royal couple for William and one from Anne for her mother. Either lying for his country, as his grandnephew Henry was later to characterize his oratory, or, more likely, left unaware of the king's incapacity, Wotton also reported to the chancellor of Cleves how well Henry admired his queen. In a March letter to the king, Wyatt was able to gloat about Henry's fortunate escape from marriage to Christina, who, it was rumored, had developed a great affection for the prince of Orange, and the next month Wyatt not only revealed to the king the pleased reaction of the emperor when he learned about England's joyous welcome of Anne but also the little joke he had cracked about Henry's lust. Later that month, Margaret of Navarre requested portraits of several members of the English royal family, including one of Anne.[51]

For her part, the queen had not informed her German attendants of her secret, for Lady Keteler, who departed for home on 19 January with a £100 reward, forwarded Anne's words of gratitude to her mother and her brother, thanking them for arranging her marriage to Henry, for "none other," she had said, "would content her mind so well." In early March her brother-in-law of Saxony, reported to the king that he had learned from his councillors that the union was "joyful and prosperous which we desire God to bless and fortunately to continue." As late as 16 May no word seems to have leaked to Cleves about the king's impotency. On that day Hochsteden sent a message to Christopher Mont who was then stationed at Cologne, requesting assistance for his two nephews who were residing in England, one with the king and the other with Cromwell.[52]

Although many of her countrymen departed for Cleves in January, some, including her young cousin Francis of Waldeck,

stayed behind to provide company for her, until, as Hall sympa-
thized, she could become "better acquainted" with her new subjects.
At Antwerp, Wotton had counted eighty-eight people who planned
to reside with the queen, a rather large German infusion, considering that many of her English subjects had also won appointments to
serve her. The two groups combined together made, according to
John Norris, a great court "as ever I think was seen in our master's
days." The increase in her household wages from £108 at Christmas
to £376 at the Annunciation attest to the costs of this expansion in
numbers.[53]

The foreigners could be a source of controversy because they were
expensive to support, might act as their rulers' partisans, and could
interfere in spousal relationships. Some of Anne's ladies surely also
had hopes of finding noble spouses, as had two of Catherine of
Aragon's maids, Inez de Venegas and Maria de Salinas who wed
William, Lord Mountjoy, and William Willoughby de Eresby, respectively.[54] Often princes exasperated by the presence of so many strangers peremptorily sent them home, thereby greatly distressing their
brides. In 1514 Mary Tudor reacted with anger when Louis XII sent
packing all her English ladies, except six maidens. In 1626, citing the
example of Louis XIII, brother of Henrietta Maria who had expelled
the Spanish servants of his wife, Charles I forced his consort's attendants to return home because he believed they were the cause of her
"unkindness" to him. He allowed her only a Scottish and an English
priest and three female servants who could speak French.[55]

Although the marriage of the dowry-less Anne of Cleves
remained unconsummated, some of her German attendants were
permitted to stay in the realm until late spring. No record of disputes
concerning them has survived nor of any Anglo-German marriages.
In early June William Paget, who was appointed to escort the queen's
gentlewomen to Düsseldorf, recorded the expenditure of royal funds
to defray those travel costs. He carried with him a letter from Henry
to Anne's mother dated 5 June in which he praised their faithful and
loyal service to his consort. A few days after the ladies arrived at
Cleves on 20 June, a far more speedy trip than their lengthy trek to
England in 1539, Henry rusticated Anne and was seen crossing the
Thames to visit with her maiden of honor.[56]

The meaning of one of the imprisoned Cromwell's comments
concerning the royal family is difficult to interpret. He recalled that

sometime during Lent the king had complained that Anne had been "stubborn and willful" about a matter concerning his daughter Mary. It is not known when Anne actually first met her older step-daughter, who was only five months her junior. The initial plans that had called for both of the princesses to participate in their step-mother's Blackheath reception had been cancelled. On 27 December, the day Anne sailed to England, Mary, who had not accompanied her father to Greenwich, was residing in a house in the gardens of Westminister Abbey. After the queen's reception, only Edward seems to have been present at court, for in a letter to Lady Lisle, John Norris claimed that the king, queen, and prince were "merry." Henry's dispute with Anne may have concerned his wish to invite Mary for a visit at Easter, one of the high holidays when she usually attended court. If so, etiquette required that he seek his consort's permission for Mary to reside in her quarters. In May 1541, Chapuys was later to note with pleasure, for example, that Queen Katherine Howard had "countenanced with good grace" the king's invitation to Mary to visit court. It is interesting that Henry seems to have waited ten months before requesting his fifth consort to welcome his daughter to court but that he had expected his fourth wife to entertain her only three months after their nuptials. If this had been Henry's request of Anne in 1540, as is likely because Mary was at Whitehall in April, why the queen was "stubborn and willful" about her presence cannot be known. Diplomatic considerations, as well as her unconsummated marriage, may have led Anne to want to reject as her companion her husband's illegitimate child who was also the first cousin of the emperor, her brother's enemy. Since Anne was not as yet fluent in English, the need to express her views to the king through an interpreter could also have caused some misunder-standing and confusion. Whatever was the reason for their dispute, Mary and Anne seem to have held no animosity toward each other. In December 1540, some five months before Katherine Howard was to welcome the princess to court, Chapuys had noted that Mary had not treated this queen with the same respect as she had her two pre-vious stepmothers (Anne of Cleves and Jane Seymour). In the privy purse expenditures of Mary in 1543, moreover, evidence can be found of her exchanges of messages and presents with Anne, and in March of that year the king licensed his ex-wife to visit the princess at court for three days.[57]

When the royal couple had this disagreement about Mary, they were at Whitehall Palace in Westminster. On 4 February, a week before the beginning of Lent, the king and queen, accompanied by many noblemen, had traveled to Westminister in six barges. He was stationed in the second of the three vessels that carried him and his servants, and following him, she was in the first of the next three that transported her and her train. A display on the Thames like the one produced for her Blackheath reception was repeated, except that on this day the lord mayor and other civic dignitaries also appeared in their customary barges, which flew banners and pennons and were, according to Hall, "replenished with minstrelsy." Men on the vessels shot off ordnance and the Tower of London's guns followed with a great peal. No pageants like those welcoming Anne Boleyn on her coronation voyage to Westminster in 1533 were in evidence, but Marillac, who had probably lacked a good view of the water spectacle during the January reception, still characterized it as a great triumph for Anne of Cleves and thought it a more honorable occasion than her Blackheath entry.[58]

The procession, even without pageants and triumphant arches, served the purpose, as did civic entries and tournaments generally, of displaying the king to his subjects as the source of political power. It was also, as Geertz has noted, a way of using ceremony to take "symbolic possession" of the realm. These public, celebratory progresses that the Tudors so carefully cultivated were to come to an end in the Stuart period, dwindling into nothing more than mere private hunting trips in the reign of Charles I.[59]

A few days after Henry and Anne traveled to Westminster, Norfolk left on a mission to France. As the highest ranking nobleman in the kingdom, the widower of Henry's aunt, Anne of York, the uncle of the late queen, Anne Boleyn, and father-in-law of the king's deceased natural son, the duke of Richmond, Norfolk commanded a special place in royal circles. As Godfrey Goodman, bishop of Gloucester, was later to say about his Howard descendants, "their ancestors . . . having much matched with the crown, they stood much upon the honor of their family."[60]

His departure has sometimes been interpreted as ushering in a period of security for Cromwell who at last had his "arch-enemy" out of the realm, as though somehow Henry's marital and domestic difficulties can be understood without reference to questions of foreign policy.[61] The deciding factor in the king's selection of Anne as his wife was the Franco-Imperial treaty that seemed to pose a grave threat to England's security. Early in 1539 the Flemish fleet cruising off the coast of Zeeland and Holland and some confused diplomatic exchanges with the queen regent and Francis had Henry persuaded that an invasion was imminent. In response to this fear, he had pressed William to agree to a marriage alliance, which he at first seemed reluctant to enter but which, as has been seen, he finally ratified in the autumn of 1539.[62]

Three months later, unable to pay the marital debt to Anne, Henry had to continue the farce of their marriage until he could be certain that a combined assault against him was not under way. The ruler from whom he could at first seek encouragement was Francis, who was less hostile about his union with Anne than Charles who viewed it as a threat to his authority in Germany. In addition, there was the lingering issue of Milan. Over one year after the Franco-Imperial treaty had been signed, Charles had still not relinquished the duchy to Francis, and Henry continued to hope that disputes over Milan might yet drive the two allies apart. To emphasize the importance of the mission, he appointed Norfolk, his uncle by marriage and the highest ranking nobleman in his kingdom. Even Marillac, who was unaware at first of Norfolk's identity, recognized that the mission was important because of the quality of the diplomat and his expensive mode of travel. It was not the duke's first trouble-shooting trip to France about Henry's marital problems: he had met with Francis in 1533 concerning the king's divorce from Catherine and his marriage to Anne Boleyn.[63]

A close examination of his instructions is useful because they relate to the greater diplomatic atmosphere in which the king wed Anne. In the tiered instructions, Henry requested Norfolk to "open his heart" to Francis. If the French monarch responded favorably to discussions about an English rebel, Robert Brancestor, an agent of Cardinal Pole who was then in the emperor's employ, and to the reported boast of Charles that he enjoyed a rank superior to that of all other rulers, then Norfolk should inquire about the status of the Franco-Imperial alliance and about the disposition of Milan. If after raising these topics, the king still seemed friendly, Norfolk should suggest the possibility of a new "amity" between Henry and him based on the remitting of a part or possibly all of the pension and debts he owed the English monarch. If the conversation remained pleasant, the duke could then inquire whether France would be interested in joining a pact with England, Cleves, and other German principalities, "not in *causa religionis* but for aid and defence," a mighty force that the emperor would find difficult to withstand. Obviously, Henry still clung to the futile hope that a by-product of the Cleves marriage would be an alliance with the Schmalkaldic League. Finally, if the French king

shall hereupon condescend to ensue this purpose, or otherwise show himself fast and assured to the king's majesty, then shall the said duke send hither in post advertisement of his proceeding . . . And, if on the other side, he shall see no likelihood of good success upon the opening of the first matters, neither upon some lights of the rest . . . he shall take his leave.[64]

In other words, Norfolk was to probe the depths of the Franco-Imperial friendship to ascertain whether a war against England was planned.

When he arrived at Abbeville on Saturday 15 February, he sent Hammes pursuivant to the constable to arrange an audience with Francis. The duke spent the rest of the day reading his instructions and learning the "news and fashions" from Bonner. Norfolk's subsequent arrival at court for the royal audience, which was scheduled almost immediately, began propitiously, for after greeting him, Jean de Humieres and Louis, count of Nevers, escorted him to lodgings set aside for him at court into which the bed of Jean de Guise, cardinal of Lorraine, one of the king's chief advisors, had been moved for his comfort. Montmorency had also arranged for a servant to attend to his personal needs. The appointment of someone of his rank as *ad hoc* ambassador had signaled to the French government the significance of his mission, and, to show their good will, they had responded quickly with an honorable welcome. In French circles, the duke was highly esteemed, for he was a member of the Order of St. Michael, the French equivalent of the Order of the Garter. He requested and was granted a private conversation with Francis because, as he informed de Humieres, he did not hear well, did not always understand the French tongue, and had a secret matter to impart to him. In addition, he spoke with several royal councillors and received a visit from Castillon, the former resident to England who had departed in such haste in 1539 but who was now "marvelous affectionate" toward

Henry. On Tuesday, after visiting with the king's sister, the queen of Navarre, Norfolk wrote two different letters to bring Henry up to date about his reception.[65]

In his first letter he expressed his belief that Francis was not dissembling when he protested his "love" for Henry and seemed aware that the emperor wished to keep the two rulers suspicious of each other. After raising the question of Milan, Norfolk thought he could tell by Francis's "countenance" that he was impatient with Charles's delays in deciding the duchy's future. His next letter described his hour-long meeting with the queen of Navarre; she had a special relationship with her brother whom she attended every morning upon his rising from bed. The duke thought she was "the most frank and wise woman" he had ever met. Since she loved Henry "so entirely," she had decided to provide information to the duke about her brother's servants. First, she warned him that the English should be careful about what they said to and about Montmorency, for he had great power at court. Marillac, she also revealed, was the constable's good friend. Next, she advised Norfolk to speak with Anne d'Heilly, dame de Pisseleu Estampes, the king's mistress. When the duke expressed surprise at this recommendation, she confessed that this lady's influence was such that even she had sought her aid. She ended the interview by stating that her brother had requested her to assure Norfolk that he loved Henry "my good brother, as well as he doth me."[66]

Why she was so eager to emphasize Montmorency's authority is puzzling, but it may have had something to do with Cromwell's handling of the Rochepot case. When Francis was later, in June, to learn of Cromwell's arrest, he revealed to Marillac that Norfolk would be able to remember their February discussion about the lord privy seal [*Et se pourra très bien souvenir mon cousin le duc de Norfolk de ce que je luy en diz quant il vint dernièrement per devers moy*]. During Norfolk's February visit it was far too early for any hint about Cromwell's fall to have surfaced in official or unofficial conversations. It seems more likely that both Francis and Montmorency, who were to express great joy when they learned about his arrest, had complained to the duke about Cromwell's decisions concerning a dispute that involved Francis de Montmorency, sieur de la Rochepot, the constable's brother, who claimed the *George*, a Hamburg ship that his men had captured on the high seas but that a storm had driven into English waters in 1537. It was probably because Rochepot had failed to regain the ship in English adjudication that the queen of Navarre went out of her way to caution Norfolk about her brother's great trust in the constable, who was still trying to obtain a change of venue to France for his brother's suit. While the duke was in France that February, Marillac, who believed that he, unlike Cromwell, would be sympathetic to Rochepot's designs, wrote to Montmorency recommending that he discuss the case with him. The queen's disclosures to Norfolk may have been an indirect means of getting word back to England and incidentally to Cromwell of Francis's strong support for the claims of the constable's brother.[67]

On 23 February the duke sent his last letter from France to Henry. By that time he had met with the king's mistress and for a second time with Francis and some of his important advisors, including his sister. This letter, in addition to two earlier ones written on 21 February, can be briefly summarized. In them he made three major points: (1) Francis was Henry's friend and was not preparing to go to war against him. (2) For the present he was content to maintain his realm's treaty with the emperor but he was concerned about the delays incurred in settling Milan's future. (3) For whatever reason, Bonner had made many enemies in France. Although Wallop had already been appointed to replace him, Norfolk still deemed it necessary to demand his recall with the explanation that bishops were not appropriate appointees to serve as French resident ambassadors, for Winchester had been "little better favored" there.[68]

After he reached home on 1 March, a lessening of tensions was so noticeable that Marillac could report to Francis that all war preparations had ceased. Shortly thereafter, Cromwell requested Wallop to forward the duke's thanks to the queen of Navarre for her great kindnesses to him. She had been continuing her campaign to reassure the English through their ambassador of her brother's friendship for Henry. On 29 March Wallop informed Cromwell of her conversation with his secretary in which she claimed she had defended the king's orthodoxy to the papal nuncio after he had labeled him a Lutheran. In the exchange she had insisted that Henry was punishing heretics who denied the "Sacrament of the Altar" and had suggested to the nuncio that his master ought to reform the habits of some of his own relatives who "do live so abominably in the sin of buggery."[69]

While the relations between France and England were improving, the duke of Cleves was continuing to move slowly concerning English matters. The first extant evidence of his intention to appoint an ambassador to the realm can be found in Wotton's correspondence with Henry and Cromwell. Although he had left London on 27 January and had arrived at Cleves on 9 February some three days later than Olisleger and Hochsteden, Wotton was still the first witness of the wedding to make personal contact with the duke who was moving almost daily from place to place in his dominions. On 16 February one of William's councillors informed the English diplomat that Dr. Carl Harst, the recently appointed ambassador to England, was either ready to leave for his post or already had done so. When Wotton responded that Harst, who had previously represented Anne's brother in Toledo and Madrid, had long been expected, he was told that the duke had wished to speak with Olisleger before he permitted the departure of his ambassador.[70]

Harst, who was fluent in Latin but had no knowledge of English, seems to have arrived in the kingdom in early-to-mid March. It is rather surprising, however, that he did not bring with him a document that contained copies of two repudiations in 1535 of the Lorraine contract, which was signed at Cleves on 26 February 1540 with a beer pot by the notary Potgieter, and which reached England sometime that spring. In December 1541 after denying to his superiors, including Olisleger, that he had any previous knowledge of this document, Harst requested that they send the original of it to him from the Cleves archives. The certificate in question contained two sworn statements. One was by Henry de Groiff, chancellor of Guelders, and two other councillors who had raised certain points on 15 February 1535 about the validity of the contract between Anne and Francis in 1527 and had determined that it should not proceed further. The second statement related an undated conversation between Elbert Pallant, marshall of Cleves, and Charles of Guelders in which the duke confessed that he was aware that the spousals were no longer binding. Pallant had conveyed this comment to the Cleves councillors on 17 April 1535.[71]

The role of this document in the royal divorce will be explained in Chapters 8 and 9. In the meantime, it is noteworthy that in Wotton's correspondence with Henry and Cromwell that spring no reference was made to the arrival of this copy of the repudiations of Anne's

Lorraine contract that the king and his councillors had so specifically demanded in January. In Wotton's letters dated 6 March, 28 March, and 15 April, he commented on a variety of issues. In addition to remarks about the treaty with Cleves that had finally reached England in February and that Henry had ratified with his gold seal, Wotton discussed the new article that the king required of Cleves, which the duke rejected for fear of offending his subjects and neighbors (probably a veiled reference to the emperor), although he admitted to Wotton he would be willing to fulfill its meaning without officially endorsing it. The diplomat speculated about why Cleves had met with Saxony at Paderborn in February, about whether the emperor would wage war against the princes, about whether William would be able to retain Guelders and wed Christina, about whether Henry's intercession with the emperor on behalf of Cleves would be permitted, and about the proposed marriage of Amelia of Cleves to John Ernest of Saxony, the duke elector's brother. In June, just before Cromwell's arrest, Henry informed Wotton that in Harst's audience with him on 31 May they had discussed the emperor's opinions about William's possession of Guelders and his marriage to Christina.[72]

Because the beer pot document was dated in February, the editors of the *Letters and Papers* placed the manuscript, for which Olisleger and Hochsteden had offered to surrender themselves as hostages until it reached the realm, among the state papers of that month, but it was not until June that any other reference to it can be found. The *Letters and Papers* also contain little evidence about Carl Harst, the Cleves ambassador, who was instructed to seek promises of military aid from Henry. The king and his council apparently arranged no special reception for him at his first arrival in March, as they had done for that of his predecessors in September 1539, but according to the diplomat's correspondence, Henry did grant him an audience on 31 March during Easter week, a usual time for diplomats to attend court. Although he was not attired richly or equipped splendidly enough to do justice to his honorable status as ambassador, the king received him, and then, Harst revealed, took the opportunity to complain rudely about the duke's secrecy and his unwillingness to approve of the additional treaty article. Indeed, William had done his sister and the ambassador a grave disservice, for by not furnishing Harst with the elegant clothing and the expensive household that the head of an important embassy was expected to possess, he had signaled to Henry that this mission held little significance for his duchy. Marillac did not note Harst's presence in the realm until 21 July 1540, and Chapuys, who had returned to England that same July, did not make his first reference to him until December 1541 when he worried about Harst's attempt to win Anne's reinstatement at court following the fall of Queen Katherine Howard. In a disparaging comment to Charles in January 1543, the Imperial ambassador revealed the major reason for Harst's failure to attract much attention to himself. Chapuys claimed that the Cleves agent, who had recently been summoned to court three or four times, had not been there in two years and protested against calling him an ambassador because he lived meanly at a tavern with only one servant to attend to his needs. By that time as a new Anglo-Imperial treaty had been signed, members of the privy council were denying to Chapuys that Harst held ambassadorial status: his duties, they claimed, were merely to assist Anne in her various private dealings. Her brother had obviously failed to provide adequate financial support for the diplomat, who seems to have been given only as much attention as etiquette absolutely required until his final departure, probably in 1543.[73]

Much was occurring behind the scenes during the weeks before Cromwell's arrest in June and the annulment of the royal marriage in July but only a few notices about Anne have survived from those days. She continued to play cards with the ladies of her household and received messages and gifts, a parrot and some eels, from her English subjects and her Cleves country folk. In March she ordered a crimson bonnet set with golden buttons and a feather to be made for her young stepson Edward, for whom she must have developed some affection. After celebrating Easter on 28 March at Hampton Court, she returned with Henry to Westminister for the opening of Parliament on 12 April. Six days later, after conferring the earldom of Essex upon Cromwell, the king dined in her apartments.[74]

Some time during these weeks, if not before, Henry began to woo Katherine Howard, one of her maidens of honor. Katherine's step-grandmother, Agnes, the widow of the second duke of Norfolk, testified that the king had developed an interest in her from the first time that he saw her, apparently in late December or early January at Greenwich. Given his strong feelings about obeying divine and ecclesiastical laws concerning matrimony, even though he was surely already considering divorce from Anne during Lent, it is likely that, regardless of when he first felt attracted to Katherine, that his serious pursuit of her occurred only after the Easter feast. Events then moved quickly, for on 24 April, only a few days after he had dined in his consort's apartments, he awarded Katherine, identified as Anne's servant, the forfeited goods and chattels of two murderers. It was rather tactless, if the dowager duchess knew of her step-grand-daughter's new admirer, for her to send a gift to the queen ten days later on 4 May.[75]

Although Henry did not introduce ladies who were already his mistresses into his consorts' privy chambers, it is clear that he viewed the maidens of a wife who had fallen into disfavor as blossoms, ripe for plucking as consorts. Anne Boleyn, Jane Seymour, and Katherine Howard all won promotion from queen's maiden to king's bride. He was the only English monarch to marry his consorts' attendants, but unlike his French counterparts neither he nor his predecessors on the throne expected their wives to employ in their privy chamber their mistresses whom they planned to retain as their illicit lovers. In 1662 this practice changed when, about six weeks after their wedding, Charles II provided Catherine of Braganza with a list of names for her privy chamber at the top of which was placed his principal mistress, Barbara Palmer, countess of Castlemaine, who had just given birth to their second child, a son named Charles. It took several weeks to wear down her resistance but his will finally prevailed. While it is most unlikely that Henry had already developed a special interest in Katherine when he approved her appointment as maiden of honor, the mortification the queen must have felt when she realized that he was greatly attracted to her attendant, as she had done by 20 June when she complained to Harst about the affair, still ran very deep.[76]

Her last public appearances as queen occurred at the May Day festivities, the formal beginning of spring. In late March the king's household had begun preparations for the tournaments that traditionally accompanied this festive holiday. In March and in April, after learning that arrangements for the games were underway, Marillac speculated that they would be held to honor Anne's coronation, which, he had heard, would take place about Whitsuntide. Having also learned about these same rumors, Anne discussed them at length with Harst who reported the conversations in two letters to Cleves in early April. In order to avoid arousing the suspicions of the king who, Anne pointed out, did not like to be pressured, she advised her countryman to raise the question of her coronation with both Cromwell and Southampton, but only in an indirect manner. By way of introducing the topic, he should mention to them that he had heard rumors that she was to be crowned and then inquire as to what Henry's intentions were regarding the ceremony. After explaining in his April letters that he regretted the king's delay in scheduling the coronation, Harst admitted that he had a feeling that something was not right, a perceptive comment, indeed, for he might well have asked Anne why she could not speak about the matter with her husband directly. Whether or not Harst communicated with any of the councillors was left unreported. He may well have solaced himself with the news from some "great gentlemen" that her English subjects loved Anne and thanked God for bringing to their realm such a "good queen." As the king's insecure consort well knew, the much-longed-for public ceremony in which she would be anointed and crowned would not only offer the appearance of divine approval for her queenship but also provide an affirmation of Henry's commitment to her as his consort. Since he had been unable to consummate their marriage, absolutely no chance existed that this highly sacred and expensive ritual would appear on the royal schedule that spring. The activity that had led Marillac and others to speculate incorrectly about the queen's coronation, as noted above, involved plans for the war games that traditionally welcomed this spring season. On Saturday, which was May Day, six knights, who presented themselves as challengers, fought defenders at the lists. On the following Monday and Wednesday, respectively, these warriors participated in a tourney and barriers. Between 30 April and 7 May, in association with the tournaments, open house was held at Durham Place where Henry and Anne attended suppers and banquets.[77]

Some other important information about Anne is contained in a letter Harst wrote to Cleves on 26 June in which he commented about three recent visits with her, the last that were to occur at court. On 20 June, as reported above, Anne complained to him about Henry's attentions to Katherine Howard. Surprised that she knew about the affair, he tried to comfort her with the remark that it was only a light romance and that the king would soon be inviting Anne to join him on his summer progress. Obviously, she had failed to reveal to her countryman that their marriage had not been consummated, for in his letter home he also lamented that she was not yet pregnant. This remark seems ultimately to have fueled the claim in Cleves that it was her infertility that had caused the divorce. Two days later, on 22 June, Harst noted that she appeared in better spirits (perhaps because Katherine Howard had left court) and that she was able to reassure him that Henry had been kind to her. On the morning of 24 June, St. John the Baptist's Day, with a sad demeanor and sorrowful eyes, as Harst referred to her appearance, she informed him that the council had instructed her to remove to Richmond Palace, allegedly because it enjoyed a healthier climate than the court. Her greatest concern about this move was, according to Harst, that she would share the fate of the rusticated Catherine of Aragon, not that of the executed Anne Boleyn. Clearly, she enjoyed the splendor, the pomp, the circumstance, and the excitement of court life. As she was to remove to Richmond on the following day, Harst tried futilely to comfort her by promising to visit her and by suggesting that Henry wanted to protect her from the plague and from the controversy surrounding the prisoners who were soon to be executed in London (presumably the three Lutherans and the Papists discussed below in Chapter 8). Privately, he was extremely concerned about her emotional state and requested in his letter that her family forward messages of support to her. Nothing could comfort her, however, for she was disheartened and complained about Henry's treatment of her. Indeed, it was somewhat shabby of him not to inform her personally of her rustication, but he had obviously made a decision he considered irrevocable and wished to be spared a scene. He chose not to see her again until August after the divorce and his remarriage.[78]

On 6 July Marillac reported rumors, which he doubted, that Anne had moved to Richmond to escape the sickness at court, and the news, which he seems to have believed, that the king was attracted to Katherine Howard. Richard Hillis, a fervent Protestant who detested Winchester, was later to recall that before 24 June, St. John the Baptist's Day, which was the day Anne learned she was to leave court, he had heard stories about Henry's crossing the Thames to visit Katherine in the bishop's Lambeth home. It is extremely doubtful, as

Glyn Redworth has argued, that Henry's next queen was ever a guest at the bishop's palace. Since her step-grandmother possessed a palatial Lambeth mansion in which Katherine had resided before her appointment as maiden of honor, it is far more likely that Henry was crossing over to Norfolk House, which lay directly opposite the residence of Cranmer, for a visit with his intended bride, where she surely had removed by 21 or 22 June, after the queen's discovery that her husband had developed an interest in her.[79] The topics of Chapters 8 and 9 are Cromwell's arrest and the annulment of the king's marriage to Anne.

8

KING'S SCAPEGOAT

It was not a coincidence that the king's divorce from Anne and Cromwell's execution both occurred in July 1540, for the two events were inextricably linked together. The widely accepted and often repeated view that a conservative religious faction manipulated Cromwell's downfall because he had foisted Anne upon Henry for the purpose of consolidating an evangelical reformation in England is, however, both misleading and inaccurate. As explained in Chapters 3 and 4, shifts in the relationship of France and the empire in 1538–39 led Henry to select his next consort from Cleves. It is interesting in light of the claim that Cromwell's evangelical goals both directed England's foreign policy and dictated the choice of the king's bride that at least one contemporary observer, Cardinal Farnese, Paul's agent in France, correctly identified Anne as a Catholic.[1]

Refuting the claim that Cromwell's evangelicalism was the force behind diplomatic decisions during his years in power requires a discussion of his religious beliefs, a reference to Anglo-German relations, and an examination of the evidence that reportedly proves the domination of factional politics at court.[2] Following this refutation, an analysis will be offered that links his downfall both to Henry's determination to end his union with Anne and to the criminal charges against Walter, Lord Hungerford, who was executed for treason and sodomy at the same time and in the same place as Cromwell. This new explanation requires a review of his actions or inactions concerning the Cleves marriage from 1539 to his arrest in 1540 and a study of the French accusations that he planned to marry into the royal family.

It is significant that most of the evidence for the competition of conservative and evangelical court factions can be found in the dispatches of diplomats who were seldom at court and who were simply repeating rumors that circulated about royal activities. Two examples will suffice to illustrate just how inaccurate their information could be. In the spring of 1540, as noted in Chapter 7, Marillac made the preposterous claim that preparations were underway for Anne's coronation. Later that year, Russell, a strong supporter of the royal supremacy who had assumed the deceased Cromwell's role as the confidant of Chapuys, actually persuaded the ambassador that he longed for papal reconciliation more than any other Englishman. Henry was well aware of their mostly inadequate news-collecting activities. In July when he informed the French and Imperial ambassadors of the inquiry into the validity of his marriage to Anne, he revealed that he was providing them with an explanation so that they would know the truth of the matter and not have to rely upon the London rumor mill.[3]

As John Guy has asserted, debate will continue about Cromwell's faith even though he unquestionably denied at the end of his life that he was a heretic. In his execution speech, according to Hall and later John Foxe, he claimed to be a true Catholic, "not doubting in any sacrament." Less than two months before his arrest, when as vicegerent he had appointed a committee to examine the church's doctrines and ceremonies, he complained, on the one hand, about the "superstition" of the papists and on the other of the "stiffness" of heretics.[4] Scholars have recently identified him as an evangelical, but this term is sometimes used loosely and without precise definition.[5]

In early modern Christendom, evangelicalism, which upheld biblical authority over papal supremacy, was often associated with Christian humanists (especially Erasmus) who were attempting to rediscover an inner personal faith in a religion that had become too concerned with externals. Most of the Injunctions that Cromwell enforced against pilgrimages, the veneration of relics, and offerings to images seem to have furthered, as John Guy has also pointed out, humanist reform. In Germany after 1520, however, the evangelical movement became disassociated from humanism because it rejected doctrinal changes. Melancthon even complained about the humanists employed in Cleves because he believed they hindered religious reform.[6]

By contrast, English evangelicalism continued to be less well defined and tended to encompass all who were anti-papal. For example, in 1535 Cranmer referred to some men as "papistical, not friendly to the gospel," and in 1546 William Thomas stated that the "just and evangelical conclusion" in England was that the "Popish authority over the kings and princes of the earth [was] usurped." Moreover, papists, together with those heretics, such as Lutherans, anabaptists, and others who actually confessed their contrary jurisdictional or doctrinal positions publicly, were routinely forced to recant or to suffer execution.[7]

The thesis that Cromwell led a court faction to manipulate evangelical reform without the king's knowledge does not accurately reflect the known facts. In July 1536 as vicegerent, he attended Convocation to sign the Ten Articles, the first of the statements of faith issued during the Reformation and the most radical one formulated in the reign. Significantly, its actual title indicated Henry's approval: "Articles Devised by the King's Highness Majesty to Stabilize Christian Quietness and Unity Among Us, and to Avoid Contentious Opinions." Because the government was considering an alliance with the Schmalkaldic League, it is not surprising, as James Pragman has observed, that the articles "exhibit certain affinities to the Augsburg Confession," which Cromwell had earlier requested Richard Tavener to translate.[8]

On major doctrinal issues, such as the bodily presence in the Lord's Supper and the need for good works to attain salvation, the Ten Articles failed to deviate from the received tradition. The statement on faith was a typical medieval formula: "justification by a faith that included charity and obedience." It is also true that Cromwell issued, in August 1536 (as noted above), Injunctions to enforce the Ten Articles that were somewhat more hostile to the usage of images, relics, miracles, prayers to saints and to other popular practices than were the Articles themselves. As vicegerent, according to John Guy, he moved somewhat beyond the Articles to make possible greater humanist reform of the church. The argument that he did so as the leader of a evangelical faction at court without the king's knowledge is problematic, however, because it distorts the reality of court politics and ignores the deep personal interest of Henry in religious matters. Early in 1540 John Wallop of the privy chamber even referred to the "Injunctions" as the "king's."[9]

This is not the place to rehash all the Reformation formularies, but the Act of Six Articles requires attention because it represents the medieval position. As observed in Chapter 4, the king approved this statute in 1539 when, in response to the recently signed Franco-Imperial alliance, he chose to present the English church as nothing less than a Catholic establishment that deviated from orthodoxy only in so far as it had rejected papal power. Without noting this foreign context, scholars have sometimes argued that, as an evangelical, Cromwell was actually a proto-Protestant who lost out to conservatives in the struggle over the enactment of the Six Articles that was passed over his personal opposition.[10]

If he were opposed to the statute's passage, then he must be judged hypocritical or, at the least, duplicitous.[11] Not only did he make no formal protest against it, as did Cranmer and some other churchman, but also, according to George Constantine, who attended court in August 1539, Cromwell was "utterly persuaded as the act is" and helped to convince Cranmer to acquiesce in its demand for clerical celibacy.[12] In addition, Ralph Morice, the archbishop's secretary, recalled that after the statute's enactment, Henry sent Cromwell and other councillors to dine with Cranmer at Lambeth to assure him of the king's continued good will.[13] The circumstances in which both the Ten Articles and the Six Articles were promulgated indicate that during Henry's reign foreign policy considerations had more impact on the nature of official doctrinal statements than did the alleged faith of his advisers or the intrigue of court factions.[14]

For both diplomatic and domestic reasons, the German initiative was sound strategy. When Francis was at odds with Charles, for example, he negotiated agreements with the emperor's enemies, including the Lutheran princes, the duke of Guelders, and the Ottoman Turks, who almost captured Vienna in 1529. The comment of E. Harris Harbison about the policy of Henry II of France is equally true about the diplomacy of his father Francis: "Henry II, Montmorency, and the Guises were all Catholics, but the secular tone of the age is nowhere more evident than in the willingness of all of them to make alliances with the infidel and the heretic in order to embarrass the emperor."[15]

In England, as David Potter has observed, little evidence exists that political factions manipulated the king's foreign policy. A brief examination of Anglo-German diplomacy in 1535 and 1540 will help to illustrate his point. In March 1535 Cromwell referred in his

"Remembrances" to the need to impede the emperor's "enterprises" by aiding the duke of Guelders and the Germans, a comment that has usually been overlooked in studies of why he specifically, and England more generally, pursued the German initiative. A few months later Norfolk and his nephew, George, Viscount Rochford, forwarded the king's order to Cromwell to instruct Robert Barnes, who had since 1531 accepted missions to Germany to gather information for the crown, to meet with Melancthon for the purpose of persuading him to refuse Francis's invitation to visit his realm and to accept Henry's similar one, instead. Cromwell had already communicated with Barnes about the mission but had been awaiting final instructions from the king and the council before sending him abroad. Much of the year's correspondence was devoted to the question of whether Melancthon would travel to France or England. After Christopher Mont, another English agent on the continent, had met with Melancthon, who proved unwilling or unable to accept either invitation, the diplomat sent messages both to Henry and Cromwell about his German adventures; the ones he wrote to the principal secretary were sometimes less full and less explanatory than those to the king, who referred to Mont as "his household servant" in a message to Saxony in 1538.[16]

Two years later Mont sometimes communicated directly with Henry about German affairs. Even after Katherine became queen and Cromwell was executed, official documents continued to identify Mont as "the king's servant" and to record his reports to Henry from Germany. Furthermore, in July 1540 Henry not only made great efforts to retain the Cleves alliance, maintaining Wotton there as ambassador until mid-1541, but also encouraged Francis to negotiate an agreement with William.[17] At no time did Mont or any other agent write or act as though he represented the views of Cromwell's faction. Such behavior would have jeopardized their positions, for councillors could never be certain when Henry might read letters that were addressed to them or intervene in their implementation of policy. In 1536, for example, Cromwell informed Vaughan that during his absence from court the king had read the letter the diplomat had addressed to him. In 1540 at Henry's direction, Ralph Sadler even required Cromwell to answer in his own name Wyatt's dispatch from the Imperial court but to forward a draft of it to Henry before sending it.[18]

Further complicating an analysis of Cromwell's direction of foreign policy is that in the spring of 1536, during the period when he was allegedly seeking a German alliance for ideological reasons, some scholars have charged him with favoring closer ties with Charles V, an enemy of the princes. Eric Ives has even argued that the information Cromwell leaked to the Imperial ambassador about Anne Boleyn's fall in 1536, which occurred two months before the Ten Articles were issued, formed part of a plot to oust the emperor's enemies at court and to adopt friendlier relations with him. During those spring months, it is true that Cromwell did pass on rumors to Chapuys, but they were often outrageous untruths, such as the claim that he was opposed to the dissolution of the monasteries. Clearly, Chapuys viewed him as an endless source of news that was welcome whether it turned out to be true or not, and in 1540 when the king raised Cromwell to the earldom of Essex, the diplomat, then stationed at Brussels, was pleased to learn of the new honor.[19] Cromwell's simultaneous negotiations with both the German princes and the emperor seem to have had far less to do with his personal views than with approved official royal policy.

As Potter has observed, the government needed to maintain its German contacts. The Hanseatic League with its headquarters at the Steelyard was an ancient, powerful mercantile association that possessed numerous ships of war. Besides exporting English wool to Germany, its merchants obtained loans and other commodities for the royal family. The Ryngk family, for example, completed a variety of commissions for Henry and his father. Sir Herman Ryngk sought to mediate a marriage for Mary Tudor not only with William of Cleves in 1530 but also with the emperor in the 1520s. The Lutheran Reformation did not negate the value of these contacts.[20]

Although, as observed earlier, commentators in Henry's reign usually referred to those who rejected papal power as evangelicals, some modern scholars have identified a few individuals, especially Norfolk and Winchester, as leaders of a conservative religious faction that sought to destroy Cromwell's alleged evangelical party. In 1531 it is true that Winchester lost office because he had protested against limiting papal authority, but his *De Vera Obedentia* which defended the royal supremacy permitted his re-entry into the English evangelical camp. It is also difficult to categorize Norfolk as merely conservative. In 1538 he predicted divine punishment for those who supported the *mumpsimus* and superstitions of the pope and the cardinals, and in 1540 he complained that the constable of France was "too much papist to do good to us."[21]

That Norfolk and Winchester were hostile to all humanist reforms is also problematic although Constantine volunteered his belief that the duke was not knowledgeable enough about God's word. Among the peerage, Francis Talbot, earl of Shrewsbury, and Norfolk were the leading recipients of monastic lands. This anti-monasticism was consistent with anti-papal sentiment, but it is damaging to claims about Norfolk's aggressive anti-biblical stance that he revealed to Cromwell in 1539 that a number of Scottish refugees, who had fled their homeland because they feared retaliation for reading the scriptures in English, came to him daily for aid at Berwick. He spoke gently to them, he admitted, and sometimes provided them with financial assistance. In February 1540, furthermore, John Wallop assured Lord Lisle that Norfolk would advise him to "sequester" the individuals who disobeyed the "king's Injunctions," as well as the "flesh eaters." As an ecclesiastic, Winchester, on the other hand, did have some reservations about religious reform, but as Redworth has pointed out in his recent biography, the bishop approved the destruction of Becket's shrine and promoted the publication of vernacular translations of the scriptures. In a plea to Cromwell after his arrest in 1540, Richard Sampson, bishop of Chichester, explained that Tunstall and Richard Stokesley, the deceased bishop of London, were both more favorable to old church usages than was Winchester, an opinion that echoed Constantine's earlier analysis of their beliefs. Furthermore, Redworth also denied that the bishop and Norfolk operated as political allies and observed that they were often in disagreement on foreign policy. While in France in 1540, as related in Chapter 7, the duke even made a gratuitous criticism of the bishop's tenure there as resident ambassador.[22]

Another difficulty with the theory that factions controlled politics was the nature of court life. It was where the king lived, ruled his realm, and pursued pleasurable pastimes, but the individuals who interacted with him in these activities were constantly changing. While Stephen Gunn has correctly emphasized that "the fluidity of early Tudor politics is too readily underestimated,"[23] Chris Given-Wilson has located three circles in a king's "affinity." The first includes those who had a personal relationship with him: members of the privy council and privy chamber and others, including the queen and her ladies, who had places assigned to them at court. The second circle numbered officials who were "bound to him by ties of service," especially members of his household. The third group was an outer circle of lords, knights, and esquires who were only occasionally at court.[24]

Complicating the smooth functioning of the court was that many in the first circle frequently had to be absent. Members of the privy chamber alternated shifts of employment on their posts with holidays at home and were sometimes tapped for diplomatic errands. It was also difficult to maintain sufficient councillors in attendance on the king to advise him on public policy, for the duties of their other offices often required their absence. Consequently, Cromwell, like Wolsey before him, met with Henry only sporadically. In addition, the means by which information flowed at court hindered the alleged politics of factional leaders. The kind of news to which individuals had access differed between those who were of the court and council, as John Dudley pointed out in 1538, and those who were only of the court. Dudley, who was of the court but not of the council, did not, for example, have access to sensitive matters concerning public policy. Finally, during the somewhat lengthy hunting season, the king routinely reduced the number of his attendants as he moved from place to place.[25] Time and space were usually lacking for the leaders of these alleged factions to develop any consistent or long-term, cooperative strategies.

Official documents admonished members of the privy chamber to "be loving together, and of good unity and accord." They, and the privy councillors, belonged to the same team and were expected to cooperate in providing appropriate advice and assistance to the king. As P. S. Lewis has explained, court politics could be a "curious love-hate relationship." The "bickerings" were among individuals who might "on the whole" be in agreement about many matters but "disagree about who was to play where."[26] Competition for favor could and often did involve intrigue, gossip, and betrayal. The goal was to obtain a favored position and to pass on some of the accumulated largess to a following of clients and hangers-on. Those who failed to win royal favor turned to his kindred or his most important advisers like Cromwell, whose faction included, first of all, his family and kin, secondly, personal friends, and thirdly, clients seeking patronage or remedies for various kinds of problems. As Diane Willen has pointed out in her study of Russell's connections: "Kinship, friendship, and patronage reinforced each other."[27]

Many clients did not live at court, for they either visited it or sent agents to it seeking assistance. Some, like Lord Lisle at Calais, for example, had a whole range of people from whom they could request aid. Lisle had a stepdaughter, Anne, and a relative, Lady Rutland, in the queen's privy chamber, friends on the council, like Cromwell and Southampton, gentlemen in the privy chamber like Bryan, and members of the episcopal establishment like Winchester all supporting him in his extended network. His friends can not be identified as members of any one particular court faction.[28]

It is possible to name some of Cromwell's supporters and clients. A few of them were to join Queen Mary's government: his colleague, Wriothesley, for example, welcomed papal power in 1554. Bonner, who was Cromwell's friend, but who was not at court, also supported the Marian reconciliation. Other friends of Cromwell, Denny and Sadler, for example, felt comfortable with the Edwardian Reformation. So did Vaughan, who was not at court. Probably, for every future Protestant who was Cromwell's friend, a future Roman Catholic counterpart can be found. Indeed, Constantine even claimed in 1539 that Cromwell had requested the transference of Bishop Durham, usually identified as conservative, from the council of the north to the council attendant on the king. Although it was Henry who appointed him to that office, letters surviving from early 1538 indicate that Cromwell had acted as patron for the bishop when he had sought assistance for some of his own clients.[29]

If patrons' criteria for distributing church office was not based mainly on a cleric's specific religious persuasion, as Rosemary O'Day has confirmed, then surely it is unreasonable to claim that court patronage was based on ideology. Let Antonio de Guevara, preacher and historiographer to Charles V, whose treatise on the court was translated into English by Bryan and published in 1548, be the final word here on this issue: "In princes' courts, the custom and use is to speak of God and to live after the world."[30]

Before turning to Cromwell's fall, three incidents in early 1540 require attention because misinterpretations of them have fueled the faction theory. The first was the public quarrel of Winchester and

Barnes. Briefly, because Redworth provided details about it in his biography of the bishop, the king appointed Winchester to preach at court on Lenten Fridays. It is possible that since, as recently as September 1538, he had been charged with, but absolved of, favoring papal reconciliation, Henry was offering him an opportunity to prove his loyalty. That Nicholas Wilson who was also suspected of harboring popish attitudes was another Lenten preacher supports this speculation. In May he was to be imprisoned for aiding admirers of papal authority.[31]

The bishop's appointment to preach at Lent may have had nothing to do with his subsequent attack on Barnes, who he knew favored Lutheranism. If the rumors in late 1539 were true that Cromwell had forced Winchester from the council because he had opposed Barnes's selection as Danish ambassador, then that earlier controversy may explain the bishop's attack. The circumstances of Winchester's removal were more complicated than Cromwell's mere personal intervention, however, for the king, who had been worried about a Franco-Imperial invasion, had personally approved the Danish mission of Barnes who was identified in credences as Henry's "household servant" [familiaris noster]. If his opposition to Barnes's mission had caused Winchester's loss of favor, then it could well have been the king who ordered Cromwell to deprive him of council membership.[32]

On the first Sunday in Lent, after Winchester had preached at court on Friday, he took St. Paul's pulpit away from Barnes who had been scheduled to appear at that time. Amidst barely veiled references to him, the bishop attacked the doctrine of justification by faith and more significantly, given his own checkered history on this issue, charged that it posed a threat to the royal supremacy. Two weeks later Barnes preached a sermon to defend his views in which he called Winchester a "cock of the game, whose spurs were blunt and could not prick" and threw his glove at the congregation in a symbolic challenge not only to his adversary but also to the religious establishment.[33]

The king could not permit to go uninvestigated a public attack on one of his bishops by a doctor of divinity and minor diplomat like Barnes. As Godfrey Goodman, bishop of Gloucester, was to write in 1650 concerning James I's comment at the Hampton Court Conference in 1604: "No bishop, no king, no nobility; which as you see, has lately fallen out according to his prediction. It is the church which supports the state, it is religion which strengthens the government; shake the one, and you overthrow the others."[34] On 5 March, Henry summoned the two antagonists to Hampton Court where he had recently removed with the queen. Attended only by Browne and Southampton, he met with Barnes in his privy closet. By 12 March Henry ordered him and two other Lutherans, William Jerome and Thomas Garrett, to recant their views publicly during Easter week. The king subsequently deemed unacceptable the recantations of the three Lutherans, whose remarks may even have caused disputes among the bishops who were assembling for parliament and convocation. Imprisoned on 3 April, they were burned to death on 30 July alongside three papists, Thomas Abel, Richard Featherstone, and Edward Powell, who were hanged, drawn and quartered as traitors.[35]

The Lenten dispute did not lead to Cromwell's downfall. He seems to have been uninvolved in the inquiry, for in two spring "Remembrances" he referred only to the papists. Moreover, in Barnes's letter to John Epinus on 21 May, he spoke of his "fierce controversy" with Winchester over justification and purgatory and lamented that his only support had come from Hugh Latimer, former bishop of Worcester. Other evidence fails to confirm a special friendship between Barnes and Cromwell, although, besides the gossip that he had forced Winchester from the council because he opposed Barnes's Danish mission, Cromwell's name was linked to the Lutheran's twice in 1539. The first time was when Barnes returned to court in August, a few weeks after the passage of the Six Articles. Constantine recalled that Cromwell had recommended that the diplomat, who excused himself on account of "weariness," discuss his reservations about the statute with Henry.[36]

It is conceivable that in August 1539 the king himself had suggested to Cromwell the possibility of an audience with Barnes. Certainly, a few months later, in early March 1540, after Henry had already interrogated Barnes about the dispute with Winchester, Southampton left Hampton Court for London to meet with Cromwell and to discuss recalling Barnes for another interrogation. When the lord admiral returned to court on 11 March, he learned that Henry was no longer so keen on meeting with the preacher. It is likely that the king simply changed his mind about scheduling another meeting with Barnes before ordering him to recant his Lutheran views.[37]

Cromwell's second association with Barnes in 1539 can be proved by the letters of William Barlow, bishop of St. David's and the Lutheran's patron. In August 1539 the bishop asked Cromwell to present Barnes with the Welsh prebend of Llanboidy, a far from unusual request of the king's vicegerent, as, for example, Bryan had earlier interceded with Cromwell to obtain the office of prior of Coventry for his client. In December 1539 Barlow later thanked Cromwell for preferring Barnes to Llanboidy. Since he had been on diplomatic assignments from March to August in 1539, this position, which was worth about £18 a year, can be viewed more as a reward for royal services than as a sign of special Cromwellian favor. Supporting this suggestion was Cranmer's unsuccessful request in 1538 that Cromwell grant to Barnes the deanery of Tamworth College, which was worth about £20 a year, £2 more than at Llanboidy. The archbishop expressed the view that Barnes "deserved a greater living," for Tamworth was "a very small prefer- ment for such pains and travail, as he most willingly had sustained in the king's affairs."[38]

After his dispute with Barnes was over, Winchester shared a recon- ciliation dinner with Cromwell that lasted for about four hours. For an explanation of this meal, it is helpful to recall the dinner that Henry had directed Cromwell to have with Cranmer after he had protested the passage of the Six Articles. In his letter to Wallop approving of the meal Winchester and Cromwell shared, Norfolk further revealed that Wriothesley, who had disputed with the bishop's agents over his election as knight of Hampshire in 1539, had also had peacemaking exchanges with him. The king's servants were once more working together, for in May 1540 Cranmer, Cromwell, Winchester, among others, served on a royal commission on the collection of London tithes.[39]

The other alleged leader of the conservative faction was Norfolk, whom Cromwell required to stay away from Hampton Court on 1 April. Cromwell's order does not represent evidence of his evangeli- cal strategy to prevent the conservative duke from conferring with Henry, as has been erroneously argued, perhaps from a lack of understanding of the privilege of "easy access" to the king that noblemen held by right of their possession of their elite status, as

M. L. Bush has confirmed. Nor is it evidence of the lord privy seal's otherwise general control of Henry's appointments. A letter of Cranmer's proves this assertion. On 19 November 1538 he informed Cromwell that he had two meetings the next day, the one with the king at 10:00 a.m. he could not make if he had to be with Cromwell at Stepney before 9:00 a.m. He continued: "I will send unto his Grace to know his determinate pleasure herein, and I will not fail to await upon you at Stepney, at your hour assigned, unless the king's pleasure is to the contrary." Despite this and other evidence, Eric Ives's claim that Cromwell was able to keep "his rivals away from real contact with Henry for several years" has usually framed the interpretation of Cromwell's above cited letter to Norfolk. Allegedly, for political reasons, the lord privy seal planned to prevent his noble enemy attending court by using the rather lame excuse that a ducal servant had died from the sweating sickness. Surely Cromwell wrote the letter at the direction of a king who was anxious about the spread of disease at court, for Henry had even deserted Anne Boleyn in 1528 when one of her ladies had caught this virulent infection. In 1538 Norfolk had, himself, volunteered to stay away from the king's presence if one of his household who had fallen ill proved to have anything more serious than the ague. In his response to Cromwell's prohibitive directive in April 1540, the duke did not seem to harbor any suspicions about the letter writer's motive. He assumed that Cromwell, as he requested him, would inform the king that he had not had any recent contact with the deceased and reported that he planned to travel to London where he would await notice as to whether or not he could continue on to Hampton Court. On 12 April, of course, he would be able to see Henry at the opening of parliament and surely could raise concerns about this incident at that time.[40]

Norfolk normally did not relish endless court attendance, if for no other reason than its great expense. In 1538, for example, he requested a license from the king to be absent on St. George's Day. He also had other commitments. On 11 March 1540 when he finished briefing Henry on his mission to France, he left to oversee the suppression of a monastery, the revenues of which had just been granted to him. After Cromwell's fall, he was present at only about one third of the sessions of the privy council for which attendance records have survived. He was far too busy to discharge the functions of government, as Cromwell did. What he and most noblemen of his high rank desired was regular input into the making of official policy. In 1540, after the distribution of Cromwell's offices, Norfolk simply continued to work with ministers, like Wriothesley and Sadler, who had been friends of the lord privy seal, and others, like Browne and Southampton, who had been his colleagues.[41]

Sometimes Norfolk and Cromwell had disagreements, but they were part of a give-and-take working relationship. Two incidents from the spring of 1539 help to confirm this state of affairs. On 4 April Anthony Rowse protested to Cromwell the actions of Robert Holdich, Norfolk's steward, who had abducted the twelve-year-old daughter of the deceased Sir Edward Ichingham and planned to marry her to his son. When a few days after Cromwell had responded affirmatively to Rowse's plea that the girl be returned to her kinsmen, Norfolk arrived home to learn of the adverse decision affecting his steward, he sent a letter of protest to the lord privy seal. On 19 April Cromwell referred the controversy to Henry with the observation that he was sorry the duke was taking it so personally.[42]

The election of the knights for the county of Norfolk was held during that same month. Chosen over the protests of Sir Edmond Knyvet, the duke's nephew, were Richard Southwell and Edmund Windham. A dispute between Knyvet and Southwell caused Norfolk on 18 April, the day before Cromwell referred the Ichingham matter to the king, to inform the lord privy seal about the irresponsible actions of his nephew who was disinclined to obey his relatives, including his noble uncle. The concerned duke requested Cromwell to bring him to good order and not to "give too much confidence to his words." To prevent Southwell and Kynvet from fighting over the election, Norfolk bound each of them in the amount of £2,000 to keep the peace and ordered them to appear before the council.[43]

On another occasion in 1538, Norfolk also required Cromwell's assistance with a local problem. Since county officials had not as yet succeeded in disbursing the vagabonds from Norfolk and Suffolk, the duke asked Cromwell to write a letter to him stating that the king was amazed that there were still so many of them in the countryside. Norfolk planned to present the document to the justices of the peace at the next quarter sessions and for it to have the desired effect, requested Cromwell not to "declare [to them] that I have written unto you in this letter."[44] Disagreements could emerge and could be worked out among Henry's councillors, but, in the meantime, they cooperated together for the good of the king and his realm.

Some extant correspondence even proves that Norfolk and Cromwell shared a personal relationship beyond this working one. In 1536 Cromwell's heir, Gregory, was a guest at the duke's Kenninghall home, where, according to his host, he was neglecting his books for hunting, a pastime he greatly enjoyed. Norfolk even occasionally sought Cromwell's advice about personal matters, as, for example, the difficulties of his daughter, Mary, widow of the king's illegimate son, Henry Fitzroy, duke of Richmond, in obtaining her jointure. In early 1538 the duke indicated that he had contemplated taking her to court but, before he did, he wished Cromwell to inquire of the king whether her visit would displease him. Later that year, Norfolk informed the lord privy seal that his daughter-in-law, Frances, countess of Surrey, had given birth to his grandson, the future fourth duke, sooner than had been expected. If she had carried the child to full term, he explained, he had planned to ask the king and Cromwell to act as godfathers. The premature birth, even though the child was "as lusty a boy as need be," required an immediate christening. In the same letter Norfolk asked for the delivery of his will, which Cromwell had been keeping in a safe place since 1536 when he had agreed to act as the duke's principal executor. That Norfolk appointed him to this personal office surely indicates the high regard in which he was held.[45]

The faction theory derives in part from a dispatch of Marillac who asserted on 10 April that Cromwell was losing power. He speculated that Winchester, Durham, and possibly John Clerk, bishop of Bath and Wells, would not only be summoned to the privy council but would also gain Cromwell's offices – Durham would become vicegerent and Bath would become lord privy seal. Crediting Marillac's statement is problematic, for he seems to have been unaware that Durham was already a councillor and referred to a Bishop Belte, who the editors of the *Letters and Papers* assume to have been the bishop of Bath and Wells.[46]

What Marillac's letter most likely reflects is the excitement generated in early April when Henry transferred Cromwell's office of principal secretary to two of his satellites, Sadler and Wriothesley. A few days later the king granted him the earldom of Essex and the office of great chamberlain, which the recently deceased John de Vere, fifteenth earl of Oxford, had held.[47] Cromwell's loss of the principal secretaryship just before he assumed these honors must have generated the rumors of his downfall that Marillac repeated.

The leaders of the alleged factions seemed unaware of the murderous struggle that supposedly was raging. The duke had left voluntarily to collect his monastic revenues; Cranmer was absent from court. Cromwell, who had been moving back and forth between Hampton Court and London, was preparing for the parliamentary session and for his new preferments. Lord Audley was at his home in Walden, Essex, during most of Lent. Winchester took time out to fight publicly with Barnes who had no standing at court.[48]

Given the inadequacy of the evidence that Cromwell led an ideological, proto-Protestant faction, it is still true, as J. J. Scarisbrick has pointed out, that a great part of the statements in the final bill of attainder that condemned him to death claimed he was a sacramentary. By contemporary standards, to label him not just a generic heretic or a Lutheran, but a sacramentary, was a terrible dishonor. When in 1539 John Barlow, dean of Westbury, had accused Constantine of harboring those views, he had complained to Cromwell: "The dean has slandered me for a sacramentary which is, if anything can be worse, more heinous than treason." For members of the ruling classes, radical religious reform was synonymous with rebellion.[49] Why, then, did the government condemn Cromwell for so detested a heresy when the lesser charge of Lutheranism was enough to cost him his life, as it was to cost Barnes his life? To arrive at the answer to this question, it is necessary to recall his actions concerning the Cleves marriage.

Although he had helped to negotiate the treaty, he seems not to have given the matter any greater attention than some of his other duties, perhaps because unlike the king, he did not fret about the Franco-Imperial alliance that he correctly suspected would be short lived. After the arrival of the Cleves ambassadors in 1539, Henry had thought it necessary to send word to Cromwell through Southampton to "pay attention to his weighty matters."[50]

When it became known that the king was displeased with Anne, Cromwell seems to have been unconcerned about losing royal favor, although he surely wished his earlier prediction to Chapuys that Henry would refuse to marry a lady with whom he was unacquainted had ruled the royal behavior in this case. Because Cromwell had seen Anne for the first time at the Blackheath reception, he possessed a distinct advantage over colleagues like Southampton. In his July deposition, the lord admiral later recalled, Cromwell had criticized him for having praised Anne so highly in his letters from Calais, and Southampton may actually have had some concern about the future of his long-time personal relationship with the king. He had, he swore, given Cromwell the rather lame excuse that by the time he had greeted Anne at Calais, the matter was too far advanced for him to presume to interfere. In July, with the lord privy seal safely in prison, Southampton seems to have conveniently forgotten the effusiveness of his December letters. His younger half-brother, Browne, recalled in his deposition that he had been worried about the lord admiral's fate. Southampton had probably spent the better part of January apologizing to the king for having made what, when seen with hindsight, was a terrible blunder in judgment. In this context Marillac's comment to Montmorency on 10 June that Cromwell's friends included Southampton was surely incorrect.[51]

According to Cromwell's letters, the king was in charge of breaking developments in January. It was he who ordered his councillors to confer with the German ambassadors and who quizzed his bishops about the Lorraine contract. As Cromwell also admitted, he had failed to respond when Anne had tried to converse with him about her marital problems. Although Henry had granted him permission to speak with her, somehow Cromwell never found the time to initiate a private conversation with his queen. In fact, he may never have spoken to her at all except through interpreters on formal occasions.[52]

While he was reluctant to discuss with Anne her wifely behavior, especially as it would have had to be done through interpreters, he may also have genuinely believed that given time Henry would be able to consummate the union. Not equipped with training in matrimonial law, Cromwell probably had no deep knowledge of the grounds for annulling a marriage, for Henry and his churchmen had been intimately involved in those details during the earlier divorce proceedings. As vicegerent Cromwell handled financial issues and constitutional procedures that involved the crown's assumption and supervision of church authority, property, and doctrine. The king never turned to him for advice about the legality of his marriages, and Cromwell even admitted his own inadequacies in this regard. In 1538, for example, when a question was raised about the validity of the union of Mary Howard and the deceased duke of Richmond, he referred the matter to Cranmer.[53]

In the meantime, as long as Francis and Charles remained allies, the king's major concern was that, prodded on by the pope, they might be preparing an invasion of England. Before he could do more than merely hope to end his marriage, he had to ascertain the extent of that danger; this was the rationale for sending Norfolk to France in February (as discussed in Chapter 7). From the duke the king had learned that it was not only unlikely that Francis and Charles would declare war on his realm but also that the strength of their friendship was diminishing. Henry understood that he could resolve his thorny marital problems without great fear of a hostile reaction from Cleves who might join with them in an assault against England.[54]

For clarification of the grounds for divorce, Henry needed to confer with his churchmen. During Lent at Hampton Court, when surely with some relief he obeyed the church's ban against sexual intercourse, he may even have begun conversations about a divorce with Tunstall, an expert on canon and civil law. These discussions had probably not progressed very far before he returned to Whitehall after Easter (28 March), when he seems to have resumed his efforts to consummate the marriage. As parliament opened on 12 April, he possessed ample opportunity to consult with the bishops in the House of Lords and with the other churchmen who assembled with them in the double convocation that was convened at parliamentary times. Henry may have then turned for assistance to Winchester, another expert on canon and civil law, whom Constantine described as very "learned," for he was to play a major role in the divorce proceedings. Chapter 9 addresses two of the legal grounds: the validity of Anne's contract with Lorraine and the king's claim that he had entered the union unwillingly.[55]

The third reason for the divorce was the non-consummation of the marriage, which needs examination here because it formed the backdrop to Cromwell's fall. An understanding of the events of the spring of 1540 necessitates an investigation of early modern beliefs about impotency. The type of dysfunction that Henry described to Cromwell was defined as relative, toward one specific woman only, rather than general, toward all women. Unless he suffered from a relative affliction, he could not wed again, for canon law prohibited men from remarrying if they were naturally impotent, a disability that was usually defined as biological or physical. In other words, if the male genitalia were intact and normal but failed to function properly, the blame was not sought in the psyche of the man but rather in some negative external stimuli. There were two problems with claiming relative impotency: it was difficult, even awkward, to prove, and once proven the church blamed it on magical or demonic interference. The difficulty of proof was surely the reason Dr. Butts mentioned the king's night emissions, *duas pollutiones nocturnas in somno*, in his deposition. They were a sin for which penance had to be done, but they also provided evidence of his ability to emit semen despite his incapacity with Anne.[56]

Edward Muir has observed that the "most widespread fertility fear was that someone might employ castration magic against the groom." This belief in demonic or magical inspiration of relative impotency had a long history. In the ninth century, Hincmar of Rheims, for example, had recommended exorcism rather than divorce as the best response to this incapacity that he blamed on sorcery. As the church gained control of matrimonial matters, its leaders, especially Honorius III (r. 1216–27) ranked impotence caused by evil spirits as a diriment impediment.[57] As scholastic churchmen began also to shape the received folklore about sorcery and wise women into a systematic demonology, they blamed relative impotency on *maleficium*, the interference of witches who were defined as heretics and worshippers of the devil. In English sources the words sorcery, magic, and witchcraft were used interchangeably.[58]

It was not easy for writers to differentiate natural, biological impotency from magical interference. Some defined it as natural if an erection was impossible but demonic if an erection occurred that was accompanied by an obstruction of the seminal duct; still others claimed that it was demonic if the penis "stirred" but could not become erect, and natural if it could not stir. Authors also differed about the specific way in which witches and devil-worshippers created the incapacity. Some argued that these creatures cast spells that made men believe their penises had been removed. The source of the illusion lay not in the human imagination but in the action of outside forces. Still others charged that the creatures caused incapacity in a symbolic way by tieing knots in the strings or ribbons that attached the breeches to the doublet. The spell could be broken only when the knots were untied. So widespread was the fear of demonic interference in marital relations that the custom developed in Tudor England to celebrate marriages at night in a private place to avoid the witch's "knot."[59]

Charges that sorcery had been used to injure monarchs had appeared from time to time throughout the medieval period. In England royal husbands had not complained of suffering from relative impotency, although some of them had accused their wives and concubines of using magic to bewitch or enchant them. In 1193, however, a protracted dispute over relative impotency had erupted in France. On the day after the wedding of Philip Augustus and Ingeborg of Denmark, he repudiated her with the claim that evil charms had prevented the consummation of their union. Other commentators spoke of offensive bodily features. Ultimately, perhaps because she refused to deny their carnal union, having failed apparently to distinguish between the "mingling of the sexual organs" and the "mingling of seeds in the female vessel," Innocent III ordered Philip to resume his marriage with her. Another case of relative impotency, which occurred more closely in time to the reign of Henry VIII, was that of Henry IV of Castile who proved unable to consummate his union with Bianca of Navarre in 1440. After the mandatory wait of three years required by canon law when they both still confessed the lack of sexual union, she underwent a physical examination to prove her virginity. Inquiries about his sexuality were also made at the Segovia brothel, which he had reportedly visited. It was officially concluded that a magical spell had caused his relative incapacity: the marriage to her was terminated and he was permitted to remarry.[60]

In his recollections about his conversations with Henry in April and May, Cromwell provided the time by which the king had begun to claim that he had been prevented from consummating his marriage to Anne by some outside force or "obstacle." On 30 June in a letter about the royal marriage, Cromwell identified Whitsuntide (16 May) as the date on which the king referred to an "obstacle" in his failed relations with Anne. In another letter to Henry, perhaps also written on 30 June, in which he denied the heresy charges that were outlined in the bill of attainder against him, he recalled that the king had mentioned the "obstacle" to him after Easter and again in Whitsunweek at Greenwich. Obviously, Henry's discussions with his bishops and other church leaders had helped to shape how he defined his incapacity, for that was not the explanation he had offered in January – he had then complained about Anne's physical traits that had made him assume that she was not a maiden.[61]

Once having admitted the existence of an obstacle, Henry had two questions that needed to be answered. Whose magical powers had affected him in this adverse way, and why? He seems to have asked the why question first. He identified all papists as potential conspirators working to trap him in an unfruitful marriage in support of the restoration of the Yorkist house. It was unnecessary for him to explain to anyone that this was the specific reason to arrest these individuals, for anyone who denied or was suspected of denying the royal supremacy was always a target for incarceration. It was widely accepted that a papist and a traitor were the same thing and they shared the same kind of punishment.[62]

One of the first victims may have been Lord Lisle who along with his wife had long been suspected of papist leanings. He had been residing in London since April when he had been relieved of his duties at Calais by a royal commission that had arrived at the frontier town to inquire about the activities there of both papists and sacramentaries. This is not the place to detail the facts they uncovered but references to two cases are essential. Lisle's chaplain, Sir Gregory Botolf, a secret papist, was found to have been involved in a conspiracy to turn over Calais to Paul III and Cardinal Pole.[63] The king's commissioners also confirmed that Adam Damplip, an alleged sacramentary who had been the source of a lengthy religious controversy, was a Lutheran because he believed in the real presence but not in transubstantiation. Further complicating matters, Damplip, too, it was discovered, had connections with Pole, who reportedly had offered him employment in his household.[64]

It was probably because the commissioners found this double evidence linking Lisle indirectly to Pole and the papacy that he was imprisoned on 19 May, three days after Whitsuntide. These two events added weight to the concern that Lisle had aroused in 1538 when it was learned that he had received Geoffrey Pole in disguise at Calais. The investigators also suspected Lisle of having corresponded with Henry Courtney, marquess of Exeter, another Yorkist claimant who had been executed in 1538. Since Lisle was a natural son of Edward IV, Henry may have, in the midst of his latest marital crisis, even believed his incompetent lord deputy was capable of harboring ambitions for the crown. After Lisle's arrest evidence of his correspondence with the emperor was discovered.[65]

On 1 June Marillac wrote home about Chichester's and Wilson's imprisonment for favoring old church usages and for having had contact with the Pole family. Wilson confessed only that he had attempted to assist the papists, Abel, Featherstone, and Powell, who were to be executed in July. As usual, Marillac's dispatches contained some correct news, such as the names of these clerics, but also included incorrect predictions. Despite his claims, Latimer was not restored to his bishopric; Barnes remained in prison; Wallop was in no danger of immediate arrest; and Cromwell's alleged assertion that five more bishops would be imprisoned was false. In his letters, Marillac also lined up Winchester, Sampson, and Wilson against Cromwell and Cranmer in a fierce court struggle. The major evidence for the factional battle that led to Cromwell's fall relies on the opinions of one confused Frenchman whose dispatches must be mined electically to reach this conclusion. Even more interesting is the preposterous version of Harst, the Cleves ambassador, about these events. Despite having a special unnamed friend with access to court and possessing Anne's confidence, Harst claimed that Cranmer joined Winchester in bringing down Cromwell! Since he also identified the archbishop as an ally, the suspicion lingers that Cranmer was the one who deliberately misled him about Cromwell's arrest. Certainly, the archbishop continued to feed Harst news, such as information about the Scottish ambassador in 1541. In 1539–40, Norfolk, posing as the French confidant, Cromwell as the Imperial friend, and Cranmer as the Cleves ally filtered incorrect, contradictory news into the diplomatic network in return for which they hoped to obtain secret information about their home courts.[66]

If there were two competing ideological factions, neither succeeded unscathed. While Winchester may have gained politically from Cromwell's fall, both Sampson, who claimed that Winchester had told him to leave religious ceremonies to the king's direction, and Wilson, who remained in prison for some time, were specifically exempted from the parliamentary Act of Pardons in 1540. Cranmer survived every political crisis in Henry's reign and contented himself

12 Anne of Cleves, queen of England

13 Henry VIII enthroned (from the marriage proclamation of Henry and
Anne of Cleves, 5 January 1540)

14 William Fitzwilliam, earl of Southampton

15 Thomas Cranmer, archbishop of Canterbury

16 Painted oak bedhead, with polychrome decoration with the date
    1540 and the initials HA (probably made in anticipation of Henry
    and Anne's wedding)

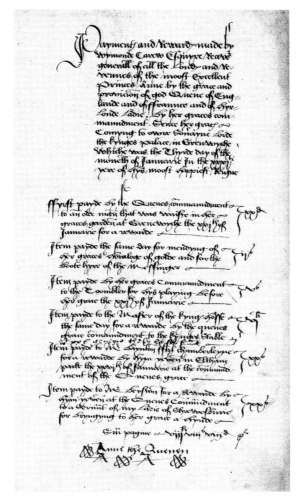

17 Document bearing the signature of 'Anne the Quenen'

PARVVLE PATRISSA, PATRIÆ VIRTVTIS ET HÆRES
  ESTO, NIHIL MAIVS MAXIMVS ORBIS HABET.
GNATVM VIX POSSVNT COELVM ET NATVRA DEDISSE,
  HVIVS QVEM PATRIS, VICTVS HONORET HONOS.
ÆQVATO TANTVM, TANTI TV FACTA PARENTIS,
  VOTA HOMINVM, VIX QVO PROGREDIANTVR, HABENT
VINCITO, VICISTI, QVOT REGES PRISCVS ADORAT
  ORBIS, NEC TE QVI VINCERE POSSIT, ERIT.

18 Edward VI, king of England, as a child, *c.* 1538

19 Stephen Gardiner, bishop of Winchester

20 Richmond Palace

21 Hever Castle, Kent

22 Handwritten dedication by Anne of Cleves in Book of Hours, Germany 1533

23 The tomb of Anne of Cleves, Westminster Abbey

with only one written protest about Cromwell's arrest. But where was Norfolk? It was not until June that Marillac added him to the successful Winchester faction after it was learned that the duke had been one of the men who arrested Cromwell. Following the lord privy seal's death, furthermore, all individuals who had viewed him as their patron continued to enjoy royal favor.[67]

Not having learned about the divorce inquiry until July, Marillac had no reason to suspect that the probable purpose of the May arrests was to uncover proof about a conspiracy to keep Henry locked in an unfruitful marriage.[68] Investigations into these prisoners' activities failed to unearth evidence that implicated them even in indirect ways and all ultimately were released. The ability as well as the desire to impede the consummation of the king's marriage had to be established. None of the prisoners, furthermore, seemed to have direct or indirect links to a witch who could have caused Henry's impotence.

As the prisoners were being interrogated, Cromwell seems to have personally drawn the king's suspicions toward himself. In a statement two days after his arrest on 10 June, he confessed that in late May when Rutland and the queen's other councillors applied to him for licenses to permit her German attendants to return home, he had once again instructed her lord chamberlain to advise Anne to treat Henry with more pleasant behavior. The anxious king who had been consulting with his doctors and priests about the mystery of who and what were causing his impotency surely reacted with outrage at this untimely action when he learned of it. The intervention of Cromwell that had met with his approval in January when he was still trying to consummate the union with Anne was clearly inappropriate after Whitsuntide when an increasing number of his councillors had become aware of his dissatisfaction with her. Cromwell's confession is not explicit as to whether the comments to Rutland about the need for Anne to alter her behavior were expressed in a discreet exchange or in the presence of her other councillors. Even assuming he possessed the good sense to speak privately with the lord chamberlain, his comments would still have appeared as official policy to Rutland who would have assumed that any matter touching Henry this intimately would have the force of royal approval. As the vicegerent, the lord privy seal, and the great chamberlain, Cromwell routinely delivered messages in the king's name.[69]

There are at least two difficulties with his having initiated this conversation with Rutland in May. First, it is unlikely that Henry had granted him permission to confide in the earl about his marital problems in January, much less for a second time in May. Equally damaging to his political fortunes, Cromwell seems to have neglected to inform the king that he had earlier delegated this delicate duty to Anne's lord chamberlain, for when he referred to his January exchange with Rutford in his 12 June letter to Henry, he inserted the words, "for which I ask your mercy." He might well ask for mercy. Since he indicated in his letters that many of the sensitive conversations about the king's negative reaction to Anne and his inability to consummate the marriage with her occurred in the privy chamber, Cromwell must have understood the need to maintain secrecy about Henry's personal affairs. The ordinance of the Eltham Ordinances of 1526 required its members to keep "secret all such things as shall be done or said in the same [privy chamber] without disclosing any part thereof to any person not being for the time present in the same chamber. . . ."[70] Moreover, it is puzzling that Cromwell had decided to appoint Rutland to approach Anne about her demeanor toward Henry when the king had authorized him specifically to accomplish that task. It cannot be argued that Rutland was the most appropriate official for this extraodinary duty because, for example, he was fluent in German or was, like Southampton, who had spent two weeks with the queen at Calais, relatively well acquainted with her. In January, Rutland, like Cromwell, had met his mistress for the first time and in July when he informed her about the inquiry into the validity of her marriage, he required an interpreter, for, as he admitted, he could not understand her.[71]

Secondly, in May when Cromwell spoke to Rutland once more about requesting her to make herself more attractive to Henry, the king was already blaming, as his lord privy seal well knew, an obstacle for thwarting his consummation of the marriage. The suggestion that Anne's unapproachable demeanor was the cause of his impotency could have extremely adverse ramifications. Cromwell dishonored her by placing the onus of her husband's incapacity on her, thereby raising the possibility that she was not only a disobedient wife but also a traitor to her homeland's interests in that she was preventing, perhaps by deliberating making herself unpleasant to him, the conclusion of the union as agreed to in the marriage treaty.

Cromwell's statements to Rutland could not only disrupt diplomatic relationships with Cleves if Anne's brother learned of them, but might also effect an estrangement between her and her lord chamberlain, who could only conclude from the second conversation with Cromwell that she had refused to change her behavior. Moreover, it could make the task of the churchmen, who were to prepare the divorce case, somewhat awkward if they learned that the lord privy seal doubted the king's well-crafted version of what had transpired in the bed chamber. As will be explained in Chapter 9, one of the official grounds for the divorce was Henry's claim that he had decided to delay coitus until he had received proof that Anne was legally free to wed him. It was necessary for the protection of his and her honor that his sexual failure be presented formally in this guise. The divorce degree did not depend upon the assertions in Cromwell's letters, which the depositions corroborated, of the king's incapacity. The major reason for the divorce, as expressed in official documents, remained her controversial pre-contract with Lorraine, which was, as was argued in Chapter 7, ironically, the most likely cause of the king's psychogenic inability to consummate the marriage.[72]

He must have shrunk from having his bewitchment cited in divorce documents that convocation originated and that parliament approved. While the belief that witches caused relative impotence was widespread, few precedents existed for its use in divorce proceedings in England, as compared to the more numerous ones in France, for example. Whenever English husbands claimed *maleficium* as the reason for a divorce, their truthfulness was challenged. In 1584 Reginald Scot, who clearly believed that men were bewitched so "they cannot use their own wives; but any other bodies they may well enough away withall," also observed, "which witchcraft is practiced among many bad husbands for whom it were a good excuse to say they were bewitched." The concern of some that they might be charged with biological incapacity, even when, as they believed, they suffered from *maleficium*, must have been great. In 1613 Henry, earl of Northampton, chided the earl of Essex, whose wife Frances accused him of impotency, as "my good lord the gelding" although James I, who believed that Essex had been bewitched, referred to the possibility of his obtaining a cure in Poland. The claim of demonic interference could even elicit the charge, at a time when divorces were difficult to obtain, that the spouses were conspiring together to free themselves from wedlock. Equally troubling to the wife of an allegedly bewitched husband was that she could, herself, be accused of utilizing sorcery to cause his sexual dysfunction. For these and other reasons, many of the men who believed that they suffered from demonic interference, according to George Kittredge, chose to accuse the alleged witches of *maleficium*, thereby seeking a restoration of their sexual capacity instead of suing for a divorce.[73]

Over the years he held royal office, Cromwell undoubtedly disagreed with Henry about some issues, such as the spending of the proceeds from the dissolution, which could have caused the king occasionally to consider replacing him as his chief minister. However, Henry mostly spent the dissolution profits on the French wars and other matters after Cromwell's death. While as a junior member of parliament in 1523, he may have drafted a speech (although doubt exists about his authorship) in which he argued against war with France for political reasons, he was not a pacifist. By 1539 when he was a knight of the garter, he had begun to take steps to remedy the over-utilization of mercenaries in the army. To the muster that was called during the parliamentary session of 1539, furthermore, he provided 1,500 soldiers at his own expense. In the spring of 1540 no evidence suggests that controversial matters, such as the financing of foreign wars, dominated Henry's public agenda, for he was still concerned with defensive measures. The records seem to indicate that his two greatest worries were his failed marriage and the Franco-Imperial alliance. The timing of Cromwell's downfall, which occurred shortly after his second conversation with Rutland, and his refutation of the charge that he revealed the king's secrets, which is explained below, seem to point to the failed marriage as the cause of his arrest. A king who was willing to bring down a cardinal in 1529–30 and to effect a schism from Rome in 1533–34 so that he could divorce his first wife would not hesitate to order the imprisonment of his vicegerent in 1540 when he believed, with the evidence of the Rutland leaks, that he was working to keep him trapped in a sterile marriage. Like Wolsey before him, Cromwell's power was shattered by a failed marriage with international complications. Unfortunately, the only account of his arrest on 10 June is in a letter of Marillac who did not witness the event. According to him, when

Norfolk, Southampton, and others took custody of him in the council chamber of the king's house at Westminster, Cromwell protested angrily and threw his hat on the ground in exasperation. Norfolk took off the order of St. George that Cromwell wore around his neck while Southampton untied the garter on his leg before they escorted him to the Tower. All of this is rather melodramatic and was probably exaggerated, but it is true that when ministers lost office, they were stripped of their insignias of honor.[74]

Since Cromwell, as vicegerent, was the most visible promoter of the royal supremacy, it would have been ridiculous for the councillors to claim he was a papist. In his letter to Henry on 12 June, Cromwell responded to three charges. The first was that he had discussed some unidentified subject with Sir Richard Riche, chancellor of Augmentations, and Sir George Throgmorton, a suitor to that court. He denied that he had ever spoken with the two men together at the same time, but, if he had, he had never discussed the matter with which he was being charged. This issue, probably his alleged threat to wage war on the king, will be explained below. Secondly, Sir William Kingston, comptroller of the royal household, complained that he had revealed a secret matter entrusted to him by Henry fourteen days earlier, about 29 May. Cromwell denied informing anyone but Southampton about it on the previous Sunday (6 June) in accordance with royal orders. The nature of the secret was not revealed, but since, in his response, Cromwell also referred to his and Southampton's support for a "remedy" for the king's problem, it was probably that, after consultation with his churchmen, Henry had decided to initiate an inquiry into the validity of his marriage. That the charge of revealing secret matters was one of only three accusations to which he responded in this letter written two days after his arrest lends great credibility to the suggestion that it was his unauthorized discussion with Rutland about Henry's domestic crisis in late May that was the immediate cause of his downfall. Thirdly, Cromwell denied the accusation that he had retained servants illegally, although he admitted that many petitioners had requested him to receive their children into his household.[75]

In this letter, he made no reference to his religious views, and the official reasons for his arrest, as explained in the council's statement to Wallop on 10 June, did not identify him specifically as a heretic:

where the king's majesty has of long season travailed . . . . to establish such an order in matters of religion, as, neither declining on the right hand nor on the left hand, God's glory might be advanced . . . so it is, that the lord privy seal . . . neither remembering his duty herein to God, nor yet to his highness . . . hath not only, of his sensual appetite, wrought clean contrary to this his grace's most godly intent, secretly and indirectly advancing the one of the extremes, and leaving the mean indifferent true and virtuous way . . . he hath not spared most privately, most traitorously, to devise how to continue the same, and plainly in terms to say, as it has been justified to his face by good witness, that, if the king and all his realm would turn and vary from his opinions, he would fight in the field in his own person, with his sword in his hand, against him and all other; adding, that if he lived a year or two, he trusted to bring things to that frame, that it should not lie in the king's power to resist . . . it, if he would; binding his words with such oaths, and making gesture and demonstration with his arms, that it might well appear he had no less fixed in his heart, that was uttered with his mouth. For the which apparent and most detestable treasons, and also for many other great treasons and enormities, whereof upon the opening of the first accusation he has been and stands by grave testimony accused, he is committed to the Tower of London and there to remain until it shall please his Majesty to have him thereupon tried according to the order of the laws.[76]

Clearly, the major concern here was his threat, which was reinforced by hostile gestures, to wage war on the king, for his contemporaries viewed the intent to commit treason as as heinous as the act, itself. It is likely that this alleged threat was the grave matter, embodied in a fictionalized narrative of their belief in his guilt that Throgmorton and Riche, both of whom benefited financially from Cromwell's fall, had imparted to Henry and which Cromwell had denied in his 12 June letter. It is ironic that Riche was also the major witness, "rogue," as M. L. Bush has labeled him, against Sir Thomas More in 1535. That he was a scoundrel on the lookout for opportunities to curry royal favor and win advancement is a tempting characterization, and perhaps he was nothing more than an opportunist eager to bring down a leading minister from whom he had been estranged, for Cromwell hinted in his letter of 12 June of their strained relationship. Nevertheless, the authorities took his evidence seriously, and in July Riche was one of the officials appointed to oversee Anne's translation from queen consort to king's sister. Although the council's letter to Wallop on 10 June referred to Cromwell's disagreement with Henry on church governance, it included no clear explanation of what the nature of that dispute was except to say he had advanced one of the extremes. On 11 June, Cranmer, seemingly unaware that Cromwell was to be accused of heresy, expressed amazement to the king that the vicegerent could have committed treason. Marillac, picking up rumors as usual, did hear that Cromwell was in trouble because he had favored the German Lutherans too much, a not unreasonable assumption since it would have been incredible to assume that he had supported the other extreme, papal authority.[77]

In the meantime, members of the French government began to accuse Cromwell of treason. At the fall of a powerful minister, those who have blamed him personally for responding negatively to their petitions for redress tend to climb on the bandwagon, raising other issues against him. The French had two reasons to welcome his ruin. The first was the Rochepot affair. By July 1540 Francis had written three times to Henry about the dispute; in one letter he accused the lord privy seal of having seized a great portion of the prize. On 24 July Cromwell denied the French claims, and reviews of the dispute after his death sustained the original judgment against Rochepot.[78]

The second reason Francis welcomed his fall was that his diplomats had long identified Cromwell as one of Chapuys's special informants. To glean information about French and Imperial matters and to spread false information to their courts, various English ministers either befriended or made enemies of their residents. In 1539 before his departure for home, for example, Castillon complained to the constable that Cromwell had caused Henry to be angry with the French embassy and assured him that Norfolk was entirely favorable to their cause. This opinion about the duke's friendship probably led Montmorency optimistically but incorrectly to believe that Norfolk would support Rochepot's claims. On 29 July, the day after Cromwell's execution, Marillac informed the constable that Chapuys would no longer be able to rely on Cromwell for the follies (*follyes*) that he had once held. A bizarre discovery further confirmed his alliance with Cromwell. In late March 1539, Maioris, the replacement for Chapuys, had reached London two days before Marillac, the successor of Castillon. It is likely that Chapuys assumed Maioris would move into his apartments in which he left some official documents. Instead, Marillac lodged in Chapuys's rooms where he discovered despatches that proved Cromwell had been regularly passing on gossip to him. Although it was not until

September 1540 that Marillac mentioned his find to Montmorency, the previous knowledge of Cromwell's association with Chapuys must have helped to shape French expressions of pleasure at his fall despite his reassurances after Norfolk's return from France in March that he felt far more friendship for Francis than for Charles. Incredibly, in June Harst had heard that the French embassy might actually put in a good word for Cromwell! He personally had little sympathy for the fallen minister and noted in a letter to Cleves that Cromwell was caught in the trap he had set for others. This unfeeling comment and Cromwell's unwillingness to discuss Anne's martial problems with her should go a long way toward putting to rest once and for all the assertion that he had engineered her royal marriage.[79]

Shortly after Wallop conveyed news of Cromwell's arrest to the French government, John, Cardinal du Bellay, took the opportunity to relate to him some damaging rumors about the fallen minister's ambitions. After returning home in 1539, Castillon had reportedly revealed that he had learned from two trustworthy Englishmen that Cromwell harbored ambitions to become their king. The cardinal also repeated to Wallop the Portuguese ambassador's remark in 1538 that diplomats generally assumed that Cromwell not only planned to become monarch but also to wed Mary Tudor. The Portuguese ambassador may have had as his source some rumors about the princess that Chapuys had reported in July 1536 after the fall of Anne Boleyn, for the news of ambassadors tended to be spread from one court to another through diplomatic networks. Chapuys had pointed out that some of Mary's attendants had expressed fears that Henry would compel her to wed Cromwell in order to prevent her from marrying abroad where she would be free to denounce the Statutes of Supremacy and Succession. He did not believe the allegation and went on to speculate that if the king did actually offer his daughter to Cromwell, he would decline the honor.[80]

Modern historians have justifiably dismissed the charge of Cromwell's ambitions to wed Mary as absurd, but her suspicious father, who was seeking someone to blame for his dilemma, did take it seriously. He must have been outraged at the possibility of her union with one of his subjects, because among other reasons her illegitimate status made it imperative that she wed some continental nobleman or prince like Philip of Bavaria or Charles of Orléans, to bolster her social standing and prestige. As the Spanish ambassador was to remark in 1553 at her accession, if she married an Englishman her "posterity would not have as much renown." On 22 June 1540 her concerned father directed Wallop to verify the rumors about Cromwell. Two weeks later in association with Carne, who had recently joined him, Wallop assured Henry that the cardinal had instructed Castillon to send a written confirmation of his claims about Cromwell's royal plans, and that when it arrived, they would forward it to England. Du Bellay had also revealed to them, the diplomats further noted, that some nine months earlier after Francis and he had considered the matter, they had come to the conclusion that Henry would make Cromwell an earl or a duke and permit him to wed the princess. They also believed that Cromwell had been endeavoring to prevent Mary's marriage so that he himself could wed her. Wallop and Carne further informed Henry that the Portuguese ambassador had repeated to them the rumors he had earlier heard about Cromwell's ambitions, which were, he claimed, well known among the diplomatic corps. Some days later, on 10 July, the English agents attended court and spoke with the constable, who, outraged at the treatment of his brother Rochepot, swore that it was common knowledge that Cromwell had planned to wed Mary. His evidence for this exaggerated claim may have been a letter he received on 10 February from two French ambassadors in the Netherlands who asserted that Henry would not permit Mary to wed anyone at all but that if he relented on this score, then she would have to marry an unnamed Englishman.[81]

In the meantime, searchers collected information at Cromwell's home that a suspicious monarch could view as evidence for some of the charges that were surfacing in France and elsewhere. The copy made at Cleves on 26 February 1540 of the notarial certificate, the beer pot document that was composed in Latin, in which the duke of Guelders and his chancellor had proclaimed in 1535 that the Lorraine–Cleves marriage would not proceed, was, according to Edward, Lord Herbert, the first biographer of Henry, found in Cromwell's papers rather than in the royal archives. Although Lord Herbert was unsure whether Cromwell had shown it to Henry, an English translation of it was added to the documentation gathered for the divorce. There is undoubtedly a simple explanation. Having learned of Henry's decision to initiate the inquiry into his marriage,

Cromwell may well have begun to collect together the relevant evidence concerning her contract with Lorraine. However, it seems extraordinary (as noted in Chapter 7), that none of the correspondence between the crown and Cleves during the spring of 1540 ever mentioned the receipt of the beer pot document or, conversely, ever complained that the promised instrument had not been forwarded. It is also surprising that Harst remained unaware of its existence until December 1541. The suspicion lingers that Cromwell viewed the certificate as a true invalidation of the Lorraine contract; perhaps this view lay behind his decision in May to send word to Anne through Rutland once again to behave more pleasantly to the king. When the document arrived in England, however, it should have been, and may have been, forwarded to Cranmer and Durham for their expert opinions about its validity.[82]

Marillac had also heard that some letters written by Lutheran lords were found among his papers. It would have been surprising if some had not been discovered since he had been involved in negotiations with them as well as with Catholic rulers. Given Cardinal du Bellay's claim that Cromwell had attempted to prevent Mary's marriage to her noble suitors, a letter that may have been found among his papers would have been particularly damaging. On 21 August 1540, almost a month after Cromwell's death, Philip of Bavaria informed Mont that he had sent the deceased a letter concerning his alliance with Mary that was addressed to Henry and dated 25 April. He knew that Cromwell had received the message at Whitsuntide but he suspected that it had never been forwarded to the king and begged him to see that Henry did receive a copy of it. Philip further indicated that he hoped Southampton whom he considered a friend would become lord privy seal. It is possible that no such message from Philip was found in Cromwell's papers, for erroneous complaints like this often surfaced at a favorite's fall. There seems little reason, however, after the lord privy seal's death, for Philip to invent his letter, and there is also no way of determining whether, if it ever existed, Cromwell had actually forwarded it on to Henry.[83]

In some respects Cromwell's inaction could be viewed as damaging to his case. As he had failed to offer a concrete solution for extracting Henry from his marital tangle, presumably because the king seems not to have not requested it of him, some colleagues might have concluded that he hoped to keep Henry locked in an unfruitful marriage. This was the claim that Hilles later forwarded to Henry Bullinger. Foxe also reported the rumors that, had Cromwell lived, he would have tried to prevent the divorce and that before his execution, he had said: "That he wished his dagger in him that had dissolved or broken that marriage." The July deposition of Wriothesley for the divorce can be viewed as support for these later rumors. On either 6 or 7 June, in an impromptu meeting with Cromwell at his Austin Friars home in London, Wriothesley swore that the lord privy seal had confided that Henry had failed to consummate his marriage with Anne. When he had inquired how the king "may be relieved by one way or other," the lord privy seal had remarked that it was a "great matter." The next day, when Wriothesley asked him again to find some way of relieving the king of his "grief and trouble," Cromwell said only that it was "a great matter." Wriothesley then pleaded, "let the remedy be searched for" to which Cromwell had merely responded, "Well." When Henry had told him in late May of his "secret matter," which was likely the planned inquiry into the validity of the marriage, he had instructed Cromwell not to reveal it to anyone else. Later on 6 June Henry had granted him permission to inform the lord admiral. Given this royal mandate, It becomes obvious why Cromwell was so taciturn with Wriothesley about a solution to the king's problem, but when the conversation is repeated out of context, it makes him appear unwilling to seek a remedy for Henry's "grief." In fact, Wriothesley's testimony, which lacks corroboration, does not ring true; it was likely a fictionalized narrative created to indicate his conviction that Cromwell not only hoped to keep the king trapped in the Cleves marriage but was also incapable of maintaining secrecy about the king's private matters.[84]

With this possibility in mind, some questions need to be raised about the disposition. Although by Whitsuntide (16 May), according to Cromwell, many councillors were aware that Henry was dissatisfied with his marriage, why did Wriothesley, one of the two principal secretaries, remain ignorant of this fact for another three weeks? His alleged ignorance until 6 or 7 June is especially puzzling because shortly thereafter Henry asked him to assist Winchester in arranging the procedures to be followed for the divorce inquiry. And why, on 12 June, less than a week after this alleged discussion with Wriothesley, and again on 30 June, did Cromwell explicitly state that he had spoken only with Southampton and Rutland about the king's inability to consummate the marriage? Even if he had revealed secret matters such as this (which should be discussed only in the privy chamber) in those impromptu meetings at his London home with Wriothesley, who was not a member of the privy chamber, what was the point? Why in June, five months after the marriage, inform him about Henry's incapacity when he could not also tell him about the divorce inquiry? The most vital message in Wriothesley's July testimony was, in fact, his confirmation of the inability of the lord privy seal to maintain secrecy about the king's problems. This was the blunder Cromwell had actually made with Anne's lord chamberlain in January and May, and probably not one he had made with the principal secretary in June. Of all deponents to call to testify in July moreover, why Wriothesley? Even if the speculation is incorrect that some version of this conversation with Cromwell did occur, he offered no new information that would assist in the divorce case. In the months leading up to 16 May, it was not to Wriothesley the king confided his marital problems. The alleged June conversation with Cromwell added no relevant facts to the divorce case. While it confirmed that he knew the marriage had not been consummated, he had already admitted to having been privy to that knowledge in his June letters. Moreover, others could swear to Henry's incapacity based on their personal conversations with him. Wriothesley, who also wrote out Cobham's deposition, which alleged statements by the younger Pallant that the young man later denied, was quite capable of inventing accounts that reflected the state of affairs that he perceived to be true. In fact, the individual who should have given the testimony to which Wriothesley signed his name was Rutland, but on the morning of 7 July the earl surely did not have permission to make the trip down the Thames from Richmond Palace, where he was monitoring Anne's reactions to the divorce inquiry, to Westminster, with Suffolk and the other deponents. Someone in authority had to stay in charge of the distraught queen's household. Thus, it seems likely that Wriothesley gave evidence about a fake conversation in June with Cromwell as a substitute for the real ones that had occurred between Rutland and Cromwell in January and in late May.[85]

Even the wedding of Cromwell's son Gregory could be viewed as a step in achieving his royal ambitions. Families who hoped "to gain the highest prestige," as Jennifer Ward has pointed out, sought marriage alliances with the ruling family. In 1537 Gregory had wed Elizabeth Seymour, widow of Sir Gregory Oughtred and sister to the queen, thereby becoming brother-in-law to the king and shortly thereafter uncle of the royal heir. It was a relationship that Henry favored. In 1538 when it was suggested that the duchess of Richmond, the widow of his natural son, might become the wife of Sir Thomas Seymour, another sibling of Queen Jane, Henry approved the proposed bridegroom's nomination of Cromwell as the family's negotiator because his son Gregory was the husband of Elizabeth. That a man like Cromwell, who had been raised from lowly circumstances, would hope for loftier relationships might occur to a distrustful king, as he sought to verify the French report that his imprisoned minister had hoped to wed Mary. The French claim about his wedding plans for the princess when coupled with Wriothesley's testimony that he had no strategy for extricating Henry from an unfruitful marriage and that he revealed sensitive royal matters without permission made Cromwell's position extremely vulnerable. It might even occur to the suspicious king that his lord privy seal hoped to replace the Tudor dynasty with a Cromwellian dynasty.[86]

The early identification of his actions as treasonable and not as heretical is evident in the process by which the bill of attainder was enacted. He was not to be tried in a court of law, for instead parliament prepared a bill of attainder, which needed only the king's assent to become statutory law, to declare him guilty of various capital offences. It is ironic that Cromwell stood condemned by attainder because it was only after he had come to power that the earliest of these statutes was enacted. On 17 June the House of Lord's *Journal* named the bill, "Billa Attincture Thome Comitis Essex" with no reference to heresy; it was read for a third time on 19 June and sent to the Commons. Probably between 23 and 29 June, the Commons crafted and approved a substitute bill; both were returned to the Lords.[87]

In the new bill, the first section enumerates numerous actions such as the illegal retention of servants in which he was said to have circumvented the king's laws. A second section, which probably originated in the Commons, refers to sacramentarianism, which will be addressed later in this chapter. A third section contains the charge of

Riche and Throgmorton that he had threatened to wage war on Henry. Here Barnes's name was linked to that threat.

In the last Day of March [1539] . . . upon demonstration and declaration then and there made unto him, that there were many new preachers, as Robert Barnes clerk, and other, whereof part were committed to the Tower of London, for preaching and teaching of lewd learning against your highness' proclamations; the same Thomas affirming the same preaching to be good . . . did not let to declare . . . these most traitorous and detestable Words ensuing . . . That if the king would turn from it, yet I would not turn; And if the king did turn, and all his people, I would fight in the field in mine own person with my sword in my hand against him and all others. . . .[88]

At issue was not the preachers' heresy but Henry's right, as supreme head, to govern the ecclesiastical establishment. It is interesting that the Lords named only Barnes and, even more interesting, that the date of 31 March 1539 was chosen. Clearly, they invoked his name because they remembered his recent dispute with Winchester and his heresy conviction. Equally clearly, they made no attempt to ascertain his whereabouts in 1539. On 5 March of that year Henry had granted him credences to go on missions to Saxony, Denmark, and the city of Wismar, and on 10 March, a royal warrant had provided him an allowance for diets and post money. At the exact time the bill of attainder accused him of preaching in London, he had been abroad on crown business. The fictionalized facts in their narrative simply reflected their firmly held conviction that Cromwell and he were guilty of treason.[89]

Sandwiched in between the two sections with the claims that Cromwell was a traitor are the following charges:

Thomas Cromwell, earl of Essex, being a detestable heretic . . . has secretly set forth and dispersed into . . . this your realm . . . great numbers of false erroneous books . . . to induce and lead your subjects to . . . refusal . . . of the belief in the most holy and blessed sacrament of the Altar . . . Certain matters . . . translated into English . . . have . . . been against the said most blessed and holy sacrament; yet the said Thomas Cromwell, earl of Essex . . . has affirmed the same heresy so translated to be good . . . and said that it was as lawful for every christian man to be a minister of the said sacrament as well as a priest . . . your vicegerent has licensed and authorized divers persons, detected and suspected of heresies, openly to teach and preach. . . .[90]

In the days after his arrest and before the enactment of the bill of attainder, he was asked neither to respond to these charges nor to defend his orthodoxy. Although most of the questions put to him as a prisoner concerned the marriage of Henry and Anne, no statement referring to it surfaced in the attainder.[91]

Why, then, charge him as a detestable sacramentary? On 25 September 1538, the landgrave of Hesse and the duke elector of Saxony explained to Henry that letters had been found in the hands of Peter Tasch, an anabaptist (a generic name for members of radical religious groups) that had mentioned England, providing proof to them that the heresy had spread to the realm. Their comments about the members of this sect who they claimed were "men mad, carried by fond phantasies, great deceivers" follow:

that they, condemning the baptism of infants, be baptized again; this is the badge of the whole sect . . . they say all things ought to be common . . . Magistrates may exercise no power . . . they utterly take away all political orders, which God both did institute and much approve . . . For surely this is true, the devil, which is an homicide, carries men that are entangled in false opinions to unlawful slaughters . . . They take away right opinions both of the deity of Christ and of his two natures; as the Manichaeans did, boast of their illuminations, revelations, with other like phantasies . . . Yet of all things they most filthy pollute the holiness of matrimony, granting commonly to one man many wives, to one wife many husbands. . . . Many embrace these monstrous opinions by malice . . . being moved thereunto by wanton desires, and having full hope of a more licentious life . . . And this barbarous confusion of super-stitions . . . breaks out into seditions, murders . . .[92]

Their "illuminations, revelations, with other like phantasies" caused them to be associated with the devil. During these visions, some of these "terrors of the devil," fell to the ground as though they were having seizures, actions that led witnesses to believe that they suffered from demonic possession. The most infamous anabaptists were those who had taken over Münster in 1534. Horrified Lutherans had joined with equally horrified Catholics to destroy their control of this town.[93]

The earliest record of anabaptism in England dates from 1535, but the most serious outbreak with reference to Cromwell's attainder was the Calais controversy. In the spring of 1540 royal commission-ers had been confiscating the town's archives, which included corre-spondence between Lisle and Cromwell about its heresies and other troubles. Independent evidence indicates that Cromwell's friends believed that he was deeply opposed to sacramentarianism, which is a specific variant of anabaptism that denies the real presence in the sacrament of the altar. Even in a letter of June 1539 to Lisle that responded to the charges the lord deputy had made against Damplip, Cromwell had characterized these radical beliefs as "most detestable heresy." In fact, Cranmer, whose later evidence indicates treated sacramentaries in his diocese with sympathy, actually interrogated Damplip and ordered his return to Calais. As vicegerent, it was not Cromwell's duty to determine whether the accused were guilty of heresy, but it was his duty to supervise their punishment when they were convicted of religious errors. In this respect, as Henry's principal minister, he possessed less power than Wolsey, who as a churchman had held the authority to view evidence, to judge, and to condemn heretics. While Cromwell was authorized to investigate governance and financial abuses of the church and to regulate popular piety, he did not have the capacity to decide who was heretical and who was not. Furthermore, areas of church law, such as the matrimonial code, as noted earlier, were entirely beyond his competence. In 1536 it had been Richard Sampson, then the future bishop of Chichester, who had assembled the case for annulling Henry's marriage to Anne Boleyn.[94]

In May 1539 Cromwell also justifiably cautioned Lisle about accepting the claims of witnesses that individuals were guilty of this "heinous crime" until it was ascertained that the accusers understood the nature of the heresy. Along with the king and other ministers, he was greatly concerned that Lisle and the Calais council had been handling religious disputes and other matters so ineptly they were fomenting widespread rancor. Warning that this divisiveness would jeopardize the security of the frontier town, Cromwell recommended that Lisle:

by all means devise how with charity and mild handling of things to quench this slanderous bruit . . . ever exhorting men discreetly, and without rigor or extreme dealing, to know and serve God truly and their Prince and Sovereign Lord with all humility and obedience.

In contrast to the troubles of the Calais governors, Muriel McClendon has recently pointed out how Norwich magistrates managed effectively to rule their town and to prevent outside interference despite their religious divisions. This was the goal Cromwell had expressed in the above letter to Lisle who had obviously failed to

respond positively to those instructions. It was a strategy of modera-
tion that modern historians, such as Irvin Horst, interpret as occurring generally in Reformation England. While, for example, Henry
did execute more anabaptists than all the Lollards burned by his
fifteenth-century predecessors, he still executed only about twenty, a
small number compared to the hundreds who were killed in
Habsburg lands.[95]

Because of Cromwell's cautious approach to handling religious
divisions at Calais, some scholars have speculated that he was
working to protect the sacramentarians from prosecution.[96] A few
Calais residents did make this charge against him during a time
when there were a series of issues disturbing them, not all of which
were religious, for one observer of Calais defenses in 1539 protested
that it would only take forty Frenchmen to seize their port. Clearly,
his letters to Lisle seem to indicate that his greatest concern was for
the security of the frontier town.[97]

If some modern scholars find it plausible to justify the problematic
claim that Cromwell's goal was to protect the Calais sacramentarians from prosecution, then how much more plausible would that
charge seem to a concerned monarch who had begun to suspect his
lord privy seal of treason. No record exists of Lisle's confessions after
he was imprisoned, but surely in trying to clear himself of incompetence, he would have lashed out at Cromwell, the person he seems to
have blamed for his troubles. The Calais controversy almost certainly explains why the variant of anabaptism with which Cromwell
was charged was sacramentarianism.[98]

The next step then is to explain why the charge of heresy was
made against him. The Lords had, after all, believed that it had
enough evidence for his treasonable activities to enact a bill of
attainder. The landgrave of Hesse and the duke elector, it will be
remembered, claimed that the heretics were "terrors of the devil"
with "wanton desires." Other contemporaries, who called them
"monstrous dragons" and "angels of satan" associated heretics,
witches, and sorcerers with individuals who committed illegal sexual
acts, or as Henry Smith was later to say, heresy was a "harlot." In his
visitation articles for his diocese, Bishop Bonner routinely asked,
"Whether there by any that is a sacramentary or anabaptist or liber-
tine?" Inevitably, all heretics were identified either as licentious, as
adulterers, as sodomites, or as the authors of some other illicit sexual

acts. Henry was surely intent upon finding the witch or sorcerer who had caused his impotence; if such a creature were identified and if there were even some indirect association with Cromwell, it is plausible, given the charges emerging at Calais, that the crown could link him to the creature by labelling him a sacramentary, a heretic widely recognized as a wanton agent of Satan. Henry, according to Horst, was more sensitive about the heresy of the Sacrament of the Altar than any other theological point. Only the first article of the Act of Six Articles, which upheld transubstantiation, carried with it the death penalty of burning as a heretic when the individual held the belief only and did not attempt to teach or preach it. In the 1540 Act of Pardons, furthermore, all those who held errors about the "most holy and blessed Sacrament of the Altar," were exempted even though Cromwell was already specifically excluded by name.[99]

As it turned out, two sorcerers and a witch were found to be associated with Walter, Lord Hungerford of Heytesbury, a client of Cromwell's. Hungerford, who was the descendant of an illustrious Lancastrian family that had lost its title by attainder in 1461, had his principal residence at Farleigh Castle in Somerset but also owned extensive estates throughout Wiltshire, including most especially in Heytesbury parish. Sir Walter, who had close connections with the neighboring Seymour family, was called to the parliament of 1536 as Baron Hungerford of Heytesbury. Cromwell seems to have begun to serve as his patron at the behest of Hungerford's father-in-law, John, Lord Hussey, who in 1532 had requested him to assist his son-in-law in obtaining appointment as sheriff of Wiltshire. From 1533 when Hungerford assumed the office of sheriff of Wells until his death in 1540 he continued to enjoy Cromwell's favor.[100]

On 15 June the council began an inquiry into some misdemeanors a woman named Mother Huntley had alleged against Hungerford.[101] The investigation was initiated four days before the Lords passed Cromwell's original bill of attainder and sent it to the Commons. It was the information that the council unearthed about Hungerford, it is being argued here, that caused the Commons, sometime after 23 June and before 29 June, to add the heresy charges to Cromwell's bill of attainder.

In Hungerford's bill of attainder, which the Lords read first on 2 July, parliament accused him of three different crimes. First, on 20 October 1536, although he had pretended to arrest the traitor,

William Bird, the vicar of Bradford on Avon who was charged with sympathizing with the rebels in the Pilgrimage of Grace, Hungerford had actually employed him as his chaplain for several months. Like his alleged patron, Bird was also attainted for treason in 1540. Because the attainder emphasized Bird's association with the northern rebellion, it is possible that it was Hungerford's marriage to Lady Elizabeth Hussey whose father had been executed in 1537 for complicity in the Lincolnshire rising that had first brought him to the attention of the council. Of the several letters from the Hungerford family that were found among Cromwell's papers, one of the most interesting was from Lady Hungerford, who accused her husband of having imprisoned her for three or four years in the tower of Farleigh Castle. After complaining bitterly to Cromwell about her treatment, she pleaded plaintively for a divorce. Actually, Lord Hungerford had already petitioned for this action, and in February 1540 William Petre and Thomas Benet had been commissioned in the king's name to proceed in a *divorticum a mensa et thoro* process that would not permit remarriage. According to Lady Hungerford, her husband had discharged the commission when he learned that after the divorce he would still have to support her financially. Stanford Lehmberg has observed that it was "ironic that the final surviving paper issued by Cromwell as vicegerent" was this aborted commission. While suffering in his unfruitful marriage, Henry may have had less sanguine thoughts about the behavior of his vicegerent, who was willing to assist Hungerford in divorcing his wife but seemed ready to keep him locked in an unfruitful marriage.[102]

Secondly, on 22 March 1537 at Farleigh in Wiltshire, and at other times and places, Hungerford had called upon Sir Hugh Wood and Dr. Maudlin to use their magic to predict how long the king would live. Hungerford had also enticed them to work with Mother Roche, probably reputed to be a witch, to determine Henry's length of life and whether he would be successful against the pilgrims. Thirdly, Hungerford, who was "replete with detestable vices," on 6 May 1537 at Wiltshire and at other times and places, had for three years "exercised, frequented, and used the abominable and detestable vice and sin of buggery with William Master, Thomas Smith" and other servants. Typically, accusations of buggery involved members of the same household.[103]

The connection between sodomites and heretics can be found in Hesse's and Saxony's letter of complaint to Henry. He noted that some of the ideas of the anabaptists could be traced to the dualistic concepts of the Manichaeans, a medieval heretical group. They were the intellectual ancestors of the twelfth-century Albigensians, who were sometimes labeled as Bulgars because they were thought to have lived in Bulgaria. The dualistic nature of their beliefs had led them on a quest for Godly purity and an determination to escape from the material world. Believers in reincarnation, they argued against siring children to perpetuate the never-ending cycle of souls being reborn into the material world. Although their goal was to escape from this cycle of rebirths, their enemies accused them of non-procreative or unnatural sexual acts; the term buggery, a name for anal intercourse which was a variant of the more general term of sodomy, was corrupted from the word Bulgar.[104]

Besides that his execution time and place were the same as Cromwell's, Hungerford's death was significant because he was the only man accused of this crime to be executed in the Tudor period, or, as Wriothesley the chronicler said, for "treason of buggery." Considering that gentlemen often slept two to a bed, it is amazing that so few individuals were charged with this act, which had been forbidden by statutory law in 1534. Marillac, who as usual was passing on gossip to his correspondents, reported both Hungerford's use of magic and the act of sodomy, even claiming that he had forced his own daughter. No reference to incest can be found in the bill of attainder, and Hilles was later to limit his comments to the assertion that Hungerford had actually died for computing Henry's death.[105]

Often the accusations against individuals charged with treason had references to their use of magic to predict how long the king would live. In those cases, it was not the traitor but the common people like Mother Roche who were identified as the sorcerer or witch. So widespread was the belief in demonically inspired magic that even royal officials were reputed to have had use of it to win Henry's favor, for rumors claimed that both Wolsey and Cromwell had relied upon magical rings to gain power.[106] With the charges of heresy and sorcery whirling around Cromwell and his client Hungerford, they remained in prison until after the king's marriage was dissolved, the topic of Chapter 9.

9

HENRY'S SISTER

The official inquiry into the validity of the king's marriage was initiated on 29 June when Winchester, assisted by Wriothesley, drew up memoranda listing a number of tasks for the council to complete. It must: advise the clergy, presumably in the double convocation, about the appropriate procedures to be followed in their deliberations; communicate to Henry the various steps that needed to be taken for the inquiry; initiate two searches: Petre and Wriothesley to seek knowledge at Cromwell's home of whether the contract with Lorraine was *per verba de futuro* or *per verba de presenti*, and Petre to question the notaries, Anthony Hussey and Richard Watkins, and others about the whereabouts of Anne's sworn statement in January that she was free to wed the king; determine how and by whom the queen was to be notified of the inquiry; ask Henry about which councillors should question Cromwell (His responses to their interrogation were detailed in Chapter 8); request the clergy to advise Henry about how he should "order himself as using his liberty from matrimony or otherwise in the meantime"; assemble as much evidence as possible to prove his "dissent" from consummating the union and obtain the queen's confession of her bodily integrity. In addition, Wriothesley listed six matters concerning the legality of Anne's English and Lorraine marriages. The councillors needed to determine: (1) the difference between *sponsalia de presenti* and *sponsalia de futuro*; (2) whether either of these vows could be declared invalid if there was an appearance of the lack of personal consent even though witnesses could testify to the presence of consent; (3) whether the lack of consummation with "a certain horror in nature" was reason enough to nullify a marriage; (4) whether the beer pot document, which had copies of the 1535 Guelders repudiations, was a sufficient discharge "for the former spousal"; (5) whether it was a lawful impediment for parties aware of the first spousal to marry without a better discharge than the beer pot document; (6) what depositions and how many deponents were necessary to prove the lack of consent.[1]

Probably on the same day that Winchester and Wriothesley drew up these memoranda, Henry requested Wallop, his resident in France, to question the cardinal of Lorraine, paternal uncle of Francis, about the status of the marriage contract between his nephew and Anne and to obtain from him copies of it, if at all possible. He admonished Wallop to make "it appear" as though the inquiry did not "proceed from" him (the king). If the ambassador succeeded in discussing the contract with the cardinal and then made a report on his findings to Henry, the correspondence has not survived.[2]

The next action, the effect of which was to establish a kind of safety net for the king's plans to remarry, occurred on 3 July when the House of Lords approved a bill to reduce matrimonial impediments that was accepted by the House of commons two days later. Having been given Henry's assent, the statute paved the way for his future wedlock by declaring that all unions contracted and consummated after 1 July were indissoluble even if one or both of the spouses had previously entered into an unconsummated marriage, as he had done, of course, with Anne. Regardless of the ecclesiastical determination about his alliance with her, this statute made it necessary for the courts to rule that the Cleves alliance would not invalidate the match with Katherine Howard that he surely already had in mind for late July.[3]

On 4 July, anticipating that parliament would ask him to permit an inquiry into the legality of his marriage, Henry instructed Richard Pate to obtain an audience with the emperor on 8 July for the purpose of informing him of that official action.[4] On 6 July, two days after this letter to Pate was sent, Audley, Cranmer, Tunstall, Suffolk, and Southampton, the original negotiators of the Cleves treaty, minus the imprisoned Cromwell but with the addition of Norfolk, reported to the House of Lords on the existence of certain impediments to the king's marriage and obtained their permission to seek his approval for an ecclesiastical inquiry into its validity.[5]

After the commons responded positively to the Lords' request, a joint parliamentary delegation procured an audience with Henry to persuade him to permit the inquiry. By canon law the only divorce possible, but without the right of remarriage, was a legal separation, *divoritcum a mensa et thoro*, the grounds for which were adultery, heresy, apostasy, or cruelty. The action parliament sought was an inquiry into whether the king's union with Anne was invalid from its inception, the remedy for which, if the answer was in the affirmative, would be an annulment, *divorticum a vinculo matrimonii*, with remarriage possible for both spouses. Although this was to be the king's third union to end in annulment, the break-up of marriages in Tudor society generally was a relatively rare occurrence.[6]

As Anne's consent was also required, Henry sent Beard to her with a written message alerting her to the inquiry. At 4:00 a.m. on 6 July, the day the validity of the marriage was to be raised in parliament, Harst arrived at Richmond at Anne's request to explain to her lord chamberlain the gist of the letter delivered to her by Beard. When later informing Southampton about the interview, Rutland reported that because he could not understand either Anne or Harst, he had drafted as his interpreter Wymond Carew, her receiver-general, who was the bearer of the present letter. As she had, Rutland further remarked, taken the matter "heavily," he had attempted to comfort her by emphasizing the need before God to "discharge" her conscience and Henry's about their union. Rutland also assured her that as parliament was concerned enough about the marriage's legality to request the king to permit an ecclesiastical investigation into it, he should accept their advice. At her lord chamberlain's comment that she had "cause to rejoice and not to be sorry," she remained silent. As her outraged ambassador refused to carry or write her response to Henry, she returned Beard to him with an oral message.[7]

On the afternoon of 6 July two further meetings about the inquiry occurred. The king dispatched Audley, Suffolk, Winchester, Kingston, and Sir Thomas Cheyney, along with Riche as interpreter, to Richmond to explain more fully to Anne the reasons for his decision to accept the parliamentary petition. In their letter to him that evening, the councillors reported that she had volunteered only that she was "content always with your majesty," and that, except for Winchester who was scheduled to address the double convocation the next day, they would spend the night there and would brief him about their exchanges with her upon their return. They were confident that all would "proceed well" and that his "virtuous desire" would be obtained, a positive tone on the unfolding events that may have come as a welcome surprise to her husband. On 24 July he was to remind the bishop of Bath and Wells who had joined Wotten's embassy at Cleves that when he had departed in late June, her conformity had been unexpected. Henry did not explain why he had anticipated her recalcitrance, but he may have thought that her strength of character, which surfaced in the recent dispute concerning Mary, might lead her to oppose him on this action, as had Catherine of Aragon in similar circumstances. In fact, his opinion about Anne's reaction to an inquiry into the validity of their marriage was initially correct. She was not as submissive as his councillors had indicated on 6 July, and their letter needs to be read in association with Harst's three dispatches to Cleves dated between 7 and 10 July. That she had actually fainted at their arrival, probably from shock that action on the inquiry was moving so quickly, had not deterred them, for they had simply waited until she revived and appeared calmer before continuing their mission. During their conversations with her, when they referred to documents they possessed relating to her Lorraine marriage, she asked, but without success, that copies of them be left for her examination. Not easily defeated, she dispatched Beard the next day to Henry with another request for this evidence, but the council returned only her husband's response that she should cease sending messages to him. Harst, who had recommended that she refrain from assenting to the inquiry, did not believe that she had approved of it on 6 July. Since the language barrier, even with interpreters present, was formidable, a good deal of miscommunication or even misrepresentation may have existed at this stage of the process. In the meantime, Harst was the central figure in the second important meeting of the day. While the above councillors were closeted with Anne at Richmond, he was listening to the explanations of Norfolk, Cranmer, Tunstall, and Browne at Westminster about the reasons for the inquiry. He refused their request to write an objective report about it to the duke of Cleves, and after the official meeting was over, even attempted, but failed, to persuade Tunstall to halt the inquiry.[8]

The next morning at Westminster, acting upon the commission of the king to examine his marriage, the double convocation met at the chapter house of St. Peter's Church. With Cranmer presiding, Winchester gave a learned oration on the reasons for invalidating the king's union with Anne. Subsequently, a committee composed of

Cranmer, Edward Lee, archbishop of York, Bonner, Tunstall, Winchester, John Bell, bishop of Worcester, and eight members of the lower houses was charged to investigate the truth of his assertions. Five members of this committee (Tunstall, Winchester, Richard Gwent, Thirlby, and Richard Layton, dean of York) scheduled depositions of several individuals for that afternoon between one and six o'clock.[9]

Later that same morning the royal council informed the agents of foreign powers in England about this crisis. Without being apprised of the reason for their summons, both the Imperial and French residents were appointed to attend court at a fixed time to hear separately in the privy council chamber, in the presence of a number of councillors, Tunstall's Latin oration on the king's decision to authorize the convocations, as parliament had petitioned, to inquire into the validity of his marriage. The government, Marillac later informed Francis, had closed all passages abroad to give the councillors time to alert their ambassadors about this grave matter before rumors about it could reach them, or, indeed, could reach Anne's family.[10]

That afternoon the double convocation's subcommittee completed most of the depositions.[11] References to the one sworn jointly by the negotiators of the marriage treaty and to the several individual statements of Henry, Suffolk, Heneage, Southampton, Browne, Butts, Chamber, Russell, Cobham, and Wriothesley were made in Chapters 6 through 8 concerning five issues. In October 1539 the king and his ministers had instructed the Cleves ambassadors to bring with them, when they returned with Anne, copies of the documentation that would prove her Lorraine marriage was repudiated. After the Rochester greeting, Henry expressed a reluctance to wed her. The union remained unconsummated. Cobham claimed that Pallant the younger, who denied making the statement, had confessed that papists were attempting to obtain a dispensation of Anne's Lorraine union to permit her English marriage. Wriothesley swore that Cromwell, who seemed unwilling to seek a remedy for Henry's problems, had revealed that the marriage had not been consummated. Philip Hoby also gave a statement that seems not to have survived.[12]

Three ladies of the queen's privy chamber, the countess of Rutland, Jane, Viscountess Rochford (widow of Anne Boleyn's executed brother), and Catherine, widow of Sir Piers Edgecombe, swore to some facts about Anne's version of her intimate moments with Henry. In order to give their testimony they must have journeyed from Richmond to Westminster on the morning of 7 July with Audley, Suffolk, and Southampton, whose depositions were also taken that afternoon. Anne's attendants dated their conversations with her on Tuesday or Wednesday (22 or 23 June) preceding midsummer. It was about this time, of course, that Henry could be seen crossing the Thames to visit Katherine, probably at her step-grandmother's Lambeth mansion.[13]

The ladies confessed that they had initiated the exchange with Anne by inquiring whether she was with child. To her denial that she was pregnant, they responded that she could not be so certain about her condition unless she still remained a maiden. She allegedly rejected their claim with the following statement:

How can I be a maid . . . and sleep every night with the King? . . . When he comes to bed he kisses me, and takes me by the hand, and bids me, good night, sweet heart: and in the morning kisses me, and bids me, farewell, darling. Is not this enough?

When Lady Rutland asked her if she had discussed these encounters with Mother Lowe, who could presumably have enlightened her about the facts of life, Anne replied that she had not confided in her countrywoman. All three attendants placed their signatures on the deposition that she had repeated these comments several times to them both individually and jointly.[14]

It is highly doubtful that she actually made the above assertions, for at least four reasons. First, in January Cromwell revealed after his arrest that she had often unsuccessfully sought his advice, an indication of her early recognition that her marriage was in trouble. Too busy, or so he alleged, to consult with her, he had assigned this duty to Rutland, who may well have informed his countess that Cromwell had requested him to advise her mistress to treat her husband more pleasantly. Secondly, as these ladies failed to identify the presence of an interpreter during these several conversations, it is extremely unlikely that they took place. In her few months in the realm, Anne had not learned English well enough to volunteer the comments attributed to her. Indeed, in his letter to Southampton about his exchange with Anne on 6 July, as noted above, Rutland was careful to reveal that he had used an interpreter who had been approved by the king. He also asked Southampton, in the event Anne or her ambassador wished to speak with him again, whom he should employ as an interpreter for he could "understand neither of them." Unlike the other deponents, except for the treaty negotiators who signed a joint statement, the ladies swore to the same record instead of to separate individual accounts.[15] They either conspired together to create fictionalized conversations with her that expressed what they believed was the actual relationship of the royal couple or one of the king's ministers, perhaps Wriothesley, devised this single deposition for each to sign.[16] Thirdly, Anne's comments were couched in language that emphasized her innocence for the purpose of making it appear as though she must surely be a virgin since she remained ignorant as to how conception occurred. This emerges as an interesting spin on the changing perception of the state of her sexuality, for Heneage, Denny, and Cromwell had recalled Henry's earlier suspicions that she had not brought her maidenhead with her to England. Fourth, in Winchester's memoranda in late June and in her first letter to her brother after the July divorce, both the bishop and the ex-queen referred to the "integrity of her body." No evidence supports the notion that Winchester or Rutland or Wriothesley had to explain to her, through an interpreter, of course, just what that phrase meant.[17]

Whether or not she was a virgin, that she should have been this ignorant about breeding protocol must be doubted, if for no other reason than that her mother would have prepared her for a marriage, the most important factor of which was neither romance nor luxurious living but the birth of children. In his epistle to Anne, published in his translation of Wolfgang Capito's book on the Psalms in 1539, Richard Tavener explicitly utilized Biblical imagery to refer to the major reason for the union. When she arrived, he hoped she would be: "a fruitful vine in [his] majesty's house, furnished with children round about [his] grace's table. For so thus shall the man be blessed (says he) which fears the Lord. . . . This lady most excellent is prepared of the almighty for your majesty. . . ."[18]

The ribaldry that accompanied weddings, such as the obscene refrains that were sung to bless German wedding beds, and the ubiquitous gossip about that night's bloody sheets formed the atmosphere for the consummation of marriages that interested parties hoped would result in childbirth. "The begetting of children," as Edward Muir has explained, was not viewed "so much a natural process as the product of a series of ritual interventions" that had to be learned. Negative comments about sexual behavior even surfaced in advice books for girls, who were considered more susceptible to sexual license and more controlled by their passion than were boys. In *The Book of the Knight of the Tower*, for example, Geoffroy de la Tour-Landry IV related a story about how to keep a man from "lechery" by having him wash in a tub of cold water. Even Henry and Anne's oak bed head had the figures of a licentious putto and a pregnant female carved upon it. This was not Victorian England where legs were delicately referred to as limbs but early modern Christendom where men boldly wore codpieces to signal their manhood. Surely one of the goals of the witnesses in the divorce case was to make Anne appear so naive about sexual matters that she would be spared a personal inquiry into the question of her virginity, perhaps even *virgo intacta*, by sober and honest matrons. Evidence of her extreme innocence would also serve to validate Henry's claims that the marriage had not been consummated.[19]

On the afternoon of 9 July, one and one-half days after the completion of the depositions, the double convocation unanimously agreed that the two had never been legally wed and that they were both free to remarry. The decision to permit her to remarry was interesting since these churchmen also signed the certificatory letter in which it was claimed that her previous contract, according to Henry Kelly, "impeded her marriage and rendered it ambiguous and confused." If her Lorraine union was the reason for the invalidation of her English one, then considering that Francis was still alive, how could it be declared that she was free to remarry? On 10 July the convocations' sentence was announced at parliament, which two days later confirmed their judgment that the marriage was invalid. As Wriothesley predicted in his June memorandum: "The Instrument signed with the beer pot contains no matter of discharge but rather ministers matter of much doubt."[20]

Henry listed four reasons for the annulment. (1) The condition required in 1539 that is the presentation of the documentation to prove the invalidity of the Lorraine marriage was not fulfilled. (2) He had wed her reluctantly. (3) He had decided to refrain from consummating the marriage until he had proof that her contract with

Lorraine had been discharged. (4) Anne's marriage to Francis was presumed to be *per verba de presenti*. This was a reasonable assumption for two reasons. As Henry Swinburne was later to point out, when questions arose about which vows had been taken, the presumption should be that they were *per verba de presenti*. In addition, the *per verba de presenti* vows of children younger than twelve and fourteen, for girls and boys respectively, could conclude a valid marriage under some conditions. As noted in Chapter 4, the fiancells between royal families were often *per verba de presenti*. Henry, himself, had entered into such a marriage with Catherine of Aragon, and on 27 June 1505, the day before he was to turn fourteen, when it would have become indissoluble, he had officially repudiated it, although the two were later wed. After listing the above four reasons for his divorce, Henry added: "Many other causes, great, and not to be published to the world, the Church of England has followed, and grounded them upon; which only were sufficient if the other before expressed, were not at all."[21] This was probably a veiled allusion to his relative impotency.

Chapter 8 earlier explained the difficulty in claiming and proving this kind of sexual dysfunction. In consultation with the churchmen, perhaps Cranmer but certainly Winchester and Tunstall who were members of the subcommittee that obtained the depositions, Henry decided that the official record of his divorce would ignore the sworn statements about his inability to consummate the union and his negative reaction to her bodily features. The depositions were neither attached to nor referred to in the final divorce decree. In 1613 when the archbishop of Canterbury was seeking precedents for the impotency case against Essex, he unearthed the records for the Cleves divorce and observed that it was based on the existence of a pre-contract. In 1540 many of Henry's subjects seemed to have believed that this was the reason the double convocation had decided to declare the marriage invalid, for on 12 July Harst reported that people were remarking that it was too bad the king had married another man's wife.[22]

In 1540 no proof was produced that either Anne before the age of twelve or Francis before the age of fourteen had revoked their contract. A statement by the Cleves' ambassadors that the couple's proxies had merely agreed to *per verba de futuro* vows was not sufficient evidence to cause any court to invalidate the marriage. For a definitive determination of the validity of that union, the churchmen required written documentation that could be interpreted. Apparently, the only evidence that arrived for their inspection was the beer pot document with copies of the remarks made in 1535 by Guelders and his chancellor that the contract of 1527 was not to go forward. Later, in December 1541 Harst was to inform Ghogreve and Olisleger that he had learned that the double convocation had deemed this evidence of the cancellation of her contract unacceptable because it was only a copy and not an original document. He asked for the original to be sent to him from the Cleves archives with the explanation that this was the first time that he had heard of it.[23]

An even more interesting fact about these repudiations of her marriage to Francis in 1535 is the existence of another agreement about it that was made in 1538, three years after Charles of Guelders had negated the original contract. In the 1538 document Charles and John of Juliers–Cleves agreed that one of the conditions for William to succeed to Guelders was the conclusion of a marriage between Anne and Francis. It could be argued that the 1538 document, which seems never to have been officially refuted, had the effect of voiding the 1535 statements of Guelders and his chancellor. In 1538 William had taken control of Guelders, but a year later, after his accession to Juliers–Cleves, he had arranged for his sister's union with Henry, contrary to the terms of his deceased father's recent agreement, the existence of which may have been the real cause for his delay of the negotiations for the English marriage in May 1539. Without these documents to interpret, especially the contract and treaty of 1527, the convocations had little choice but to annul the royal marriage.[24]

During the churchmen's deliberations, Anne summoned Harst to Richmond twice. The first time was on the morning of 8 July when she asked him to explain to her the meaning of the council's letter that had forbidden her to send any more messages to Henry. The second time was that evening, close to midnight, when she informed him about the instructions Beard had brought to her from the king that she should assent to the clergy's determination, which had not yet been made official, that her marriage was invalid. According to the sympathetic Harst, who recommended that she refuse to accept their verdict, she was sobbing so loudly and crying so violently it almost broke his heart. With his assistance she discussed the business with her lord chamberlain, who tried to calm her, reassuring her that she had nothing to fear from Henry and recommending that she send him the response that she thought was right. The message that Beard carried back to Henry was that she had accepted him as her husband and master and only death could part them. The next morning at court, when Harst protested both about the speed with which the inquiry was being conducted and the king's treatment of Anne, the council responded that Henry did not intend to renounce the Cleves alliance and that he had pledged to treat Anne as his sister.[25]

After Harst learned of the convocations' official verdict, he recommended to Anne that she concede the inevitable because he feared that enormous pressure would be brought to bear on her to accept it. Indeed, his analysis was correct. On 11 July councillors arrived at Richmond once again, this time determined to obtain her written agreement to the divorce. Reluctantly giving up the struggle to remain queen, she complied with their wishes, for she must have begun to understand the inadequacies of the well-meaning Cleves ambassador in this crisis and to realize that the speedy conclusion of the divorce process made it impossible for her brother, even if he wished, to voice any viable protest. As she also well knew, Katherine Howard was waiting in the wings at Lambeth. Powerless in a foreign land, Anne wrote a letter to Henry "in her own tongue and language" in which she stated that she had agreed to the inquiry into the validity of their marriage because she had more regard for God and his truth than for her "worldly affection" for him, and that she accepted the clergy's conclusions concerning their "pretended matrimony." His councillors, she continued, had informed her that she would be able to visit court occasionally and that he would adopt her as his sister. After closing her letter as his "Sister and Servant," she signed a notarial record that she had freely consented to the divorce, which was witnessed by Hussey, Suffolk, Southampton, Riche, Wriothesley, Beard, Ladies Rutland, Rochford, and Edgecombe, Dorothy Wingfield, Anne Josselyn, and Elizabeth Rastall. On Monday 12 July her submission was announced in the houses of parliament, which allowed them to confirm, as noted above, the sentence of the double convocation.[26]

Suffolk, Southampton, and Wriothesley returned to Richmond with Henry's response of 12 July to her written compliance. After informing her of his pleasure at her "good conformity," they withdrew, leaving her alone with her interpreter to read his message.

Having done so, she recalled them to inquire about living arrangements and other matters contained in his letter. Henry had informed her that he would grant her extensive property in Sussex, Essex, and Suffolk as well as Richmond Palace and Bletchingley Manor, both of which had splendid parks and lay close to London, and she inquired about the latter's exact location. In addition, as his sister he granted her precedence over everyone except his future queen and children, and agreed to give her 8,000 nobles a year to support herself and her household, but in England only. He also arranged for sufficient household furnishings and jewelry to be provided for her comfort. As Patrick Carter has pointed out, Anne's settlement was "not ungenerous," but it also cost Henry very little, for the attainder of Cromwell and the earlier one of Sir Nicholas Carew, who had owned Bletchingley, largely financed it. When the councillors requested that she correspond with her brother, she protested that it was not "meet" for her to contact him before he had written to her and that she preferred to wait for his communication with Henry. She trusted, she also announced, that regardless of how he or the duke elector reacted to this business that the king would "be good" to her for she remained "at his pleasure." The councillors ended their letter to Henry with the assertions that they would wait to learn from him whether or not they should press her to send a written message to her brother and that they were also forwarding a ring that she was sending him to prove her continued good will.[27]

Upon receipt of the above documents and token, Henry met with the councillors attendant on him concerning her reluctance to write a message to her brother. He decided that they must not only procure a letter from her to William but they must also obtain a German translation of her message of consent to the divorce. The letter to her brother would prevent her from changing her mind if he should try to dissuade her from agreeing to the divorce and the translation would prevent her from alleging that she was ignorant of what she had written. Since Henry feared her "womanish nature" might cause her to alter her opinion, he also asked that she compose a second letter of consent in her own language as an "evident demonstration" of her submission. Finally, they were to assure her that she would not be penalized for her relatives' reactions to these proceedings.[28]

In the next few days she had a series of meetings with Suffolk,

England. The constable later predicted to Wallop that William would remain Henry's friend. On the last day of July Pate reported the emperor's favorable reaction to the news, and his resident in England accepted the assignment to prevent, if at all possible, Henry's remarriage to her. The great desire of Francis to obtain Milan, which Charles granted to his son Philip in October 1540, and the unswerving determination of Cleves to retain control of Guelders led these two allies finally to wage war on the emperor in 1542. The Franco-Imperial treaty that had prompted Henry to wed Anne had been fragile, indeed. The Venetian ambassador's comment in 1520 about the relationship of Henry and Francis could easily have been said about that of Francis and Charles in 1539–40: "These sovereigns are not at peace. They adapt themselves to circumstances, but hate each other very cordially."[32]

The most important question about the marriage's dissolution is why her family failed to provide Henry with an official copy of the original contract and treaty with Lorraine. Over the succeeding years Guelders had alternated in his opinions about the union that he had mediated, deciding to renounce it in 1528 and 1535 but reconfirming it in 1538. Since three official versions of the contract of 1527 existed, one for Guelders, one for Lorraine, and one for Cleves, it would seem unlikely that the archivists of all three duchies would have misplaced their copies. Concerning Anne's legal right to be Henry's consort, her brother's failure to send the documents, which were written in Low German, becomes even more puzzling, for a close study of them indicates that Francis and she were sworn in *per verba de futuro* vows only. When they were to come to an appropriate age, but without a definite date specified, they were to conclude the union in a nuptial ceremony. They had never been legally wed.[33]

Perhaps her brother's ministers had thought it was unnecessary to forward the documents to England because they held the misguided belief that Henry had consummated the union and that all was well with the royal couple. This was the tone of the messages that were sent abroad until July, and even most of Henry's attendants who became aware that the marriage had not been consummated were alerted to his problem only about Whitsuntide. In addition, diplomatic silence both about the receipt of the beer pot document and about the need for further information concerning the Lorraine union must have misled Anne's family about the real state of affairs.

It must also be claimed, however, that the ducal government was operating deceitfully, for it was disingenuous of William to forward the beer pot document repudiations of Anne's marriage in 1535, but not only fail to send with it the original treaty and contract of 1527, but also to remain silent about his father's agreement that reaffirmed the Lorraine union in 1538. It is likely that William did not wish to publicize these documents because the ones dated in 1527 indicated that Francis should inherit Guelders and the one dated in 1538 detailed one of the conditions for Cleves' control of Guelders that had not been met, that is, the union of his sister with him. It appears as though William was willing to sacrifice Anne's English marriage rather than reveal to Henry or to anyone else the details of those awkward agreements concerning Guelders. Ultimately, of course, the dissolution of the marriage depended upon more grounds than the exact status of the Lorraine contract, but, as has been argued here, it was Henry's uncertainty about whether she was actually his lawful wife that had prevented him from consummating the union, and it was that incapacity in turn that led to the divorce. It must also be noted that even had William sent the necessary documentation in March, it may well have been too late to effect the reversal of the impotence, for it is difficult to alter a repeated pattern of sexual dysfunction. The appropriate occasion for Cleves to have provided the records of 1527 was in May 1539 when Wotton first requested them. The major blunder here was not William's, however, but the king's, who insisted upon going forward with the negotiations without absolute guarantees up front that Anne was free to wed him. This episode highlights the deep, but misguided, concern for the security of his realm that he had felt following the ratification of the Franco-Imperial treaty that seemed to set England up for an invasion, indeed a papal crusade.[34]

In both popular and scholarly accounts, after noting the executions of Anne Boleyn and Katherine Howard, authors have hinted and sometimes stated explicitly that Anne of Cleves was fortunate that Henry repudiated her. One author has even argued that she set out to achieve this desirable result by contriving to make herself unattractive and "dull" to her husband. These "present-centred" sentiments are the product of modern cultural and social factors that fail to understand the major family and dynastic expectations and considerations of early modern society. As Victor Turner has observed, "To penetrate to the structure of a mind different than our own is hard work," for they were not "simpler people"; they merely had "wide diversities of cultural experiences."[35]

Anne's mother had raised her to marry a great duke with all the advantages that this status would bring to her family and her homeland. When the union with Lorraine fell through, her relatives were fortunate to find her a wealthier and more powerful husband in England. Had she given birth to a son or even a daughter, the existence of the child would have held out the promise that the marriage might create a long-standing relationship between England and Cleves. Not only might her union with Henry have tied her native land closer to the kingdom diplomatically but it might also have offered her the opportunity to broker good alliances for some of her brother's noble subjects and to find employment for them in her adopted realm. Some of her countryfolk had already taken advantage of her position. In January 1540 Henry and Cromwell employed Olisleger's two nephews in their households and, even following the annulment, some of her German attendants, including her cousin Waldeck, remained with her. The younger Pallant had, of course, futilely hoped for a pension.[36]

Two other dimensions of her loss need consideration. First, some contemporaries viewed her status as a divorced woman as dishonorable, for she had lived with Henry as his wife for six months. A few were even aware that he was quite knowledgeable about some intimate parts of her body, for he had revealed to Cromwell that he had "felt" her breasts and belly. Some contemporaries, endowed both with prevailing beliefs about the excessive sexuality of women and skepticism about his ability to refrain from coitus with her in the bedchamber, believed that she had lost her virginity. In this regard it is interesting that the testimony of the dowager duchess of Norfolk had been sought for Henry's divorce in 1529 when the only relevant fact that she possessed was that Catherine and Arthur had lain in bed together as husband and wife, behavior that seems to have persuaded her, as well as others, that he had consummated the marriage. In late 1541, furthermore, reports began to circulate in England, a few months after Anne had returned from a visit to court, that she had given birth to Henry's child, a rumor he considered serious enough to have investigated.[37]

A second, equally compelling issue was the loss of her social position and economic well-being. As queen she had been a central figure in a grand court in which she had enjoyed a place second only

to Henry in protocol, address, and ceremony, and she had also presided over a great landed estate with a household of attendants and
officials, who, although accountable to the king's ministers, enjoyed
large powers of discretionary and independent action. On each
page of her receiver-general's accounts, she signed her name with a
flourish, "Anne the quenen." The divorce exiled her from this pomp
and circumstance and authority: two visible signs of her demotion
were the decrease in her household from about 130 to 30 members
and the replacement of a nobleman, the earl of Rutland, as her lord
chamberlain by a knight, Sir William Goring. The Cleves ambassador believed the divorce had brought great shame upon her and her
family and characterized her subsequent life as that of an English
prisoner, although David Loades has more accurately observed that
she lived on "the fringe of English public life." Lamenting her treatment, Harst not only recommended that she find a way to go home
but also pleaded with her relatives to persuade her to depart the land
of her disgrace. Worried about the deep humiliation she might have
to endure if she returned to Cleves, she assured Harst that she
wished to remain in England, that she trusted Henry who was to
grant her naturalization in January 1541, a status that required her
to obtain a royal license to travel abroad, and that she was thankful
for his expensive gifts. With hindsight when readers turn to the
accounts of his wives to consider the executions of Anne Boleyn and
Katherine Howard, the rustication of Catherine of Aragon and the
childbirth death of Jane Seymour, it is easy for them to assert that she
was personally better off away from court, living out her life as the
royal sister rather than as the queen consort. Her private anguish
leaves, however, an emotional trail of thwarted ambitions and hopes.
In a reference to Christina of Milan in 1539, Wriothesley, perhaps
transferring his own views to the young woman, remarked that she
would rather marry the king of England than the duke of Cleves or
of Lorraine. Anne had lost both a duke and a king, a terrible dishonor by her family's and her society's standards, if not her own.[38]

On 6 August, nine days after his marriage to Katherine Howard
at Oatlands in Surrey, Henry traveled to Richmond to meet with
Anne for the first time since her rustication. Undoubtedly, he sought
an opportunity to inform her about his bride before she appeared
publicly as queen, as she had been scheduled to do at Hampton
Court on 8 August. He may also have wished to observe for himself

that Anne's household arrangements were fully satisfactory. As his sister, she appeared to some observers, like Marillac, to be joyous and content. He could not decide if this demeanor was prudent dissimulation on her part, which it definitely was, or mere stupidity. Aware of her private grief, Harst kept up the subterfuge, for he mendaciously remarked to the French ambassador that she cheerfully accepted her demotion. Her submissiveness won her an invitation to court in January 1541. According to Chapuys, after she had given Henry two horses with violet velvet trappings for his New Year's gift, she traveled to Hampton Court on 3 January with Lord William Howard, the queen's uncle whom she had met on the road and with whom she had first become acquainted at Calais. Ladies Suffolk, Hertford, and others welcomed her and then escorted her to the queen's lodgings. Chapuys had heard that, as she was kneeling to greet Katherine, her former maiden-of-honor, Henry entered, bowed, embraced, and kissed her. Following dinner with his queen and his ex-queen, the king retired to his quarters while Anne remained to dance with Katherine. The next day after the three had once again dined together, the queen reportedly handed over to Anne a ring and two little dogs, the New Year's gifts the king had previously given to her. It is to be hoped that by this time her English was sufficient for her to converse with them without relying on interpreters. Afterwards she returned to her place of exile at Richmond Palace. While publicly she seemed resigned to her fate, some of her relatives did express their displeasure; one informed Pate at Brussels that he longed for her return home and hoped to see the day when Henry would repent his repudiation of her. As long as he was pleased with Katherine, her brother accepted the finality of the divorce and did not foolishly press for a reconciliation.[39]

Although Anne led a somewhat uneventful life following Henry's marriage to Katherine, her presence in England remained a topic of interest abroad. In late 1541 John of Luxembourg, third son of Charles, count of Brienne, abbot of Ivry, printed a French tract called, "The 'Remonstrance' of Anne of Cleves," which William Paget, ambassador to France, unsuccessfully requested Francis to suppress in January 1542. The tract, which was not only printed twice in French but also appeared in Italian in 1558, represents Anne as overwhelmed with sorrow about her dishonor. She was alleged to have recalled her first contentment about the marriage as she received gifts, rich clothes, and letters written in Henry's own hand. But she also lamented: "Wives are given to men to obey them . . . if then the king chooses to leave you and take another, ought you to go contrary to his will?" She was not conscious of having committed any offense, for he had left her on an "arbitrary whim."[40] The "Remonstrance" thus represents the sentiments of an individual ignorant about Henry's selective impotence, which seems to have remained a tightly kept secret in England.

What Anne thought about the arrest of her successor for adultery in November 1541 was not recorded, although Chapuys had heard rumors that she was delighted. Royal agents did question Jane Rattsey, one of Anne's servants, about her alleged prediction to Elizabeth (probably Catherine) Basset that God had moved against Katherine because he intended to elevate Anne to the queenship again. As soon as they learned of the queen's arrest, William of Cleves and his ministers began to send Anne secret oral messages via Harst promoting her reinstatement at court. The concerned ambassador claimed Anne's plight had kept him from sleeping well for over a year and characterized the Englishmen with whom he had to deal as deceitful and unpredictable. He informed Cleves that he had discussed with Anne both her remarriage to the king and the restoration of her honor but had, he also revealed, warned her to deny to others that she had been seriously considering her reinstatement. With great expectations, on 12 December, he delivered letters from her brother to Suffolk and from Olisleger to Cranmer and Southampton, whom Anne was said especially to trust perhaps because she remembered his kindness at Calais. As Harst handed over the dispatches that sought their assistance in effecting a reconciliation between Anne and Henry, he reported to them that he possessed letters of credence that empowered him to negotiate their remarriage. All recipients forwarded their messages to Henry; in addition, Cranmer, whom Harst identified as an ally, not only refused to discuss the issue with him but also expressed outrage to the king: "I thought it not a little strange, that Olisleger should think it meet for me to move a reconciliation of the matrimony, of the which I, as much as any other person know most just causes of the divorce."[41]

That same month Marillac reported that Harst had tried unsuccessfully to obtain an audience with Henry whose grief over

Katherine's betrayal prevented him from agreeing to any such meeting. Remaining persistent, Harst met with members of the council on 14 December; although Suffolk and Cranmer were unwilling to speak with him about the remarriage, Winchester agreed to discuss the matter with him publicly before the other councillors. Harst informed Ghogreve and Olisleger about his exchanges with the idiotic (*dollen*) bishop, whose attitude concerning Anne's reinstatement he characterized as rude. The diplomat also revealed that Anne was greatly saddened by the negativism of Winchester, who later predicted accurately to Marillac that Henry would never take her back. As France was then an ally of Cleves, it was Marillac's duty to encourage the reconciliation, but he confessed to Francis that he had not pressed the matter with the bishop because he did not want Anne treated any worse than she already was.[42]

By January 1542 Marillac was informing the queen of Navarre that he had advised Harst to wait until Katherine's fate was sealed before seeking Anne's remarriage. Keeping the Franco-Cleves alliance in mind, it is interesting to note his opinion of her. Not only was she patient, he reported, but she also never said anything that would make her seem unhappy with her fate. She always did what she thought would please the king and had the heart and grace to accept what could not be remedied. Those who visited her greatly praised her virtue and Marillac exclaimed, "She is well and said to be half as beautiful again since she left court."[43]

In the meantime, Chapuys worried that as soon as Henry was divorced from Katherine he would remarry Anne. In early 1542 he reported their exchange of New Year's gifts. She sent Henry some pieces of crimson, and he presented her with pots and flagons. Later, the ambassador heard that Henry had dispatched his physicians to Richmond to treat her for a bout of tertian fever. Harst's disclosure in February, the month of Katherine's execution, that he was in possession of messages from many German princes urging Henry to remarry Anne and that he was waiting only for Francis's approval to present them to Henry caused the Imperial ambassador further anguish.[44]

Katherine's death seems to have given Harst and Anne, momentarily at least, hopes for a reconciliation, a reaction that was not as strange as it might seem. When Francis of Lorraine, Anne's putative husband, wed Christina of Milan in 1541, only Henry among the leaders of Christendom challenged the legality of their marriage. Most of his contemporaries also believed that witchcraft was the force behind selective impotency, although Harst surely had not learned of Henry's incapacity with Anne. As, under the ambassador's intense questioning, she had denied that the king had ever treated her in a disrespectful manner, Henry may have succeeded in persuading his sexually inexperienced ex-wife that his failure to consummate the union was by choice and not involuntary. By the end of 1542 her extreme melancholy about her status led her receiver-general to seek some assistance for her from John Gates of the privy chamber. Apparently on her behalf, Carew had earlier requested Butts not only to give Henry her commendations and to ask about his health but also to send to Lady Suffolk some of his cramp rings that he blessed on Good Friday, which were said to cure cramps, convulsions, and epileptic seizures, among other afflictions. According to Carew, Butts did forward some cramp rings to the duchess but returned no response to Anne concerning her inquiry about the king's health, a silence and even a neglect that greatly saddened her. Carew was, therefore, requesting Gates to ask his brother-in-law, Anthony Denny, to approach Henry about sending a token, perhaps some cramp rings, and a message of friendship to her. This letter provides substantial evidence that her receiver-general, who continued to serve her until 1543, had developed a certain respect, indeed, perhaps admiration for her, for as he admitted to Gates, "Charity binds to comfort the comfortless and me in especial her." He was writing the letter at 3:00 a.m., he further admitted, "being not best at ease." Her plight had thus caused a second anxious attendant to have sleepless nights.[45]

In the meantime, Chapuys continued to fret about her presence in England and to record her various activities. In March 1543, for example, he reported her three-day visit to court and the rumor, which he hoped was true, that Henry had paid little attention to her. Later, he heard that Anne longed to return home because she felt humiliated by Henry's marriage on 12 July to Katherine Parr, who, twice widowed and childless, seemed to have no hopes of offspring and who was "not nearly so beautiful as she." Perhaps, the king had understood she would again feel rejection or may have learned of her anguish, for on 27 July the council informed Carew that he was determined to have dinner with her, "at the park over against the house," and required her receiver-general to make the arrangements.[46]

What her treatment would have been had she returned to Cleves after the divorce cannot be known, but it is possible that she would not have fared well for she feared she would suffer great humiliation. In the fifteenth-century, Bianca of Navarre had suffered the scorn and neglect of some of her relatives and friends after Henry IV of Castile, having failed to consummate their marriage, had returned her home. As Anne's brother, who had been unable to give her a dowry, also had a younger unmarried sister to support, it was surely impossible for him to offer Anne the financial independence that she enjoyed in England, at least during Henry's reign.[47]

By remaining in the kingdom, she was also able to avoid the perils of the war in which the emperor invaded Cleves, defeated William, and captured Gelderland. In November 1542 John Butler informed Henry Bullinger that the whole of Juliers "has been ravaged and desolated with fire and plunder by the Imperial forces." In September 1543 William signed a treaty at Venlo, in which in return for ceding Guelders to the emperor he was allowed to retain his other territories. Once again ignoring Erasmus's warning against rulers' marrying foreign-born brides, Charles required William, whose alliance with Jeanne of Navarre had been nullified, to wed his brother Ferdinand's daughter, Maria. This was an excellent marriage for her since her father had numerous children for whom he had to provide. The loss of Guelders and the devastation of her homeland greatly saddened Anne's mother, who died in August shortly before the Venlo treaty was signed. Wotton reported that he had heard she was "out of her wits" because of the "loss of her country" and that at her funeral her son was so distraught that he had threatened to kill one or two of his councillors. Her death may have brought some satisfaction to Charles V, who was to write in his autobiography that the inexperienced young duke had wrong-headedly followed his mother's council in the dispute over Guelders, which she viewed as a part of her Juliers inheritance. Wotton's letters provide support for this assertion, as they refer to William's frequent visits with his mother to discuss ducal business.[48] The final settlement of Guelders indicates how badly English ambassadors, and Henry himself, underestimated the Habsburg resolve to seize the duchy from Cleves. No danger of William's joining with the Franco-Imperial alliance to defend his sister's honor had ever existed.

During the remainder of his life, Henry ensured that Anne was well cared for: he granted her additional support for her "necessities" and more estates, including Kemsing, Seal and Hever in Kent; Hever, the former home of Anne Boleyn, was later to become her principal residence. In one of his records, Henry wrote in his own hand "expenses for my beloved sister Anna." At some point after the divorce, she gave him a Book of Hours that had been printed in Germany in 1533, which she had probably brought with her to England. In the spring and summer of 1546, she returned to court for two more visits that set the rumors flying that she was pregnant and had borne two of his children. In the last months of Henry's life, she even possessed sufficient resources to be able to send to William of Cleves expensive presents, such as horses and greyhounds.[49]

Shortly after the king died in January 1547, Hertford and Browne instructed the council, if it had not already done so, to inform her of his death. Before it became common knowledge that Katherine Parr, the queen dowager, had wed Thomas, Lord Seymour of Sudeley, rumors had begun to circulate that Anne might marry him. Even the new monarch, Edward VI, briefly suggested her as a wife to Seymour. Remarriage might have alleviated some of her financial difficulties that were partly caused by the inflation that the coinage debasement had helped to fuel. In response to her pleas for assistance, her brother sent to England Ambassador Heresbach, who met with the king on 11 April 1547 and with Anne at Hever from 14 to 17 April. While Edward seems to have been fond of her, Hertford, his lord protector recently ennobled as the duke of Somerset, and John Dudley, the future duke of Northumberland who was to supplant Somerset as chief minister, were less sympathetic. Dominating the council, they whittled away at her possessions. Although Richmond and Bletchingley had been granted to her for life, both were confiscated in early 1547. The loss of Richmond, the splendid palace that Henry VII had built as his principal residence, was a major blow, for its seizure signaled her mounting financial problems and continuing social demotion. No longer the king's sister, only the king's aunt, she had to make do with lesser dwellings. As compensation the council granted her two more Kentish estates: Penshurst, a former Boleyn home that she rarely visited because of its distance from London, and Dartford Priory, a small, comfortable house where she had stayed the night before her Blackheath reception and where she was to spend some of her later years. Her pleas for aid to Somerset won her Cranmer's sympathy but little assistance, since the crown began to delay paying the salaries and pensions of her household officials. In 1549 William dispatched to England Dr. Herman Cruser and Christopher Rolshmisen, who achieved only limited success even after meeting with Edward on 15 December. Anne thanked her brother for their help but warned that she might have to move to Cleves. William's response was to dispatch Cruser to England again in the spring of 1551. His arrival with Olisleger's son to discuss her affairs with the council caused speculation that she would return home with them. Although this was her inclination, as she wrote to her brother on 5 April, Cruser revealed to the Imperial ambassador only that he had pleaded for her financial relief. With none in sight, by 1552 she was repeating to William that she would be no trouble to him if she were to return home. She also continued to express dissatisfaction with her financial plight to the council.[50]

After Mary's accession in 1553, some diplomats viewed Anne's presence as a threat to the renewed Anglo-Imperial alliance. Simon Renard, the Imperial resident, accused Henry II of France of working to prevent the queen's union with Philip of Spain and of promising aid to William of Cleves who planned to revenge his sister's repudiation by encouraging other German princes to rebel against Charles. Renard even charged that Mary believed Anne approved of these plots and was conspiring with her brother to further the dynastic ambitions of Princess Elizabeth. No evidence substantiates Renard's fears about Anne's disloyalties; in 1551, for example, she had written to William that she had recently enjoyed a pleasant visit with the future queen. Along with Elizabeth she attended Mary's coronation festivities, riding in a coach with the princess in the London entry on 29 September 1553 and sitting with her at the queen's table at the coronation banquet on 1 October. They proved to be her last public appearances.[51]

On 4 August 1554 Anne sent a letter from Hever to Mary thanking her for the response to her last suit and requesting an audience with her, perhaps to seek financial redress, for rumors continued to spread about her money problems and even a possible remarriage.

In late 1553 diplomats attending Mary's coronation, reported that Anne was considering a match with Ferdinand of Austria, the brother of Charles and the future emperor. If this plan had occurred to her, it was a futile hope, for Ferdinand, who was also, of course, her brother's father-in-law, had determined not to remarry. Renard later heard that she was petitioning to have her union with her late ex-husband reinstated so that she could enjoy the benefits and status of the dowager queen of England. Katherine Parr, Henry's only other surviving consort, had died giving birth to Lord Seymour's child, a daughter named Mary, in 1548.[52]

By 1556 Anne's brother felt it was necessary for him to request Mary's assistance concerning three of his subjects, Jasper Brockehouse, his wife, and Otho Wylik who were residing with his sister, and who, he believed, had by their "pernicious doctrine" and "marvelous impostures" driven her mad. Having tried unsuccessfully to have them discharged, he was hoping the queen would expel them from England. These concerns can be traced back to the spring of 1552, when Brockehouse, her cofferer since 1547, his wife, and their countryman attempted to bring her finances under control, for her expenses exceeded her income of £2,666 by £922 a year. His attempt to limit her expenditures made Brockehouse extremely unpopular, and he soon became involved in a dispute with Anne's cousin and attendant, Francis, who had inherited his father's title of Waldeck. In June, Brockehouse reported to Olisleger, who informed William, that Count Waldeck had been attempting to persuade Anne to recognize him as her heir and to release to him some of her personal effects. In response to this news, Olisleger recalled the count to Cleves. William, who seems, however, to have accepted Waldeck's version of the dispute, began to send agents more frequently to check on Anne and her household. Cruser arrived in 1553 for a third visit just after Mary's accession and returned in March 1554 to inform Anne of her sister Sybilla's death and to congratulate the queen on having put down Wyatt's rebellion. The Cleves ambassador, who reported that Anne's house was untidy, that she did not heed Brockehouse's advice, and that she was too lenient with her servants, was in the realm with his wife again that September and by himself a final and sixth time in May 1555. That spring Anne allowed Brockehouse to travel home to defend himself against his detractors in return for promises that he would be permitted to resume his duties in England. A year later, William, who was increasingly hostile to Brockehouse's presence in her household, sent Waldeck to persuade Anne to discharge her cofferer, his wife, and colleague, but she refused, praising their years of loyal service. As Waldeck's mission was unsuccessful, her determined brother, who decided that she disliked Cruser perhaps because she had learned or at least suspected that he had criticized the management of her household, instructed Carl Harst, who had stood by her loyally during the distressful days of 1540, to carry a letter to her in which he warned her against continuing to retain Brockehouse. In August the duke also dispatched Arnold of Leiven to the queen to explain to her these difficulties, and in September her council obliged him by deporting the three Germans. When informed of this action, King Philip, whose first cousin Maria was married to William, sent word from Ghent that it met with his approval. Less than a year later on 16 July 1557, deprived of her trusted servants, Anne died in a land she considered alien. In 1552 after twelve years in the realm, she had confessed to her brother that England was not her home and she was a stranger there.[53]

At her death when she was not quite forty-two-years old, she was in residence at Chelsea Manor, the former home of Thomas More which had been made available for her use. Her body was transported from there to Westminster Abbey where a requiem mass was celebrated for her on 4 August. Elizabeth Paulet, marchioness of Winchester, the chief mourner at her funeral, and her husband, William, first marquess of Winchester, hosted a feast at their London home to honor her memory. In her will, which was written on 14 and 15 July, Anne bequeathed goods to her servants, some of whom were Germans, including Otho Wylik, and to the poor, and she appointed "our most dearest and entirely beloved sovereign lady Queen Mary," who was to receive her best jewel, as her overseer. She gave her second best jewel to her other stepdaughter, Elizabeth, whom she asked to care for Dorothy Curzen, one of her maids, and also left jewelry to her brother, his wife, Lady Suffolk, Mary, countess of Arundel, Lord Paget, and Waldeck. The executors of her will were Nicholas Heath, archbishop of York, Henry, earl of Arundel, Sir Edmund Peckham and Sir Richard Preston. As she lay dying, she requested that she have "the suffrages of the holy church according to the Catholic faith wherein we end our life in this transitory world."[54]

Afterwards, references to her could still be found in diplomatic dispatches. In 1559, because a woman had appeared in Saxony pretending to be her, Emperor Ferdinand asked Baron Kasper von Breuner, his English agent in England, to investigate what had happened to the real Anne. After interrogating some servants who had witnessed her death, Breuner reported that she had been "held in honor all her life long, and at all times till the day of her death had a free household." "Everybody," he continued, "has nothing but good to say of the duchess."[55]

Two Englishmen who praised her in dedications probably published before the divorce, were Thomas Elyot and Thomas Becon. In the 1540 edition of *The Defence of Good Women*, which he asked her to accept as her own, Elyot referred to her desire to "embrace virtue and gentleness wherein consists very nobility." In 1561 Becon reissued *The Pomander of Prayer* that he had dedicated to her and William at an earlier, unknown date. In it he referred to her affection for God and to her "diligent" prayers and spiritual devotions. Exhorting her to take his book according to her "accustomed gentleness," he ended his dedication with the words: "God whose glory you heartily love whose word you joyfully embrace, whose name you earnestly call upon might vouchsafe to preserve your grace in continual health and increase of honor."[56] Raphael Holinshed later wrote in his chronicle that she was "a lady of right commendable regard, courteous, gentle, a good housekeeper, and very bountiful to her servants."[57]

In 1621 the writer Slayter Sleydon echoed these favorable comments in his lament: "Fair Anne of Cleves and she forsaken."[58] It was left to later observers to add to this unpleasant episode in Henry's life the well-known and often repeated negative interpretations of her appearance. The most infamous of these authors was Gilbert Burnet, bishop of Salisbury, who made the double-barrelled, misogynist comment that she was a "Flanders Mare" and that Holbein had "bestowed the common compliment of his art too liberally" upon her. In accepting his analysis, subsequent writers have committed the error that Judith Shapiro has warned about. They have failed "to distinguish consistently between the sex bias emanating from the observer and the sex bias characteristic of the community under study." Nicholas Wotton, as explained in Chapter 4, believed Holbein's portrait of her was realistic, and, of course, it was Burnet, himself, not one of her contemporaries, who coined the phrase, "Flanders Mare." As Mary Crawford and Roger Chaffin have reminded scholars, "gender or gender-role identification should play a large part in determining how texts are understood."[59]

Of the major protagonists involved in the divorce crisis, it is possible that in the long run Thomas Cromwell's reputation has suffered the least. Undoubtedly, he was not a traitor or a heretic as he was charged. His downfall was almost certainly the result of misunderstandings about his reaction to Henry's inability to consummate the marriage with Anne and of royal suspicions about the reasons for his violation of the privy chamber ordinance of secrecy. Although parliament and the king labeled him a traitor and a sacramentarian, Foxe extolled his virtues in the *Acts and Monuments*, which was, except for the scriptures, the most popular book in Elizabethan England. In the twentieth century, analyses of Cromwell's character have proceeded from Peter Wilding's claim in 1935 that he was "molded on Machiavelli:" "a nationalist, a rationalist, a realist," and "near to being an atheist" to more recent accounts in which his religious commitment looms large. Most historians, like John Guy and Richard Rex, now argue that his promotion of humanist reform was genuine. While he is no longer credited as the sole or even the major intellectual architect of the Reformation, his contributions as a parliamentarian and as the vicegerent are considered significant.[60]

At the time, however, Cromwell died in disgrace. As Constantine had explained to him in 1539: "The world ever flatters them that be in authority. And whatsoever they say or do is clerkly, wisely, and exceedingly well done, and said."[61] When a royal favorite fell from power, those same flatterers scrambled to win other patrons, as evidenced by Pate's letter to Norfolk in 1540 in which he related that the imprisoned minister, characterized by him as a traitor and heretic, had been the duke's enemy. The diplomat who uttered this indictment had until recently been reputed to be Cromwell's client; in 1538, for example, John Mason had credited him with enjoying the good favor of the lord privy seal.[62] Political desertions like this were typical, not only in England, but also in other lands, for as Margaret of Valois, the first wife of Henry IV of France, was later to write: "Thus it is ever in courts, adversity is solitary, while prosperity dwells in a crowd."[63]

Among Cromwell's former friends only Cranmer expressed astonishment to Henry about the charge of treason against him. Perhaps, if he could have known about it, Cromwell would have approved of the greatest desertion of all, that of his son and daughter-in-law, for in June "upon [his] knees," he begged the king "to be good and gracious lord to [his] poor son and the good and virtuous lady his wife, and their poor children." Shortly after his death, that daughter-in-law thanked Henry for the mercy he had shown her husband in the face of the "heinous trespasses," "detestable offences" and "grievous offences" of his father. She ended her letter with:

Most humbly beseeching your majesty in the mean season mercifully to accept this my most obedient suit and to extend your accustomed pity and gracious goodness toward my said poor husband who never has nor god willing never shall offend your majesty but continually prays for the prosperous estate of the same long time to remain and continue.

This submission made it possible for Gregory and his wife to retain his father's title of Lord Cromwell and some of his property for themselves and their descendants.[64]

The London Chronicle relates his final disposition. On 28 July, a Wednesday:

was beheaded at Tower Hill Thomas Cromwell, which that been afore M. of the Rolls, and after that the king's secretary, and after that the vicar general, knight of the Garter, earl of Essex, and lord chamberlain of England; and my Lord Hungerford was beheaded then that same time too . . . and the heads of my Lord Cromwell and my Lord Hungerford were set up on London bridge and their bodies buried in the Tower.

That his death had a profound impact on his contemporaries can be proved by a broadside issued in 1540 on the execution: the earliest broadside on record, some of its verses follow:

> Both man and child is glad to hear tell
> Of that false traitor Thomas Cromwell
> Now that he is set to learn to spell.
>> Sing troll on away, sing troll on away.
>> Heave and how rombelow troll on away.
> When fortune looked thee in thy face,
> Thou had fair time, but thou lacked grace;
> Thy coffers with gold thou filled a pace.
>> Sing, etc.
> Thou did not remember, false heretic,
> One God, one faith, one king catholic,
> For thou has been so long a schismatic.
>> Sing, etc.

Thou would never to virtue apply,
But coveted ever to climb too high,
And now hast thou trodden thy shoe awry.
   Sing. etc.
God save King Henry with all his power,
And Prince Edward that goodly flower,
With all his lords of great honor.
   Sing, etc.[65]

Historians have, as Alan Stewart has recently observed, tended to omit from their accounts of the Reformation evidence of its hostility toward the acts of sodomy that were often associated with the allegedly celibate clergy. The origins of the Buggery Statute of 1534, he believes, can be traced to a failed sanctuary bill. The year after the passage of the Buggery Statute, commissioners investigating the monasteries to obtain evidence to justify or perhaps to force their suppressions recounted numerous sexual crimes, including over 100 acts of sodomy. In modern narratives of Cromwell's fall, the fate of Hungerford has likewise been distanced from that of the minister's, perhaps in an unintentional fulfillment of George Kittredge's resolve that Hungerford "was somehow involved in a horrible scandal, into which we need not enquire." The execution of the two at the same time and place, the burial of their bodies together, and, most importantly, the display of their heads side by side on London Bridge created powerful messages for their contemporaries to observe and ponder. Visual experiences as manifested in executions and hangings, in the rhetorical gestures and the facial expressions of speakers, or in the images of biblical and religious history displayed in church sculpture and paintings, wielded a more far-reaching impact in early modern society than they do today.[66]

Contemporary accounts, like that of the London *Chronicle*, noted the execution of the two men together. Hall added a twist to the compelling drama. Under the incorrect date of 19 July he reported Cromwell's arrest and then after relating his "godly" and dignified last speech in which he denied that he was a heretic, Hall explained: "[he] so patiently suffered the stroke of the axe, by a ragged and butchery miser, which very ungoodly performed the office." After recording other events of that month, the chronicler arrived at 28 July. Although he had already described Cromwell's death, he observed: "The twenty and eight day of July, as you have heard before in this year, was the Lord Cromwell beheaded, and with him likewise was beheaded the Lord Hungerford of Heytesbury." In contrast to Cromwell's calm demeanor, Hall revealed that Hungerford was "certainly at the time of his death . . . very unquiet in mind and rather in a frenzy than otherwise." By referring once again to Cromwell's execution, Hall not only effectively associated the two noblemen together in his text but also reminded his readers of the different methods by which they had approached the end of their lives. Their contemporaries would have understood that, unlike Hungerford, Cromwell had in the spirit of the *ars moriendi* prepared so well for the dreadful moment that when it came he could declare his orthodox faith and face eternity with courage, with calm resignation, and the hope of salvation. The faithful closely observed individuals who were dying, whether they were resting quietly in private bedsteads or standing condemned in public execution sites, to note if they were fearful or courageous in their last moments in order to predict their final resting places, and, in turn, to learn from them how to prepare for their own deaths. Here Hall made it clear to his readers that the man charged with sodomy had not made his peace with God. A modern commentator on the executions might prefer to believe that his "frenzy" arose because he had been forced to watch the axeman butcher Cromwell to death. According to the hierarchy of the day an earl would have been executed before a baron. In his history of Wiltshire published in 1822, Sir Richard Colt Hoare ended his discussion of Heytesbury parish with the comment that Hungerford had suffered on the scaffold, and "The crimes laid to his charge were, if true, such as must excite but little pity for his fate."[67]

After his divorce from Anne, the king continued to make it clear that he believed she was legally the wife of Lorraine's heir. When he learned that it was arranged for the duchess of Milan to marry Francis of Lorraine in 1541, as noted above, he protested the event to Chapuys and forbade his ambassadors to attend the wedding feast. At that time he also explained to the ambassador, some two years before Cleves finally lost Guelders, that he believed that Duke Antony had agreed to hand over to King Francis his claims to Guelders before his heir was allowed to wed the duchess of Milan. Until Cranmer informed him about Katherine's chequered sexual past, Henry had doted on his bride. It can be assumed that one of the reasons for this obsession was the ability of the sexually experienced young woman to help her husband prove to his satisfaction that his impotency was truly selective, but it was not long before her reported relationships with other men led to her downfall. Perhaps it was because of his experiences with Katherine, and earlier with Anne Boleyn and Anne of Cleves, that Henry was willing to assent to an act in 1542 that made witchcraft a secular crime, with special emphasis on the ability of these creatures to provoke a person into illicit love.[68]

His six marriages, the Roman schism, and the numerous executions that occurred during his reign have led some modern scholars to be highly critical of Henry. Diarmaid MacCulloch, a biographer of Cranmer, is the most recent historian to compare him to Stalin, thus trivializing the truly monumental crimes against humanity of that dictator and his ruthless bureaucracy. Others have claimed that Henry was the victim of factional politics and thus had little control over his own court.[69] Many of his contemporaries were not only far more laudatory of him but they also recognized the extent of his authority. In 1546 William Thomas said:

Prudent he was in council and forecasting; most liberal in rewarding his faithful servants, and ever unto his enemies as it behooves a prince to be.

and

I will confess he did many evil things as the publican sinner but not as a cruel tyrant or as a pharisaical hypocrite.[70]

In 1571 Richard Reynolds even argued Henry had been more successful than Caesar in ruling his kingdom, for "he in all parts directed his princely heart to virtuous usage."[71]

By the seventeenth century writers had become more critical, foreshadowing the modern development. In 1649 his first biographer, Edward, Lord Herbert, said that Henry "was very knowing in the art of governing, and cut out as it were for a king; for he kept all in an exact obedience; and had his passions been as subject to him as his people, he had been the absolutist of kings. . . ." Although Herbert also ended his book with the statement: "To conclude; I wish I could leave him in the grave," Abraham van Wicqueford was later moved to complain in his treatise on ambassadors that Herbert "too much flattered the memory of a prince who had very great qualities, but a great many more bad ones than good."[72]

Accused of foisting Anne upon Henry to consolidate the

Reformation in England, Cromwell, some modern scholars have argued, lost out to factional politics. His successful rivals effected his downfall, engineered the divorce, and confirmed their power over the king by providing him with a new, receptive wife. The actual chain of events was much more complicated than allowed by this shallow narrative which is replete with characters who are simple-minded stereotypes. Deprived of their culture and its expectations, they have assumed roles in this political drama as ahistorical manipulators, ideologues, and murderers. Obscuring our ability to understand these past events, the factional theory forces us to see as "through a glass darkly," to quote St. Paul in I Corinthians 13:13. Instead of having Anne foisted upon him, Henry chose her as his bride in response to the Franco-Imperial alliance. When he was unable to consummate the union, he sought the reasons for his incapacity in the religious and scientific knowledge and lore of his day. His selective impotency, although it was not the official reason for the divorce, made it necessary for him to seek a scapegoat to blame for his bewitchment. Far from being manipulated, Henry, aided by his churchmen and councillors, made the decisions in this deadly domestic crisis. As Erasmus had Eusebius say in "The Godly Feast," a colloquy first published in 1522:

A king's mind, when aroused, is violent and unrestrained; it cannot be led this way or that but is driven by its own force . . . You suffer less hard if you go along with the stream than if you resist violently.[73]

☙ 10 ❧ CONCLUSION

From Jane's death on 24 October 1537 until Anne's divorce on 9 July 1540, Henry's behavior compared favorably with that of other bereaved rulers who sought to remarry for the purpose of begetting legitimate children to secure their dynasty's future. The steps that he, his councillors, and diplomats took to select a new wife, to negotiate the marriage treaty, to swear the initial vows, to transport the bride to her new home, and to arrange her greeting and the nuptial ceremony, itself, were ordinary and essential parts of early modern culture. The most unusual aspects of the union with Anne were its non-consummation and subsequent annulment. Even here, however, precedents existed for the actions and decisions that were made and helped to direct the final outcome.

Very soon after Jane's death in what was not considered unusual haste by her contemporaries, the king's councillors recommended that he seek another wife. Diplomatic considerations helped to shape the nature of that selection. The process of identifying a pool of foreign-born candidates from which a queen consort could be chosen had long been a familiar one at early modern courts. That Henry as a reigning monarch had wed four ladies who were not members of foreign dynasties is one of the most unusual characteristics of his unions. In simultaneously considering French and Imperial candidates in 1537–39, he set two goals: (1) to create a closer friendship between one of their realms and England with the intention of avoiding diplomatic isolation and (2) to prevent the recently widowed James V of Scotland from basing his continuing friendship with France on another marriage alliance.

A number of available candidates having been identified, Henry then required his privy councillors, especially Cromwell, and members of his privy chamber to discover information about them.

Cromwell instructed diplomats abroad to question the ladies and sent artists to paint portraits of them. The king, who was also involved in the negotiations, attempted to persuade the French and Imperial ambassadors that the selection of his consort was so serious a personal matter that he, himself, needed to become acquainted with the candidates. He first requested a Calais conference with their rulers, who were asked to bring along their courts and ladies. Later, he asked that the French candidates visit their relatives' homes near Calais where he would send a trusted advisor to meet with them. While it may have been somewhat unusual for him to attempt to have the ladies brought to him, monarchs had long sought to see, and sometimes succeeded in seeing, their brides before their marriages. James V had, of course, traveled incognito to France in 1536 to inspect two noble prospects and had chosen to wed one of them, Francis's daughter Madeleine.

Although Henry also enjoyed incognito visits and parties, he was unable to trek around the French and Flemish countrysides in search of the proposed brides partly because of his ill health and partly because of the real fear of being abducted and held for ransom. As 1538 was ending, it became evident that Charles and Francis, whom Paul was pressing to accept a truce and end the bloody struggle over Milan, had been stalling the marriage deliberations with Henry. Francis adamantly refused to permit his cousins to meet with the English king at Calais, and Charles ended the negotiations for his niece Christina of Milan's union with Henry because, as he pointed out to Wyatt, the English ambassador at his court, Paul, who had just renewed the excommunication of him for divorcing Catherine of Aragon in 1533, would not issue the necessary dispensation for this marriage to her young relative.

The event that led to Henry to select a German bride was the peace alliance signed by Francis and Charles at Toledo in 1539. It was an entirely customary action for an antagonist of the emperor to ally with his enemies, especially the German princes and the duke of Guelders. When Francis was at war with Charles, his ministers had even crafted an agreement with the sultan of the Ottoman Turks who almost took Vienna in 1529. It was not to consolidate the Reformation in England but to find an ally abroad that motivated Henry to agree to wed Anne of Cleves and to send agents to her relatives with a marriage proposal.

In early 1539 her brother, the new duke of Cleves, was none too eager to enter into an English alliance. He was intent upon discovering whether the emperor would permit him to retain Guelders, a lost ancestral territory over which he had regained dynastic control in 1538. The Franco-Imperial treaty, as it turned out, posed a serious threat to William's security, and having failed to obtain the emperor's and the queen regent's consent to his continued rule of Guelders, he authorized his commissioners in September 1540 to negotiate the marriage alliance with England. Holbein had earlier painted the now famous portrait of Anne which, according to Nicholas Wotton, was an accurate likeness of her and reflecting the romantic tradition was supposed to cause the king to fall in love with her at first sight.

The financial negotiations, the proxy betrothal vows, the appointments to her household, and the arrangements for her to travel to England mostly followed traditional usage. It was unusual to waive the dowry, but she was not the first queen consort who failed to bring great wealth to the realm. Most initial vows, furthermore, were usually sworn in the future wife's homeland, but a precedent for the bride's proxy to wed the king in England existed. Nothing unusual seems to have occurred in the arrangements for her household except that Henry decided to send an English lady to join her privy chamber perhaps to provide her with insights about his realm's customs.

The procession of Anne's train from Cleves to Calais and then across the Channel to England was unexceptional. She rode in the typical chariot for great ladies of the period, was received appropriately in the towns on the itinerary, and then was stranded by the weather at Calais, as many others had been. Having crossed the Channel at Deal, she traveled on Watling Road northward and reached Rochester on New Year's Eve. It was there the next day that the king made an unofficial visit in disguise to greet her in the chivalric style. Long viewed by modern scholars as an eccentric action on his part, it is clear that Henry was following customary royal protocol for receiving foreign-born brides. The most unusual aspect of the unofficial visit was that he delayed it until she arrived at Rochester rather than performing it at Canterbury or further afield.

His negative reaction to her appearance may have been partly motivated by his having learned that her ambassadors had not brought with them the documentation for his inspection that would have proved to him and his churchmen beyond the shadow of a doubt that she was legally free to wed. Even had he admired her looks, he would still have had to complain about the failure to provide him with the records that could prove to his satisfaction that he would be entering a valid marriage with her so that God might bless them with legitimate children. It was an absolute and widely enforced requirement that brides and grooms present evidence to prove that they were unencumbered by previous commitments before the priest began the nuptial service.

After her public reception, which was not so lavish as that of Catherine of Aragon's London entry since it took place at Greenwich three days before Epiphany, the king in consulation with his councillors decided he had to go forward with the marriage because of the threat posed by Francis's entertainment of Charles who had been traveling across France to Flanders. Henry expressed the fear that if he failed to wed her, her brother would join these two allies in an all-out assault on England. He required, however, that she swear that she was free to wed, and that the ambassadors not only swear a similar oath but also promise to forward from Cleves the necessary documentation to prove the validity of their claims.

On 5 January Henry settled a jointure on her that replaced the traditional dower and the next day, the Epiphany, Cranmer conducted their marriage ceremony and then celebrated the Trinity Mass. It was probably because their wedding fell on the Epiphany that Henry delayed his first attempt at sexual consummation until the third night of their marriage, for it was widely believed that when conception occurred on a feast day, like the Epiphany, or a Sunday, the infant would be born deformed. He failed, as it is argued in Chapter 7, because of his psychogenic inability to complete the union with a woman whose bodily features, as he described them to Cromwell, indicated to him that she was already married. She had not, he was convinced, brought her maidenhead to England with her. As the weeks passed and his attempts continued to fail, he altered the way in which he referred to his sexual dysfunction. Undoubtedly, after discussions with his doctors and his churchmen, he learned from them to express his incapacity with the phrase, "ever an obstacle," thus raising the possibility of some devious external force. The church had long maintained that witches caused the male impotency toward one woman which Henry believed he suffered, for he was, as Dr. Butts mantained, guilty of "night emissions." Henry needed to make it clear that general impotence toward all women, which was viewed as biological in origin, was not his affliction, for the church would prevent his remarriage in that case.

The search for the papists who hoped to keep Henry trapped in an unfruitful marriage and for the witch or witches who had caused the selective incapacity commenced in May. Why at that late date Cromwell decided to intervene in the royal couple's marital relationship with a belated attempt to encourage their sexual union will never be known. After his arrest in June, he admitted that he had asked Anne's lord chamberlain for a second time in late May to encourage her to be more pleasant to her husband. This must have been the action that caused the suspicious king, who had promoted him to the office of lord chamberlain and to the earldom of Essex in April, to have him arrested and imprisoned. Initially, he was to be charged simply with treason, as indicated by the House of Lords' first bill of attainder, but after an investigation of the activities of his client Lord Hungerford, who was found to have had dealings with witches, the commons crafted a second bill of attainder, adding to it a section charging Cromwell with being a sacramentary, the version that the Lords then approved. Early modern Christians associated heresy, especially this radical form, with witchcraft.

It would have been foolish to charge the minister who had been so prominent in the public attack on the papal supremacy, as evidenced by his enforcement of the Reformation statutes, with conspiring with the Pole family and other supporters of Paul. The other side of the religious coin was the hated sacramentarians, the heretics who were perceived to be sinners against social morality and rebels against law and order. Perhaps the imprisoned Lisle, who had, himself, been involved in indirect contacts with Cardinal Pole, accused Cromwell of trying to prevent the prosecution of the Calais sacramentarians, for certainly some of his partisans at that port town did.

While Cromwell remained in prison, the divorce process was officially initiated. Parliament requested Henry to permit the double convocation to inquire into the validity of the royal marriage. Anne's consent was apparently obtained; depositions were taken, and the anticipated verdict was handed down. It is interesting that both in the bill of attainder and in the divorce depositions, some of the evidence was fictionalized. This was not an unusual process in treason and divorce cases. The charges against Anne Boleyn in 1536, for example, were entirely contrived.

As part of the divorce process, Anne of Cleves, whom Henry adopted as his sister, was to remain financially independent as long as she remained in England where her communications with her German relatives could be exchanged under the watchful eyes of Henry's ministers. Her household as queen was discharged and a new one for her as the king's sister was established. The repudiation of her as his wife and his subsequent remarriage to Katherine Howard had no major impact on England's foreign policy. Henry continued his friendship with her brother and maintained agents, such as Christopher Mont, in Germany to report on political and religious events. Shortly after the divorce, he developed a new understanding with Francis, whose alliance with the emperor had not long endured, as Cromwell had predicted.

In the meantime, although exiled from court, Anne had hopes of a reconciliation after the arrest and execution of Katherine Howard, her successor as queen, but it was not to be. Following Henry's death, she lost Richmond Palace and Bletchingley Manor and suffered financial difficulties. She also had to deal with disputes among the members of her household, and her brother's interference that led to the exile of three trusted servants. Shortly before she died in 1557, she was still describing herself to him as a stranger in a foreign land.

An examination of the marrying of Henry and Anne in 1539–40 is an occasion for more than the mere description of the protocol involved in that process. It offers an opportunity to interpret their wedding and wooing procedures within a wider cultural and social framework: one that is comparative in both a contemporary and chronological sense across early modern Christendom. To arrive at some understanding of the meaning of the marrying protocol that directed and guided their behavior, it is necessary to study diplomatic conventions, religious rituals, folklore, wedding customs, and the impact of romance literature and the chivalric ideals that helped to shape this society's ideals. Victor Turner's comment, already quoted in Chapter 9, helps to put this investigation in focus: In the past there were "no simpler people"; merely people with "wide diversities of cultural experiences."

NOTES

The following abbreviations are used in the notes

Abbott	George Abbott, *The Case of Impotency as Debated in England in that Remarkable Tryal An. 1613 Between Robert, Earl of Essex, and the Lady Frances Howard*, vol. I (1715)
ACP	*Acts of the Privy Council of England*, ed. J. Dasent, 32 vols. (1890–1907)
Bisson	Douglas Bisson, *The Merchant Adventurers of England: The Company and the Crown, 1474–1564* (Newark, DL, 1993)
BL	British Library
BIHR	*Bulletin of the Institute of Historical Research*
Bouterwek (4)	A. W. Bouterwek, "Anna von Cleve," *Zeitschrift des Bergischen Geschictsvereins* 4 (1867)
Bouterwek (6)	A. W. Bouterwek, "Anna von Cleve," *Zeitschrift des Bergischen Geschictsvereins* 6 (1869)
Brundage	James Brundage, *Law, Sex, and Christian Society in Medieval Europe* (1995).
Burnet	Gilbert Burnet, *The History of the Reformation of the Church of England*, new edn, 3 vols. in 6 pts. (Oxford, 1826)
CS	Camden Society
CSP Spain	*Calendar of Letters, Despatches, and State Papers Relating to Negotiations Between England and Spain*, ed. G. Bergenroth, P. de Gayangos, G. Mattingly, M. Hume, and R. Taylor, 13 vols., 2 supplements (1862–1954)
CSP Ven	*Calendar of State Papers and Manuscripts Relating to English Affairs Existing in the Archives and Collections of Venice, and Other Libraries of Northern Italy*, ed. Rawdon Brown, 38 vols. (Washington, DC, 1864–1947)
Cartwright	Julia Cartwright, *Christina of Denmark, Duchess of Milan and Lorraine, 1522–1590* (New York, 1913)
Constantine	T. Amyot, "The Memorial from George Constantyne to Thomas Lord Cromwell," *Archaeologia* 13 (1831)
Cust	Nina Cust, *Gentlemen Errant: Being the Journeys and*

	Adventures of Four Noblemen in Europe During the Fifteenth and Sixteenth Centuries (New York, 1909)
DNB	*Dictionary of National Biography*
EETS	Early English Text Society
Ellis (1)	Henry Ellis, *Original Letters Illustrative of English History*, 1st ser., 2nd edn. (1825)
Ellis (2)	Henry Ellis, *Original Letters Illustrative of English History*, 2nd ser. (1827)
Ellis (3)	Henry Ellis, *Original Letters Illustrative of English History*, 3rd ser. (1846)
Foxe	*The Acts and Monuments of John Foxe*, ed. G. Townsend (New York, 1965)
Guy	John Guy, "Thomas Wolsey, Thomas Cromwell, and the Reform of Henrician Government," *The Reign of Henry VIII: Politics, Policy and Piety*, ed. D. MacCulloch (1995)
Hall	Edward Hall, *Henry VIII*, intro. Charles Whibley, vol. II (1904)
HMC	Historical Manuscripts Commission
Holbein	Arthur Chamberlain, *Hans Holbein the Younger* (1913)
Iongh	Jane de Iongh, *Mary of Hungary, Second Regent of the Netherlands*, tr. M. Herter Norton (New York, 1958)
Kaulek	Jean Kaulek, ed., *Correspondance Politique de MM. de Castillon et de Marillac: Ambassadeurs de France en Angleterre, 1537–1542* (Paris, 1885)
Klarwill	Victor von Klarwill, ed., *Queen Elizabeth and Some Foreigners: Being a Series of Hitherto Unpublished Letters from the Archives of the Hapsburg Family* (1928)
Lacomblet	Theodor Lacomblet, *Urkundenbuch für die Geschichte des Niederrheins, odor des Erzatifts Köln, der Fürstenthumer Jülich und Berg, Geldern, Meurs, Cleve und Mark und der Reichsstifte Elten, Essen und Werden*, 4 vols. (Aalen, 1966)
Land	*Land im Mittelpunkt der Mächte: Die Herzogtümer Jülich-Kleve-Berg* (Kleve, 1985)
Lisle Letters	Muriel St. Clare Byrne, ed., *The Lisle Letters*, 6 vols. (Chicago, 1981)
LP	*Letters and Papers, Foreign and Domestic of the Reign of Henry VIII*, ed. J. Brewer, J. Gairdner, and R. Brodie, 21 vols. (1862–1932)
Lubkin	Gregory Lubkin, *A Renaissance Court: Milan Under Galeazzo Maria Sforza* (Berkeley, CA, 1994)
McEntegart	Rory McEntegart, "England and the League of Schmalkalden, 1531–1547 Faction, Foreign Policy, and the English Reformation," Ph.D. thesis, London School of Economics and Political Science (1992)

Midelfort   Erik Midelfort, *Mad Princes of Renaissance Germany* (Charlottesville, VA, 1996)

Müller   Albert Müller, "Die Beziehungen Heinrichs VIII zu Anna von Cleve," D. Phil. thesis, Tübingen University (1907)

Nott   George Nott, *The Works of Henry Howard, Earl of Surrey, and of Sir Thomas Wyatt the Elder*, vol. II (1815)

Parsons   John Parsons, "Mothers, Daughters, Marriage, Power: Some Plantagenet Evidence, 1100–1500," *Medieval Queenship* (New York, 1993)

Peters   Henry Peters and Helmut Lahrkamp, "Zwei Bildnisse Heinrichs VIII auf Schenkungsurkunden für Anna von Kleve," *Düsseldorfer Jahrbuch* 48 (1956)

Pietzsch   Gerhard Pietzsch, *Archivalische Forschungen zur Geschicte der Musik an den Hofen der Grafen and Herzoge von Kleve-Jülich-Berg (Ravensberg) bis zum Erloschen der Linie Jülich-Kleve im Jahre 1609* (Verlag Köln, 1971)

Potter   David Potter, "Diplomacy in the Mid-Sixteenth Century: England and France, 1536–1550," Ph.D. thesis, Cambridge University (1973)

PRO   Public Record Office

Queller   Donald Queller, *The Office of Ambassador in the Middle Ages* (Princeton, NJ, 1967)

Redworth   Glyn Redworth, *The Defence of the Church Catholic: The Life of Stephen Gardiner* (Oxford, 1990)

Scarisbrick   J. Scarisbrick, *Henry VIII* (Berkeley, CA, 1968)

Sprengel   Norbert Finzsch-Sprengel, "Heinrich VIII und Anna von Kleve," *Annalen des Historischen Vereins für den Niederrheins* 192–3 (1990)

StP   *State Papers of Henry VIII*, 11 vols. (1830–1852)

Strype   John Strype, *Ecclesiastical Memorials*, 3 vols. in 6 pts. (Oxford, 1822)

TRHS   *Transactions of the Royal Historical Society*

Warnicke   Retha Warnicke, "Family and Kinship Relations at the Henrician Court: The Boleyns and the Howards," *Tudor Political Culture*, ed. D. Hoak (Cambridge, 1995)

Wicquefort   Abraham van Wicquefort, *The Embassador and His Functions*, tr. Mr. Digby (1716)

Wriothesley   Charles Wriothesley, *A Chronicle of England During the Reigns of the Tudors from A.D. 1485 to 1559*, ed. William Hamilton, CS, vol. I (1875)

Unless otherwise specified, references to calendars, *LP*, and the *Lisle Letters* are to documents and the place of publication is London.

1 INTRODUCTION

1 Erasmus, *The Education of a Christian Prince*, tr. L. Born (Morningside Heights, NY, 1936), 42, 240–3; William Camden, *Remains Concerning Britain*, ed. R. Dunn (Toronto, 1984), 244; F. Furnivall, *The Regement of Princes A.D. 1411–1412: From the Harleian MS. 4866* (*Hoccleve's Works*, vol. III), EETS, ex. ser., 72 (1897), ll. 5335–41, 5363–6, 5386–90, 5394; Jerome Mitchell, *Thomas Hoccleve: A Study in Early Fifteenth Century Poetic* (Urbana, IL, 1968), 31, for the quotation.

2 Erasmus, *Education of a Prince*, 142, and *A Right Fruitful Epistle Devised by the Most Excellent Clerk Erasmus, in Laud and Praise of Matrimony* (1536), sig. Aiii–Bi, Eiii; Erasmus, *Erasmus on Women*, ed. E. Rummel (Toronto, 1996).

3 Not all marriages followed this pattern. Indissoluble marriages resulted both from vows in the future tense if sexually consummated and from vows in the present tense even if the marriage was not held at church or sexually consummated.

4 Ralph Houlbrooke, *The English Family: 1450–1700* (1984).

5 Erasmus, *Education of a Prince*, 243; David Potter, *A History of France, 1460–1560: The Emergence of a Nation State* (1995), 257.

6 *CSP Spain*, II, 669, for example.

7 Nott, 473.

8 Parsons, 64.

9 Erasmus, *Education of a Prince*, 243; Parsons, 69; *CSP Spain*, II, 201; Francis Blucke, *Louis XIV*, tr. M. Greengrass (Oxford, 1990), 9, noted that Louis learned that his queen was corresponding with the Spanish during a Franco-Spanish war.

10 Tr. in Cartwright, 22.

11 *CSP Spain*, XI, p. 153; Klarwill, 190.

12 P. Fichner, "Dynastic Marriage in Sixteenth-Century Habsburg Diplomacy and Statecraft: An Interdisciplinary Approach," *American Historical Review* 81 (1976), 243–65; Klarwill, 137–44; BL MS Julius FV1, fos. 61a–61b.

13 Charles Ingrao, *The Habsburg Monarchy, 1618–1815* (Cambridge, 1994), 4; Dorothy McGuigan, *The Habsburgs* (Garden City, NY, 1966), 32.

14 *CSP Spain*, III-ii, 8 (p. 28).

15 J. Lander, *The Limitations of English Monarchy in the Later Middle Ages* (Toronto, 1989), 6; James I quoted by David Bergeron, *Royal Family, Royal Lovers: King James of England and Scotland* (Columbia, MO, 1991), 92; Klarwill, 292.

16 *CSP Spain*, XI, p. 132.

17 *CSP Spain*, II, 669; VI-i, 73; Hoccleve, *Regement of Princes*, ll. 5335–41, 5363–6, 5386–90, 5394.

18 Mark Hansen, *The Royal Facts of Life: Biology and Politics in Sixteenth Century Europe* (Metuchen, NJ, 1980), 6–7, 216.

19 *LP*, XIV-ii, 574; P. Fichner, *Protestantism and Primogeniture in Early Modern Germany* (New Haven, CT, 1989), 36.

20 Quoted by R. Stradling, *Philip IV and the Government of Spain, 1621–1665* (Cambridge, 1988), 374.

21 In 1613 Abbott, 19, commented: "Henry VIII was a strange prince in that kind: He put himself into many marriages."

22 There were similarities. A prevalent view was that families intermarried. The duke of Suffolk, for example (*LP*, XIV-ii, 4), confided that if his son-in-law, Lord Clifford, did not accept Cromwell's advice, he would be "sorry that ever I married with him."

23 Max Gluckman, "Les Rites de Passage," *Essays on the Ritual of Social Relations*, ed. Gluckman (Manchester, 1962), 28; Clifford Geertz, "Centers, Kings, and Charisma: Reflections on the Symbolics of Power," *Rites of Power: Symbolism, Ritual, and Politics Since the Middle Ages*, ed. S. Wilentz (Philadelphia, PA, 1985), 15–16; R. McCoy, "From the Tower to the Tiltyard: Robert Dudley's Return to Glory," *Historical Journal* 27 (1984), 425–35, for noblemen using chivalry.

24 Malcolm Vale, *War and Chivalry*, (Athens, GA, 1981), 35; Gerald Harriss, "Political Society and the Growth of Government in Late Medieval England," *Past and Present* 138 (1993), 28–57.

25 Edward Muir, *Ritual in Early Modern Europe* (Cambridge, 1997), 1–9; David Cannadine, "The Context, Performance and Meaning of Ritual: The British Monarchy and the Invention of Tradition, c. 1820–1977," *The Invention of Tradition*, ed. E. Hobsbaum and T. Ranger (Cambridge, 1983), 3–4; Richard Green, *Poets and Princepleasers: Literature and the English Court in the Late Middle Ages* (Toronto, 1980), 491, observed that kings were not "as far sighted about the propaganda value" as has been claimed. They needed to display their wealth, however, to signal their royal status.

26 Johan Huizinga, *The Waning of the Middle Ages: A Study of the Forms of Life, Thought, and Art in France and the Netherlands in the XIVth and XVth Centuries* (1948).

27 Maurice Keen, *Chivalry* (New Haven, CT, 1984), 3; Larry Benson, *Malory's Morte D'Arthur* (Cambridge, MA, 1976), 141.

28 Henry was described as St. George (*LP*, II, 410); Sharon Jansen, "Prophecy, Propaganda, and Henry VIII: Arthurian Tradition in the Sixteenth Century," *King Arthur Through the Ages*, ed. V. Lagorie and M. Day, 2 vols. (New York, 1990), I, 284, for Arthur as a portrait of Henry.

29 S. Gunn, "Chivalry and the Politics of the Early Tudor Court," *Chivalry in the Renaissance*, ed. Sydney Anglo (Woodbridge, 1990), 123; Potter, *History of France*, 257; M. Rodriquez-Salgado, *The Changing Face of*

Empire: Charles V, Philip II and Habsburg Authority, 1551–1559 (Cambridge, 1988), 2–3; S. Anglo, "How to Kill a Man at Your Ease: Fencing Books and the Dueling Ethic," *Chivalry in the Renaissance*, ed. Anglo, 1–12.

30 Catherine Bates, *The Rhetoric of Courtship in Elizabethan Language and Literature* (Cambridge, 1992), 2.

31 Jessie Weston, *From Ritual to Romance* (Cambridge, 1920), title page.

32 Bates, *Rhetoric of Courtship*, 7, notes that in the second half of the sixteenth century "to woo" became interchangeable with "to court."

2 ENGLISH NEGOTIATORS

1 *LP*, XII-ii, 889, 970, 972.

2 *StP*, VIII, 1.

3 Scarisbrick, 355, conjectures that it was a hasty move and doubts Henry's reluctance; PRO, SP1/126/58 (*LP*, XII-ii, 1030); *StP*, VIII, 5; Nott, 329; *CSP Spain*, VI-i, 7; A. Gurevich, *Categories of Medieval Culture*, tr. G. Campbell (1985), 5, for misunderstandings of early modern motives.

4 Werner Gundersheimer, *Ferrara: The Style of a Renaissance Despotism* (Princeton, NJ, 1973), 272.

5 Edmond Bapst, *Les Mariages de Jacques V* (Paris, 1889), 311–13; *CSP Spain*, V-i, 78.

6 *Memoirs of the Duke of Sully, Prime-Minister to Henry the Great*, tr. C. Lennox, 5 vols. (1810), II, 339.

7 Nott, 321.

8 Jennifer Ward, *Noblewomen in the Later Middle Ages* (New York, 1992), 17–18.

9 R. Griffiths, "The Crown and the Royal Family in Later Medieval England," *Kings and Nobles in the Later Middle Ages: A Tribute to Charles Ross*, ed. Griffiths and J. Sherborne (New York, 1986), 14; Joel Rosenthal, *Nobles and the Noble Life, 1295–1500* (New York, 1976), 42.

10 *StP*, VIII, 1; William Camden, *Remains Concerning Britain*, ed. R. Dunn (Toronto, 1984), 244; *LP*, XII-ii, 1008 (22).

11 Susan Doran, *Monarchy and Matrimony: The Courtships of Elizabeth I* (1996), 40–73.

12 John Guy, "The Privy Council: Revolution or Evolution?" *Revolution Reassessed: Revisions in the History of Tudor Government and Administration*, ed. C. Coleman and D. Starkey (Oxford, 1986), 70–85; Guy, 42–3.

13 Geoffrey Elton, *The Tudor Constitution: Documents and Commentary*, 2nd edn. (Cambridge, 1982), 88–124; Guy, 42–3; Elizabeth Rogers, ed., *The Letters of John Hackett, 1526–1534* (Morgantown, WV, 1971), 376.

14 Nott, 471; *StP*, VIII, 29–30. In 1536 Cromwell told Chapuys that Henry would not marry a foreigner because if she committed a crime he could never get rid of her (*CSP Spain*, V-ii, 61).

15 *StP*, VIII, 1; *Memoirs of Sir James Melville of Halhill, 1535–1617*, ed. A. Steuart (1929), 76.

16 Rosalind Marshall, *Mary of Guise* (1977), 46; Richard Eaves, *James V's Regency, 1524–1528: A Study in Anglo Scottish Diplomacy* (New York, 1987), 68; *LP*, XII-ii, 539.

17 G. Elton, *Reform and Reformation: England, 1509–1558* (Cambridge, MA, 1977), 126–201.

18 *DNB*; *LP*, XIII-i, 1.

19 Redworth, 31–60; *LP*, IX, 443; Gary Bell, "Elizabethan Diplomacy: The Subtle Revolution," *Politics, Religion & Diplomacy in Early Modern Europe: Essays in Honor of De Lamar Jensen*, ed. M. Thorp and A. Slavin (Kirksville, MO 1994), 274; David Potter, "Foreign Policy," *The Reign of Henry VIII: Politics, Policy, and Piety*, ed. Diarmaid MacCulloch (1995), 105.

20 *StP*, VIII, 5, 42; *LP*, XI, 239; XIII-ii, 1280 (fos. 35, 40b); *DNB*; W. Richardson, *Stephen Vaughan: Financial Agent of Henry VIII: A Study of Financial Relations with the Low Countries* (Baton Rouge, LA, 1953), 16–27; Bisson, 3–7.

21 *DNB*.

22 Richardson, *Vaughan*, 3, 16.

23 *DNB*; Potter, 286–7.

24 Retha Warnicke, *The Rise and Fall of Anne Boleyn: Family Politics at the Court of Henry VIII* (Cambridge, 1989), 191–233; in a draft letter of 1539, Cromwell addressed Wyatt as gentleman of the privy chamber (*LP*, XIV-i, 166).

25 Queller, especially 16–92, for much of the following; Pierre Chaplais, "English Diplomatic Documents to the end of Edward III's Reign," *The Study of Medieval Records: Essays in Honor of Kathleen Major*, ed. D. Bullough and R. Storey (Oxford, 1971), 38.

26 Dudley Digges, *Letters of Negotiations* (1655), 29.

27 Queller, 68–91; J. Jones, *Full Powers and Ratification: A Study in the Development of Treaty-Making Procedure* (Cambridge, 1949); *Roger of Wendover's Flowers of History*, tr. J. Giles, 2 vols. (1849), II, 608; Mary Greene, *Lives of the Princesses of England From the Norman Conquest*, 6 vols. (1849), III, 286–8.

28 Queller, 82–91; Betty Behrens, "The Office of the English Resident Ambassador: Its Evolution As Illustrated by the Career of Sir Thomas Spinelly, 1509–1522," *TRHS*, 4th ser., 16 (1933), 162 n.3, notes Venice established limited terms; Vincent Ilardi, "The First Permanent Embassy Outside Italy: The Milanese Embassy at the French Court, 1464–1483," *Politics, Religion & Diplomacy*, ed. Thorp and Slavin, 1–18.

29 Behrens, "English Resident Ambassador," 166–7, believes Henry VII appointed Spinelly; Bell, "Elizabethan Diplomacy," 274; Charles Carter, "The Ambassadors of Early Modern Europe: Patterns of Diplomatic Representation in the Early Seventeenth Century," *From the*

Renaissance to the Counter Reformation: Essays in Honor of Garrett Mattingly, ed. Carter (New York, 1966), 270. The ordinary post between France and England took eleven or twelve days, royal couriers five to six days (*LP*, XIII-i, 1452).

30 Redworth, 55–83; Potter, "Foreign Policy," 104–5; *LP*, XIII-ii, 131, 270.

31 *LP*, XII-i, 987; XII-ii, 368; XIII-i, 116; Starkey, "Court and Government," *Revolution Reassessed* ed. C. Coleman and D. Starkey, 30–5, and "Intimacy and Innovation: The Rise of the Privy Chamber, 1485–1547," *The English Court from the Wars of the Roses to the Civil War*, ed. David Starkey, D. A. L. Morgan, J. Murphy, Pam Wright, Neil Cuddy, and Kevin Sharpe (1987), 74–85; see also in *English Court*, Cuddy, "The Revival of the Entourage: the Bedchamber of James I, 1603–1625," 173–7; Murphy, "The Illusion of Decline: the Privy Chamber, 1547–1558," 119–21, and Wright, "A Change in Direction: the Ramifications of a Female Household, 1558–1603," 147–72; Potter, 273, 342.

32 Queller, 84–140; *The Works of Francis Osborne*, 9th edn, 2 vols. (1689), II, 501; *StP*, VIII, 367; *CSP Spain*, VI-i, 41.

33 Jocelyne Russell, *Peacemaking in the Renaissance* (1986), 69; BL Add. MS 25,114, fo. 302 (*LP*, XIII-i, 918); *LP*, XII-i, 366; when in 1536 Norfolk's pension from the emperor was canceled, he accepted a French stipend, and in 1537 Charles V recommended giving a present to Cromwell to induce him to support Don Luis's union with Mary (*CSP Spain*, V-ii, 71, 130).

34 E. Adair, *The Exterritoriality of Ambassadors in the Sixteenth and Seventeenth Centuries* (1929), 31, for the quotation; Wicquefort, 353 (first published in French at The Hague in 1681); Queller, 82–164; R. A. Stradling, "Spanish Conspiracy in England, 1661–63," *English Historical Review* 87 (1972), 269–86.

35 Wicquefort, 298; Warnicke, *Anne Boleyn*, 191–233; Richardson, *Vaughan*, 19; John Hotman, *The Ambassador*, tr. from French (1603), sig. D5–6; Garrett Mattingly, "The First Resident Embassies: Mediaeval Italian Origins of Modern Diplomacy," *Speculum* 12 (1937), 28; *CSP Spain*, VI-i, 232, p.ix. In 1541 Chapuys had a spy in the French ambassador's confidence (*CSP Spain*, VI-i, 201, 203).

36 *LP*, XIV-i, 449; Charles Carter, *Secret Diplomacy of the Habsburgs, 1498–1625* (New York, 1964), 99.

37 Betty Behrens, "Treatises on the Ambassador Written in the Fifteenth and Early Sixteenth Centuries," *English Historical Review* 51 (1936), 623; Wicquefort, 246–65; *LP*, XII-ii, 131, 1202; *CSP Spain*, III-ii, 340; VI-i, 38, 202.

38 Redworth, 83; John Archer, *Sovereignty and Intelligence: Spying and Court Culture in the English Renaissance* (Stanford, CA, 1993), 3–9.

39 Chaplais, "Diplomatic Documents," 39–40; *CSP Spain*, VI-i, 199; Hotman, *Ambassador*, sig. B7; Wicquefort, 49.

40 Hotman, *Ambassador*, sig. B7, C5–6.

41 Queller, 68–98, 177–87; Thomas Hearne, *Collection of Curious Discourses*, 2 vols. (1771), I, 152, for Thynne; *LP* XII-i, 770, XII-ii, 586; XIII-i, 327; XIII-ii, 144; Hotman, *Ambassador*, sig. C7, D5–7.

42 David Kertzer, *Ritual, Politics, and Power* (New Haven, CT, 1988), 104.

43 Stephen Collins, *From Divine Cosmos to Sovereign State: An Intellectual History of Consciousness and the Idea of Order in Renaissance England* (Oxford, 1989), 20; Queller, 190–208; William Roosen, "Early Modern Diplomatic Ceremonial: A Systems Approach," *Journal of Modern History* 52 (1980), 454–8; Gordon Mattingly, *Renaissance Diplomacy* (Boston, 1955), 37–8; *CSP Spain*, VI-i, pp.ix, xxx; Wicquefort, 203, reported that Spain's embassies made it "appear still more powerful than it really is."

44 Queller, 190–208; Roosen, "Diplomatic Ceremonial," 454–8; Kaulek, 51; Mattingly, *Renaissance Diplomacy*, 37–8; Norbert Ohler, *The Medieval Traveller*, tr. C. Hillier (Woodbridge, Eng., 1989), 67–75; Peter Burke, *The Historical Anthropology of Early Modern Italy* (Cambridge, 1987), 80.

45 Queller, 190–208; De Lamar Jensen, "Franco-Spanish Diplomacy and the Armada," *Renaissance to Counter Reformation*, ed. Charles Carter, 225–9; *LP*, XIV-i, 144; XVI, 117–19; Kaulek, 159; David Potter, *A History of France, 1460–1560: The Emergence of a Nation State* (1995), 83; Sydney Anglo, "The Imperial Alliance and the Entry of the Emperor Charles V into London: June 1522," *Guildhall Miscellany* 2 (1962), 137.

46 Hotman, *Ambassador*, sig. G8.

47 Roosen, "Diplomatic Ceremonial," 460–3; *Satow's Guide to Diplomatic Practice*, ed. Lord Gore-Booth (1979), 20–2. The king of the Romans had precedence over other monarchs; see Wicquefort, 128–45, 208–20; Mary Sullivan, *Court Masques of James I: Their Influence on Shakespeare and the Public Theatre* (New York, 1913), 5–58.

48 BL Add. MS, 21,564, fo. 1 (*LP*, XIII-ii, 143); James Muller, *The Letters of Stephen Gardiner* (Cambridge, 1933), 90; *LP*, XIII-i, 1254–5, 1336–7, 1452; Hotman, *Ambassador*, sig. G8; *CSP Spain*, VI-i, 2; banquet seating was controlled (*LP*, II-ii, 3446); Ralph Winwood, *Memorials of Affairs of State in the Reign of Queen Elizabeth and King James I*, 3 vols. (1725), III, 350; Sullivan, *Court Masques of James*, 22.

49 Wicquefort, 128–69; E. Chambers, *The Elizabethan Stage*, 4 vols. (Oxford, 1923), I, 144–5.

50 Richardson, *Vaughan*, 3–4; Bisson, 3–7; Carter, "Ambassadors of Europe," 270–7. After Charles' inheritance was split, the emperor ceased to send residents. It was a convention that only peer states exchanged them; Hotman, *Ambassador*, sig. B3; Ilardi, "Permanent Embassy Outside Italy," 2.

51 F. Levy, "A Semi-Professional Diplomat: Guido Cavalcanti and the Marriage Negotiations of 1571," *BIHR* 35 (1962), 211–12; BL Galba MS B.X, fo. 82 (*LP*, XIII-ii, 47).

52 Roger Milton, *Heralds and History* (1978), 10–12; Anthony Wagner, *Heralds of England* (1967), 6–136; Wagner, *Heralds and Heraldry in the Middle Ages* (Oxford, 1939), 61–82.

53 Wagner, *Heralds and Heraldry*, 2–82; Joycelyne Russell, *Diplomats at Work: Three Renaissance Studies* (Wolfeboro, NH, 1992) 96; Ellis (1), I, 84–5, for Norfolk's challenge to James.

54 Hotman, *Ambassador*, sig. B4; Wagner, *Heralds and Heraldry*, 38; Hugh London, *Life of William Bruges, the First Garter King of Arms*, vols. 111–12 (1970), 12–20; Kenneth Fowler, *The Age of Plantagenet and Valois: The Struggle for Supremacy, 1328–1498* (New York, 1967), 140; *DNB*; Louise Campbell and Francis Steer, *Catalogue of Manuscripts in the College of Arms Collections*, vol. I (1988), 470; *LP*, XII-ii, 870; Gunn, "Chivalry and Politics," 120.

55 Henry Sedgwick, *The House of Guise* (New York, 1938), 27; Cartwright, *The Perfect Courtier: Baldassare Castiglione: His Life and Letters, 1478–1529*, 2 vols. (New York, 1927), II, 25.

56 *Boutell's Heraldry*, rev. G. Scott-Giles and J. Brooke-Little (1966), 10; F. Cripps-Day, *A Herald's Mourning Hood* (1935), 156; *DNB*; Louise Campbell and Francis Steer, *Catalogue of Manuscripts in the College of Arms Collections* (1988), I, 470; Anthony Wagner, "The Origin of the Introduction of Peers in the House of Lords," *Archaeologia* 101 (1967), 119–50; Bell, "Elizabethan Diplomacy," 270–2.

57 Queller, 110–25; Mattingly, *Renaissance Diplomacy*, 112; *StP*, VIII, 1; *LP*, XIV-i, 926.

58 Phyllis Lachs, *The Diplomatic Corps Under Charles II and James II* (New Brunswick, NJ, 1965), 4–5.

3 CANDIDATE POOL

1 *CSP Spain*, V-ii, 61 (p.141), 64, 116, for "seriously"; *LP*, XII-ii, 46.

2 Emmanuel Ladurie, *The Royal French State, 1640–1610*, tr. J. Vale (Oxford, 1994), 72–94, noted control of Milan and its region meant at least partial control of the Po Valley from the Alps to the Apennines.

3 Lubkin, 17–19; William Robertson, *The Progress of Society in Europe*, ed. F. Gilbert (Chicago, 1972), 110–12; Paul Kendall and Vincent Ilardi, *Despatches with Related Documents of Milanese Ambassadors in France and Burgundy, 1450–1483*, 3 vols. (Athens, OH, 1970), I, v–vi.

4 Ladurie, *French State*, 109–13; R. Knecht, *Francis I* Cambridge, 1982), 47–164, 300–01; Hayward Keniston, "Peace Negotiations Between

Charles V and Francis I (1537–38)," *Journal of the Proceedings of the American Philosophical Society* 102 (1958), 142–7.

5 Charles III was married to Beatrix, sister of the empress; *StP*, VII, 701; VIII, 9; *LP*, XII-ii, 46, 125, 1217; XIII-ii, 51; Ladurie, *French State*, 113; Desmond Seward, *Prince of the Renaissance: The Golden Life of François I* (New York, 1973), 188; Ian Roy, ed., *Blaise de Monluc: The Habsburg-Valois Wars and the French Wars of Religion* (Hamden, CT, 1972), 1–89.

6 E. Chamberlin, *The Count of Virtue: Giangaleazzo Visconti Duke of Milan* (New York, 1965), 40–2. Clarence's brother the duke of Lancaster married into the Portuguese royal family. Richard Jones, *The Royal Policy of Richard II: Absolutism in the Later Middle Ages* (New York, 1968), 21; Nigel Saul, *Richard II* (New Haven, CT, 1997), 84–5.

7 John Currin, "Henry VII, Italy, and the Fear of French Domination, 1494–1509: A Study of Early Tudor Foreign Policy," M.A. Thesis, Arizona State University (1984).

8 *StP*, VIII, 1–2; *LP*, XII-i, 34, for "natural"; XII-ii, 539, 1285; XIII-i, 239; *CSP Spain*, V-ii, 574, for Henry's statement; C. Hotle, *Thorns and Thistles: Diplomacy Between Henry VIII and James V, 1528–42* (Lanham, MD, 1996), 114–23.

9 *StP*, VIII, 5–6.

10 *StP*, VII, 668, 680; VIII, 5–6; *LP*, XII-i, 433, 760, 931, 997, 1032, 1242; XII-ii, 71, 125, 559. Another complication was the cardinal's death in 1538 (*LP*, XIII-i, 252); H. van Nierop, *The Nobility of Holland: From Knights to Regents, 1500–1650*, tr. M. Ultee (Cambridge, 1993), 143; A. Dek, "Genealogie der Heren Van Brederode," *Jaarboek van het Centraal Bureau voor Genealogie* 13 (1959), 121-2; *The Seditious and Blasphemous Oration of Cardinal Pole, Entitled the Defence of the Ecclesiastical Unity*, tr. F. Withers (1560), sig. Aiiii–Biii; Susan Brigden, "The Shadow That You Know: Sir Thomas Wyatt and Sir Francis Bryan at Court and in Embassy," *Historical Journal* 39 (1996), 8–9, for plots against Pole.

11 *StP*, VIII, 5–6; Dek, *Genealogie der Heren en Graven Van Egmond* ('S-Gravenhage, 1958), 25, 52; van Nierop, *Nobility of Holland*, 39, 147; Iongh, 171; Jonathan Israel, *The Dutch Republic: Its Rise, Greatness, and Fall, 1477–1806* (Oxford, 1995), 107; Edward Browne, *An Account of Several Travels Through a Great Part of Germany* (1677), 21; *CSP Spain*, V-ii, 182, added the dowager duchess of Florence, later the duchess of Parma, to the pool. There is no reference to her as a candidate in the English documents.

12 *StP*, VII, 709; VIII, 5–6; *LP*, XII-ii, 245, 825, 1303. The usual German name for this state is Jülich–Cleves since a marriage led to its unification in the sixteenth century. English records identify Anne and her brother William as of Cleves and I shall continue that practice

while retaining the German usage for their father except that the English spelling, Juliers, will be adopted.

13 Nott, 329, 470; BL Add. MS 21,564, fo. 6b (*LP*, XIII-ii, 143); *LP*, XII-ii, 212–13; XIII-i, 843; Kaulek, 40; *CSP Spain*, VI-i, 179.

14 *CSP Spain*, V-ii, 182 (p. 430), 212, 572; *LP*, XII-ii, 212–13, 1143, 1217; XIII-i, 273; XIII-ii, 51; Edward Armstrong, *The Emperor Charles V*, 2 vols. (New York, 1916), I, 305; *The Chronicle of Froissart*, tr. Lord Berners, 6 vols. (1902), V, 89, for equal ages; Lubkin, 9, for Elisabetta.

15 BL Harl. MS 282, fos. 159a-b (*LP* XIII-i, 255); *LP*, XIII-i, 273, 510, 1220; XIV-i, 335; Nott, 475–7, 494.

16 Potter, xii-xiii; Potter, *History of France*, 99.

17 Nott, 318, 461, 490; *StP*, VIII, 23–7; *LP*, XII-i, 1310; XII-ii, 372, 844, 868, 1001; XIII-i, 56, 273, 915, 917; *CSP Spain*, V-ii, 182; R. Merriman, ed., *Life and Letters of Thomas Cromwell*, 2 vols. (Oxford, 1902), II, 244; in June 1538 (*LP*, XIII-l, 1221), they agreed to a ten-year truce; Joceylyne Russell, *The Congress of Arras, 1435: A Study in Medieval Diplomacy* (Oxford, 1955), 78–9, for papal mediation; Nicholas Cheetham, *Keepers of the Keys: A History of the Popes from St. Peter to John Paul II* (New York, 1983), 201–3; Friedrich Gontard, *The Chair of Peter: A History of the Papacy* (New York, 1964), 414–17.

18 Iongh, 155–81; Cartwright, 22–104; *CSP Spain*, V-ii, 223; VI-i, 24–5; *StP*, VIII, 34–6; *LP*, XIII-i, 612, 1314.

19 *StP* VIII, 6, 14, 59; *LP*, XIV-i, 321.

20 Kaulek, 11; Caroline Bingham, *James V: King of Scots, 1512–42* (1971), 144–5; in 1538 an Imperial ambassador mentioned the sister of the duke of Nevers (*CSP Spain*, VI-i, 4) as a bride for Henry; there is no reference to her in the English records.

21 Knecht, *Francis*, 192; Henry Sedgwick, *The House of Guise* (New York, 1938), 29–32; Roy, *Blaise de Monluc*, 2.

22 H. Noel-Williams, *The Brood of False Lorraine: The History of the Ducs de Guise (1496–1588)*, 2 vols. (1919), I, 37; Gabriel de Pimsdan, *La Mère des Guises: Antoinette de Bourbon, 1494–1583* (Paris, 1925), 60; Bingham, *James*, 144; Rosalind Marshall, *Mary of Guise* (1977), 191–2.

23 Kaulek, 5, 10; *LP*, XII-ii, 1201; XIII-i, 1355; W. Richardson, *Vaughan: Financial Agent of Henry VIII: A Study of Financial Relations with the Low Countries* (Baton Rouge, LA, 1953), ll; Potter, "Foreign Policy," 106; Susan Anton, *Elizabeth*, 191–4.

24 *StP*, VIII, 10–12; *LP*, XII-ii, 1292; XIII-i, 56, 204; Marshall, *Mary of Guise*, 44; *Holbein*, II, 155.

25 *LP*, XII-ii, 245; XIII-i, 56, 691; Nott, 469–70; *StP*, VIII, 27–8; Müller, 5–6.

26 Kaulek, 8–11; *LP*, XIII-i, 56; D. Hay, ed., *The Letters of James V* (Edinburgh, 1954), 237–307; *Holbein*, II, 154. The spelling of Marie is used for Vendôme to make it easier to distinguish her from Guise.

27 D. Seward, *The Bourbon Kings of France* (New York, 1973), 4–5; Potter, *History of France*, 376.

28 Seward, *François*, 192; Bingham, *James*, 144–5.

29 Peggy Liss, *Isabel the Queen, Life and Times* (New York, 1992), 70–3; *StP*, VIII, 39–40; Constantine, 61.

30 *StP*, VIII, 39–40, 124n., 139; PRO SP1/142/230 (*LP*, XIV-i, 209); PRO SP1/143/90 (*LP*, XIV-i, 308). Wriothesley's remark (*StP*, VIII, 143–7) that she was "tickled" does not in the context reveal that she was being sarcastic; *Holbein*, II, 133; Archives du Royaume Bruxelles, *Papiers d'État*, 82, 20, quoted in Cartwright, 170, 187.

31 John Pope-Hennessy, *The Portrait in the Renaissance* (New York 1966), 8–81; Marianna Jenkins, *The State Portrait: Its Origins and Evolutions* (New York, 1947), 2; Selby Wittingham, "Portraits of Charles V," *Burlington Magazine* 113 (1971), 553; W. Lethaby, "The Westminster Portrait of Richard II," *Burlington Magazine* 65 (1934), 220–2.

32 Andrew Martindale, *Heroes, Ancestors, Relatives and the Birth of the Portrait* (The Hague, 1988), 8–32.

33 Norma Goodrich, *Charles, Duke of Orléans* (New York, 1963), 10; Lorne Campbell, *Renaissance Portraits: European Portrait Painting in the Fourteenth, Fifteenth and Sixteenth Centuries* (New Haven, CT, 1990), 197; Le Cte de La Borde, *La Renaissance des Arts à la Cour de France: Études sur le seizième siècle*, 2 vols. (New York, 1965), I, 53; Rachel Gibbons, "Isabeau of Bavaria, Queen of France (1385–1422): The Creation of an Historical Villainess," *TRHS*, 6th ser., 6 (1996), 51–74.

34 Martin Warnke, *The Court Artist: On the Ancestry of the Modern Artist*, tr. D. McLintock (Cambridge, 1993), 219; Richard Green, *Poets and Princepleasers: Literature and the English Court in the Late Middle Ages* (Toronto, 1980), 109.

35 Roger Loomis, *Studies in Medieval Literature: A Memorial Collection of Essays* (New York, 1970), 275–88; J. Vale, *Edward III and Chivalry: Chivalric Society and Its Context, 1270–1350* (Woodbridge, 1982), 4–82; Larry Benson, "The Tournament in the Romances of Chrétien de Troyes and L'Histoire de Guillaume le Maréchal," *Chivalric Literature: Essays on Relations between Literature and Life in the Later Middle Ages*, ed. Benson and J. Lyerle (Toronto, 1980), 1–19; Juliet Barker, *The Tournament in England, 1100–1400* (Woodbridge, 1986), 87–93; *Poems of Cupid, God of Love: Christine de Pizan's Épistre au Dieu d'Amours and Dit de la Rose and Thomas Hoccleve's The Letter of Cupid*, ed. T. Fenster and M. Erler (New York, 1990), 9; J. Palmer, "English Foreign Policy, 1388–99," *The Reign of Richard II: Essays in Honour of May McKisack*, ed. F. DuBoulay and C. Barron (1971), 76; Patricia Eberle, "The Politics of Courtly Style at the Court of Richard II," *The Spirit of the Court: Selected Proceedings of the Fourth Congress of the International Courtly Literature Society*, ed. G. Burgess and R. Taylor (Cambridge, 1985), 177–8, for the quotation.

36 John Archer, *Sovereignty and Intelligence: Spying and Court Culture in the English Renaissance* (Stanford, CA, 1993), 48–9, for "eyeliking"; Guillaume de Lorris and Jean de Meun, *The Romance of the Rose*, tr. C. Dahlberg, 3rd edn. (Princeton, NJ, 1995), 1–21; ll. 20817–21214; E. Vivaver, ed., *The Works of Sir Thomas Malory*, 2nd edn., 3 vols. (Oxford, 1967), I, 270; Martindale, *Heroes, Ancestors*, 31.

37 C. Armstrong, "The Golden Age of Burgundy: Dukes that Outdid Kings," *The Courts of Europe: Politics, Patronage, and Royalty, 1400–1800*, ed. A. Dickens (New York, 1977), 55; Michael Senior, *The Life and Times of Richard II* (1981), 91; Joan Evans, *English Art, 1307–1461* (New York, 1981), 63–82.

38 Wittingham, "Portraits of Charles," 553; Warnke, *Court Artist*, 220.

39 N. Nicolas, ed., *A Journal by One of the Suite of Thomas Beckington . . . During an Embassy to Negotiate a Marriage Between Henry VI and a Daughter of the Count of Armagnac, A.D. 1442* (1828), ix; S. Dicks, "Henry VI and the Daughters of Armagnac: A Problem in Medieval Diplomacy," *Medieval and Renaissance Studies* (Emporia, KS, 1967), 5–12; Philippe Erlander, *Margaret of Anjou, Queen of England* (Coral Gales, FL, 1970), 63.

40 Goodrich, *Orléans*, 23; Lebel Gustave, "British–French Artistic Relations in the XVI Century," *Gazette des Beaux Arts* 33 (1948), 267–80; Warnke, *Court Artist*, 220–1; Campbell, *Renaissance Portraits*, 197; Robert Wellens, "Un Episode des Relations Entre l'Angleterre et les Pays-Bas au Début du XVI Siècle: le Projet de Mariage Entre Marguerite d'Autriche et Henri VII," *Revue d'Histoire Moderne et Contempraire* 29 (1982), 267–90.

41 Alfred Woltmann, *Holbein and His Times* (1892), 434; Roy Strong, *Portraits of Queen Elizabeth I* (Oxford, 1963), 6–40; Giovanni Maria de Franches, *Of the . . . Auspicious Marriage: Betwixt . . . Prince Frederick, Count Palatine of the Rhine . . . and . . . Lady Elizabeth* (1613), sig. A; Warnke, *Court Artist*, 220–1; J. Dunlop, *Memoirs of Spain During the Reigns of Philip IV and Charles II from 1621 to 1700*, 2 vols. (1834), II, 145, for Charles II addressing amatory discourses to a portrait of Louise of Orléans worn on his breast

42 *StP*, VIII, 10–12.

43 Ibid.,17–19; *Holbein*, II, 139–55, for the incorrect dating of his missions in the *LP*.

44 *StP*, VIII, 17–19; *CSP Spain*, V-ii, 217, 220; *LP*, XIII-i, 419; *Holbein*, II, 128–53; Cartwright, 150–8; Pierre de Bourdeille, Seigneur de Brantôme, *The Lives of Gallant Ladies*, tr. A. Brown (1960), 280.

45 BL Add. MS 5,498, fos. 2a–b (*LP*, XIII-i, 380).

46 *Instructions Given by King Henry the Seventh to his Embassadors, When He Intended to Marry the Young Queen of Naples: Together with the Answers of the Embassadors* (1756); George Hersey, *Alfonso II and the Artistic Renèwal of*

Naples, 1485–1495 (New Haven, CT, 1969), 7; Walter Richardson, *Mary Tudor the White Queen* (1970), 50.

47 Scarisbrick, 361; *LP*, XIII-i, 840, 900, 917, 1003, 1062, 1070, 1217, 1356, 1452; XIII-ii, 262; *Holbein*, II, 146; Cartwright, 263–78; T. F. Shirley, *Thomas Thirlby, Tudor Bishop* (1964), 12.

48 BL Add. MS 5,498, fos. 1–1b; Cartwright, 165, 278; Kaulek, 48, 58, 74; *LP*, XIII-i, 1452; *The Letters of James V*, ed. Denys Hay (Edinburgh, 1954), 428.

49 *StP*, VIII, 10–12; *LP*, XIII-i, 1217, 1356; XIII-ii, 262; BL Add MS. 5,498, fos. 1a-b; *Holbein*, II, 139–55; Cartwright, 167–8; *CSP Spain*, VI-i, 4 (p.10); Joanne Baker, "Female Monasticism and Family Strategy: The Guises and Sainte Pierre de Reims," *Sixteenth Century Journal* 28 (1997), 1091–107.

50 BL Add. MS 5,498, fos. 1–1b; Knecht, *Francis*, 25; Iongh, 209–27; *LP*, XIII-ii, 262; *Holbein*, II, 146; *Letters of James*, 424, 428; Cartwright, 238, 323; Sedgwick, *House of Guise*, 16.

51 *LP*, XIII-i, 56; Nott, 477, 488, 494–8; *CSP Spain*, V-ii, 213; VI-i, 4.

52 *LP*, XIII-i, 1217, 1355–6, 1496; XIII-ii, 78; Kaulek, 78; BL Add. MS 21,564, fos. 6b-7b (*LP*, XIII-ii, 143).

53 L. Salzman, *Edward I* (New York, 1968), 16; *LP*, XIII-ii, 1048; M. Offord, ed., *The Book of the Knight of the Tower*, EETS, suppl. ser., 2 (New York, 1971), 25; Klarwill, 211.

54 *CSP Spain*, V-ii, 116, 212–13; William Oldys, ed., *Harleian Miscellany*, 10 vols. (1811), VIII, 9; Charles Petrie, *Philip II of Spain* (1963), 74, for Mary; Juan Vives, *A Very Frutefull and Pleasant Boke Called the Instruction of a Christian Woman*, tr. R. Hyrde (1540), sig. Riiii; Retha Warnicke, *Women of the English Renaissance and Reformation* (Westport, CT, 1983), 34.

55 *LP*, XIII-ii, 77; Edmond Bapst, *Les Mariages de Jacques V* (Paris, 1889), 289; Bingham, *James*, 114–45; Seward, *François*, 192–4; Agnes Strickland, *Lives of the Queens of Scotland*, 8 vols. (Edinburgh, 1854), I, 288–9.

56 John Brand, *Observations on the Popular Antiquities of Great Britain*, ed. H. Ellis, 3 vols. (New York, 1970), I, 19–55, 463–4; Enid Welsford, *The Court Masque: A Study in the Relationship Between Poetry and the Revels* (New York, 1962), 3–19; Glynne Wickham, *Early English Stages, 1300–1660*, 3 vols. (New York, 1957), I, 197–207, for mumming acquiring a literary framework.

57 Victor Turner and Edith Turner, *Image and Pilgrimage in Christian Culture: Anthropological Perspectives* (New York, 1978), 3; V. Turner, *The Ritual Process: Structure and Anti-Structure* (Chicago, 1969), 94.

58 Mircea Eliade, *Rites and Symbols of Initiation: The Mysteries of Birth and Rebirth*, tr. W. Trask (New York, 1958), 124–5; Chrétien de Troyes, *Arthurian Romances*, tr. D. Owen (New York, 1987); *The Works of Sir*

Thomas Malory, ed. Eugene Vinaver (Oxford, 1967), 2nd edn., 3 vols., I, 277; II, 513, 577; G. Bunt, ed., *William of Palerme: An Alliterative Romance* (Groningen, 1985), ll. 1638–1764.

59 Peter Dembroski, *Jean Froissart and His Meliador: Context, Craft, and Sense* (Lexington, KY, 1983), 13, 78; George Wolf, tr., *The Poetry of Cercamon and Jaufre Rudel* (New York, 1983), 95–102, for Rudel falling in love with the countess of Tripoli sight unseen.

60 Baldessar Castiglione, *The Book of the Courtier*, tr. G. Bull (1967), 119.

61 Lee Ramsey, *Chivalric Romances: Popular Literature in Medieval England* (Bloomington, IN, 1983), 45–58; Norris Lacy, "The Typology of Arthurian Romance," *The Legacy of Chrétien de Troyes*, 2 vols. (Amsterdam, 1987), I, 53; Dembroski, *Froissart and Meliador*, vv. 6595–7012; J. Rawson, *King Horn, Floriz and Blauncheflur, The Assumption of Our Lady*, EETS, vol. 14 (1866, re-edited 1901), ll. 1128–44; *Works of Malory*, I, 39, 270, 331; II, 555–7, 829, 1068; J. Zupita, ed., *The Romance of Guy of Warwick*, EETS, ex. ser., vol. 25–6 (1966), 298–300; Lloyd Davis, *Guise and Disguise: Rhetoric and Characterization in the English Renaissance* (Toronto, 1993), 9.

62 *CSP Ven*, III, 4, for an exception to dice-playing; Sydney Anglo, "The Evolution of the Early Tudor Disguising, Pageant and Mask," *Renaissance Drama*, new ser., 1 (1968), 10–44, distinguishes between masked individuals who entered court on foot to dance (maskers) and those who arrived on carts to perform an elaborate dramatic piece (disguisings). Contemporary references were vaguer. Wickham, *Early English Stages*, I, 20; Welsford, *Court Masque*, 42, 141; Vale, *Edward and Chivalry*, 62–9; Ann Payne, "The Salisbury Roll of Arms, c. 1463," *England in the Fifteenth Century*, ed. D. Williams (Wolfeborro, NH, 1987), 192.

63 Pauline Stafford, *Queens, Concubines, and Dowagers: The King's Wife in the Early Middle Ages* (Athens, GA, 1983), 32; Anita George, *Annals of the Queens of Spain* (New York, 1850), 52, for Don Garica, an eleventh-century conde of Castile, who, "Impatient" to see his betrothed Sancha of Leon, was killed on his visit.

64 Edgcumbe Staley, *King René D'Anjou and His Seven Queens* (New York, 1912), 34; Jules Baudot, *Les Princesses Yolande et les Ducs de Bar de la Famille des Valois* (Paris, 1900); Roger Boase, *The Troubadour Revival: A Study of Social Change and Traditionalism in Late Medieval Spain* (1978), 88, for Juan in 1370. When he heard that his betrothed Jeanne de Valois was dying, he traveled incognito to her bedside; T. N. Bisson, *The Medieval Crown of Aragon* (Oxford, 1986), 120; *Knight of the Tower*, 28, has a legend about a king of Aragon whose daughters the disguised king of Spain looked over; James Cabell, *Chivalry* (New York, 1909), 198, tells how Henry V was said to have wooed Katherine of France by accident when he met her in a forest.

65 Peter Thomas, "Charles I of England: The Tragedy of Absolutism,"

Courts of Europe, ed. A. G. Dickens, 193; J. Shuttleworth, *The Life of Edward, First Lord Herbert of Cherbury Written by Himself* (1976), ix, 115–18; Frederick Hard, ed., *The Elements of Architecture by Sir Henry Wotton* (Charlottesville, VA, 1968), xviii, 101.

66 *LP*, XIII-i, 995; XIII-ii, 77–8; *CSP Spain*, VI-i, 7.

67 Kaulek, 74; *LP*, XIII-i, 995.

68 Kaulek, 80.

69 David Hill, *A History of Diplomacy in the International Development of Europe*, 3 vols. (New York, 1967), II, 448; Karl Brandi, *Emperor Charles V: The Growth and Destiny of a Man and of World Empire*, tr. C. Wedgwood (New York, 1939), 388; *LP*, XIII-i, 1396.

70 BL Add. MS 21,564, f. 6b; *LP*, XIII-i, 1356, 1396, 1405, 1440, 1496; XIII-ii, 8, 11, 23, 77, 280; *CSP Spain*, V-ii, 113, 224; James Muller, *The Letters of Stephen Gardiner* (Cambridge, 1933), 87–8.

71 *StP*, VIII, 65–9, 73; *LP*, XIII-ii, 640, 748, 752–3, 1120, 1162–3; Kaulek, 140; *Holbein*, II, 154; Cartwright, 176.

72 *LP*, XIII-i, 628, 843, 1003, 1102, 1470; Nott, 478; the commissioners obtained full powers and the discussions were held (*LP*, XIII-i, 814, 909, 917).

73 *StP*, VIII, 53, 89–102; PRO SP1/140/207–8 (*LP*, XIII-ii, 1169) is damaged; Nott, 478–84; *LP*, XIII-i, 612, 640; XIII-ii, 280, 859, 974 (p.414), 1169; *CSP Spain*, VI-i, 2, 7 (p.19), 16, 24, 30–2.

74 *LP*, XII-ii, 46, 122; XIII-ii, 974 (1); Nott, 499–504; Charles Smith, *Papal Enforcement of Some Medieval Marriage Laws* (Port Washington, NY, 1972), 5–51; Frederick Pollock and Frederick William Maitland, *The History of English Law Before Edward I*, 2nd edn. reissued, 2 vols. (Cambridge, 1968), II, 387–8.

75 *LP*, XIII-i, 1320; Nott, 499–504; *StP*, VIII, 6.

76 *StP*, VIII, 107, 109, 111; *LP*, XIII-ii, 1054; XIV-i, 26, 121.

77 *StP*, VIII, 32–3, 111–14; *LP*, XII-ii, 46; XIII-ii, 1087; Müller, 4–5.

78 *LP*, XIII-i, 917; *CSP Spain*, VI-i, 33.

79 Smith, *Papal Enforcement*, 163–72; W. Ormrod, "Edward III and his Family," *Journal of British Studies* 26 (1987), 398–422; Richard Fletcher, "Diplomatic and the Cid Revisited: The Seals and Mandates of Alfonso VII," *Journal of Medieval History* 2 (1976), 358; John McNeil and Helena Gamer, *Medieval Handbooks of Penance: A Translation of the Principal Libri Poenitentiales and Selections from Related Documents* (New York, 1988), 336–7; Colin Richmond, "The Pastons Revisited: Marriage and the Family in Fifteenth Century England," *BIHR* 58 (1985), 31, for the quotation.

80 Nott, 306; PRO SP1/142/8–10,105–09 (*LP* XIV-i, 7, 103); Kaulek, 45; *LP*, XIV-i, 37, 299; *CSP Spain*, VI-i, 21, 33; *StP*, I, 604; VIII, 156. In 1539 (*LP*, XIV-ii, 168–9, 222–3), the emperor suggested resuming negotiations to stall the Cleves marriage.

81 Hall, 282–3.

4 CLEVES SELECTION

1 Midelfort, 94–9; Walter Prevenier and Wim Blockmans, *The Burgundian Netherlands* (Cambridge, 1986), 227, for John II's fathering sixty-three illegitimate children; Cartwright, 208.

2 F. Carsten, *Princes and Parliaments in Germany From the Fifteenth to the Eighteenth Century* (Oxford, 1959), 261–2. Juliers had also acquired Ravensberg which lay to the north and east of Mark.

3 Benjamin Arnold, *Princes and Territories in Medieval Germany* (Cambridge, 1991), 110–237; Carsten, *Princes and Parliaments*, 262–9; F. Du Boulay, *Germany in the Later Middle Ages* (1983), 65–95; Joachime Bumke, *Courtly Culture: Literature and Society in the High Middle Ages*, tr. T. Dunlap (Los Angeles, CA, 1986), 31; W. Janssen, "Kleve-Mark-Jülich-Berg-Ravensberg" and H. Hilger, "Kleve und Burgund," *Land*, 17–18, 209.

4 Carsten, *Princes and Parliaments*, 269; *LP*, VII, 1030.

5 Rory McEntegart, "Fatal Matrimony: Henry VIII and the Marriage to Anne of Cleves," *Henry VIII: A European Court in England*, ed. D. Starkey (1991), 140, claimed she was thirty-four in 1540; Pietzsch, 177–182; N. H. N., "Descent of Henry VIII's Wives," *Gentleman's Magazine* 145 (1829), 396–7; F. Barnard, "The Kinship of Henry VIII and his Wives," *Miscellanea Genealogica et Heraldica*, 5th ser. (1918–19) III, 194–6; Karl Brandi, *Emperor Charles V: The Growth and Destiny of a Man and of World Empire*, tr. C. Wedgwood (New York, 1939), 35.

6 Cust, 18n.; Prevenier and Blockmans, *Burgundian Netherlands*, 173–229; Janssen, "Kleve-Mark-Jülich," 35; T. Philipps, ed., "Account of the Ceremonial of the Marriage of the Princess Margaret, Sister of King Edward the Fourth, to Charles, Duke of Burgundy, in 1468," *Archaeologia* 31 (1846), 328, for the chronicler; Norma Goodrich, *Charles, Duke of Orléans* (New York, 1963), 230.

7 Prevenier and Blockmans, *Burgundian Netherlands*, 19, 109, 173–273; Paul Kendall and Ilardi, *Despatches with Related Documents of Milanese Ambassadors in France and Burgundy, 1450–1483*, 3 vols. (Athens, OH, 1970), I, 30, 270, 314–16; David Hill, *A History of Diplomacy in the International Development of Europe*, 3 vols. (New York, 1967), II, 130; Carsten, *Princes and Parliaments*, 264; A. Ward, G. Prothero, S. Leathes, eds., *The Cambridge Modern History: The Renaissance*, 3 vols. (New York, 1902–12), I, 450; *CSP Spain*, VI-i, 7; Cust, 175–96.

8 *LP*, II, 1608; III, 128, 2288 (4); G. Benecke, *Society and Politics in Germany, 1500–1750* (1974), 291; William Jerdan, ed., "The Visit of the Emperor Charles V to England, A. D. 1522," *Rutland Papers. Original Documents Illustrative of the Courts and Times of Henry VII and Henry VIII*, CS, vol. 21 (1842), 61.

9 Midelfort, 99; Bumke, *Courtly Culture*, 91.

10 Brandi, *Charles*, 30.

11 Agnes Strickland, *Lives of the Queens of England*, 12 vols. (1842), IV, 325; Brandi, *Charles*, 30; R. Evans, *The Making of the Habsburg Monarchy, 1550–1700: An Interpretation* (Oxford, 1979), xxi; Otto Cartellieri, *Court of Burgundy* (1929), 139–40; Prevenier and Blockmans, *Burgundian Netherlands*, 283, for the quotation; Franz Matenaar, *Kleve, Burg und Stadt Unter dem Schwan* (Kleve, 1959).

12 Henry Cohn, *The Government of the Rhine Palatinate in the Fifteenth Century* (Oxford, 1965), 225; Pietzsch, 136–47; *Land*, 136; Brandi, *Charles*, 22.

13 Thomas Brady, Jr., "Phases and Strategies of the Schmalkaldic League: A Perspective After 450 Years," *Archiv fur Reformationsgeschichte* 74–5 (1983), 162; Müller, 21–2; McEntegart, 238–80; McEntegart, "Henry and Anne," 140–2; *LP*, XIII-i, 23, 145, 1320; XIII-ii, 1162; *CSP Spain*, V-ii, 225; VI-i, 7 (p.18); *StP*, VIII, 41. Albert of Prussia recommended that Henry marry Christian III's sister or Sigismund of Poland's daughter *LP*, XVI, 4n.; Lacomblet, IV, 658–66, for the 1538 Lorraine agreement.

14 *StP*, VIII, 9; BL Galba MS B.X, fo. 82 (*LP*, XIII-ii, 47); *LP*, XIII-i, 145, 1314; XIII-ii, 859; Brandi, *Charles*, 432–3; *Cambridge Modern History*, I, 423–4; Lord Berners, *Chronicle of Froissart*, 6 vols. (1902), V, 87–8; Edward Armstrong, *The Emperor Charles V*, 2 vols. (New York, 1916), I, 4; II, 318–20; James Tracy, *Holland Under Habsburg Rule, 1506–1566: The Formation of a body Politic* (Los Angeles, CA, 1990), 68, 75; Lacomblet, IV, 646; Müller, 16–17.

15 Carsten, *Princes and Parliaments*, 269; Charles Carter, *Secret Diplomacy of the Habsburgs: 1498–1625* (New York, 1964), 16–19; Tracy, *Holland Under Habsburg Rule*, 20, 68; Martha Freer, *The Life of Jeanne D'Albret, Queen of Navarre*, 2 vols. (1855), I, 24; *CSP Spain*, VI-i, 24; Abraham Glezerman and Michael Harsgor, *Cleve–ein Unerfultes Schicksal: Aufstieg, Ruckzug, und Verfall eines Territorialstaates* (Berlin, 1985), 263–5.

16 *LP*, XIII-i, 1212; Tracy, *Holland Under Habsburg Rule*, 58, 65–8; *CSP Spain*, VI-i, 24 (p.62); Jerdan, *Rutland Papers*, 61.

17 Jervis Wegg, *Richard Pace: A Tudor Diplomat* (New York, 1971), 146–8; *LP*, I-i, 1162; III, 274; VIII, 1158 (24–5).

18 BL Add. MS 25,114, fo. 30 (*LP*, IV-iii, 6364); *StP*, I, 104; *LP*, I-i, 1440; II-ii, 3473; III-i, 354; IV-i, 214 (p.85), 1811; IV-ii, 2530, 2718, 4810, 4827; XIII-ii, 47; Ellis (3), II, 127–31; John Fudge, *Cargoes, Emissaries: The Commercial and Political Interaction of England and the German Hanse, 1450–1510* (Toronto, 1995), 120–70; Klarwill, 230.

19 BL Galba MS B.X, fo. 82 (*LP*, XIII-ii, 47); *LP*, III, 274; IV-ii, 2530, 2932, 3898; IV-iii, 6364; XIII-ii, 33; Bouterwek (4), 385–91, for the 1527 contract; Rosalind Marshall, *Mary of Guise* (1977), 15. Rumors in 1528 about the break-up of Anne's betrothal to Francis possibly spread because of Guelders's agreement to recognize the emperor as his heir. Observers could view it as a repudiation of the Lorraine covenants, but

the rumors were circulating in February and the treaty was not signed until October (Armstrong, *Charles*, II, 318–20).

20 *LP*, V, 497, 548, 707, 805, 1131; VI, 1324. No record confirms John's insanity but an ancestor of William's mother, Gerhard II (*c.* 1417–75), was declared incompetent to rule. William's heir, John William (1562–1609), was deranged (Midelfort, xi, 99).

21 Brady, "Schmalkaldic League," 162.

22 *Cambridge Modern History*, I, 437; John Dolan, *The Influence of Erasmus, Witzel and Cassander in the Church Ordinances and Reform Proposals of the United Duchees of Cleve During the Middle Decades of the 16th Century* (Münster, 1957), vi-vii, 3–10, 25, 108; *LP*, VI, 1039; Midelfort, 95; Nicholas Cheetham, *Keepers of the Keys: A History of the Popes from St. Peter to John Paul II* (New York, 1983), 65; Janssen, "Kleve-Mark-Jülich," 38; J. Engelbrecht, "Anglo-German Relations in the Reign of Henry VIII," *Henry VIII. In History Historiography and Literature*, ed. U. Baumann (New York, 1992), 121.

23 *StP*, VIII, 175, 182; *LP*, XIV-i, 1230.

24 Geoffrey Elton, *Reform and Reformation: England, 1509–1558*, 277–9; Scarisbrick, 364–5; *CSP Spain*, VI-i, 7 (p.91); *LP*, XIII-ii, 695, 743, 752, 979; XIV-i, 37, 370.

25 Bisson, 88; Brady, "Schmalkaldic League," 171; *LP*, XII-ii, 1088; XIII-i, 648–9; XIV-i, 691–2, 698–9, 908; Abbott, 19, for the marriage resulting from Henry's fear that France and the Empire would unite with the papacy against him.

26 *LP*, XIII-i, 214, 352, 645, 650, 815, 1102, 1147, 1305; XIII-ii, 37, 165; Burnet, I-ii, 491–535.

27 *LP*, XIII-i, 499, 815; XIV-i, 368, 711, 731, 981.

28 *CSP Spain*, V-ii, 223 (p.525); *LP*, XIII-ii, 1162; XIV-i, 4, 37, 1260.

29 *StP*, VIII, 134; *LP*, XIV-i, 4, 37, 1137; *CSP Spain*, VI-i, 37; Wriothesley, 100.

30 Glyn Redworth, "A Study in the Formulation of Policy: The Genesis and Evolution of the Act of Six Articles," *Journal of Ecclesiastical History* 37 (1986), 49; Scarisbrick, 403–10; Elton, *Reform and Reformation*, 287–8; *LP*, XIV-i, 1063, 1065.

31 *CSP Spain*, VI-i, 54, 76; *LP*, XIV-i, 1168.

32 PRO SP1/142/105–09, parts of which are unreadable (*LP*, XIV-i, 103[1,2]); *LP*, IV-i, 4, 37; David Potter, "Foreign Policy," *The Reign of Henry VIII: Politics, Policy, and Piety*, ed. Diarmaid MacCulloch (1995), 103.

33 Esther Hildebrandt, "Christopher Mont, Anglo-German Diplomat," *Sixteenth Century Journal* 15 (1984), 278–92; *LP*, V, 506 (1); VI, 918; XIII-i, 352–3, 367, 648–50, 815.

34 PRO SP1/142/105–09.

35 Ibid.; *LP*, XIV-i, 592, 768, 1028; XIV-ii, 37–9, *CSP Spain*, VI-i, 60; Müller, 5–27. William signed a marriage contract in 1537 with the duchess but in 1538 agreed to wed a daughter of Lorraine.

36 PRO SP1/142/105–09.

37 *StP*, I, 599, 606; VIII, 182; Brady, "Schmalkaldic League," 169n; Engelbrecht, "Anglo-German Relations," 121; Müller, 17–27; McEntegart, 311.

38 *DNB*; *LP*, XIV-i, 157; Müller, 24–5.

39 *LP*, XIV-i, 490.

40 BL Harl. MS 296, fos. 163a-b (*LP*, XIV-i, 489): *LP*, XIV-i, 534; Müller, 26–7.

41 *StP*, I, 605; Müller, 26–7; Cartwright, 41. They referred to the duchess only, but it can be assumed that they meant "the duchess" of Milan since she had only recently been a candidate for the queenship.

42 *LP*, XIV-i, 580, 701–4, 834, 844; *StP*, I, 608; Müller, 26–7.

43 *LP*, XIV-i, 35, 470, 495, 570; *StP*, VIII, 156. On 16 April (*StP*, I, 608), Cromwell said that he had written to Paynell and Mont.

44 *DNB*; *LP* XIV-i, 2, 701; XIV-ii, 781 (fo. 85).

45 *StP*, I, 182, 599, 613; VIII, 182.

46 *StP*, VIII, 152–5; William Thomas, *The Pilgrim: A Dialogue of the Life and Actions of King Henry the Eighth*, ed. J. Froude (1861), 122–4; *CSP Spain*, VI-i, 43–4, 50; R. Wernham, *Before the Armada: The Emergence of the English Nation, 1485–1558* (New York, 1966), 143–5, believed Henry drew back that summer because he did not want to provoke the emperor.

47 BL Vitel. MS B.XXI, fos. 178–84 (*LP*, XIV-i, 920); Carter, *Diplomacy of the Habsburgs*, 18; Carsten, *Princes and Parliaments*, 269.

48 BL Vitel. MS B.XXI, fo. 178; *LP*, XIV-i, 1215.

49 BL Vitel. MS B.XXI, fos. 178–80; Müller, 32–3.

50 BL Vitel. MS B.XXI, fos. 179–80; G. Ives, tr., *The Essays of Montaigne*, 4 vols. (Cambridge, MA, 1925), I, 60.

51 BL Vitel. MS B.XXI, fos. 179–80; *Harleian Miscellany*, VIII, 9.

52 BL Vitel. MS B.XXI, fos. 179–80; Roger Sablonier, "The Aragonese Royal Family Around 1300," *Interest and Emotion: Essays on the Study of Family and Kinship*, ed. H. Medick and D. Sabian (Cambridge, 1984), 212–13, for the brother of Maria of Cyprus-Lusignan who decided not to let James II's envoys see her before they had confirmed that she would be his bride but to permit French envoys to see the naked breasts of his daughter.

53 BL Vitel. MS B.XXI, fos. 180–1.

54 Ibid.

55 Ibid.; Müller, 31–2; Lacomblet, IV, 658–66, Bouterwek (4), 360.

56 BL Vitel. MS B.XXI, fo. 182; Müller, 31–2, believed John preferred the

Lorraine match; *LP*, XIII-i, 23; Petrus Blok, *History of the Peoples of the Netherlands*, tr. R. Putnam, 5 vols. (New York, 1907), II, 230.

57 *LP*, XIII-i, 122, 165; *CSP Spain*, V-ii, 155, 228; Brandi, *Charles*, 433; Armstrong, *Charles*, II, 319. It was rumored in 1535 (*LP*, IX, 1018) that to heal the rift they would replace William as the ruler of Cleves with the duke elector; Blok, *People of the Netherlands*, II, 230.

58 BL Vitel. MS B.XXI, fos. 182–4.

59 Ibid., fo. 178.

60 Ibid.; *LP*, XIV-i, 948.

61 BL Vitel. MS B.XXI, fos. 182–4.

62 Ibid.; Cust, 445.

63 Robert Palmer, "Contexts of Marriage in Medieval England: Evidence from the King's Court Circa 1300," *Speculum* 59 (1984), 46–7, for dowries paid before a marriage that led to law suits.

64 *DNB*; BL Vitel. MS C.XVI, fo. 264–5b (*LP*, XIV-i, 1193); *LP*, XVI-i, 74, 78, 781 (fo.85b), 862; Müller, 33–4.

65 BL Vitel. MS C.XVI, f. 264; *LP*, XIV-ii, 781 (fo. 85b); Parsons, 64–76; *CSP Spain*, V-ii, 212; Georgina Masson, *Queen Christina* (1968), 15, noted a Hohenzollern custom for the mother to have "the final say in the bestowing of her daughter's hand in marriage."

66 BL Vitel. MS C.XVI, fo. 264; Cartwright, 75; *StP*, VII, 465.

67 *LP*, XIV-ii, 781 (fo.85); *Holbein*, II, 176–82; Oskar Batschmann and Pascal Griener, *Hans Holbein* (1997), 149–53, said he flattered Anne and speculated that his sketch was used for the miniature at the Victoria and Albert Museum; Susan Foister, "Holbein as Court Painter," *Henry VIII*, ed. Starkey, 62; John Cooper, "Die Bedeutung der Bildnisse Annas von Kleve bei dem Heiratsverhandlungen mit Heinrich VIII," *Land*, 156. If not Cranach, perhaps Barthel Bruyn the Elder painted her (Peter Hacker and Candy Kuhl, "A Portrait of Anne of Cleves," *Burlington Magazine* 134 (1992), 172–5).

68 BL Vitel. MS B.XXI, fo. 187b (*LP*, XIV-ii, 33); *LP*, XIV-ii, 781 (fo.85); *Holbein*, II, 176–82; Batschmann and Griener, *Holbein*, 192; Rader Boureaunu, *Holbein*, tr. F. Ionescu (1977), 5, for the quotation.

69 *LP*, XIV-i, 1092; *CSP Spain*, V-ii, App. 220.

70 *LP*, XIV-i, 1261, 1348; Ellis (1), II, 119–20; Constantine, 60–1.

71 Ellis (1), II, 121, has extracts from BL Vitel. MS B.XXI, fo. 187b; Bouterwek (4), 397; Müller, 26–7; McEntegart, 375–6; *LP*, XV, 310.

72 BL Vitel. MS B.XXI, fo. 187b.

73 Ibid.

74 BL Harl. MS 296, fos. 165–7 (*LP*, XVI-ii, 220); Müller, 34–5.

75 BL Vitel. MS B.XXI, fo. 1887b; Müller, 33–4, noted political concerns overcame the personal reluctance of Anne's mother.

76 *StP*, VIII, 5–6; Müller, 22.

77 Cartwright, 129–35; Bouterwek (4), 349.

78 BL Vitel. MS B.XXI, fo. 187b.

79 David Mathew, *The Courtiers of Henry VIII* (1970), 167; Dolan, *Influence of Erasmus*, 2–3; Bouterwek (4), 298n; Euan Cameron, *European Reformation* (Oxford, 1991), 105–87; Parsons, 75; Thomas Birch, ed., *An Historical View of the Negotiations Between the Courts of England, France, and Brussels From the Year 1592 to 1617* (1749), 491; Anthony Molho, *Marriage Alliances in Late Medieval Florence* (Cambridge, MA, 1994), 141; *The Book of the Knight of the Tower*, ed. M. Y. Offord, tr. William Caxton, EETS, suppl. ser., II (New York, 1971), 25; Janssen, "Kleve-Mark-Jülich," 38.

80 *LP*, XIV-i, 1092; Juan Vives, *A Very Frutefull and Pleasant Boke Called the Instruction of a Christian Woman*, tr. R. Hyrde (1540) sig. Hii–Nii, Riiii–Tiii; W. George and E. Waters, ed., *The Vespasiano Memoirs: Lives of Illustrious Men of the XVth Century*, (1926) 446; Retha Warnicke, *Women of the English Renaissance and Reformation* (Westport, CT, 1983), 33; Ethel Williams, *Anne of Denmark: Wife of James VI of Scotland: James I of England* (1970), 2–4, for her residence with her mother's parents until she was fourteen or fifteen.

81 Bodleian Lib. Jesus MS 74, fo. 299b; Warnicke, *Women of the Renaissance*, 33; Cartwright, 28; *LP*, VI, 1082; Martha Freer, *Henry III, King of France and Poland: His Court and Times*, 3 vols. (New York, 1888), I, 59; C. Proescholdt, "The Introduction of German Language Teaching into England," *German Life and Letters* 44 (1991), 93–4; Mary Hervey, *Holbein's Ambassadors* (1900), 75; Klarwill, 144; Cust, 251–65.

82 Pietschze, 136–47.

83 Warnicke, *Women of the Renaissance*; A. Audrey Locke, *The Seymour Family: History and Romance* (1911), 8–9; J. Jackson, *Wulfhall and the Seymours, With an Appendix of Original Documents Discovered at Longleat* (1874), App. XXIV, p. 3; *DNB*.

84 In 1541 Chapuys (*CSP Spain*, VI-i, 209), who was hostile to Anne, heard rumors in the Low Countries that she indulged in wine and hinted perhaps even sexual excesses, but no one in England made these claims; Bob Scribner, ed., *Germany: A New Social and Economic History, 1450–1630*, vol. I (1996), 13; David Buisseret, *Henry IV* (1984), 77; W. Bradford, ed., *Correspondence of Charles V* (1850), 456; Cust, 309–57, for Leodius; John Hotman, *The Ambassador*, tr. from French (1603), sig. D7; *LP*, VI, 1040; Cartwright, 211.

85 Cust, 527–8; Antoni Maczak, *Travel in Early Modern Europe*, tr. U. Phillips (Cambridge, 1995), 282; J. Carmer, *The Second Book of Nicander Nucius of Corcyra*, CS, vol. 17 (1831), 16, for the quotation.

86 *LP*, XIV-ii, 117.

87 *Ibid.*, 128, 220, 286; E. Smut and J. Zweers, "Anna von Kleve und Heinrich VIII von England," *Land*, 149; Müller, 35–6.

5 TRAVELING BRIDE

1 *LP*, XIV-ii, 221–2; Kaulek, 138; Edward Armstrong, *The Emperor Charles V*, 2 vols. (New York, 1916), II, 20. In 1613 Abbott, 19, noted the marriage took place to strengthen the king against the pope, the emperor, and Francis.

2 *LP*, XIV-ii, 59, 423; Müller, 18–19.

3 *StP*, I, 608, 616; *LP*, XIV-ii, 84, 574; Kaulek, 121–2; Edward Armstrong, *Charles V*, I, 133; Ellis (1), II, 119–20; Ellis (2), II, 137.

4 *LP*, XIV-ii, 63, 117; Kaulek, 126.

5 *LP*, XIV-ii, 128, 149, 168–9, 221; *Lisle Letters*, V, 1536; Peters, 294 n.5; Bouterwek (4), 372; Müller, 38; McEntegart, 131, 377–82.

6 BL Harl. MS 296, fo. 167 (*LP*, XIV-ii, 220); Cust, 387; Müller, 37–8; Cartwright, 187–216; *LP*, XIV-ii, 46, 168–9, 183, 210, 215, 247.

7 Christine Weightman, *Margaret of York*, 78; Martin Hume, *Two English Queens and Philip* (New York, 1908), 41; C. Grose, "The Anglo-Portuguese Marriage of 1662," *Hispanic American Historical Review* 10 (1930), 313–52.

8 *DNB*; Müller, 19–41; McEntegart, 377–80; *LP*, XIV-i, 1353; assumed that Henry and Cromwell were speaking truthfully, but they were merely mollifying the Saxons to encourage them to enter a defensive alliance. Later (*LP*, XV, 310), the duke elector informed Henry that the League would not enter a treaty except for religious reasons.

9 *StP*, I, 616–18.

10 *LP*, XIV-ii, 210; Müller, 37–8; W. Robson-Scott, *German Travelers in England, 1400–1800* (Oxford, 1953), 22; Cust, 124– 386; Hans Medick and David Warren, eds., "Introduction," *Interest and Emotion*, 13.

11 Joachime Bumke, *Courtly Culture*, 208; Peter Burke, *The Historical Anthropology of Early Modern Italy* (Cambridge, 1987), 134; Michel Jeanneret, *A Feast of Words: Banquets and Table Talk in the Renaissance* (Cambridge, 1991), 39; S. Bertelli, F. Cardini, and E. Zorzi, *Italian Renaissance Courts* (1986), 21–4, for "intrusion"; Felicity Heal, *Hospitality in Early Modern England* (Oxford, 1990), 2.

12 Bernard Guenee, *States and Rulers in Later Medieval Europe*, tr. J. Vale (Oxford, 1985), 79–80; *LP*, XIV-ii, 389.

13 Cust, 390–5; Hall, 293–4; *LP*, XIV-i, 781; XIV-ii, 32, 275, 286, 367; Kaulek, 127, 133–4; *Lisle Letters*, V, 1547, 1550, 1553, 1560. The editors of *LP* placed the treaty with other documents dated 6 October (XIV-ii, 286); Bouterwek (4), 396, for the final contract.

14 BL Vitel. MS C.XI, fos. 213–220b (*LP*, XIV-ii, 286); Iongh, 40–4; Strype, I-ii, 452–4; Müller, 19–52; McEntegart, 83–131, 381–96.

15 BL Vitel. MS C.XI, fos. 213–220b; Bouterwek (4), 396–407.

16 BL Vitel. MS C.XI, fos. 213–220b; Müller, 34–6; Diane Hughes,

"From Brideprice to Dowry," *Journal of Family History* 3 (1978), 276; R. Outhwaite, "Marriage as Business: Opinions on the Rise in Aristocratic Bridal Portions in Early Modern England," *Business Life and Public Policy: Essays in Honour of D. C. Coleman*, ed. N. McKendrick and R. Outhwaite (Cambridge, 1986) 23; Jennifer Ward, *English Noblewomen*, 26–7; *LP* XIV-ii, 432, was a preliminary jointure.

17 BL Vitel. MS C.XI, fos. 213–220b.

18 BL Harl. MS 296, fo. 167; *LP*, XIV-ii, 258, 286; Müller, 31–9.

19 BL Vitel. MS C.XI, fos. 213–20b.

20 Müller, 16–59; McEntegart, 384; A. Pollard, *The Reign of Henry VII From Contemporary Sources*, 3 vols. (New York, 1967), I, 2–6; *LP*, XIV-ii, 657, 733, 1425–7; XV, 310; *StP*, VIII, 238, 279; Peters, 295n.10, for a contract between Philip and Mary; Cust, 523.

21 Müller, 39–40; Bouterwek (4), 396–8; Peters, 294; BL Harl. MS 296, fo. 165; James Cabell, *Chivalry*, 181; Edward Black, *Royal Brides: Queens of England* (Sussex, Eng., 1987), 116.

22 Georgina Masson, *Frederick II of Hohenstaufen: A Life* (1957), 103–66; *Roger of Wendover's Flowers of History*, tr. J. A. Giles, 2 vols. (1849), II, 608; Henry Swinburne, *A Treatise of Spousals, or Matrimonial Contracts* (New York, 1985), 162–92; Black, *Royal Brides*, 66–7, for male relatives accompanying brides; Elizabeth Hamilton, *Henrietta Maria* (New York, 1976), 45–8, for nuptial proxies.

23 Strickland, *Queens of England*, II, 232.

24 *CSP Spain*, XII, pp. 6, 137.

25 Grose, "Anglo-Portuguese Marriage," 336; Hamilton, *Henrietta Maria*, 45–8.

26 Frederick Pollock and Frederick William Maitland, *The History of English Law Before Edward I*, 2nd edn., 2 vols. (Cambridge, 1968), II, 368–70; Charles Donahue, Jr., "The Canon Law on the Formation of Marriage and Social Practice in the Later Middle Ages," *Journal of Family History*, 8 (1983), 144–7, notes that church courts upheld these rules; Michael Sheehan, "Marriage and Family in English Conciliar and Synodal Legislation," *Essays in Honour of Anton Charles Pegis*, ed. J. O'Donnell (Toronto, 1974), 205–14.

27 H. Richardson, "King John and Isabelle of Angouleme," *English Historical Review* 65 (1950), 366; Jane de Iongh, *Margaret of Austria: Regent of the Netherlands*, tr. Herter Norton (New York, 1953), 42–84.

28 John Leland, *Antiquarii de Rebus Britannicis Collectanea*, ed. T. Hearne, 6 vols. (1774), IV, 261.

29 *CSP Spain*, II, 668; Parsons, 67; Eric Carlson, *Marriage and the English Reformation* (Oxford, 1994), 20, reported "Contracts by future words which had not been completed could be enforced by the courts, but they were reluctant to do so. . . ."

30 Walter Richardson, *Mary Tudor, The White Queen* (1970), 80–1; "The Spousels of Princess Mary, 1508," *The Camden Miscellany, Volume The Ninth* (1895), 22–3; *CSP Ven*, I, 482.

31 *Chronicle of Froissart*, IV, 30; Iongh, *Margaret of Austria*, 115; J. Carmer, *The Second Book of Nicander Nucius of Corcyra*, CS, vol. 17 (1831), 49; Lubkin, 49; Dorothy McGuigan, *The Habsburgs* (Garden City, NY, 1966), 14, for the ceremony of Mary of Burgundy with Maximilian's proxy in which a sword was placed between them.

32 Williams, *Anne of Denmark*, 15; Ralph Dutton, *English Court Life from Henry VII to George II* (1963), 110; Antonia Fraser, *Six Wives of Henry VIII* (1992), 28, believed it occurred in the proxy union of Arthur and Catherine, but *CSP Spain*, I, 241, does not refer to it.

33 Pollock and Maitland, *English Law*, II, 370; Sheehan, "Marriage in Legislation," 205–14; Chilton Powell, *English Domestic Relations*, 19–20, for banns by a bellman; *LP*, X, 916; XVIII-i, 854, for the licenses to marry Jane Seymour and Katherine Parr.

34 Müller, 40–1; *LP*, XIV-ii, 387; HMC, "Townley Manuscripts," *Fourth Report* (1874), IV, App. 412; Hume, *Two English Queens*, 54; Marcel Mauss, *The Gift: The Form and Reason for Exchange in Archaic Societies*, tr. W. Halls (1990), viii; Edmund Gardner, *Dukes and Poets in Ferrara: A Study in the Poetry, Religion and Politics of the Fifteenth and Early Sixteenth Centuries* (St. Clair Shores, MI, 1972), 134, for love letters; Bouterwek (4), 373.

35 *LP*, XIV-ii, 221, 274; XV, 170; Kaulek, 168; Peter Barber, "Henry VIII and Mapmaking," *Henry VIII: A European Court in England*, ed. David Starkey (1991), 149; see also *LP*, XV, 23.

36 *LP*, XIV-ii, 258; C. Bastide, *The Anglo-French Entente in the Seventeenth Century* (1914), 7; Weightman, *Margaret of York*, 47–8; BL Cotton MS Nero C.IX, fos. 173–7.

37 Weightman, *Margaret of York*, 47–8; Cust, 493, for the proverb.

38 PRO SP1/153/171 (*LP*, XIV-ii, 287); *LP*, XIV-ii, 314, 356, 388–9, 591, 600; *CSP Spain*, VI-i, 91; Müller, 43.

39 *CSP Spain*, VI-i, 58.

40 BL Harl. MS 296, fo. 166; *LP*, XIV-ii, 285; Peters, 294–6. It was waived again on 5 January.

41 Anthony Molho, *Marriage Alliances in Late Medieval Florence* (Cambridge, MA, 1994), 16; *CSP Spain*, V-ii, App. 223.

42 *Hall's Chronicle: Containing the History of England, During the Reigns of Henry the Fourth, and the Succeeding Monarchs to the end of the Reign of Henry the Eighth*, ed. Sir Henry Ellis (1809), 204.

43 Richard Baker, *A Chronicle of the Kings of England: From the Time of the Romans' Government unto the Death of King Charles I* (1665), 187; J. Davies, ed., *An English Chronicle of the Reigns of Richard II, Henry IV, Henry V, and Henry VI, Written Before the Year 1471*, CS, vol. 64 (1856), 144; *The*

Chronicle of Froissart, tr. Lord Berners, 6 vols. (1902), V, 268–71, for the duke of Berry's financial difficulties.

44 PRO SP1/154/5 (*LP*, XIV-ii, 297); *LP*, XIV-ii, 425–7, 572, 781 (fos. 97,104b); Richardson, *Mary, White Queen*, 67; Lubkin, 51.

45 *LP*, XIV-ii, 284; *Lisle Letters*, V, 1574, 1620; John Dunlop, *Memoirs of Spain during the Reigns of Philip IV and Charles II from 1621 to 1700*, 2 vols. (1834), II, 146–7.

46 PRO SP1/157/13–17 (*LP*, XV, 21); *LP*, XIV-ii, 487, 527, 529, 548, 550, 609; *Lisle Letters*, V, 1593, 1600, 1612; Anne Crawford, "The King's Burden? – The Consequences of Royal Marriage in Fifteenth Century England," *Patronage, The Crown and the Provinces in Later Medieval England*, ed. Ralph Griffiths (Atlantic Highlands, NJ, 1981), 48–9.

47 *StP*, VIII, 218–19; *LP*, XIV-ii, 274, 658, 745, 781 (fos. 101b–102b), 783; XVI, 380 (fos. 113, 120), 398; *Henry VIII*, ed. Starkey, 136; W. Tighe, "The Gentlemen Pensioners in Elizabethan Politics and Government," Ph.D. Dissertation, Cambridge University (1983).

48 BL Harl. MS 296, fo. 165; PRO SP1/155/141 (*LP*, XIV-ii, 737); *LP*, XIV-i, 658; XIV-ii, 469, 574, 583; Cust, 360n.2.

49 PRO SP1/154/118 (*LP*, XIV-ii, 495); *LP*, XIV-ii, 380, 424, 469, 494–5, 548, 573; XVI, 380 (fos.111b–112b).

50 Müller, 44; *LP*, XIV-ii, 541, 548, 607, 781 (fos. 71,100b); HMC, "Townley MSS," App. 413; John Allen, *Post and Courier Service in the Diplomacy of Early Modern Europe* (The Hague, 1972), 106.

51 McEntegart, 393; J. Crofts, *Packhorse, Wagon and Post: Land Carriage and Communications Under the Tudors and Stuarts* (Toronto, 1967), 110–11; Hall, 300; PRO SP1/155/85–88 (*LP*, XIV-ii, 634); *LP*, XIV-ii, 388, 604; *Lisle Letters*, V, 1616. Tokkyn was substituted for Ecloo. The journey is in Bouterwek (4), 410–13; E. Smit and J. Zweers, "Der Erwerb Geldern als Berweggrund für die Hierat Zwishen Anna von Kleve und Heinrich VIII von England, *Land*, 150; Müller, 44–5; *CSP Ven*, II, 509; Henrietta Haynes, *Henrietta Maria* (New York, 1912), 18; Suzanne Westfall, *Patrons and Performance: Early Tudor Household Revels* (Oxford, 1990), 65–6.

52 John Hale, *The Civilization of Europe in the Renaissance* (New York, 1994), 150; Carl Cipolla, *Before the Industrial Revolution: European Society and Economy, 1000–1700* (New York, 1993), 261–2; Frederick Fairholt, *Lord Mayors Pageants: Being a Collection Towards a History of These Annual Celebrations* (1843), 2; R. Withington, "The Early Royal Entry," *Publications of the Modern Language Association* 32 (1917), 616–23; Peter Burke, *The Fabrication of Louis XIV* (New Haven, CT, 1992), 191.

53 PRO SP1/155/85–8; *StP*, VIII, 354–5; R. Smuts, "Public Ceremony and Royal Charisma: The English Royal Entry in London, 1485–1642," *The First Modern Society: Essays in English History in Honour of*

Lawrence Stone, ed. A. Beier, D. Cannadine, and J. Rosenheim (Cambridge, 1989), 65–6; Hugh Trevor-Roper, *Princes and Artists, Patronage and Ideology at Four Habsburg Courts* (New York, 1976), 18; Lawrence Bryant, *The King and the City in the Parisian Royal Entry Ceremony: Politics, Ritual, and Art in the Renaissance* (Geneva, 1986), 22, 130; Haynes, *Henrietta Maria*, 20.

54 PRO SP1/154/118;155/85–8; BL Vitel. MS CXI, fos. 220–4 (*LP*, XV, 14); Bisson, ix, 4, for marts at Bergen-op-Zoom; J. Wegg, *Antwerp, 1477–1559: From the Battle of Nancy to the Treaty of Cateau-Cambresis* (1916), 13–98; E. Carus-Wilson, *Medieval Merchant Venturers*, 2nd edn (1967).

55 PRO SP1/155/85–8; *Chronicle of Calais*, 172; *LP*, XX-ii, 992; Bouterwek (4), 397, Müller, 45; Samuel Bentley, *Excerpta Historica, or Illustrations of English History* (1833), 297–8.

56 PRO SP1/157/126–30 (*LP*, XIV-ii, 677); PRO SP1/155/85–8; *LP*, XX-ii, 992; *Chronicle of Calais*, 172, differs somewhat in detail from Wotton; Westfall, *Patrons and Performance*, 65–6, for trumpeters; Cecily Booth, *Cosimo I: Duke of Florence* (Cambridge, 1921), 102; Michael Prawdin, *The Mad Queen of Spain*, tr. E. Paul and C. Paul (1938), 14.

57 PRO SP1/155/85–8; V. Sackville-West, *Daughter of France, The Life of Anne Marie Louise d'Orléans, Duchesse de Montpensier, 1627–93* (New York, 1959), 14; Edward Muir, *Civic Ritual in Renaissance Venice* (Princeton, NJ, 1981), 187–211.

58 Henry provided plate worth over £1,400; *StP*, VIII, 208; *LP*, XIII-i, 1055–6; XIII-ii, 617, 1280 (fos. 11b, 56); XIV-i, 592 (p. 599); PRO, SP1/155/85–8; Cust, 269–403, for other gifts; Lubkin, 57.

59 PRO SP1/155/141; *LP*, XIV, 753; *Lisle Letters*, V, 1594. Nobles were worth 7 shillings, 6 pence each and sovereigns were worth 22 shillings, 6 pence each.

60 PRO SP1/155/85–8;157/126–30; *LP*, XIV-ii, 493, 604, 761; BL Vitel. MS CXI, fos. 220–4 (*LP*, XV, 14); Bouterwek (4), 410; Müller, 45.

61 *LP*, XIII-ii, 732; XIV-ii, 494, 548, 781 (fo. 100b), 782 (p. 344); T. H. Lloyd, *The English Wool Trade in the Middle Ages* (Cambridge, 1977), 211–56; Peter Bowden, *The Wool Trade in Tudor and Stuart England* (1962), 107; *Lisle Letters*, I, p. 443.

62 BL Harl. MS 296, fo. 165; *LP*, XIV-ii, 212–13; 781 (fo. 100); XVI, 98 (pp. 32–5); BL Vitel. MS CXI, fos. 220–4; Bouterwek (4), 411; *Chronicle of Calais*, 168, 173; Hall, 294; *Lisle Letters*, I, between 434–6; Ellis (3), III, 252.

63 Bouterwek (4), 411; *Chronicle of Calais*, 168; Hall, 295. The accounts vary; PRO SP1/157/126–30; *LP*, XIII-i, 1502; BL Vitel. MS CXI, fos. 220–4; *Lisle Letters*, V, p. 725; Smuts, "Entry in London," 69.

64 PRO SP1/157/126–30; *LP*, XIV-ii, 630, 674. Since she arrived later

than expected, her passage was probably rescheduled for 13 December, the day they wrote their letter.

65 PRO SP1/157/126–30; PRO E101/422/15; PRO SP1/155/125 (*LP*, XIV-ii, 703); BL Vitel. MS CXI, fos. 220–4; Patrick Carter, "Financial Administration, Patronage, and Profit in Tudor England: The Career of Sir Wymond Carew (1498–1549)," *Southern History*, 21 (1998).

66 PRO SP1/157/126–30; John Kirk, *History of Charles the Bold, Duke of Burgundy*, 3 vols. (1863–88), I, 456, for isolation; M. Lowenthal, ed., *The Autobiography of Michel de Montaigne* (Boston, 1935), 105.

67 Margaret Visser, *The Rituals of Dinner* (New York, 1991), 50.

68 PRO SP1/157/126–30; David Potter, *A History of France, 1460–1560: The Emergence of a Nation State* (1995), 85; Dunlop, *Philip and Charles*, II, 159–62; Ruth Kleinman, *Anne of Austria: Queen of France* (Columbus, MO, 1985), 24.

69 PRO SP1/155/115–16,125 (*LP*, XIV-ii, 685, 703).

70 *LP*, XIV-ii, 300, 386; Nott, 362–5, 516–18; Burke, *Historical Anthropology*, 81.

71 *StP*, VIII, 204, 218; Cust, 530.

72 Knecht, *Francis*, 296; Nott, 350, 360; *LP*, XIV-ii, 717, 754, 769; W. Bradford, ed., *Correspondence of Charles V* (1850), 513–14; *CSP Spain*, VI-i, 95.

73 Geoffrey Elton, *Reform and Reformation: England, 1509–1558* (Cambridge, MA, 1977), 182–3.

74 Elizabeth Rogers, ed., *The Letters of John Hackett 1526–1534*, (Morgantown, WV, 1971), 376; PRO SP1/155/115–16; Kaulek, 88, 150–2; Ellis (1), II, 419–20. Variations could occur; in 1539 Bonner explained to Henry that he had written in more detail to Cromwell (*LP*, XIV-i, 620).

75 PRO SP1/153/159 (*LP*, XIV-ii, 266); *StP*, VIII, 218; *LP*, XIV-ii, 201, 283, 290; XVI, 380 (fos. 111b–112).

76 PRO SP1/154/124–5 (*LP*, XIV-ii, 500); *LP*, XIV-i, 801; *StP*, VIII, 211; *Nicander Nucius*, 45; Brantôme, *Gallant Ladies*, 19, 280.

6 ROYAL GREETER

1 Kaulek, 147; *LP*, XIV-ii, 757; *StP*, VIII, 218; Lambarde, *A Perambulation of Kent* (1596), 429; Simon Thurley, *The Royal Palaces of Tudor England: Architecture and Court Life, 1460–1547* (New Haven, CT, 1993), 197.

2 Kaulek, 144; *LP*, XIV-ii, 754; XV, 14, says she landed between 6 p.m. and 7 p.m. and that the duke and duchess received her at Deal; Bastide, *Anglo-French Entente*, 7; *The Itinerary of John Leland in or about the Years 1535 to 1543*, ed. L. Smith (Carbondale, IL, 1964), IV, 48; Hall, 295.

3 Edward Hasted, *The History and Topographical Survey of the County of Kent*, 12 vols. (Canterbury, 1797–1801), IX, 476; X, 12; Howard Colvin, *The History of the King's Works*, 6 vols. (1982), IV, 455; Keith Spence, *The Companion Guide to Kent and Sussex* (1973), 137, for the quotation; Hall, 295; *Itinerary of Leland*, IV, 50; J. Coad, *Dover Castle and Defences of Dover* (1995), 54; *LP*, XV, 14.

4 Hasted, *History of Kent*, IX, 476; Hall, 295; Geoffrey Parker, *The Military Revolution: Military Innovation and the Rise of the West, 1500–1800* (Cambridge, 1988), 27; *LP*, XIV-ii, 754.

5 PRO SP1/155/83 (*LP*, XIV-ii, 630); Jack Haswell, *The Ardent Queen: Margaret of Anjou and the Lancastrian Heritage* (1976), 48–53; Ralph Griffiths, *The Reign of Henry VI: The Exercise of Royal Authority* (Berkeley, CA, 1981), 487–8; Cust, 29–30, 492–3 n.4 for channel horrors.

6 *LP*, XIV-ii, 754; see also *LP*, XI, 108; XIII-ii, 677; XXI-i, 250; Add. I, 79.

7 *LP*, XIV-ii, 754; *The Itinerary of John Leland on or about the Years 1535 to 1543*, ed. Lucy Smith, 5 vols. (Carondale, IL, 1964), IV, 68; CS, *Rutland*, 74, and *LP*, III-ii, 2288, for Charles.

8 Hall, 295; Spence, *Kent and Sussex*, 179; W. Page, ed., *The Victoria County History of Kent*, 3 vols. (1974), II, 131; Wriothesley, 109; *LP*, XIV-ii, 754; *Lisle Letters*, VI, 1634; Colvin, *King's Works*, IV, 59.

9 *LP*, XIV-ii, 753; Henry Jenkyns, ed., *The Remains of Thomas Cranmer, Archbishop of Canterbury*, 4 vols. (Oxford, 1883), I, 296–7.

10 Thurley, *Royal Palaces*, 57, 115; Page, *Victoria History of Kent*, II, 113, 228; Hall, 295; *LP*, XIV-ii, 750; XV, 379; *Lisle Letters*, VI, 1634.

11 *LP*, XVI, 380 (fo. 116); Wriothesley, iii.

12 Wriothesley, 109.

13 BL Titus MS B.1, fo. 409 (*LP*, XV, 822); Burnet, I-ii, 296; BL Otho MS C.X, fo. 242 (*LP*, XV, 824).

14 Retha Warnicke, "Henry VIII's greeting of Anne of Cleves, and Early Modern Protocol," *Albion* 28 (1996), 565–86; Martin Hume, *The Wives of Henry the Eighth and the Parts They Played in History* (New York, 1905), 331, also suggests chivalry.

15 Terence McCarthy, *Reading the Morte Darthur* (Woodbridge, Eng., 1988), 54.

16 Staley, *René D'Anjou*, 47–8; Mary Hookham, *The Life and Times of Margaret of Anjou, Queen of England and France; and of her Father René 'The Good,' King of Sicily, Naples and Jerusalem With Memoirs of the House of Anjou*, 2 vols. (1872), I, 75.

17 Derek Brewer, "Malory's 'Proving' of Sir Lancelot," in *The Changing Face of Arthurian Romance: Essays on Arthurian Prose Romances in Memory of Cedric E. Pickford*, ed. A. Adams, A. Diverres, K. Stern, and K. Varty (Woodbridge, Eng., 1986), 127–8.

18 Haswell, *Margaret of Anjou*, 48–53; Griffiths, *Henry VI*, 487; A. Hinds,

ed., *Calendar of State Papers and Manuscripts, existing in the Archives and Collections of Milan, 1385–1618*, vol. I (1969), 18–19.

19 Staley, *René D'Anjou*, 138–40.

20 Miller, *Henry of Castile*, 84, for the quotation; A. de Palencia, ed., *Crónica de Enrique IV* (Madrid, 1973), 75; J. de Mata Carriaz, ed., *Memorial de Diversas Hazañas, Cronica de Enrique IV* (Madrid, 1941), 18.

21 Lubken, 53; Staley, *René D'Anjou*, 130.

22 Arthur Ferguson, *The Chivalric Tradition in Renaissance England* (Washington, D.C., 1986), 46–7; Müller, 47n.2.

23 William Walsh, *Philip II* (1937), 67–75; John Lynch, *Spain 1516–1598: From Nation State to World Empire* (Oxford, 1992), 72.

24 Mary Greene, *Lives of the Princesses of England From the Norman Conquest*, 6 vols. (1849), IV, 83; Patricia Buchanan, *Margaret Tudor, Queen of Scots* (Edinburgh, 1985), 22–3; see also Louise Fradenburg, *City, Marriage, Tournament: Arts of Rule in Late Medieval Scotland* (Madison, WI, 1991).

25 See also R. C. McCoy, "From the Tower to the Tiltyard: Robert Dudley's Return to Glory," *Historical Journal* 27 (1984)," 425–35.

26 David Loades, *Mary Tudor: A Life* (1989), 224–5; Gordon Kipling, *The Receyt of the Ladie Kateryne*, EETS, vol. 296 (Oxford, 1990), 6–7.

27 Max Gluckman, "Les Rites de Passage," *Essays on the Ritual of Social Relations*, ed. Gluckman (Manchester, 1962), 28; Clifford Geertz, "Centers, Kings, and Charisma: Reflections on the Symbolics of Power," *Rites of Power: Symbolism, Ritual and Politics Since the Middle Ages*, ed. Sean Wilentz (Philadelphia, 1985), for the quotation.

28 David Cannadine, "The Context, Performance and Meaning of Ritual: The British Monarchy and the Invention of Tradition, *c.* 1820–1977," *The Invention of Tradition*, ed. E. Hobsbawn and T. Ranger (Cambridge, 1983), 3–4.

29 David Loades, *The Politics of Marriage: Henry VIII and his Queens* (Dover, NH, 1994), 116; Scarisbrick, 334–5.

30 Pere III of Catalonia (Pedro IV of Aragon), *Chronicle*, tr. M. Hillgarth, 2 vols. (Toronto, 1980), I, 98; II, 449; Jonathan Nicholls, *The Matter of Courtesy: Medieval Courtesy Books and the Gawain Poet* (Dover, NH, 1985), 2–4.

31 Edward Storer, *Peter the Cruel: The Life of the Notorious Don Pedro of Castile, Together with an Account of his Relations with the Famous Maria de Padilla* (1911), 70, for "casual treatment" of a bride; Iongh, 61–2, for Louis's leaving the battlefield to greet her.

32 William Tyler, *Dijon and the Valois Dukes of Normandy* (Norman, OK, 1971), 62–3.

33 *CSP Spain*, V-ii, App., 226 (p. 552).

34 Elizabeth Hamilton, *Henrietta Maria* (New York, 1976), 30; Hebe Elsna, *Catherine of Braganza: Charles II's Queen* (1967), 20; Dunlop, *Philip and Charles*, II, 163.

35 Ruth Kleinman, *Anne of Austria: Queen of France* (Columbus, MO, 1985), 270–1; J. Dinfreville, *Louis XIV: Les Saisons D'un Grand Regne* (Paris, 1977), 143; Philippe Erlanger, *Louis XIV*, tr. S. Cox (New York, 1970), 89.

36 Loades, *Mary, A Life*, 224–5; J. Kirby, *Henry IV of England* (1990), 149–50; J. de Trokelowe and H. de Blaneforde, *Chronica Monasterii S. Albani*, ed. H. Riley (1886), 350. Henry VIII had traveled to Dover in March 1539 (*LP*, XIV-i, 452).

37 David Willson, *King James VI and I* (New York, 1956), 85–95; *Memoirs of Sir James Melville of Halhill, 1535–1617*, ed. Francis A. Steuart (1929), 329; Caroline Bingham, *James V: King of Scots, 1512–42* (1971), 112–26; James Merriman, *The Flower of Kings: A Study of the Arthurian Legend in England Between 1485 and 1835* (Lawrence, KS, 1973), 49.

38 Julia Cartwright, *The Perfect Courtier: Baldassare Castiglione: His Life and Letters, 1478–1529*, 2 vols. (New York, 1927), I, 117–18; Norma Goodrich, *Charles, Duke of Orléans* (New York, 1963), 15.

39 Enid Welsford, *The Court Masque: A Study in the Relationship Between Poetry and the Revels* (New York, 1962), 3–5, 42, 141; Vale, *Edward and Chivalry*, 62–71; C. Armstrong, "The Golden Age of Burgundy: Dukes that Outdid Kings," 69.

40 Gordon Kipling, *The Triumph of Honour: Burgundian Origins of the Elizabethan Renaissance* (Leiden, 1977), 96; Gordon Kipling, "Henry VII and the Origins of Tudor Patronage," *Patronage in the Renaissance*, ed. G. Lytle and S. Orgel (Princeton, NJ, 1981), 149–50; Hall, I, 15; *LP*, XIV-ii, 176; *CSP Spain*, V-ii, 71 (p.193), App., 220.

41 W. Wiley, *The Gentlemen of Renaissance France* (Cambridge, 1954), 60–80; Philippe Erlanger, *The Age of Courts and Kings: Manners and Morals, 1558–1715* (1967), 24.

42 *CSP Spain*, V-ii, App. 226; William Prescott, *History of the Reign of Philip the Second, King of Spain*, 3 vols. (Philadelphia, PA, 1872), III, 431.

43 BL Titus MS B.I, fo. 409; Burnet, I-ii, 296; BL Otho MS C.X, fo. 242.

44 Scarisbrick, 375; Jackson, *Wulfhall and Seymours*, 5–11, App. 16, for Hertford's payment to Holbein in September 1537 for Jane's picture.

45 PRO SP1/161/1 (*LP*, XV, 821), for the divorce.

46 Strype, I-ii, 452–63; Burnet, I-ii, 299.

47 Malcolm Gaskill, "Reporting Murder: Fiction in the Archives in Early Modern England," *Social History* 22 (1998), 1–30.

48 Strype, I-ii, 456–8; Kaulek, 150; John Brand, *Antiquities of Britain*, III, 12–18, for gifts; Sprengel, 59–67.

49 Raymond Firth, *Symbols: Public and Private* (Ithaca, 1973), 302; *Autobiography of Montaigne*, 119; Wriothesley, 109; Strype, I-ii, 456–8; Hall, 296; *LP*, VI, 10; XV, 14, 18; *Lisle Letters*, VI, 1634; Müller, 47.

50 Strype, I-ii, 453–9.

51 Page, *Victoria History of Kent*, II, 75; Hasted, *History of Kent*, XII, 3–5; *LP*, XVI, 380 (fos. 121b, 122), 1489 (fos. 165, 182b); XXI-ii, 200 (ii).

52 *LP*, XVI, 125, 147, 1489 (fo. 179); Carel van Mander, *Dutch and Flemish Painters* (New York, 1969), 88; *Holbein*, II, 81.

53 Kaulek, 150–2; *LP*, XV, 179; Pierre de Bourdeille, seigneur de Brantôme, *The Lives of Gallant Ladies*, tr. Alex Brown (1961), 19, 280; Grose, "Anglo-Portuguese Marriage," 322–3.

54 Kaulek, 202, 218, 383.

55 Ibid., 150–2.

56 Hall, 303; Frederick Hard, "Introduction," Henry Wotton, *The Elements of Architecture*, (Charlottesville, VA, 1968), xxx; Klarwill, 291–2; BL Julius MS F.VI, fos. 61a–b; Susan Doran, *Monarchy and Matrimony: The Courtships of Elizabeth* (New York, 1966), 79.

57 Hale, *Civilization of Europe*, 161.

58 Hard, "Introduction," xxx; *LP*, XIV-ii, 744.

59 Frank Jessup, *A History of Kent* (1974), 77; Spence, *Kent and Sussex*, 33, for the quotation.

60 G. Vigarello, *Concepts of Cleanliness: Changing Attitudes in France Since the Middle Ages*, tr. J. Billell (Cambridge, 1988), 46; Wriothesley, 109; Styrpe, I-ii, 456–8; Patrick Morrah, *A Royal Family: Charles I and his Family* (1982), 25.

61 Strype, I-ii, 456–8; Müller, 47–52, for Henry's learning at Rochester that Olisleger had not brought the friendship treaty.

62 BL Titus MS, B.I, fo. 409; Strype, I-ii, 452–3; Burnet, I-ii, 297; Müller, 31–9.

63 Strype, I-ii, 456; *StP*, VIII, 425; Henry Kelly, *The Matrimonial Trials of Henry VIII* (Stanford, CA, 1976), 274.

64 Hasted, *History of Kent*, II, 305–6; Page, *Victoria History of Kent*, II, 181, 188; John Nichols, *The Progress and Public Processions of Queen Elizabeth*, new edn. 3 vols. (New York, 1965), I, xi n.

65 This largely follows Hall, 296–302, but see PRO SP1/157/ 4–9 (*LP*, XV, 10); *Lisle Letters*, VI, 1634; Wriothesley, 111; Hasted, *History of Kent*, I, 373, for the quotation; Esther Goody, "Greeting, Begging, and the Presentation of Respect," *The Interpretation of Ritual: Essays in Honour of A. I. Richards*, ed. R. Firth and J. LaFontane (1972), 39–40.

66 PRO SP1/157/49 (*LP*, XV, 10); BL Royal MS App. 89, fos. 104– 09 (*LP*, XV, 80); *Chronicle of Calais*, 170; Wriothesley, 110–11, gives different placements; Müller, 48, identified Olisleger as the responder.

67 Hall, 299; *Lisle Letters*, VI, 1634.

68 *Victoria History of Kent*, II, 194; *Chronicle of Calais*, 171.

69 Hall, 301; Kaulek, 150–1; R. Smuts, "Public Ceremony and Royal Charisma: The English Royal Entry in London, 1485–1642," *The First Modern Society: Essays in English History in Honour of Lawrence Stone*, ed.

A. Beier, D. Cannadine, and J. Rosenheim (Cambridge, 1989) 74; *LP*, XV, 14; John Hayward, *Annals of the First Four Years of the Reign of Queen Elizabeth*, CS, vol. 7 (1840), 15.

70 Kipling, *Receyt of Kateryne*; Nicole Belmont, "The Symbolic Function of the Wedding Procession in the Popular Rituals of Marriage," *Ritual, Religion and the Sacred: Selections from the Annales Societes Civilisation*, ed. R. Forster and O. Ranum, tr. E. Forster and P. Ranum (Baltimore, 1982), 1–7; Smuts, "Entry in London," 66–88; Laurence Bryant, *The King and the City in the Parisian Royal Entry: Ceremony, Politics, Ritual, and Art in the Renaissance* (Geneva, 1986), 22; David Bergeron, "Charles I's Royal Entries into London," *Guildhall Miscellany* 3–ii (1970), 95.

71 BL Titus MS B.I, fo. 409; Burnet, I-ii, 297; BL Otho MS C.X, fo. 242; Strype, I-ii, 455; Hall, 298.

72 Wriothesley, 111; BL Otho MS C.X, f. 242; Burnet, I-ii, 497–8; HMC, "Townley MSS," App. 412; *LP*, XV, 267; Müller, 52, notes that on 27 January 1540 William sent the agreement to Henry.

73 Kenneth Stevenson, *Nuptial Blessing: A Study of Christian Marriage Rites* (New York, 1983), 89–90; Michael M. Sheehan, "Marriage Theory and Practice in the Conciliar Legislation and Diocesan Statutes of Medieval England," *Medieval Studies* 40 (1978), 433–7; J. Cox, *The Parish Registers of England* (Totowa, NJ, 1974), 76; William Harrington, *In This Book Are Contained The Commendations of Matrimony . . . With the Declaration of All Impediments* (528), sig. Bviii–Ci; Strype, I-ii, 452–3; William Black, *Illustrations of Ancient State and Chivalry from Manuscripts Preserved in the Ashmolean Museum* (1840), 29; André Burguière, "The Marriage Ritual in France: Ecclesiastical Practices and Popular Practices (Sixteenth to Eighteenth Centuries)," *Selections from Annales*, ed. R. Forster and O. Ranum, 11, notes that in the south of France the sacramental approach occurred with the verification that the two could wed made after the nuptial ceremony.

74 Peggy Liss, *Isabel the Queen: Life and Times* (New York, 1992), 71–3; Freer, *Henry*, I, 103.

75 BL Titus MS B.I, fo. 409; Burnet, I-ii, 297; BL Otho MS C.X, fo. 242.

76 Strype, I-ii, 452–3; BL, Titus MS B.I, fo. 409; Burnet, I-ii, 297; BL Otho MS C.X, fo. 242.

77 BL Titus MS B.I, fo. 409; Burnet, I-ii, 297; BL Otho MS C.X, fo. 242; Michael Van Cleave Alexander, *The First of the Tudors: A Study of Henry VII and his Reign* (Totowa, NJ, 1980), 181; Kipling, *Receyt of Katheryne*, 6–7; Kirby, *Henry IV*, 150–1; Quentin Bone, *Henrietta Maria: Queen of the Cavaliers* (Urbana, IL, 1972), 31, for a bridal dressing that took seven hours; John Leland, *Antiquarii De Rebus Britannicis Collectanea*, 6 vols. (1774) V, 338, for instructions to Frederick of Orange about the liturgy.

78 *LP*, XV, 861.

79 *LP*, XV, 91, 861; *StP*, VIII, 269; BL Otho MS C.X, fo. 242; Burnet, I-ii, 497–8.

80 *LP*, XIV-ii, 432; XV, 20, 21 (2), 91; XV, 144 (2), 642; PRO SC6/H.VIII, 6377–93 in *List of Original Ministers' Accounts Preserved in the Public Record Office*, pt. II, List and Indexes, vol. 34 (New York, 1963), 296. For German documents, Peters, 295–8; Rory McEntegart, "Fatal Matrimony: Henry VIII and the Marriage to Anne of Cleves," *Henry VIII: A European Court in England*, ed. David Starkey (1991), 141, for the amount in pounds; *Land*, between 128 and 130.

81 Lloyd Bonfield, *Marriage Settlements, 1601–1740* (Cambridge, 1983), 1–3.

82 William Thomas, *Pilgrim: A Dialogue of the Life and Actions of King Henry the Eighth*, ed. J. Froude (1861), 14, 57.

7 QUEEN CONSORT

1 *LP*, xv, 861; Simon Thurley, *The Royal Palaces of Tudor England: Architecture* and Court Life, 1460–1547 (New Haven, CT, 1993), 247.

2 Hall, 303.

3 Burnet, I-ii, 299; John Brand, *Observations on the Popular Antiquities of Great Britain*, ed. H. Ellis, 3 vols. (New York, 1970), II, 113–14; John Leland, *Antiquarii de Rebus Briticannicis Collectanea*, ed. T. Hearne, 6 vols. (1774), II, 676; *LP*, XIII-ii, 732; Scarisbrick, 376, said, "one would have expected" him to have been elevated to an earldom "some time before" April 1540; Gunn, "Henry Bourchier, earl of Essex, 1472–1540," *The Tudor Nobility*, ed. G. Bernard (Manchester, 1992), 135.

4 Hall, 302; Maria McBride-Mellinger, *The Wedding Dress* (New York, 1993), 18–24; Phillis Cunnington and Catherine Lucas, *Costume for Births, Marriages, and Deaths* (1972), 92–4, for Mary Stuart's hair tied up with silver ribbons in 1641; Leland, *Britannicis Collectanea*, V, 343.

5 Sybilla's portrait shows her with a garland of Rosemary (Plate section 1, p. 8); Brand, *Antiquities of Britain*, II, 119–25.

6 Bouterwek (6), 104–7; Brand, *Antiquities of Britain*, II, 86, Hall, 303, omitted Essex.

7 Kenneth Stevenson, *Nuptial Blessing: A Study of Christian Marriage Rites* (New York, 1983), 83; *LP*, XVIII-i, 873.

8 Normally the ceremony took place at the church door. Sheehan, "Choice of Marriage Partner in the Middle Ages: Development and Mode of Application of a Theory of Marriage," *Studies in Medieval and Renaissance History* 1 (1978), 27; Mark Searle and Kenneth Stevenson, *Documents of the Marriage Liturgy* (Collegeville, MN, 1992), 165; Bouterwek (6), 104–7, for Olisleger; see also *The Accession, Coronation,*

and Marriage of Mary Tudor, As Related in Four Manuscripts of the Escorial, tr. C. Malfatti (Barcelona, 1846), 86; Ralph Houlbrooke, *Church Courts and the People During the English Reformation, 1520–1570* (Oxford, 1979), 70, for impediments.

9   Bouterwek (6), 104–7; Searle and Stevenson, *Marriage Liturgy*, 166–75.

10   Hall, 302; Bouterwek (6), 104–7; Brand, *Antiquities of Britain*, II, 103–35. The Sarum Use calls for the right hand, but before 1487 the betrothal ring was placed on the right hand. In the nuptials when a betrothal ring was available it became the wedding ring and was shifted to the left hand.

11   Bouterwek (6), 104–7; Hall, 302; *Accession, Coronation and Marriage of Mary*, 86; Brand, *Antiquities of Britain*, II, 137–9; PRO E101/422/15; *LP*, XV, 289, 541; Patrick Carter, "Financial Administration, Patronage, and Profit in Tudor England: The Career of Sir Wymond Carew (1498–1549)," *Southern History*, 21 (1998).

12   Brand, *Antiquities of Britain*, II, 113–14.

13   Hall, 302–3; Brand, *Antiquities of Britain*, II, 87–8, 161; J. Nichols, ed., *Narratives of the Days of the Reformation*, CS, vol. 77 (1859), 170; *Collections of Ordinances*, 151, for dinner at 10:00 a.m. but after divine service on feast days; supper was at 4:00 p.m.

14   Sydney Anglo, "The Evolution of the Early Tudor Disguising, Pageant, and Mask," *Renaissance Drama*, new ser., 1 (1968), 3–44; Kipling, *Burgundian Origins of the Renaissance*, 96–102.

15   Anglo, "Tudor Disguising," 3–44.

16   Ibid.; Hall, 302–3.

17   Kipling, *Burgundian Origins of the Renaissance*, 96–102; Erica Veevers, *Images of Love and Religion: Queen Henrietta Maria and Court Entertainments* (Cambridge, 1989); John Guy, *Tudor England* (Oxford, 1988), 426–7, for entertainment.

18   Ronald Hutton, *Charles the Second, King of England, Scotland, and Ireland* (Oxford, 1989), 278–448; Hester Chapman, *Mary II, Queen of England* (Westport, CT, 1976), 35.

19   Mary Green, *Lives of the Princesses of England From the Norman Conquest*, 6 vols. (1849), I, 23; Gordon Mattingly, *Catherine of Aragon* (Boston, 1941), 38–42; Gordon Kipling, *Receyt of the Ladie Kateryne*, EETS, vol. 296 (Oxford, 1990); Desmond Seward, *Prince of the Renaissance: The Golden Life of François I* (New York, 1973), 194; Josephine Ross, *The Winter Queen: The Story of Elizabeth Stuart* (New York, 1979), 30–48.

20   Esther Cohen and Elliott Horowitz, "In Search of the Sacred: Jews, Christians, and Rituals of Marriage in the Later Middle Ages," *Journal of Medieval and Renaissance Studies* 20 (1990), 225–49; Nicole Belmont, "The Symbolic Function of the Wedding Procession in the Popular Rituals of Marriage," *Ritual, Religion, and the Sacred: Selections from the Annales, Societes, Civilisation*, ed. R. Forster and O. Ranum, trans. E.

Foster and P. Ranum (Baltimore, 1982), 1–7; Anglo, "Tudor Disguisings," 24–31, for Epiphany celebrations.

21 Searle and Stevenson, *Marriage Liturgy*, 177; Andre Burguière "The Marriage Ritual in France: Ecclesiastical Practices and Popular Practices (Sixteenth to Eighteenth Centuries)," *Selections from Annales*, 19; Edward Muir, *Ritual in Early Modern Europe* (Cambridge, 1997), 38.

22 Pierre de Bourdeille, Seigneur de Brantôme, *The Lives of Gallant Ladies*, tr. A. Brown (London, 1960), 240.

23 Parsons, 4.

24 Peggy Liss, *Isabel the Queen, Life and Times* (New York, 1992), 79.

25 *CSP Spain*, VI-i, 34; Ross, *Winter Queen*, 45.

26 Lubkin, 53; *CSP Ven*, II, 511, for Louis; Hutton, *Charles*, 187; A. Bryant, ed., *The Letters, Speeches, and Declarations of King Charles II* (New York, 1936), 127–8; A. Moote, *Louis XIII, The Just* (Berkeley, CA, 1989), 84–5.

27 *LP*, IV, 5791; Richard Fiddes, *The Life of Cardinal Wolsey* 2 vols. in 1 (1724), II, 213; Bassompierre, *Memoires de Maréchal de Bassompierre, Contenant L'Histoire de sa Vie et de Ce Qui S'est de Plus à la Cour de France Pendant Quelque Années*, 2 vols. (1723), I, 32–3; Olga Opfell, *Queens, Empresses, Grand Duchesses and Regents: Women Rulers of Europe, A.D. 1328–1989* (Jefferson, NC, 1989), 39, for notaries.

28 Strype, I-ii, 461; in BL Otho MS C.X, fo. 247, Cromwell wrote that the king said his nature abhored her on the wedding night. Whether by that statement Henry meant that coitus had been tried was not explained; Brundage, 139; William Harrington, *In This Book Are Contained the Commendations of Matrimony . . . With the Declaration of All Impediments* (528), sig. DVIII; Pierre Payer, "Early Medieval Regulations Concerning Sexual Relations," *Journal of Medieval History*, 6 (1980), 362; Cohen and Horowitz, "Rituals of Marriage," 237n.

29 Mircea Eliade, *Rites of Symbols of Initiation: The Mysteries of Birth and Rebirth*, tr. W. Trask (New York, 1958), 25; Richard Greenham, *Seven Godlie and Fruitefull Sermons Upon Sundre Portions of Holie Scripture* (1601), 89; Vern Bullough, "Formation of Medieval Ideas: Christian Theory and Christian Practice," *Sexual Practices of the Medieval Church*, ed. V. Bullough and Brundage (Buffalo, NY, 1982), 14–21; Thomas Tentler, *Sin and Confession on the Eve of the Reformation* (Princeton, NJ, 1977), 176.

30 N. Harpsfield, *A Treatise on the Pretended Divorce Between Henry VIII and Catherine of Aragon*, ed. N. Pocock, CS, new ser., vol. 21 (1878), 250–1; W. Perkins, *Christian oeconomie: or, a short survey of the right manner of ordering a familie . . .* (1609), 98–114.

31 Dorothy Mayer, *The Great Regent: Louise of Savoy, 1476–1531* (New York, 1966), 17; Mattingly, *Catherine of Aragon*, 142, 160, 176; S. Giustiani, *Four Years at the Court of Henry VII: Selection of Despatches Written by the Venetian Ambassador, Sebastian Giustinian*, tr. R. Brown, 2 vols. (1854), I,

312; Cartwright, 106; Oman, *Henrietta Maria*, 56, for a soothsayer; Hutton, *Charles*, 204.

32 J. Halliwell, ed., *The Romance of Sir Tryamoure*, Percy Society, vol. 16 (1846), ll. 32–42.

33 Scarisbrick, 105–6.

34 Burnet, I-i, 296–302; BL Titus MS B.I, fo. 409, BL Otho MS B.X, 242; *LP*, XV, 825.

35 Strype, I-ii, 454–8; *Collection of Ordinances*, 156, Geoffrey Parker, *Philip II*, 3rd edn. (Chicago, 1995), 83, for sleeping habits.

36 BL Titus MS B.I, fo. 267 (*LP*, XV, 776); BL Arundel MS 97, fo. 133b (*LP*, XVI, 380[133b]); Abbott, 35, 116, remarked with reference to Lady Essex's claim about her husband's impotence that it was the duty of the wife to act pleasantly to her husband; Henrietta Haynes, *Henrietta Maria* (New York, 1912), 38. Inexplicably, Cromwell could find time to handle minor problems concerning Anne's attendants but not the major issue of her relationship with Henry (*LP*, XV, 195).

37 William Thomas, *The Pilgrim: A Dialogue of the Life and Actions of King Henry the Eighth*, ed. J. Froude (1861), 14; Castigione, *Courtier*, 330, noted "outward beauty is a true sign of inner goodness" and "for the most part the ugly are also evil."

38 Retha Warnicke, *The Rise and Fall of Anne Boleyn* (Cambridge, 1998) 243–7; Warnicke, "More's *Richard III* and the Mystery Plays," *Historical Journal* 35–4 (1992), 761–78; Warnicke,"The Physical Deformities of Anne Boleyn and Richard III: Myth and Reality," *Parergon* new ser. 5 (1986), 135–53; Warnicke, "Conflicting Rhetoric about Tudor Women: The Example of Queen Anne Boleyn," *The Rhetoric of Politics and Renaissance Women*, ed. C. Levin and P. Sullivan (Albany, NY, 1995), 39–56.

39 Brantôme, *Gallant Ladies*, 171, 177; Martin Hume, *The Wives of Henry the Eighth and the parts they Played in History* (New York, 1905), 340; Helen Le May, "Some Thirteenth and Fourteenth Century Lectures on Female Sexuality," *International Journal of Women's Studies* 1 (1978), 392–401; W. Wiley, *The Gentlemen of Renaissance France* (Cambridge, 1954), 212; V. Bullough and B. Bullough, *Sexual Attitudes: Myths and Realities* (Amherst, NY, 1995), 164, note that Gabriele Fallopio (1523–1562) demonstrated the existence of a hymen which was "a matter long under dispute."

40 W. Trethowan, "The Demonopathology of Impotence," *Witchcraft, Women and Society*, ed. B. Levack (New York, 1992), 265–8; V. Bullough and B. Bullough, *Sexual Attitudes*, 175; Mark Breitenberg, *Anxious Masculinity in Early Modern England* (Cambridge, 1996), 1–5; Harrington, *Matrimony*, sig. Aiii-Bi; Henry Smith, *A Preparative to Marriage* (1591), 3; Eric Carlson, *Marriage and the English Reformation* (Oxford, 1994), 69. Henry was to claim later that he had abstained from relations until he could determine whether or not she was free to marry him (*StP*, I, 635);

Ruth Perry, "De-Familiarizing the Family; or Writing Family History from Literary Sources," *Modern Language Quarterly* 55 (1994), 415–29, for incest taboos.

41 Hall, 303; Bouterwek (6), 106–7; Tentler, *Sin and Confession*, 173; R. Barber and J. Barker, *Tournaments, Jousts, Chivalry, and Pageants in the Middle Ages* (Woodbridge, 1989), 8–110; Barker, *Tournament in England*, 13, 84–101; Benson, "The Tournament in The Romances of Chrétien de Troyes and L'Histoire de Guillaume le Maréchal," *Chivalric Literature: Essays on Relations between Literature and Life in the Later Middle Ages*, ed. Benson and J. Lyerle, 1–24.

42 Clifford Geertz, "Centers, Kings, Charisma: Reflections on the Symbolics of Power," *Rites of Power: Symbolism, Ritual, and Politics Since the Middles Ages*, ed. S. Wilentz (Philadelphia, 1985), 152–68; Roy Strong, *Art and Power: Renaissance Festivals, 1450–1650* (1973), 11; Arthur Ferguson, *The Chivalric Tradition in Renaissance England* (Washington, DC, 1981), 47.

43 *LP*, XV, 617; Alan Young, *Tudor and Jacobean Tournaments* (1987), 193–5; J. Vale, *Edward III and Chivalry: Chivalric Society and its Context, 1270–1350* (Woodbridge, 1982), 94; William Tyler, *Dijon and the Valois* Dukes of Normandy (Norman, OK, 1971), 125.

44 Hall, 303; Teresa McClean, *The English at Play in the Middle Ages* (Windsor, 1984), 70.

45 Young, *Tudor and Jacobean Tournaments*, 184–208; Strong, *Renaissance Festivals*, 51; Ferguson, *Chivalric Tradition*, 50, 110; Sydney Anglo, "Introduction," *Chivalry in the Renaissance* (Woodbridge, 1990), xi-xvi.

46 G. Kernodle and P. Kernodle, "Dramatic Aspects of the Medieval Tournament," *Speech Monographs* 9 (1942), 161–72; Frederick Baumgartner, "The Final Demise of the Medieval Knight in France," *Regnum et Ratio: Essays Presented to Robert M. Kingdom*, ed. J. Friedman (Kirksville, MO, 1987), 15.

47 Hall, 303; Peter Wilding, *Thomas Cromwell* (1935), 286; *StP*, VIII, 269; Nott, 378; Kaulek, 152; Müller, 51–63; BL Royal MS App. 89, fos. 104–9, for the rewards.

48 Hastings Robinson, ed., *Original Letters Relative to the English Reformation, Written During the Reigns of Henry VIII, King Edward VI and Queen Mary*, Parker Society (Cambridge, 1847), I, 627–9.

49 PRO SP1/157/13–17 is inaccurately dated in January in *LP*, XV 21, but the maidens' names are incorrect for January and are crossed out in the original document. It must be a list from November. On Lady Day (PRO E101/422/15), those who received 50 shillings included a mistress Clinton who is omitted from the list (*LP*, XIV-ii, 573[4]) of maidens who actually received the queen at Blackheath in January, but which is dated by *LP* in late November. Clinton seems to have replaced Stourton; *Lisle Letters*, VI, 1636.

50 *Lisle Letters*, VI, 1642, 1649–50, 1653.

51 PRO SPl/157/48–9,172–4 (*LP*, XV, 68, 243); *LP*, XV, 79; *StP*, VIII, 318, 269; Nott, 396, 411.

52 PRO SPl/157/172–4; BL Royal MS App. 89, fos. 104–9; *LP*, XV, 642, 678; Strype, I-ii, 437; Philip left England in January (*LP*, XV 144[14]).

53 Hall, 303; PRO SP1/155/85–8; *LP*, XV, 135; XX-ii, 992; *Lisle Letters*, VI, 1642; Samuel Bentley, *Excerpta Historica, or Illustrations of English History* (1833), 297; Carter, "Carew."

54 This practice was controversial because often the king had to pay the ladies' dowries (L. Hector and B. Harvey, trs., *The Westminister Chronicle, 1381–94* [Oxford, 1982], 160).

55 Ellis (1), I, 116–19; *CSP Ven*, II, 511; J. Hakewell, *Letters of the Kings of England*, 2 vols. (1846–48), II, 263–9; Bassompiere, *Memoires*, 48; Green, *Princesses of England*, II, 24, 184; III, 316, for early examples; Louise Fradenburg, *City, Marriage, Tournament: Arts of Rule in Late Medieval Scotland* (Madison, WI, 1991), 79, for xenophobia.

56 BL Arundel MS 97, fo. 133b; PRO E104/422/15; Bouterwek (6), 111–12n.1; *LP*, XV, 937, for her household after the divorce; Peters, 297n.19.

57 *CSP Spain*, VI-i, 143, 149, 161; VI-ii, 116; F. Madden, ed., *The Privy Purse Expenses of the Princess Mary* (1831), xxix, 119, 151– 9; *LP*, XIV-ii, 572 (3), App. 46; XV, 518; Kaulek, 148; *Lisle Letters*, V, 1621; VI, 1642. On 12 March (*LP*, XV, 334), Henry visited his children at Richmond. It is possible the dispute was about his visit, but the other two children were not mentioned.

58 Hall, 303; Kaulek, 159, 167; Wriothesley, 112; Eric Eric Halfpenny, "The Citie's Loyaltie Display'd. A Literary and Documentary Causerie of Charles II's Coronation 'Entertainment,'" *Guildhall Miscellany* 10 (1959), 3.

59 Geertz, "Centers, Kings, Charisma," 153; Judith Richards, "'His Nowe Majestie' and the English Monarchy: The Kingship of Charles I before 1640," *Past and Present* 112 (1986), 70–96; R. Bucholz, "'Nothing but Ceremony': Queen Anne and the Limitations of Royal Ritual," *Journal of British Studies* 30 (1991), 288–323, for her appreciation of public appearances.

60 J. Brewer, ed., *The Court of King James the First by Godfrey Goodman, Bishop of Gloucester* 2 vols. (1839), I, 50.

61 Scarisbrick, 376–8.

62 *LP*, XV, 323.

63 David Head, *The Ebbs and Flows of Fortune: The Life of Thomas Howard: Third Duke of Norfolk* (Athens, GA, 1995), 116–19; *StP*, VIII, 261–5; Kaulek, 161.

64 *StP*, VIII, 245–52; *LP*, XV, 38; Müller, 56.

65 *StP*, VIII, 254–60; Warnicke, *Anne Boleyn*, 145.

66 *StP*, VIII, 254–60.

67 Bisson, 55; *LP*, XIV-i, 779; XV, 171, 223, 240, 652; Kaulek, 119, 162–3, 191–2; Slavin, "The Rochepot Affair," *Sixteenth Century Journal* 20 (1979), 3–19.

68 *StP*, VIII, 244, 258–60, 265–76; Kaulek, 159.

69 *StP*, VIII, 276–9, 289–95; Kaulek, 167.

70 *StP*, VIII, 269–70; PRO SP1/157/166–71 (*LP*, XV, 242); Müller, 54.

71 PRO SP1/157/195–7 (*LP*, XV, 267); *LP*, XV, 861 (2); *StP*, VIII, 279, 281n., 284; Müller, 58n. 4; Sprengel, 54, 63–7.

72 *StP*, VIII, 279–81, 284–7, 312; *LP*, XV, 309, 735; PRO, SP1/157/166–71; Müller, 55–9. Frederick attempted to persuade William to convert to Lutheranism and to join the League.

73 Bouterwek (6), 108, says that it reached England on 5 March; Müller, 59; Kaulek, 201; *LP*, XVI, 1401; XVIII-i, 44; *CSP Spain*, VI-ii, 94; *StP*, I, 635.

74 PRO E101/422/15; *LP*, XV, 289, 541; Strong, *Tudor and Stuart Monarchy* (New York, 1995), No. 75, for a hat of Edward's.

75 *LP*, XV, 613 (12); XVI, 1385, 1409; PRO E101/422/15; See also L. Smith, *A Tudor Tragedy: The Life and Times of Catherine Howard* (New York, 1961).

76 Hutton, *Charles*, 187; Müller, 68–73; Bouterwek (6), 162.

77 *LP*, XV, 616–17; Wriothesley, 117–18; Raphael Holinshed, *The Third Volume of Chronicles Beginning at Duke William the Norman*, newly augmented (1587), 950–1; Kaulek, 143, 160, 167, 173–5; Müller, 66–7.

78 Müller, 67–73; Bouterwek (6), 162.

79 Her father stayed at the Lambeth home in 1538 (*LP*, XIII-i, 800); *LP*, XVI, 1385, 1395, 1409, 1416 (ii), 1423, 1470; XVIII-i, 66; XVIII-ii, 5; Robinson, *Original Letters*, I, 200–15; Ellis (2), II, 158; Kaulek, 199; Redworth, 120n.42; Smith, *Catherine Howard*, 56; Warnicke, 42.

8 KING'S SCAPEGOAT

1 Redworth, 118, notes that Winchester believed the marriage brought Cromwell down; Scarisbrick, 374, doubts Cromwell foisted Anne upon Henry; Müller, 70, reported rumors abroad that Cromwell lost power because he did not act quickly enough in furthering the divorce; *LP*, XV, 179.

2 E. Ives, *Faction in Tudor England* (1979), 20; and "Faction at the Court of Henry VIII: The Fall of Anne Boleyn," *History* 57 (1972), 185; Joseph Block, *Factional Politics and the English Reformation: 1520–1540* (1993), 157–64; Richard Mackenney, *Sixteenth Century Europe: Expansion and Conflict* (1993), 208–9, warns against attaching modern labels to earlier factions.

3 Kaulek, 174, 176, 200; *LP*, XV, 856; *CSP Spain*, VI-i, 144 (p. 300);

Diane Willen, *John Russell, First Earl of Bedford: One of the King's Men* (1981); John Neale, "The Diplomatic Envoy," *History* 13 (1928–9), 209–11, noted that John Hawkins deceived the Spanish ambassador into believing he would betray England.

4 BL Otho MS C.X, fo. 242; Guy, 43; Hall, 306; Foxe, V, 402; Strype, I-i, 550–3; Burnet, I-i, 497.

5 Susan Brigden, "Thomas Cromwell and the 'brethren,'" *Law and Government Under the Tudors: Essays Presented to Sir Geoffrey Elton, Regius Professor of Modern History in the University of Cambridge on the Occasion of his Retirement*, ed. C. Cross, Loades, and J. Scarisbrick (Cambridge, 1988), 49, almost calls him a Lutheran; Irvin Horst, *The Radical Brethren: Anabaptism and the English Reformation to 1558* (Nieuw Koop, 1972), 57, for "brethren" used commonly by extreme reformers; Brigden, *London and the Reformation* (Oxford, 1989).

6 Guy, 43; Terence Cave, *Devotional Poetry in France, c. 1570 -1613* (Cambridge, 1969), ix; Bernd Moeller, *Imperial Cities and the Reformation: Three Essays*, tr. Midelfort and M. Edwards, Jr. (Philadelphia, 1972), 30–3.

7 *LP*, IX, 592; William Thomas, *The Pilgrim: A dialogue of the Life and Actions of King Henry the Eighth*, ed. J. Froude (1861), 20–1; Warnicke, 51–3; Thomas Mayer, *Thomas Starkey and the Commonwealth: Humanist Politics and Religion in the Reign of Henry VIII* (Cambridge, 1989), 7, identified Pole as an "Italian Evangelical."

8 James Pragman, "The Augsburg Confession in the English Reformation: Richard Taverner's Contribution," *Sixteenth Century Journal* 11 (1980), 83–4; F. Logan, "Thomas Cromwell and the Viceregency in Spirituals: A Revisitation," *English Historical Review* 103 (1988), 658–67.

9 Dewey Wallace, Jr., *Puritans and Predestination, Grace in English Protestant Theology, 1525–1695* (Chapel Hill, NC, 1982), 14; John Guy, *Tudor England* (Oxford, 1988), 178–80; Richard Rex, *Henry VIII and the English Reformation* (1993), 92; James McConica, *English Humanists and Reformation Politics* (Oxford, 1965), 124–5; *Lisle Letters*, VI, 1659.

10 Brigden, "Cromwell and the 'brethren,'" 49; Block, *Factional Politics*, 157–64; Scarisbrick, 376, was uncertain that it meant Cromwell's defeat.

11 Alexander Alesius excused Henry, Cromwell, and Cranmer, and blamed the bishops for the Six Articles (*LP*, XVI-i, 1353). It is also assumed that Cromwell favored bishops, as for example, Nicholas Shaxton of Salisbury who spoke out against the act, but there was some unpleasantness between them (R. Merriman, ed., *Life and Letters of Thomas Cromwell*, 2 vols. (Oxford, 1902), II, 128–31; Burnet, I-i, 436–7).

12 Strype, I-ii, 408–9; Constantine, 58–9, wrote his report while a prisoner (*LP*, XIV-ii, 399–400n). An anonymous letter writer whose

addressee is unknown believed that the lord chancellor and the lord privy seal were accepting of it (*LP*, XIV-i, 1040); Stanford Lehmberg, *The Later Parliaments of Henry VIII* (Cambridge, 1977), 40–84.

13 J. Nichols, ed., *Narratives of the Reformation*, CS, vol. 77 (1859), 258; Foxe, V, 388, 398, noted that Norfolk and Suffolk witnessed a bitter dispute about Wolsey between Cromwell and an unidentified lord. Burnet, I-i, 481, claimed, without giving his source, that the other disputant was Norfolk.

14 Redworth, "A Study in the Formulation of Policy: The Genesis and Evolution of the Act of Six Articles," *Journal of Ecclesiastical History* 37 (1986) 49–51, blamed the Calais sacramentaries. This statute had been anticipated by a proclamation in November 1538, a draft of which has corrections in the king's hand (*LP*, XIII-ii, 848).

15 *LP*, XII-ii, 18; E. Harbison, *Rival Ambassadors at the Court of Queen Mary* (Princeton, NJ, 1940), 10–11.

16 Potter, "Foreign Policy," *Reign of Henry VIII*, ed. McCulloch, 131; *StP*, VII, 622–3; *LP*, VI, 1115, 1212; VIII, 181, 344, 892, 1061–2; IX, 300; XIII-i, 352; Strype, I-ii, 243–7; in 1538 Mont urged Lutherans to visit England (*LP*, XIII-i, 815); Esther Hildebrandt, "Christopher Mont," *Sixteenth Century Journal* 15 (1984), 281–92; William Clebsch, *England's Earlier Protestants, 1520–1535* (New Haven, CT, 1964), 52–77, for Barnes's theology; McEntegart, 3–20, 131–51, argues that the king's religious motives "lay at the heart of England's Schmalkaldic diplomacy."

17 *StP*, VIII, 288, 358–61, 369–71, 376–8, 417, 427–8; IX, 98– 100; *LP*, XV, 463, 666, 814, 943, 960; XVII, 442 (7).

18 Guy, 39; *StP*, I, 624; *LP*, X, 377. The king was concerned about some topics. In 1538 Wriothesley noted that Henry was surprised Hutton had not sent more news about the duchess of Milan (*StP*, VIII, 29–30). Worried about the Franco-Cleves alliance in 1541, Henry ordered William Howard to monitor events closely (*StP* VIII, 553).

19 Retha Warnicke, *The Rise and Fall of Anne Boleyn Family Politics of the Court of Henry VIII* (Cambridge, 1989), 191–233; *StP*, VIII, 344; Kaulek, 159, for ambassadors making themselves agreeable. E. Ives, "Anne Boleyn and the Early Reformation in England: The Contemporary Evidence," *Historical Journal* 37 (1994) 389, misinterpreted my view of Anne's religion. She, like most individuals at court, including Catherine of Aragon, supported humanism. See Warnicke, 50.

20 Bisson, 54; David Potter, *A History of France, 1460–1560: The Emergence of a Nation State* (1995), 20; *LP*, IV-ii, 4810; John Fudge, *Cargoes, Emissaries: The Commercial and Political Interaction of England and the German Hanse, 1450–1510* (Toronto, 1995), 120, 221–31; Philippe Dollinger, *The German Hansa*, tr. D. Ault and S. Steinberg (1970).

21 PRO SP1/131/108 (*LP*, XIII-i, 784); PRO SP1/157/147 (XV, 224);

Redworth, 66–70; Geoffrey Elton, *Thomas Cromwell* (Bangor, Wales, 1991), 40, revised his opinion in "Thomas Cromwell's Decline and Fall," *Studies in Tudor and Stuart Politics and Government*, 3 vols. (Cambridge, 1974–83), I, 289–328, and denied that a conservative faction brought down Cromwell.

22 Constantine, 62–3; *StP*, V, 153; VIII, 260; Redworth, 63–85, 105–07; David Head, *The Ebbs and Flows of Fortune: The Life of Thomas Howard, Third Duke of Norfolk* (Athens, GA, 1995), 275; Strype, I-ii, 378–83; *Lisle Letters*, VI, 1659.

23 S. Gunn, "Chivalry and Politics of the Early Tudor Court," *Chivalry in the Renaissance*, ed. Sydney Anglo (Woodbridge, 1990), 116: Lubden, xii-xiii.

24 Chris Given-Wilson, *The Royal Household and the King's Affinity: Service, Politics and Finance in England: 1360–1413* (New Haven, CT, 1986), 203.

25 *Collection of Ordinances*, 156–9; Loades, *Tudor Court*, 40–1; Merriman, *Cromwell*, II, 279–82; *LP* XIII-i, 503, for Dudley.

26 *Collection of Ordinances*, 156; P. Lewis, *Essays in Later Medieval French History* (1985), 12; Norbert Elias, *The Court Society*, tr. E. Jephcott (1983).

27 Lorenzo Ducci, *Ars Aulica or the Courtiers Arte*, tr. E. Blount (1607), 200; Willen, *Russell*, 43; Mervyn James, *Family, Lineage, and Civil Society: A Study of Society, Politics, and Mentality in the Durham Region, 1500–1640* (Oxford, 1974), 26; and *English Politics and the Concept of Honour, 1485–1642* (Oxford, 1978), 15; Warnicke, 36–42; *LP*, XIII-i, 1190.

28 M. Bush, "The Lisle-Seymour Land Disputes: A Study of Power and Influence in the 1530s," *Historical Journal* 9 (1966), 258–60; *LP*, XI, 434; *Lisle Letters*, V, 1310, 1400, 1400a, 1427, 1541; VI, 1643–4, 1649–51, 1653–4.

29 BL Titus B.I, fo. 343 (Ellis[3], II, 225–26); *StP*, V, 128 -30; *LP*, XIII-i, 113, 397, 964; XV, 370; *DNB*; Constantine, 63, warned Cromwell not to trust Durham or Winchester. In December Christopher Chaitour, Durham's registrar, testified that the bishop had refused to lead Browne, Kingston and Southampton in an attack on Cromwell (*LP*, XIV-ii, 750[i]); Charles Sturge, *Cuthbert Tunstal, Churchman, Scholar, Statesman, Administrator* (1938); MacCulloch, *Suffolk and the Tudors: Politics and Religion in an English County, 1500–1600* (Oxford, 1986), 229–30, for Cromwell's local contacts.

30 Rosemary O'Day, *The English Clergy: The Emergence and Consolidation of a Profession: 1558–1642*, (Leicester, 1979), 4; Margaret Bowker, *The diocese of Lincoln Under John Longland*, (Cambridge, 1981), 182; Antonio de Guevara, *A Dispraise of the Life of a Courtier and a Commendation of the Life of the Laboring Man* (1548), sig, Fvii; Warnicke, 31–53.

31 Redworth, 13–14, 86–107; *DNB*; Kaulek, 187.

32 *The Whole Workes of W. Tyndall, John Frith, and Doct. Barnes* (1573); *LP*,

XIV-i, 441–3; XIV-ii, 750; Redworth, 102, believed that Cromwell dismissed Winchester and Chichester.

33 Redworth, 107–113; Kaulek, 169; Marillac had heard that Barnes took the pulpit away from someone who had been appointed on the second Sunday in Lent (*LP*, XV, 306, 383); Jonathan Van Patten, "Magic, Prophecy, and the Law of Treason in Reformation England," *Journal of Legal History* 27 (1983), 13, for symbolism.

34 Godfrey Goodman, *The Court of King James the First*, ed. J. Brewer, 2 vols. (1839), I, 421.

35 Kaulek, 169, 174, 178; *LP*, XV, 345, 411, 414, 429; Ellis (3), III, 258–64; Redworth, 113–15; C. Hopper, *A London Chronicle During the Reigns of Henry the Seventh and Henry the Eighth*, CS, vol. 4 (1849), 15; James Lusardi, "The Career of Robert Barnes," *The Complete Works of St Thomas More* (New Haven, CT: 1963–), VIII-iii, 1411.

36 *LP*, XIV-i, 441–3; XV, 598, 615; Hastings Robinson, ed., *Original Letters Relative to the English Reformation, written During the Reigns of Henry VIII, King Edward VI and Queen Mary*, Parker Society (Cambridge, 1847), II, 616–17; Constantine, 57; for what it is worth, Marillac mentioned no gossip concerning Cromwell and the Lutherans in April (Kaulek, 178).

37 *LP*, XV, 335.

38 *LP*, XIII-i, 30; XIV-ii, 103, 688, 781 (fo.63); Lusardi "Barnes," VIII-iii, 1407; Redworth, 111, implied it was a sign of friendship between Barnes and Cromwell. Christopher Chaitour later reported rumors that associated Cromwell with Barnes (*LP*, XIV-ii, 750); *Remains of Cranmer*, I, 267.

39 *Lisle Letters*, VI, 1663; Redworth, 92, believed Winchester was defending his episcopal patronage; *LP*, XV, 722. In April (PRO SP1/157/19[*LP*, XIV-i, 662]), John Kingsmill, sheriff of Hampshire, said that he knew Wriothesley would find a way to make friends with Winchester and referred to rumors that the king called him "his own bishop."

40 PRO SP1/131/24–5 (*LP*, XIII-i, 690); PRO SP1/136/7 (*LP*, XIII-i, 233); PRO SP1/158/157 (*LP*, XV, 442); Ives, "Faction at the Court of Henry," 169–88; Warnicke, *Anne Boleyn*, 75–7; *Remains of Cranmer*, I, 275; PRO SP1/158/125 (*LP*, XV, 438) and *LP*, XV, 386, 442) for Cromwell's references to plague; Bush, *Noble Privilege* (Manchester, 1983), 122. Cromwell had to apply for licenses to be absent from his duties (PRO SP1/136/7[*LP*, XIII-ii, 233]).

41 PRO SP1/131/24–5; *LP*, XV, 334, 370. In 1538 Norfolk referred to financial problems (PRO SP1/130/43[*LP*, XIII-i, 504]); Anthony Tuck, *Crown and Nobility, 1272–1461: Political Conflict in Late Medieval England* (1985), 10; Helen Miller, *Henry VIII and the English Nobility* (Oxford, 1986), 117.

42 *LP*, XIV-i, 693, 764–5, 806.

43 *LP*, XIV-i, 706, 800, 808.

44 PRO SP1/136/151 (*LP*, XIII-ii, 386).

45 *LP*, XI, 233, 434; PRO SP1/130/43; PRO SP1/131/24–5; in 1537 Norfolk offered Cromwell "a young woman with pretty proper tetins" (*LP*, XII-ii, 35).

46 *LP*, XV, 486.

47 Wriothesley, 115; Slavin, *Politics and Profit: A Study of Sir Ralph Sadler, 1507–47* (Cambridge, 1966), 46–9; Gunn, "earl of Essex," 135; *StP*, I, 623–4 (*LP*, XV, 437); *LP*, XV, 380, 540–1.

48 PRO SP/158/127; *LP*, XV, 321–2, 351, 402, 456, 468–9.

49 Scarisbrick, 379; Constantine, 77. Richard, the son of Cromwell's sister, also wrote letters against Constantine; R. Po-chia Hsia, *Society and Religion in Münster, 1535–1618* (New Haven, CT, 1984), 8.

50 Ellis (1), II, 119; *StP*, I, 617; *LP*, XIV-i, 1275, 1348.

51 *CSP Spain*, V-ii, 225; Strype, I-ii, 454–7. Caution must be used in citing their depositions, but it seems likely that Southampton and his brother were concerned. Rumors had earlier indicated that they were aligned with Kingston against Cromwell (*LP*, XIV-ii, 750); Kaulek, 190.

52 BL Titus MS, B.I, fos. 267, 409; BL Otho MS C.X, fo. 242; Burnet, I-ii, 296–301.

53 *StP*, I, 574–5.

54 *StP*, VIII, 258–60; *LP*, XV, 334, 960; Nott, 408–11.

55 William Harrington, *In this Book Are Contained the Commendations of Matrimony*, sig. Dviii; Constantine, 62. In 1540 the privy council noted that Durham and Winchester were experts on civil and canon law (*StP*, I, 655).

56 Brundage, 136–66, 372–400; and "The Problem of Impotence," *Sexual Practices in the Medieval Church* (Buffalo, NY, 1982), ed. V. Bullough and Brundage, 136; M. Summers, ed., *The Maleus Maleficarum of Heinrich Kramer and James Sprenger* (New York, 1971), 54; Strype, I-ii, 461; John McNeill and Heleno Gamer, *Medieval Handbooks of Penance: A Translation of the Principle Libri Poenitentiales and Selections from Related Documents* (New York, 1988), 303. Whether Henry had emissions is not as important as that Butts alleged he had them, thus offering evidence that he could emit semen.

57 Edward Muir, *Ritual in Early Modern Europe* (Cambridge, 1997), 40; R. Helmholz, *Marriage Litigation in Medieval England* (Cambridge, 1974), 87–8; Paul Stafford, *Queens, Concubines, and Dowagers: The King's Wife in the Early Middle Ages* (Athens, GA, 1983), 29; Pierre Darmon, *Trial by Impotence: Virility and Marriage in Pre-Revolutionary France*, tr. P. Keegan (1985), 31–73; Christopher Brooke, *The Medieval Idea of Marriage* (New York, 1989), 132–265; Kelly, "English Kings and their Fear of Sorcery," *Mediaeval Studies* 39 (1977), 206; Winifred Schleiner, "The

Nexus of Witchcraft and Male Impotence in Renaissance Thought and its Reflection in Mann's *Doktor Faustus*," *Journal of English and Germanic Philology* 84 (1985), 168–9.

58 *Solutio: Manifesta est diuersitas frigiditatis et maleficii, quia qui naturaliter frigidus est nec suam nec aliam numquam cognoscere potest. Unde si sua dimissa ob hanc causam, aliam ducit postea presumitur a canone quod suam sicut aliam posset cognoscere et immo quasi ecclesia circumuenta ad suam cogitur redire. Maleficium autem quandoque id effcit ut tantum unam quis nullo modo unquam possit cognoscere, alias autem bene, uel aliter*, Gloss to C.33 q.1 c.4v. *prioribus*, Caius 283/676, fo. 196va, quoted by Brundage, 378n.263; see also Kelly, "The Case Against Edward IV's Marriage and Offspring: Secrecy, Witchcraft; Secrecy Precontract," *Ricardian* 11 (1998), 326–35; Gamer, *Handbooks of Penance*, 340. Interestingly, *Code of Canon Law: Latin-English Edition* (Washington, DC, 1983), 396–7, still recognizes relative impotence; Keith Thomas, *Religion and the Decline of Magic* (1971), 463–5.

59 W. Trethowan, "The Demonopathology of Impotence," *Witchcraft, Women and Society*, ed. B. Levack (New York, 1992), 265–345; Darmon, *Trial by Impotence*, 15–32, 73; Schleiner, "Witchcraft and Male Impotence," 168–9; Abbott, 104, for night marriages; Brundage, "Impotence, Frigidity and Marital Nullity in the Decretists and the Early Decretalists," *Proceedings of the Seventh International Congress of Medieval Canon Law*, ed. P. Lineham (Vatican City, 1988), 415, for mental incapacity.

60 G. Duby, *Medieval Marriage: Two Models from Twelfth Century France*, tr. E. Forster (Baltimore, 1978), 75–9; Andre Poulet, "The Capetian Women and Regency: The Genesis of a Vocation," *Family, Sex, and Power*, ed. J. Parsons, 102–4; Kelly, "English Kings and Sorcery," 214–34; Miller, *Henry of Castile*, 64–70; Trethowan, "Demonopathology of Impotence," 268; Helmholz, *Marriage Litigation*, 87–9, identifies four ways to determine relative impotence: (1) a three-year waiting period; (2) a seven-handed compurgation; (3) inspection of the woman; and (4) inspection of the man.

61 BL Otho MS C.X, fo. 242; BL Titus MS B.I, fos. 267, 409; Burnet, I-ii, 296–301. The king's 9 May letter to Cromwell summoning him to court about his "honor and surety" probably concerned Imperial rebels at Calais (*StP*, I, 628–9; VIII, 344).

62 *LP*, XIII-i, 120.

63 *StP*, VIII, 368; *LP*, XV, 37, 471, 478, 495–7, 478, 747, 751; *Chronicle of Calais*, 184–8; Kaulek, 184–9. When concerns had been raised about papists, Lisle had denied their presence in Calais; *Lisle Letters*, V, 1178; VI, pp. 63–6, 142–7; Slavin, "Cromwell, Cranmer, and Lord Lisle: A Study in the Politics of Reform," *Albion* 9 (1977), 320–3. John Legh, who returned to England in May, was also arrested for communicating with Pole (*LP*, XV, 468–9, 721).

64 *Lisle Letters*, V, 1160, 1188, 1464 1469; *LP*, XIII-i, 1219; XV, 460; 539; *Remains of Cranmer*, 257–9; *Chronicle of Calais*, 185. His real name was George Bowker. MacCullouch, *Thomas Cranmer: A Life* (New Haven, CT, 1996), 182; Slavin, "Cromwell, Cranmer, and Lisle," 325–7.

65 *LP*, XIII-ii, 943, 955–7; XV, 728, 751; *Lisle Letters*, V, 1295; VI, pp. 142–7; Kaulek, 184–5.

66 Kaulek, 185–8; *LP*, XV, 747; *StP*, I, 627–8; VIII 349–50; Sprengel, 55–67.

67 T. F. Shirley, *Thomas Thirlby, Tudor Bishop* (1964), 33; Smith, *Tudor Prelates and Politics, 1536–1558* (Princeton, 1953), 142–3; *Remains of Cromwell*, I, 298–9; Lehmberg, *Later Parliaments*, 118.

68 Kaulek, 200.

69 For Henry's suspicious nature, see Willen, *Russell*, 32; Kaulek, 212; BL Arundel MS 97, fo. 133b (*LP*, XVI, 380[133b]); BL Otho MS C.X, fo. 242; BL Titus MS, B.I, fos. 267, 409; Burnet, I-ii, 296–30; PRO SP1/157/13–17 for her council; Peters, 297n.19.

70 BL Otho MS C.X, fo. 242; BL Titus MS B.I., fos. 267, 409; Burnet, I-ii, 296–30l; *Collection of Ordinances*, 156, for secrecy in the privy chamber and *LP*, XIV-i, 2, for its membership. It is interesting that one of the charges Norfolk admitted from his prison cell in 1547 (*LP*, XXI-ii, 696) was that he had revealed the king's secret matters to unauthorized people.

71 Burnet, I-i, 296–301; BL Otho MS C.X, fo. 247; BL Titus MS B.I, fo. 267; PRO SP1/157/13–17; HMC, *Rutland*, I, 27.

72 BL Arundel MS 97, fo. 133b; BL Otho MS C.X, fo. 242; BL Titus MS B.I., fos., 267, 409; Burnet, I-ii, 296–30l.

73 Reginald Scot, *The Discoverie of Witchcraft* (1584), 77–8; David Lindley *The Trials of Frances Howard: Fact and Fiction at the Court of King James* (New York, 1993), 54–113; Abbott, 24, 103. Unlike the more believing James, Abbott thought that relative impotency was the "garbage of popery." Helmholz, *Marriage Litigation*, 87–9, notes that before about 1450 to challenge relative impotency women tried to seduce the afflicted man; George Kittredge, *Witchcraft in Old and New England* (New York, 1972), 441–2.

74 Kaulek, 193–5; Guy, "Wolsey and the Parliament of 1523," *Law and Government Under the Tudors*, ed. Cross, Loades, and Scarisbrick, 16–17; Lehmberg, *Later Parliaments*, 59–62; Ben Lowe, *Imagining Peace: A History of Early Pacifist Ideas* (University Park, PA, 1997), 175–262; John Guy, *Tudor England* (Oxford, 1988), 146–7, suggested that disagreements over spending the dissolution money could have been a cause of his downfall. See also *LP*, XV, 566–7, 581, 583, 943; *StP*, VIII, 417. Ironically, it was Cromwell whom the council charged with threatening warfare to accomplish his political ambitions (*StP*, VIII, 349–50); Kaulek, 193.

75 BL Titus MS, B.I, fo. 267; *LP*, XIII-i, 111; XIV-i, 347, 1211, 1347; XV, 434. In his confiscated papers the investigators may have believed they found evidence to refute his disclaimer about retaining, for Hungerford wrote to Cromwell that he was not as willing for his son to enter into his service as his son was. Undoubtedly, Hungerford had requested that Cromwell accept his heir, but statements taken out of context can be interpreted in various ways (*LP*, XIII-ii, App. 43).

76 *StP*, VIII, 349–50.

77 BL Titus B.I, fo. 267; *LP*, XV, 872 (3); XVI, 305 (2), 878 (80); Kaulek, 190, 194; Redworth, 123n.52, 125n.56, also noted the early treason charges and observed that no one had as yet offered an explanation for why heresy was added; *Remains of Cranmer*, I, 298–9; Bush, "Lisle–Seymour Dispute," 264; Gaskill, "Fiction in the Archives," 1–30.

78 Kaulek, 119, 162, 204, 218; *StP*, I, 642; VIII, 381–2, 429–31; PRO SP1/152/185–6 (*LP*, XIV-i, 1310); *LP*, XIII-i, 1135; XIV-i, 926, 1311; XV, 171; Slavin, "The Rochepot Affair," *Sixteenth Century Journal* 10 (1979), 3–20.

79 *CSP Span*, VI-i, 44, 51; *StP*, VIII, 344; PRO SP1/152/185–6; *LP*, XIV-i, 579, 926; XV, 622, 652, 785–6; Kaulek, 29, 44, 54, 58, 87–8, 170, 181, 191–2, 207, 217; Müller, 67–71; Bouterwek (6), 165.

80 *LP*, XI, 41; XV, 792. Rumors about Cromwell's ambitions to wed Mary were still being made at the French court in 1541 (*LP*, XVI, 488).

81 *StP*, VIII, 362, 376; PRO SP1/161/75–80 (*LP*, XV, 870); *LP*, XV, 189, 954; *CSP Spain*, XI, p. 153. In October the king expressed concern about the origin of rumors that Mary would wed a base born person.

82 PRO SP1/157/195–97; see also PRO SP1/161/1; Herbert, *Henry the Eighth*, 455–6; Sprengel, 63–7.

83 *LP*, XV, App. 6–7; Kaulek, 194.

84 Strype, I-ii, 456, 459–60; Robinson, *Original Letters*, I, 200–15; Foxe, V, 401–2; Gaskill, "Fiction in the Archives," 1–30.

85 Strype, I-ii, 456, 459–60; BL Titus MS B.I, fos. 267, 409; Burnet, I-ii, 296–301; BL Otho MS C.X, fo. 242; Gaskill, "Fiction in the Archives," 1–30; *Collection of Ordinances*, 156; *StP*, I, 638; *LP*, XV, 861 (2); Cromwell did not specify that Henry asked him to discuss the nonconsummation with Southampton in January but he also did not apologize for that action. It is likely, given Henry's authorization to inform the earl on 6 June about the "secret matter," that he had earlier requested Cromwell to discuss his incapacity with him. A childhood friend, the lord admiral enjoyed a special relationship with Henry. Wriothesley was not at Richmond until 11 June (PRO SP1/161/81[*LP*, XV, 872]).

86 *LP*, XII-ii, 423, 629; *StP*, I, 576; *LP*, XIII-i, 754; Ward, *English Noblewomen*, 22–3.

87 *Journals of the Lords*, I, 143, 145–9; BL Titus MS B.I, fo. 203 (Burnet, I-i, 503); Redworth, 123n.52, 125n.56; Lehmberg, *Later Parliaments*, 107–12, 269.

88 BL Lansdowne MS 515, fos. 44–51 (Burnet, I-ii, 292); Lehmberg, "Parliamentary Attainder in the Reign of Henry VIII," *Historical Journal* 4 (1975), 675–702.

89 *LP*, XIV-i, 441–3; XIV-ii, 781 (fos. 63a–63b, 79b); S. Brigden, "Popular Disturbances and Fall of Cromwell and the Reformers, 1530–40," *Historical Journal* 24 (1981), 257–78, failed to note that Barnes was in Denmark in 1539; Gaskill, "Fiction in the Archives," 1–30.

90 BL Lansdowne MS 515, fos. 44–51.

91 Ibid., 287–301. Only after the attainder was passed did he deny he was a sacramentary (BL Otho MS C.X, fo. 242).

92 *StP*, VIII, 47–9. The letter, signed by both Germans, was written by Hesse; C. Clement, *Religious Radicalism in England: 1535–1565* (Edinburgh, 1996), 17; *LP*, XIII-ii, 890; Horst, *Radical Brethren*, 82–3.

93 *StP*, VIII, 50; Basil Clarke, *Mental Disorder in Earlier Britain* (Cardiff, 1975), 270; G. Benecke, *Society and Politics in Germany, 1500–1750* (1974) 52; Mackenny, *Sixteenth Century Europe*, 206–10; Redworth, 123n.52, 125n.56.

94 Clement, *Religious Radicalism*, xix, 50–2, 187–8; J. Martin, *Religious Radicalism in Tudor England* (London, 1989), 13–41; Horst, *Radical Brethren*, 32; Burnet, I-i, 461; Nott, 326–7, 344; *LP*, XIII-i, 936; 1446; XIII-ii, 265, 498, 848–9, 890; XIV-i, 370, 1086; Kaulek, 175; *Remains of Cranmer*, I, 257–9; *Lisle Letters*, V, 1189–90, 1443; Alastair Hamilton, *The Family of Love* (Cambridge, 1981), 14–28; Rex, *Henry and the Reformation*, 144.

95 *Lisle Letters*, V, 1429; Muriel McClendon, "'Against God's Word:' Government, Religion, and the Crisis of Authority in Early Reformation Norwich," *Sixteenth Century Journal*, 25 (1994), 353–70, and *The Quiet Reformation: Magistrates and the Emergence of Protestantism in Tudor Norwich* (Stanford, CA, 1999); Horst, *Radical Brethren*, 31.

96 *LP*, XIV-i, 307, 1234, 1322; XV, 295; Slavin, "Cromwell, Cranmer and Lisle," 316–36; Byrne, *Lisle Letters*, VI, p. 43, called this a "bogus" letter and validated the claim of Ellis Gruffud, whose information must have come from Lisle, that Cromwell was protecting the heretics. Cromwell did not sit as judge, although he did question them. Cranmer, Sampson, Richard Nix, bishop of Norwich, and Richard Gwent, among others, judged them (*LP*, XIII-i, 936, 1386–7; XIV-i, 1194, 1209–10, 1219, 1234, 1238, 1290, 1319, 1322; XIV-ii, 496, 1322).

97 *LP*, XIII-i, 879; XIV-i, 307; XIV-ii, 397; XV, 108.

98 *Lisle Letters*, VI, pp. 135–88; Clement, *Religious Radicalism*, 19.

99 Peter Claus, *Anabaptism: A Social History, 1525–1618* (Ithaca, NY, 1972), 77; Smith, *Marriage*, 7; Frederick Pollock and Frederick William

Maitland, *The History of English Law Before Edward I*, 2nd edn, 2 vols. (Cambridge, 1968), II, 552–3; Brunndage, 473; V. Bullough, "Heresy, Witchcraft, and Sexuality," *Sex, Society and Sexuality*, ed. Bullough (New York, 1976), 81–91; and V. Bullough, "Postscript; Heresy, Witchcraft, and Sexuality," *Sexual Practices*, ed. Brundage and V. Bullough, 206–17; Levack, *The Witch-Hunt in Early Modern Europe* (1987), 36–47, 153; in 1538 Bonner called John Mason a "papist" and a "harlot" (*LP*, XIII-ii, 270); Clement, *Religious Radicalism*, 24, 263, for Bonner; Bale made no distinction between idolatry and sodomy (Stewart, "Bounds of Sodomy," 201–04); Lehmberg, *Later Parliament*, 71–2, 118–19; individuals who believed the other five articles were punished on first offence by loss of land and goods and on second as felons. If individuals taught or preached the other articles, they were punished as felons.

100 *DNB*; Stewart, "Bounds of Sodomy," 196–8; G. Bradford, ed., "Proceeding in the Court of Star Chamber in the Reigns of Henry VII and Henry VIII," *Somerset Record Society* 27 (1911), 138n.3; Miller, *Henry and the Nobility*, 27; Jackson, "Farleigh-Hungerford Castle, Somerset," *Somersetshire Archaeological and Natural History Society* 3 (1852), 114–15; Richard Hoare, *The Modern History of Wiltshire*, 6 vols. (1822–43), I, 82; J. Jackson, *Wulfhall and the Seymours, With an Appendix of Original Documents Discovered at Longleat* (1874), App. xxiv, 5–11, App. 8–11; *LP*, VI, 763; XIII-ii, 1184.

101 *LP*, XV, 784.

102 PRO C65/148; *Journals of the Lords*, I, 150, 156; E. Crittal, ed., *History of Wiltshire*, Victoria County History, vol. 8 (1965), 99; Hungerford and Bird may not have been friends (PRO SP1/141/255[*LP*, XIII-ii, App. 43]); *LP*, XIII-i, 1241; XV, 185; Redworth, 122–3; BL Titus MS B.I, fo. 388 (*LP*, XV, 1029[34]), for Lady Hungerford's letter; Eliza Oliver, *Memoirs of the Hungerford, Milward and Oliver Families* (1930), 12–14; J. E. Jackson, *A Guide to Farleigh-Hungerford, co. Somerset* (Taunton, 1860), 19; Lehmberg, *Later Parliaments*, 314n.116 and BL Add. MS 48,022, fos. 96–7, for the commission. Since Hungerford had four children, including a male heir, he had a less compelling reason for remarriage than did the king who sought *divorticum a vinculo matrimonii*; Houlbrooke, *Church Courts and the People During the English Reformation, 1520–1570* (Oxford, 1979), 55–78, for the difference.

103 PRO C65/148; H. Trevor-Cox, "Further Notes on the History of the Manor of East Winterslow," *Wiltshire Archaeological and Natural History Magazine* 51 (1945), 18–23; Kittredge, *Witchcraft*, 65; Stewart, *Close Readers: Humanism and Sodomy in Early Modern England* (Princeton, NJ, 1997), xvi.

104 *StP*, VIII, 47–9; Bullough, "Postscript, Heresy, Witchcraft," 208–15.

105 Wriothesley, 120; F. Snell, *The Customs of Old England*, (1977), 29; Richard Wunderli, *London Church Courts and Society on the Eve of the*

Reformation (1981), 84; Michael Goodich, *The Unmentionable Vice: Homosexuality in the Later Medieval Period* (Santa Barbara, CA, 1979), 7–10; McNeill and Gamer, *Handbooks of Penance*, 274, has an extract that forbade individuals charged with sodomy to sleep with another person; Kaulek, 207; Robinson, *Original Letters*, I, 200–15.

106 Richard Kieckhefer, *Magic in the Middle Ages* (Cambridge, 1989), 97; Keith Thomas, *Religion and the Decline of Magic* (1971), 233; Van Pattan, "Magic, Prophecy, and Treason," 1–32. It is ironic that Cromwell was executed with a man convicted of buggery. St. John Chrysostom (d. 407) had cautioned boys not to wear long hair for it would make them attractive to sodomites (V. Bullough, "Formation of Medieval Ideals," *Sexual Practices*, ed. V. Bullough and Brundage, 18); Foxe, V, 376, reports Cromwell's dislike of men who wore long hair; Stewart, "Bounds of Sodomy," 240, claims that the origins of the Buggery Statute lay in the attack on the church, especially the dissolution of the monasteries.

9 HENRY'S SISTER

1 PRO SP 1/161/1; Müller, 58, 72, believed that this document revealed that Cleves had sent the 1527 agreements to England, but Winchester asked the searchers only to seek knowledge of the vows at Cromwell's home. In July 1540 Harst referred to a controversy about a word "hylich," which led Bouterwek (6), 170–5, to claim that the contract of 1527 reached England, but if it had, Henry's request of Wallop in June 1540 to obtain copies of it seems inexplicable (PRO SP1/161/13[*LP*, XV, 828]).

2 PRO SP 1/161/13.

3 *Statutes of the Realm*, 20 vols. (1822–8), III, C. 38; H. A. Kelly, *The Matrimonial Trials of Henry VIII* (Stanford, CA, 1976), 261–75. The statute was repealed in 1549.

4 *StP*, VIII, 373; *LP*, XV, 481.

5 Samuel Bentley, *Excerpta Historica or Illustrations of English History* (1833), 293–4.

6 PRO SP1/161/30 (*LP*, XV, 843); PRO SP1/161/149 (*LP*, XV, 909); *Journals of the Lords*, I, 153; Kelly, *Matrimonial Trials*, 265–7; Houlbrooke, *Church Courts and the People During the English Reformation, 1520–1570* (Oxford, 1979), 55–115.

7 HMC, *Rutland*, I, 27, dates the letter 9 July but the editors of *LP*, XV, 844, date it in sequence on 6 July; Bouterwek (6), 170–5; Müller, 73–4.

8 Ellis (2), II, 158–9; Bouterwek (6), 170–4; Müller, 73–5; *StP*, VIII, 403.

9 Kelly, *Matrimonial Trials*, 267; Strype, I-ii, 452–62, 553; PRO E30/1470 (*LP*, XV, 861); *LP*, XV, 860.

10 Kaulek, 200–1.

11 Cobham's was dated the preceding day and in Wriothesley's hand (Kelly, *Matrimonial Trials*, 267).

12 Strype, I-ii, 452–62; *LP*, XV, 860.

13 The ladies were at Richmond on 11 July (PRO SP1/161/81[*LP*, XV, 872]); Redworth, 120n.42.

14 Strype, I-ii, 456–8, 462–3; Kelly, *Matrimonial Trials*, 267; Browne recalled his late wife's alleged observation that Anne had "such fashion and manners of bringing up so gross that in her judgment the king should never heartily love" her.

15 HMC, *Rutland*, I, 27; Burnet, I-i, 496, assumed she knew English well enough for these conversations.

16 Kelly, *Matrimonial Trials*, 267–74; Malcolm Gaskill, "Reporting Murder: Fiction in the Archives in Early Modern England," *Social History*, 22 (1988), 1–30; Brundage, 494, noted that the accused "commonly tell interrogators whatever they believe the interrogators want to hear."

17 BL Titus, B.I, fo. 267; Burnet, I-i, 296–301; Strype, I-ii, 458–9; PRO SP1/161/1; PRO SP1/161/112–14 (*LP*, XV, 898); PRO SP1/161/149.

18 R. Tavener, *An Epitome of the Psalms or Brief Meditations With Diverse Other Prayers* (1539), dedication.

19 Joel Harrington, *Reordering Marriage and Society in Reformation Germany* (Cambridge, 1995), 209; Edward Muir, *Ritual in Early Modern Europe* (Cambridge, 1997), 39; M. Offord, *The Book of the Knight of the Tower*, EETS, 177; Simon Thurley, *Royal Palaces of Tudor England: Architecture and Court Life, 1460–1547* (New Haven, CT, 1993), 237; *LP*, XV, 821 (4), for Wriothesley's suggested inspection of Anne's body; never a likelihood in this divorce was the rare sentence of a three-year enforced habitation.

20 *Statutes of the Realm*, III, C.25; Kelly, *Matrimonial Trials*, 272; *LP*, XV, 860; PRO E30/1470; PRO, SP1/161/1.

21 PRO SP1/161/112–14; PRO SP1/161/149; PRO E30/1470; Burnet, I-i, 508–10; I-ii, 27; Kelly, *Matrimonial Trials*, 273; Henry Swinburne, *A Treatise of Spousals, or Matrimonial Contracts* (New York, 1985), 30–72.

22 PRO SP1/161/112–14; PRO SP1/161/149; PRO E30/1470; Burnet, I-i, 508–10; I-ii, 27; Kelly, *Matrimonial Trials*, 273; Abbott, 19–20; Bouterwek (6), 110 n.1; Müller, 89 n.2.

23 PRO E30/1470; PRO SP1/157/195; Sprengel, 57; Frederick Pollock and Frederick William Maitland, *The History of English Law Before Edward I*, 2nd edn, 2 vols. (Cambridge, 1968), II, 391, remarked that the "betrothal of babies was not consistently treated as a nullity;" Swinburne, *Treatise of Spousals*, 22, 50–1.

24 For the 1538 document, Lacomblet, IV, 658–67; PRO SP1/1/161/1.

25 Müller, 75–8; Bouterwek (6), 170–5.

26 Ibid., PRO SP1/161/81 (*XV*, 872, in Wriothesley's hand); PRO SP1/161/194–200 (*LP*, XV, 925).

27 Müller, 78–9; PRO SP1/161/194–200; *StP*, VIII, 406 n.; BL Otho MS C.X, fo. 254 (*LP*, XV, 874); *LP*, XVI, 503 (17,32), 1500 (46b, p. 717); XVII, 135; Patrick Carter, "Financial Administration, Patronage, and Profit in Tudor England: The Career of Sir Wymond Carew, (1498–1549)," *Southern History*, 21 (1998); Thomas Rymer, *Foedera, Conventiones, Literae, et cuisucunque generis Acta Publica Inter Reges Angliae* (Farnborough, Eng., 1967), VI, pt. III, 63–5.

28 PRO SP1/161/93 (*LP*, XV, 883).

29 Müller, 79–80; PRO SP1/161/111 (*LP*, XV, 891) is in Wriothesley's hand; PRO SP1/161/194–200.

30 Müller, 79–81; PRO SP1/161/112–14.

31 Müller, 81–2; PRO, SP1/161/194–200; *LP*, XV, 991, 1016; XVII, 135; Bouterwek (6), 118–19; J. Engelbrecht, "Anglo-German Relations in the Reign of Henry VIII," *Henry VIII: in History, Historiography and Literature*, ed. U. Baumann (New York, 1992)," 81, 93–5, 123–7; Sprengel, 54 ns. 10–11; Carter, "Carew."

32 PRO SP1/161/105–10 (*LP*, XV, 890); PRO SP1/161/132–45; *StP*, VIII, 40l n, 419–25; *LP*, XV, 931, 943, 960; *CSP Spain*, V-ii, 61; VI-i, 115; Müller, 81–3; Charles Petrie, *Earlier Diplomatic History, 1491–1713* (New York, 1949), 32; *CSP Ven*, III, 119.

33 *LP*, IV-iii, 3898; XIII-i, 23, 145; Lacomblet, IV, 646–8; Bouterwek (6), 385–91; Müller, 31–58, noted that the Cleves Council on 5 November 1539 said that the wedding should have taken place after four years, meaning apparently 1531. This condition was not in the original contract but may have been an oral commitment.

34 Lacomblet, IV, 658–67; Müller, 92, believed Anne was sacrificed.

35 Scarisbrick, 373; Antonia Fraser, *Six Wives of Henry VIII*, 338–9; John Kentleton, "Appearances can be Deceptive: The Case of Anne of Cleves," *History and Archaeology Review* 4 (1989), 20; T. Ashplant and A. Wilson, "Present-Centred History and the Problem of Historical Knowledge," *Historical Journal* 31 (1988), 253–74; V. Turner, *The Ritual Process: Structure and Anti-Structure* (Chicago, 1969), 2–3.

36 Parsons, 10–41; 72–6; Bentley, *Excerpta Historica*, 297–8.

37 *LP*, IV-iii, 5778; XVI, 1425; *CSP Spain*, VI-i, 213; Burnet, I- i, 296–301; Müller, 73–93; Sprengel, 57–69.

38 Hilda Johnstone, "The Queen's Household," *The English Government at Work, 1327–1336*, ed. J. Willard and W. Morris (Cambridge: MA, 1940), 251–81; Mary Saaler, *Anne of Cleves: Fourth Wife of Henry VIII* (1995), 78; PRO SP1/142/8–10 (*LP*, XIV-i, 7); PRO, E101/422/15; Loades, *Politics of Marriage*, 123; Bouterwek (6), 118–75; Müller, 73–93; Bentley, *Excerpta Historica*, 294; *Foedera*, VI, pt. III, 63.

39 Müller, 93–5; Kaulek, 210, 213–18, 258; *StP*, VIII, 446, 563; *CSP Spain*, VI-i, 149, 217; Saaler, *Anne*, 96.

40 William Macray, ed., "The 'Remonstrance' of Anne of Cleves," *Archaeologia* 47 (1883), 259, 265; *StP*, VIII, 652.

41 *StP*, I, 714, 716; *CSP Spain*, VI-i, 207, 396; *Remains of Cranmer*, I, 311–13; *LP*, XVI, 1382, 1387, 1407; Sprengel, 53–69, 81–95; Müller, 93–6; Saaler, *Anne*, 96.

42 Sprengel, 55–67; Bouterwek (6), 136–8; *StP*, I, 718; Kaulek, 375.

43 Kaulek, 381–3.

44 *LP*, XVII, App. B4, B11 (p.719), B13; *CSP Spain*, VI-i, 204, 227, 232.

45 Carter, "Carew"; *LP*, Add. II, 1542, 1572; Sprengel, 59–67; *CSP Spain*, VI-i, 385, 462.

46 *CSP Spain*, VI-ii, 115–16, 188–9; *LP*, XVI, 1080, 1425; Add. II, 1599; Sprengel, 53–67; Carter, "Carew"; Fraser, *Six Wives*, 306, 368, claims that Anne made the comment about Katherine's looks, but the statement of Chapuys, who was passing on rumors, was ambiguous.

47 Müller, 79; Olga Opfell, *Queens, Empresses, Grand Duchesses and Regents: Women Rulers of Europe, A.D. 1328–1989* (Jefferson, NC, 1989), 50.

48 Hastings Robinson, *Original Letters Relative to the English Revolution, Written During the Reigns of Henry VIII, King Edward VI and Queen Mary*, Parker Society (Cambridge, 1847), II, 633–4; *LP*, XVIII-ii, 126, 140; Müller, 79; PRO SP1/158/198–99 (*LP*, XV, 483); L. Simpson, ed., *The Autobiography of the Emperor Charles V* (1862), 42; *StP*, VIII, 330, 548; *LP*, XV, 309, 596; XVIII-ii, 126, 140.

49 Bouterwek (6), 136–8, for "beloved;" *LP*, XVIII-i, 436 (fo.83); XVIII-ii, 231; XIX-i, 812 (4,29), 1035 (41), 1165; XIX-ii, 340 (15); XX-i, 620 (51), 1081 (34); XXI-i, 894, 935, 1165, 1410; XXI-ii, 648 (50), 690 (58), 1384 (2), 1546; *CSP Spain*, VIII, 226; Bouterwek (6), 136–47; Saaler, *Anne*, 104–6; Fraser, *Six Wives*, 337, for the Book of Hours; Edward Hasted, *The History and Topographical Survey of the County of Kent*, 12 vols. (Canterbury, 1797–1801), II, 305; III, 193–4.

50 PRO, SP10/1/2; William Seymour, *Ordeal by Ambition: An English Family in the Shadow of the Tudors* (London, 1972), 217; *LP*, XXI-ii, 648 (50); C. Challis, *The Tudor Coinage* (Manchester, 1978), 200–1 *CSP Spain*, IX, 104, 266, 490; X, 282, 282, 323; Howard Colvin, *The History of the King's Works*, 6 vols. (1982), IV, 219–34; Saaler, *Anne*, 81–110; Bouterwek (6), 136–47; Müller, 83; *Calendar of State Papers, Domestic Series of the Reigns of Edward VI, Mary, Elizabeth and James*, vol. 1 (1856), p. 47; *ACP*, II, 81–3, 372, 375; III, 51, 54, 60, 280, 480, 507; IV, 12, 52, 250.

51 *CSP Spain*, XII, pp. 88–9, 94. Renard believed that the marriage between Cleves and Henry was negotiated to ensure an Anglo-Germanic alliance; Bouterwek (6), 150n.1; J. Nichols, ed., *The Chronicle of Queen Jane and of Two Years of Queen Mary*, CS, vol. 48 (1850), 27–32,

178; and *The Diary of Henry Machyn, 1550–1563*, CS, vol. 42 (1848), 45–6; Saaler, *Anne*, 108–15.

52 *CSPDom*, I, p. 63; *CSP Spain*, XI, pp. 259, 279, 300; Fichner, *Ferdinand of Austria: The Politics of Dynasticism and the Age of the Reformation* (Boulder, CL, 1982), 2.

53 Bouterwek (6), 139–55; *LP*, XX-ii, 992; Saaler, *Anne*, 109; *ACP*, V, 29, 354, 362; *CSPDom*, I, p. 87; *Foedera*, VI, pt. III, 228; pt. IV, 35; Bentley, *Excerpta Historica*, 293–313.

54 Bentley, *Excerpta Historica*, 293–313; Fraser, *Six Wives*, 414, incorrectly identified the marchioness as Elizabeth, widow of Gregory Cromwell, but in 1556, she was the wife of the marquess's heir; the marchioness was Elizabeth, daughter of William Capel (G. Cokayne, *The Complete Peerage*, ed. G. White, vol. 12 (1959), 757–62); Nichols, *Diary of Machyn*, 146, 358.

55 Klarwill, 121–6. The pretender died in 1560.

56 Thomas Elyot, *The Defence of Good Women* (1540); Thomas Becon, *The Pomander of Prayer* (1561); thirty-two of the fifty-three prayers in the Primer of 1553 came from the *Pomander* (D. Bailey, *Thomas Becon and the Reformation of the Church of England* [1952], 55).

57 Holinshed, *Chronicles*, 1133.

58 Slayter Sleydon, *The History of Great Britain to this Present Reign* (1621), 275; William Camden, *Annales or, The History of the Most Renowned and Victorious Princess Elizabeth, Late Queen of England*, 3rd edn (1635), 3, reported her "not being beauty worthy of a prince."

59 Burnet, I-i, 492–3, apparently had in mind real horses. Peter Edwards, *The Horse Trade of Tudor and Stuart England* (Cambridge, 1988), pointed out that Flemish mares were greatly prized for their power and strength; J. Shapiro, "Anthropology and the Study of Gender," *Soundings* 46 (1981), 460; Mary Crawford and Roger Chaffin, "The Reader's Construction of Meaning: Cognitive Research on Gender and Comprehension," *Gender and Reading: Essays on Readers, Texts, and Contexts*, ed. P. Schwickart and E. Flynn (Baltimore, MD, 1986), 4.

60 Foxe, V, 402–4; Peter Wilding, *Thomas Cromwell* (1935), 64–6; Ives, "Faction at the Court of Henry," 169–88; Pole had first made this charge against him; John Guy, *Tudor England* (Oxford, 1988), 155, 178–80; Richard Rex, *Henry VIII and the English Reformation* (Oxford, 1965), 92; John Guy, "The Privy Council: Revolution or Evolution?" *Revolution Reassessed: Revisions in the History of Tudor Government and Administration*, ed. C. Coleman and D. Starkey (Oxford, 1986), 70–85; Guy, 42–3.

61 Constantine, 70.

62 PRO SP1/160/153 (*LP*, XV, 794); PRO SP1/161/87 (*LP*, XV, 876); *StP*, VIII, 355, 357, 367; *LP*, XIII-i, 1165.

63 *Memoirs of Marguerite de Valois, Madame de Pompadour and of Catherine de Medici* (New York, 1910), 77.

64 BL Vesp. MS F.XIII, fo. 157 (*LP*, XV, 940); BL Otho MS C.X, fo. 247; Lehmberg, "Sir Thomas Audley: A Soul as Black as Marble?" *Tudor Men and Institutions: Studies in English Law and Government*, ed. Slavin (Baton Rough, LA, 1972), 9–10.

65 C. Hopper, *A London Chronicle during the Reigns of Henry the Seventh and Henry the Eighth*, CS, vol. 4 (1849), 15; Thomas Percy, *Reliques of Ancient English Poetry*, ed. H. Wheatley, 3 vols. (1876), II, 71–5.

66 Stewart, "Bounds of Sodomy," 228; George Kittredge, *Witchcraft in Old and New England* (New York, 1972), 65; Scarisbrick, 495 n., followed Jasper Ridley, *Thomas Cranmer* (1966), 256, and related his condemnation to predicting Henry's death. No reference was made to his execution with Cromwell.

67 *The Chronicle of Fabyan* (1542), 489; Hall, 306–8; K. Jankofsy, "Public Execution in England in the Late Middle Ages: The Indignity and Dignity of Death," *Omega: Journal of Death and Dying* 10 (1979), 43–4; Richard Hoare, *The Modern History of Wiltshire*, 6 vols. (1822–43), I, 103.

68 *LP*, XVI, 1080; *CSP Spain*, VI-i, 163, 167, 177 (p. 349); Kaulek, 202; Angus McLaren, *Reproductive Rituals: The Perception of Fertility in England from the Sixteenth Century to the Nineteenth Century* (1984), 39; Kittredge, *Witchcraft*, 104–23.

69 MacCulloch, *Cranmer*, 613; E. Ives, *Faction in Tudor England*, 20; Block, *Factional Politics*. Shortly before his death in 1994, Geoffrey Elton said he believed his *Henry VIII: An Essay in Revision* (1962), which was published before the factional theory gained acceptance, was a good analysis of the king's character.

70 William Thomas, *The Pilgrim: A Dialogue of the Life and Actions of King Henry the Eighth*, ed. J. Froude (1861), 78–9; Baumann, "'The Virtuous Prince:' William Thomas and Ulpian Fulwell on Henry VIII," *Henry VIII*, ed. Baumann, 167–201.

71 Richard Reynolds, *A Chronicle of All the Noble Emperors* (1571), fo. 41.

72 Herbert, *Henry the Eighth*, forward, 575; Wicquefort, 53. Catholic writers had long been critical of him, of course.

73 C. Thompson, ed., *The Colloquies of Erasmus* (Chicago, 1965), 58.

INDEX

Abbot, George, archbishop of Canterbury, 237
Abel, Thomas, 197, 208
Adams, Jan, widow of, 119
Albert, prince consort of England, 156
Albigensians, 228
Alesius, Alexander, 97
Alexander III, pope, 104
Alexander VII, pope, 104
Alfonso X, king of Castile, 54
Altorf, Wilhelm of Harf zu, 93, 100, 103
ambassadors, 20, 22–35
    and *ad hoc* appointment, 22–4, 27, 177
    bribery, 25
    ceremony and protocol of, 28–9, 181
    dispatches of, to principals, 24–5, 188, 191
    dissembling of, 25–6
    documents of, 23, 34
    false information of, 25, 188
    heralds, 22
    as intelligence gatherers, 24–5
    legatus, 22
    nuncii, 22
    and oral messages, 23
    orator, 22–3
    and papacy, 30
    precedence among countries of, 30–1
    and procurator, 23
    protected status of, 26
    as proxies in marriage, 23
    and residency, 22–4, 26, 34
    retinue of, 26, 28
    social status and looks of, 27–8
    treatment of, 31, 215
    see also diplomatic corps; heralds; marriage
American Historical Review, 4
anabaptists, 74, 189, 223–5, 228
Anglo, Sydney, 29, 159
Anglo-Scottish truce, 33

Anjou and Alençon, Francis, duke of, 45
Anna, infanta of Spain, 80
Anne Boleyn, queen of England, 20, 166
    execution of, 185, 192, 216, 242, 244, 246, 261, 268
    and marriage to Henry VIII, 14, 175, 176, 183, 199, 224
    religion of, 311 n. 19
Anne of Austria, queen of France, 122, 135
Anne of Austria, queen of Spain, 137
Anne of Bohemia, queen of England, 37, 48, 111
Anne of Brittany, queen of France, 163
Anne of Cleves, queen of England
    and annulment of her marriage, 182, 187, 218, 229–40, 261
    as appropriate wife for Henry VIII, 88–93
    at Calais, 203, 265
    and contract of marriage with Lorraine's heir, 67, 70, 81–2, 87, 110, 144–5, 150–3, 166, 180–1, 203–4, 211, 229, 232–3, 236–8, 243–5
    dispute with brother of, 254, 268
    dowry of, 88, 101, 110–11
    during reign of Edward VI, 252–3
    during reign of Mary, 253–5
    education of, 90–2
    and entertainment of, 125
    and German visitors, 254–5
    gifts to, 117, 182–3
    greeting at Rochester of, 130–7, 233, 265
    homesickness of, 122
    jointure of, 130, 153–4, 266
    journey from Deal to Dartford of, 127–9, 146
    journey to England of, 107–11, 114–24, 265
    and Katherine Howard, 182–5, 239, 247–8
    and Katherine Parr, 250

326

and marriage negotiations, 21, 41, 43, 47, 78, 118
as principal secretary, 22, 198, 200–1, 241, 246
in Queen Mary's government, 195
Wriothesley, Thomas, Garter king of arms, 162
Wyatt's rebellion, 254
Wyatt, Sir Thomas
correspondence of, 60, 170, 172
and French–Imperial meeting, 122
as Imperial ambassador, 3, 22, 40, 191, 264
Wylik, Otho, 254, 255

Yolanda de Brienne, Empress (wife of Frederick II), 104

Yolande of Aragon, queen of Naples, Sicily, and Jerusalem, and duchess of Anjou (wife of Louis II), 49, 56, 131–2
Yolande of Bar, queen of Aragon (wife of Juan I), 56
York, Anne of Mowbray, duchess of, 151, 175
York, Richard, duke of (younger son of Edward IV), 151
Yorkists, 63, 72
Ysabeau of the Netherlands, queen of Denmark (wife of Christian II), 43

Zwetkovich, Adam von, baron von Mitterburg, 69